FRAMEWORKS

MANAGEMENT

Third Edition

Roger Bennett

BA, MSc(Econ), DPhil
London Guildhall University

Prentice Hall

FINANCIAL TIMES

An imprint of Pearson Education

Harlow, England • London • New York • Boston • San Francisco • Toronto
Sydney • Tokyo • Singapore • Hong Kong • Seoul • Taipei • New Delhi
Cape Town • Madrid • Mexico City • Amsterdam • Munich • Paris • Milan

Pearson Education Limited
Edinburgh Gate
Harlow
Essex CM20 2JE
England

and Associated Companies throughout the world

Visit us on the World Wide Web at:
http://www.pearsoned.co.uk

Third edition published in Great Britain 1997

© Pearson Professional Limited 1997

The right of Roger Bennett to be identified as Author of
this Work has been asserted by him in accordance with the
Copyright, Designs and Patents Act 1988.

ISBN 0 273 63408 9

British Library Cataloguing in Publication Data
A CIP catalogue record for this book can be obtained from the British Library.

10 9 8 7 6 5
07 06 05 04 03

Printed & bound by Antony Rowe Ltd, Eastbourne

CONTENTS

PREFACE

This book is intended for use by business and management students in universities and other colleges; and should also be valuable for students preparing for the examinations of the major professional bodies in the business field.

The new edition incorporates fresh material on the latest topics in business management, and represents an extensive expansion on earlier versions. There are new sections on total quality management, environmental issues in business, the Four Cs model of human resources management, and the measurement of service quality. Sections concerning interpersonal management skills have been revised and extended, as has pre-existing material on the history and development of management thinking. Recent advances in relationship marketing and the extension of marketing methods to internal company management are now included.

I am again indebted to Rosalind Bailey for word-processing the amendments to the original manuscript, and to Financial Times Pitman Publishing for their efficient production of the book.

Roger Bennett

Part One

INTRODUCTION TO MANAGEMENT

1

NATURE AND DEVELOPMENT OF MANAGEMENT THEORY

CONVENTIONAL MANAGEMENT THEORY

1. Nature of management

Management is concerned with the deployment of material, human and financial resources, with the design of organisations, their structure and development, the specification of objectives and the choice of criteria for evaluating organisational efficiency. Management sets standards, imposes budgets, plans, controls, co-ordinates, leads and motivates staff, and takes decisions. It monitors performance and initiates remedial action when plans are not achieved.

Business management

All types of organisation – public or private, profit or non-profit, government agencies, theatres, opera houses, educational institutions, sports and social clubs, etc – need to be managed; otherwise they collapse. Accordingly, the techniques of efficient management are relevant to a wide variety of organisational forms.

Businesses are a special category of organisation. 'Business' concerns the creation of wealth. Hence, business management is the governance of all the administrative, technical and human processes involved in wealth generation. Competent business management leads to prosperity which enables society to produce the goods and services required by individuals and the community. It is therefore a socially useful activity.

2. History of management thinking

Although management has been practised throughout human history, only recently has it emerged as an important academic discipline in its own right. The systematic analysis of management began during the late nineteenth and early twentieth centuries, primarily through the work of Henri Fayol (*see* 9), Max Weber (*see* 10), and F.W. Taylor (*see* 3).

3. F.W. Taylor (1856–1917) and the scientific approach

F.W. Taylor established what came to be known as the 'scientific' school

3

of management thought. According to him, manual workers are motivated primarily by the prospect of high financial reward: offer an employee the possibility of earning good wages and he or she will naturally work hard to achieve that objective. Taylor's other assumptions are that manual workers:

(a) do not identify with their employing companies

(b) cannot be trusted to complete their duties without tight supervision

(c) perform better when undertaking simple, narrowly defined tasks that do not require the exercise of discretion

(d) are not capable of planning, organising and improving their own work.

4. Implications of scientific management

The operational implications of scientific management are as follows:

(a) Employees should be paid on a piece rate basis (*see* 10:46) with wages directly related to the volume of work completed.

(b) Management should apply the division of labour to the maximum extent. Each worker should undertake a few easy tasks for which little training is necessary. Constant repetition of tasks develops speed, skill, and a high volume of production. No time should be wasted in fetching raw materials, arranging tools, or transporting finished work. Jobs should be completed in a carefully controlled environment.

(c) Workers should be set high targets, but should be well rewarded for achieving them.

(d) Working methods should be analysed 'scientifically', including the timing of work.

(e) The types of person best suited to particular kinds of work should be identified and allocated tasks appropriate for their levels of ability.

(f) Management should plan and control all the worker's efforts, leaving little discretion for individual control over working methods. Job specifications should be clear and precise.

(g) The organisation should be controlled through application of the 'principle of exception' (*see* 12:20) whereby subordinates submit to their superiors only brief, condensed reports on normal operations, but extensive reports on deviations from past average performance.

5. Need for new attitudes

For scientific management to succeed, Taylor argued, a revolution in management thinking was required. Management and labour should recognise the existence of a common interest in achieving higher productivity, and not engage in quarrels and industrial disputes over their relative shares in the profits of the organisation. Everyone would have a job, incomes would be high, and all the benefits of a mass production consumer society would be achieved.

6. Followers of Taylor

Taylor's contemporaries extended and developed the scientific approach. H.L. Gantt (1861–1919), for example, pioneered the use of statistical production control. He devised performance charts for operatives, machines and processes allowing simultaneous comparison of several activities in terms of costs, idle time, stoppages, etc. Gantt worked with Taylor on a number of assignments and, while subsequently following Taylor's overall approach, he developed and modified Taylor's methods. In particular he suggested that:

(a) Outstandingly good or bad work by individuals should be publicly recognised via conspicuous notices on progress charts displayed at the workplace.

(b) Supervisors should be paid bonuses based on the output levels of their subordinates, in order to induce supervisors to control and motivate their staff more effectively.

Frank and Lillian Gilbreth (1868–1924 and 1878–1972) investigated the principles of human body movement in work situations. Following an initial study of the body movements required for bricklaying, they extended the analysis to other types of work until, eventually, they had a complete system for the measurement and classification of all the basic body motions used in manual labour. The purpose of their analysis was the identification of the sources of fatigue so that exceptionally tiring movements could be removed or eliminated. They were also interested in methods of staff development, suggesting that each employee should simultaneously (*i*) learn more about his or her present job, (*ii*) prepare for a position one step up in the hierarchy, and (*iii*) train a subordinate to take over his or her current duties.

7. Problems with scientific management

Criticisms of the scientific approach include:

(a) Work is dehumanised. Application of the division of labour can create boredom and alienation (*see* 14:2) among workers.

(b) Social and psychological influences on employee behaviour are ignored.

(c) It is assumed that managers know more about the detail of operatives' duties than the operatives themselves; yet managers do not undertake this work personally.

(d) Simplification of work can result in craft skills being lost forever.

(e) Certain jobs are extremely difficult to measure and, in any case, the fastest way of completing work is not necessarily the most efficient.

(f) Managements may lose the loyalty of their employees.

(g) Since *all* operational decision taking is devolved upwards, individual executives can become overloaded with technical and operational problems.

8. Legacy of scientific management

The application of scientific management created 'them and us' attitudes that have plagued industrial relations right up to the present day. Note how Taylor's ideas were formulated in the USA at the turn of the twentieth century, during a severe skills shortage in that country which created the need to deskill operations. Yet, as industry developed, it became increasingly important for workers to be creative and to exercise discretion, especially where quality control was concerned. Scientific management removed all responsibility for quality and product and process improvement from the worker. Arguably, this has placed western companies at a great disadvantage in relation to the Japanese, who adopt an entirely different approach to these matters (*see* Chapter 10).

Scientific management and the classical school

Scientific management provided a major input into a set of theories jointly known as the 'classical' approach to management. This emphasises formal rules, the specialisation of functions, clear division of responsibilities and the application of common principles to all management duties.

9. The work of Henri Fayol (1841–1925)

All organisations, Fayol argued, are involved in five types of 'activity': technical, commercial, security, finance and accounting, and management. Of these, management may, he suggested, be split into five broad areas: planning and forecasting, organisation, command, co-ordination and control.

Forecasting and planning means looking into the future and deciding today what should be done in the future depending on the occurrence of certain events. *Organisation* is the process of dividing work into units and allocating these to people and departments. *Command* involves issuing instructions to ensure that targets are met. *Co-ordination* is the unification of effort, while *control* requires setting targets, monitoring activity to ensure that targets are met, and taking remedial action to deal with divergences of actual from target performance.

Fayol was less interested in questions of day-to-day operations than in the broad structure of administration. The fundamental principles of administration – applicable, he suggested, to any form of organisation – are as follows:

(a) Specialisation and the division of labour

(b) Unity of command (i.e. one person, one boss)

(c) Linkage of authority to responsibility, so that the occupant of a post must possess the authority needed to carry its responsibilities

(d) A fair internal disciplinary system

(e) The setting of objectives throughout the organisation, and the centralisation of plans to provide a 'unity of direction' for the entire firm

(f) Use of organisation charts and job descriptions

(g) Creation of stable work groups and job security for personnel.

Further important contributions to the classical school came from Max Weber (1864–1920) and Mary Parker Follett (1868–1933).

10. The work of Max Weber

Weber investigated bureaucracy, which he regarded as the most efficient of all forms of organisation. In a bureaucracy, Weber noted, there are numerous written rules, standard procedures, and a complete separation of policy making from operational control. Precedents exist for most activities. Rules are in writing and are always followed. Bureaucracy is rational, stable and self-perpetuating.

In a bureaucracy there is much planning, many levels of authority, and the managerial division of labour is extensively applied. There is specialisation of functions, with precise definition of authority and responsibility structures. Decisions are based on expert technical advice; control of staff is purely impersonal.

According to Weber, bureaucracy was a logical institutional response to the organisational needs of industrial society. It was, he said, the natural consequence of the divorce of business ownership (shareholders) from day-to-day management. The occupant of a particular position never actually owns any part of the system. There are distinct divisions between various grades of staff, plus detailed procedures for appeals against higher level decisions. And the fact that management relies on existing rules and precedents relieves officials of the need to exercise discretion. Managers are 'professionals', they are technically competent and pursue structured careers, with regular promotions, training and staff development, and a pension on retirement.

11. Advantages and disadvantages of bureaucracy

Within a 'Weberian' bureaucracy, staff have security of tenure, a social esteem directly linked to occupational status, a regular salary, career development and protection from arbitrary dismissal. However, bureaucracies are threatened by the large volumes of 'red tape' they generate and by the possibility that actual behaviour within the organisation might be influenced by charismatic leaders who are not part of the official chain of command.

A further problem is that bureaucracy can stifle initiative. Job descriptions are precise and objectively determined (so that if a particular person resigns or retires the job can go on), but this precision itself encourages personnel not to think or act independently. Frequently, moreover, bureaucracies cannot accommodate change. Outdated solutions may be applied to problems without question, and the ritualistic work routines imposed in bureaucratic systems can cause the detailed minutiae of work to become an end in themselves. There is much 'passing the buck' and resistance to new ideas, especially where multidisciplinary approaches are required. Slow decision making might result from the existence of many levels in the hierarchy.

The bureaucrat is never 'wrong'. He or she can defend every action by referring to the appropriate rule or procedure. Relationships are predictable and thus create trust among colleagues; an *esprit de corps* arises. Staff identify with the organisation, although frustrations can emerge among junior staff if the chain of command is exceptionally long. Often, junior staff in bureaucracies have no means of immediate access to those who take decisions; resulting perhaps in unthinking conformity to the status quo.

12. Mary Parker Follett

Mary Parker Follett studied the role of group leadership in industrial manage-ment, focusing on group co-ordination and the factors that cause the authority of a group leader to be accepted by members of a working group. Follett suggested that work groups were most effective when the personal authority of senior managers – the formal authority vested in them as individuals – was replaced by functional authority, i.e. the authority necessary for particular activities to function efficiently, according to a given workplace situation. 'Management', therefore, could be defined as 'the art of getting things done through people'.

Follett adopted a 'holistic' approach to management, emphasising the needs (*i*) to recognise the complexity of human workplace behaviour, and (*ii*) to interconnect the human and mechanical aspects of industrial situations. She was therefore an important precursor of both the human relations and the systems approaches to management (*see* **14–16**). Follett's views were particularly influ-ential in Japan, where a *Follett Society* was set up to propagate her ideas among Japanese companies.

13. Characteristics of the classical approach

The classical approach is *deterministic* in that it presupposes that business and employee behaviour result from certain common causes that *always* apply, regardless of circumstances. It is logical, analytical and provides an immediately applicable framework for the management of large organisations. Application of classical (including scientific) management principles led to great increases in productivity. The nature of work was studied carefully, especially the role of leadership and the causes of employee motivation. Theories were created where none existed before. It encouraged managers to examine the organisational implications and consequences of their actions.

Classical approaches, however, can create rigid management systems that are highly resistant to change. Communication problems may emerge, with little personal contact between management and workers. Note particularly that many of the techniques of mass production for which the classical management approach was especially suited are no longer practised as extensively as was once the case.

14. The human relations school

This emerged as a reaction against scientific management and the classical approach. It began through the work of G. Elton Mayo (1880–1949) who, with others, conducted a series of experiments at the Hawthorne plant of the General Electrical Company in Chicago during the years 1927–32 (actually the 'Hawthorne experiments' had started in 1924 under the direction of GEC executives). Mayo sought to evaluate the effects of changes in physical working conditions which, according to scientific management, should cause significant variations in productivity. Thus, lighting, noise levels, etc were adjusted and resulting output changes noted. In fact, production altered counterintuitively as physical conditions were varied. Output increased whenever conditions were changed, even if conditions were made worse!

The researchers concluded that, in fact, group relationships were far more important in determining employee behaviour than were physical conditions and the working practices imposed by management. Also, wage levels were *not* the dominant motivating factor for most workers. Rather, behaviour depended on norms and standards established through contacts with other people within and beyond the working group. Further research established the following propositions of the human relations school:

(a) Employee behaviour depends primarily on the social and organisational circumstances of work.

(b) Leadership style (*see* Chapter 15), group cohesion (*see* 14:10) and job satisfaction are major determinants of the outputs of working groups.

(c) Employees work better if they are given a wide range of tasks to complete.

(d) Standards set internally by a working group influence employee attitudes and perspectives more than standards set by management.

(e) Application of the division of labour can make work so boring, trivial and meaningless that productivity actually goes down.

Human behaviour theorists, notably Douglas McGregor (*see* 15:4) and A.H. Maslow (*see* 15:21) made significant contributions to the theories of leadership, motivation, and organisational design.

15. Contributions and problems of the human relations approach

The school explicitly recognised the role of interpersonal relations in determining workplace behaviour, and it demonstrated that factors other than pay can motivate workers. However, the approach possibly overestimates the commitment, motivation and desire to participate in decision making of many employees: not everyone wants to exercise initiative or control their work.

Other criticisms are that the human relations school:

(a) fails to recognise the inevitability of fundamental conflicts of interest within industry

(b) ignores the influences of wider environmental conditions (political factors and market forces, for example)

(c) gives excessive weight to small group behaviour while neglecting the wider social structures within which groups operate

(d) is politically naive, simplistic and excessively altruistic.

16. Post-Fordism

The term 'post-Fordism' is sometimes used to describe the changes in working methods necessitated by the shift from standardised mass production associated with classical scientific management techniques and towards customised production using flexible manufacturing (*see* 10:6), total quality management (*see* 10:**31–35**), and so on (Sorge and Streeck 1988; Warde 1990). 'Fordism' involved the application of the division of labour to its maximum extent, low-cost production for mass consumer markets, and standardised work routines offering employees little discretion over how they completed their duties. The term arose in consequence of the Ford Motor Company's adoption of scientific management (*see* **3** to **8** above) in the 1920s. Key elements of post-Fordist production systems are as follows:

(a) Labour flexibility, with employees undertaking a wide range of tasks.

(b) Batch production (*see* 10:2) for multiple niche markets. Firms react quickly to changes in customer tastes and preferences.

(c) Widespread use of the latest information technology and manufacturing techniques.

(d) Greater need for trained and qualified labour.

(e) A large peripheral workforce (*see* 14:**6**) with little job security.

(f) Extensive use of sub-contracting, as opposed to company takeovers and mergers.

(g) Output that increasingly competes in international markets in terms of quality and product design rather than the price of the item.

(h) Teamwork and the empowerment (*see* 15:**28**) of working groups and of individuals.

(i) Decentralised collective bargaining, performance-related pay and the hiring of large numbers of workers on individual contracts.

(j) Employees themselves deciding how to complete jobs.

(k) Intense concern for quality management (*see* 10:**31**).

Several wider economic and political changes are said to have accompanied the move to post-Fordism, notably the privatisation of state-owned enterprises, a reduction in the level of state intervention in industry, less legally enforceable employment protection for workers (*see* 11:**17**), and a rise in corporate concern for employee welfare. Post-Fordist production requires different approaches to job design; the recruitment, selection and training of workers; work supervision and employee reward systems; than for standardised mass production technologies.

Criticisms of post-Fordist theory are that:

(a) It only applies within a limited number of companies. Mass production is still common, while the latest IT and flexible manufacturing systems are simply not available to numerous small businesses.

(b) Governments continue to intervene in private sector economic activity.

(c) Extensive state-sponsored employee welfare and social security programmes are to be found in all economically advanced countries.

17. The systems approach

Systems theory sees organisations as consisting of a number of interrelating sub-systems that jointly convert *inputs* of labour, materials, finance and other resources into *outputs* of goods and services. The sub-systems are:

(a) *The psycho-social sub-system*, comprising the interactions of individuals and groups

(b) *The technical sub-system*, which determines the characters of the inputs used and outputs created, and the nature of the processes of transformation

(c) *The information sub-system* that collects and analyses the information needed for decision making

(d) *The managerial sub-system* that designs and administers the organisation.

Open and closed systems

Closed systems do not depend for their survival on interrelations with the outside world. They determine their own destinies and fully control all internal relationships. Open systems, conversely, continuously interact with their environments, and have boundaries that cannot be clearly defined.

Businesses are open systems. They need to relate to suppliers, customers, neighbours, local authorities and central government. And the actions of management are necessarily affected by external circumstances. For instance, laws exist to govern the conduct of industrial relations; limited liability companies are compelled to follow certain rules in relation to the rights of shareholders; there are laws to protect consumers, and so on.

18. Systems factors

Systems factors necessarily affect management style (*see* Chapter 15). Examples of systems factors are:

(a) Form of ownership of the business and hence the stakeholders (*see* 6:**29**) to whom management is accountable

(b) Availability of labour and the structure of the local labour market

(c) Influence of trade unions and employers' associations

(d) Availability of sources of external finance

(e) The boundaries of the system, e.g. whether customers are regarded as an integral part of the system or as outside the system once a sale has occurred. This will affect the firm's approach towards the provision of after-sales service, guarantees, customer care facilities, and so on.

19. Advantages and drawbacks of the systems approach

The systems approach enables the managerial consequences of changes in environmental conditions to be analysed methodically. It looks at the organisation as a whole and considers all aspects of its relations. However, while it may be useful to *think* in systems terms, the abstract nature of systems theory makes it difficult to apply in practice. Also, relationships and environments can be extremely complex and almost impossible to analyse systematically.

The theory is *descriptive* rather than prescriptive. It details how organisations hang together, but cannot explain the causes of motivation at work, or why individuals perceive each other and the organisation in certain ways.

20. The contingency approach

This is the managerial equivalent of the adage 'different horses for different courses'. It asserts that managers should be flexible when designing organisations (*see* Chapter 6) or when choosing a management style (*see* Chapter 15). Certain situations, contingency theorists allege, require strict supervision and an authoritarian approach; others call for a relaxed and democratic manner. A management style suitable for one set of circumstances need not be appropriate elsewhere.

According to contingency theory, effective management is that which quickly and accurately identifies the key factors underlying a particular situation and hence applies measures specifically relevant to the case in question. The difficulties with applying the contingency approach are as follows:

(a) Contingency theory lacks unifying general principles and thus might lead to inconsistency when taking decisions. A certain style is applied today; possibly an entirely different style tomorrow.

(b) Substantial training and experience are needed for successful application of the contingency approach. Yet all managers have to take decisions, regardless of their training or past experience. The application of a common set of easily taught and readily understood managerial principles to all situations might be more effective.

(c) Individual managers may dislike altering their approaches and modes of behaviour as circumstances alter.

(d) A huge variety of variables potentially affect each management situation.

Often it is impossible to distinguish the key factors defining the true character of a particular state of affairs.

(e) Sometimes a technology or set of working conditions make it impossible to use anything other than a single approach. For instance, certain kinds of job are inevitably boring and dirty, yet have to be completed. It might be impracticable to adjust a working environment or adopt a participative management style.

RECENT DEVELOPMENTS IN MANAGEMENT THEORY

Among the most influential writers on management in recent years have been M.E. Porter (b. 1947), whose work is discussed in 5:24; Rosabeth Moss Kanter (*see* 15:16), and Tom J. Peters and Robert H. Waterman (*see* below). Contributions of twentieth century writers to the various schools of thought in recent management theory are examined in relevant chapters. The work of a number of other eminent contemporary writers in the management field is outlined in **21** to **27**.

21. Tom J. Peters and Robert H. Waterman

Peters and Waterman challenged the usefulness of traditional line and staff organisation systems (*see* Chapter 6), and attacked western industry for its lack of concern for customer care. Their work began with a study in the early 1980s of 43 US organisations that the authors considered 'excellent', in an attempt to discover the root causes of their success. The study revealed, the authors claimed, that the most successful companies are those which concentrate on well-established activities. These firms 'stick to the knitting', as the authors put it, focusing on the business they know best. Otherwise, excellent companies were those with:

(a) Simple organisation structures, minimal bureaucracy and relatively few administrative staff

(b) Great concern for customer welfare

(c) A propensity to undertake direct positive action rather than refer issues to committees for review

(d) Promotion systems emphasising entrepreneurship and independent attitudes in executive staff

(e) 'Hands-on' management styles whereby top managers are fully involved in all aspects of day-to-day administration

(f) No binding commitment to either centralised or decentralised organisational forms. Companies were structured according to the needs of the situation, although total commitment to the company's central values was always required.

These findings resulted from intuitive research methods (interviews with chief executives, anecdotes, quotations from well-known business leaders, etc) and not from rigorous and critical examination of facts. Also, follow-up studies of the same 43 companies by other investigators have argued (*i*) that many of the companies studied did not in fact exhibit these characteristics, and (*ii*) that some of them were not excellent at all. Indeed, many of the firms cited in the study (entitled *In Search of Excellence*) experienced serious financial difficulties in subsequent years. Nevertheless, intriguing questions are raised by the investigation.

In Search of Excellence concluded that strong corporate leadership was more important for commercial success than conventional organisational hierarchies based on divisionalisation (*see* Chapter 6) and the creation of orthodox cost and profit centres. Effective corporate leadership requires, the authors assert, (*i*) an appropriate corporate culture (*see* 6:**24**), (*ii*) the motivation of employees through managers' personal communication and direct involvement with day-to-day operations (i.e. 'management by walking around'), and (*iii*) the incorporation of customer care considerations into all aspects of company planning and control ('boundary bashing', as the authors put it, referring to the openness of business systems (*see* **17**) and the need to define carefully where the company's responsibilities end).

22. Thriving on Chaos

Peters developed his own work in a book entitled *Thriving on Chaos* in which he made the following points:

(a) Changes in market demand and production methods are today so frequent that it is no longer possible to predict the future environments in which an organisation will operate. Thus, flexibility and total acceptance of the need for change are required.

(b) Firms must continuously monitor consumer attitudes and respond immediately to alterations in consumer demand.

(c) A business's primary concern should be the improvement of quality and service to customers.

(d) Managers must be encouraged to innovate and to assume risk. This necessarily means that some projects will collapse, so the organisation must be prepared to condone the occasional failure.

(e) Organisation structures should be basic and simple with a minimum of bureaucratic control. All the company's administrative mechanisms should be conducive to it attaining its mission (*see* Chapter 5).

Peters asserts that too often organisations erect internal 'Chinese walls' between senior, middle and lower management that prevent people at the top knowing what actually happens in divisions and departments. This also results in managers spending more time passing information up and down the hierarchy than initiating activities horizontally. The solution, Peters argues, is open communications, with no possibilities for the concealment or censorship of information. Accordingly, hierarchical boundaries need to be thin and 'porous':

everyone should interact and suggest new ideas at will, regardless of their function or status. Similar considerations apply to relations with suppliers and (particularly) customers, who should be seen as *part of* rather than external to the organisation.

23. The work of Chris Argyris

Argyris is best known, perhaps, for his ideas concerning the personal development of individuals within organisations, and about how organisations learn. Employees, he argued, have potential that may be cultivated or suppressed through their association with organisations and by the conditions in which they work. He concluded (depressingly) that individual involvement in organisations actually created feelings of failure, personal inadequacy and frustration. According to Argyris, apathy, indifference and alienation were common among lower-level participants in large organisations, while unwarrantable conservatism – fear of risk, unwillingness to accept new ideas, unthinking conformity – characterised higher levels. The answer involved open relations between management and labour, worker participation,.and recognition that conflicts of interest in industry do exist.

Together with D. Schon, Argyris proposed a theory of learning based on human reasoning, in contrast to the behaviourist theories of learning prevalent at the time. Argyris and Schon distinguished between 'single loop' and 'double loop' learning. The former occurs when employees detect errors, correct them, learn from the experience and pass on the new knowledge so that it becomes embedded in the norms and behaviour patterns of the organisation. However, the underlying norms and assumptions of the enterprise are not *themselves* questioned. Double loop learning challenges basic norms (possibly creating thereby conflicts between managers and departments), and can lead to fundamental restructuring of values, strategies and attitudes.

24. H. Igor Ansoff

Igor Ansoff is sometimes described as 'the father of strategic management'. His starting point was the observation in the 1950s and early 1960s that business planning procedures had in many companies become highly bureaucratic causing, in Ansoff's words 'paralysis by analysis'. Ansoff argued the necessity of studying a firm's *overall* process of strategic management, not just those elements involving corporate planning. According to Ansoff, firms should focus their strategic thinking on three fundamental issues:

1. Definition of the enterprise's core objectives
2. Whether the firm should diversify and if so then into what areas and how vigorously
3. How the business should exploit and develop its current product-market position.

Ansoff then suggested a series of algorithms and techniques for allocating resources, for setting strategic objectives, and for developing synergies (*see* 2:8) within and between firms.

25. J.M. Juran and W.E. Deming

Together J.M. Juran and W.E. Deming were substantially responsible for the 'quality revolution' which started in Japan and quickly spread to the USA and other Western countries. W. Edwards Deming was an American statistician active in the field of quality control during the 1920s and 30s and whose ideas were ignored or rejected by most of US industry. However, he became quality control consultant to a number of major Japanese companies immediately following the Second World War, and in that capacity became internationally famous. His basic proposition was that all production processes are vulnerable to quality problems caused by variation. Hence, levels of variation should be minimised in order to improve output quality. Deming alleged, moreover, that quality was about *people* rather than physical products, and that the blame for at least 85 per cent of quality problems lay with management rather than workers. The key to success was, he suggested, the circle of 'planning, implementation, check and action'. Concern for the customer had to be paramount, as a delighted customer not only provided repeat business but would also promote the supplying firm's product to their friends. Deming recommended the adoption of 14 points by companies wishing to improve product quality, as follows:

1. Create 'constancy of purpose' for the continual improvement of products and service.
2. Adopt the philosophy of quality improvement.
3. Do not rely on mass inspection. Instead, build quality into the product in the first place.
4. Do not award contracts on the basis of lowest tender price. Look at the quality of the supplier's outputs as well as price.
5. Improve constantly and forever the firm's production and service systems.
6. Institute on-the-job training for all employees – including managers.
7. Institute leadership designed to help people do a better job.
8. Eliminate fear and implement effective two-way communication.
9. Break down departmental boundaries.
10. Eliminate exhortations and slogans for the workforce.
11. Eliminate quotas and numerical targets.
12. Remove barriers to pride in the quality of employees' work.
13. Encourage self-improvement by all workers.
14. State top management's permanent commitment to ever-improving quality and productivity.

Joseph M. Juran devised a 'Company-Wide Quality Management' programme following a cycle of quality planning, quality management and quality improvement. Juran emphasised the needs to:

- apply commitment to quality throughout the organisation including all levels of employee (from chief executive downwards) and all business functions
- identify customer requirements
- create measurements of quality

- implement planning systems capable of attaining quality objectives under operating conditions.

26. Edgar Schein

Schein worked with Douglas McGregor (*see* 15:4) and Chris Argyris (*see* **23**) and is commonly credited with the first comprehensive definition and systematic analysis of corporate culture. He also coined the term 'psychological contract' in relation to workers' interactions with their employing firms.

Organisational culture

According to Schein, an organisation's culture is 'what it has learned as a total social unit over the course of its history' and comprises artifacts (office layouts, how people dress, etc.); values, i.e. the principles on which employees base their behaviour (frequently reinforced by myths and stories); and underlying assumptions. The latter concern managers' and other employees' beliefs about the causes of human behaviour, how people should relate to each other, how the organisation should connect with the outside world, and so on. Schein argued that consensus between management and workers was essential in each of five areas, as follows:

1. The company's mission (*see* 5:3).
2. Objectives, including objectives for particular employees.
3. Reward and incentive systems.
4. How progress should be monitored and measured.
5. What to do when things go wrong.

Psychological contracts

These were said to be the informal unwritten understandings that exist between workers and their employing companies. Examples of the elements of a psychological contract from the employee's point of view are how he or she is treated by the organisation, opportunities for training and staff development, freedom to express opinions, etc. Employers conversely expect their workers to be loyal, diligent, and to respect management decisions. Schein argued that strikes and bad employee relations frequently result from broken psychological contracts.

27. Kenichi Ohmae

Japanese management consultant Kenichi Ohmae argued that to succeed in today's business environment a substantial company needs to establish itself in all three of the world's major trading regions: Western Europe, North America and the Pacific Rim (the so called Triad of economically advanced areas). A firm that fails to do this becomes vulnerable, Ohmae suggests, to attacks by rival businesses which are able to use their *worldwide* resources to expand their markets. The key to success within the Triad, Ohmae alleged, depends on the 3Cs of commitment, creativity and competitiveness. Finding good joint venture partners and the training of employees are especially important factors. Ohmae rejected the idea that long-term cost savings could be obtained by locating in low-wage newly industrialised countries (NICs). New technologies have resulted in labour costs becoming a smaller and smaller proportion of overall costs. And NICs are far away from the world's major markets.

According to Ohmae, strategy formulation should focus on the identification of 'key factors for success' in a given business environment and concentration on the development of these areas, particularly in fields where it enjoys relative superiority.

LEVELS OF MANAGEMENT

There are three levels of management: strategic, executive and supervisory (*see* 28). Strategic management (*see* Chapter 5) concerns broad decisions about the general direction of the organisation, e.g. what products it will produce, or how it will finance its operations. In a limited company (*see* 3:7), top managers are members of the firm's board of directors.

28. Boards of directors

Directors are elected by shareholders to protect their interests. In Britain, boards frequently contain part-time members, who typically possess specific commercial or technical skills lacking in the remainder of the board. Part timers are impartial and can take a broad and objective view of the company's operations. However, they lack detailed knowledge of the company's day-to-day operations and might not be totally committed to its long-term survival. Sometimes, firms themselves place representatives on the boards of other companies. It is not unusual to find major suppliers, customers or creditors occupying seats on the board.

Full timers are normally in charge of specific functions (accounts, marketing, etc) in addition to their role as directors. They know the organisation intimately, but because they depend on the firm for their jobs they might not be truly objective when assessing its long-term prospects.

The board needs to be large enough to incorporate a sufficiently broad range of skills and experiences, but small enough to take fast and effective decisions. Few companies have more than 15 directors; eight or nine is typical. Boards devote most of their attention to economic and organisational issues, e.g. when and how to raise share capital (*see* Chapter 9), major capital investments, whether to create or disband divisions, initiating or avoiding takeovers, and so on.

29. Continental comparisons

The main differences between UK and continental European boards are that the laws of some European states require (*i*) the existence of two-tier boards for public limited companies (i.e. an 'executive' board comprising managerial employees of the firm and, above that, a 'supervisory' board which takes strategic decisions), and (*ii*) worker directors (*see* Chapter 17) on supervisory boards. The advantages of having a separate supervisory board are that:

(a) General policy making is undertaken objectively and independently without interference from executives with vested interests in outcomes.

(b) Interpersonal rivalries at lower levels can be ignored.

(c) Employee interests may be considered in the absence of line managers who control workers.

(d) Tough decisions that adversely affect senior line managers can be taken more easily.

30. Japanese boards

These typically exhibit the following characteristics:

(a) They normally contain more directors than their counterparts in other countries.

(b) Directors are usually full-time employees of the organisation.

(c) Most directors will have spent their entire careers with the company and hence will possess detailed knowledge of its operations and be totally committed to its success.

(d) There is a distinct hierarchy within a Japanese board, with individuals moving up the system according to how long they have been with the company.

31. Executive (tactical) and supervisory management

Tactical management concerns the implementation of strategic decisions. Thus, it involves the acquisition and deployment of resources, allocation of duties, specification of secondary objectives, monitoring performance and reporting back to higher levels of authority. Control is exercised by executives. The word 'execute' means 'carry into effect'; thus an executive is someone who realises on behalf of others certain targets set in strategic plans. Examples of tactical decisions are the choice of a particular advertising agency, budget allocation, selection of suppliers, and so on.

Supervisory (first line) management does *not* involve policy making. Rather, the supervisor acts as a link between management and other grades of employee. Accordingly the supervisor is a manager who controls operatives but is controlled by higher managers. Typical supervisory duties are production planning at the workplace level, induction of new employees (*see* 16:**19**), inspection of operatives' work, timekeeping and record keeping, and dealing with the grievances of employees (*see* 16:**46**).

DECISION-MAKING APPROACH TO MANAGEMENT

This derives from the theory of managerial economics. It makes the following assumptions:

(a) The pursuit of profit is not necessarily the cause of managerial behaviour and does not explain all business decisions.

(b) Profit maximisation often requires managers to assume high levels of risk that could lead to business failure. Hence to avoid excessive amounts of risk, managers frequently choose low return but relatively safe options, i.e. they seek *satisfactory* returns that fail to maximise profits yet virtually guarantee long-term survival.

(c) Managers only have limited amounts of time and other resources for making decisions, many of which involve numerous possibilities and huge amounts of information. People possess finite powers of comprehension and cannot possibly consider every aspect of a difficult problem. Accordingly, managers typically look for easy, rule-of-thumb solutions that provide adequate, rather than optimum, returns.

H.A. Simon went so far as to equate all management with the process of taking decisions. He split the decision-making process into three stages: 'intelligence', 'design' and 'choice'. *Intelligence* means the analysis of the circumstances that made a decision necessary. *Design* involves the investigation of possible courses of action. *Choice* is the technique of selecting a particular outcome from the range of available solutions. Note that the implementation of an important decision normally requires further (operational) decisions.

32. Management science

This embraces a variety of statistical and operations research (OR) methods. The following steps are necessary:

(a) Simplify a complex problem by stripping away all non-essential details.

(b) Specify the assumptions to be made and build a *decision model* that accurately represents the situation. Assumptions could relate to the availability of resources or to the probabilities of the occurrence of certain events. The model predicts and compares the likely outcomes of various alternative decisions.

(c) Collect and analyse the necessary data.

(d) Examine the implications of the model and its sensitivity to changes in assumptions.

(e) Determine the best solution.

33. Applications of OR

Quantitative methods have been applied to many business functions, including the following:

(a) Minimisation of the amount of a firm's stockholding while ensuring there is only a small chance of running out of stock. The variables to be considered are:

(*i*) stockholding costs (warehousing expenses, administrative costs of ordering fresh supplies, the income foregone through having money tied up in inventory rather than investing in interest-earning financial assets, etc)

(*ii*) the average rate of stock depletion

(*iii*) the lead time that elapses between ordering stock and its arrival at the firm's premises.

(b) Determination of the optimum number of check-out tills to install in a supermarket, taking account of the probabilities of certain numbers of customers awaiting service at any given moment, of average servicing times, the likely sequence of fresh arrivals in the queues, and whether customers will be paying for many or few items.

(c) Deciding when to replace equipment in order to maintain maximum efficiency, given certain relationships between the age of equipment and maintenance costs.

(d) Selection of the most cost-effective transport routes for delivering goods or people to various destinations from particular supply points (warehouses or garages, for example).

(e) Determination of the mix of products to manufacture each day so as to maximise total profits subject to predetermined constraints concerning machine availability, labour time, storage capacity, and so on.

34. Advantages and disadvantages of the OR approach

Use of management science encourages the logical analysis of business problems and forces managers to consider all the assumptions behind their decisions. Complex problems are reduced to a handful of variables, which may be precisely stated using mathematical symbols that can be manipulated easily. Hence, peripheral issues are not considered. Rather, the *essence* of the problem is examined in depth. Subjective value judgements, committees and other joint decision making might not be required; conclusions can be drawn quickly and based on relevant information.

The *problems* attached to OR and statistical decision making in management include:

(a) Often, the results of OR exercises must be communicated to managers who are totally ignorant of quantitative methods. This could result in serious communication difficulties.

(b) Crucial elements of problems may be ignored in order to make them 'fit-in' with the assumptions needed to apply OR.

(c) So many variables affect business problems that it might be inappropriate to consider just a selection of them.

(d) Naive application of OR by managers not fully expert in quantitative methods can lead to extremely bad decisions.

(e) The quality of a solution is only as good as the accuracy of the data used in its formation. Much business information is subject to significant numerical error.

(f) Those conducting the investigation could become infatuated with its mathematical aspects, at the expense of common-sense solutions.

(g) Human aspects of management (employees' feelings, interpersonal relationships, etc) cannot be incorporated into statistical models.

(h) Many managers accept the results of OR exercises on their face value, without really understanding the assumptions and mathematics involved.

35. Management as an academic subject

Management belongs to the category of subjects known as 'humanities', i.e. those concerned with individual development, communication, and the analysis of the human condition taken as a whole. It is an 'art' because, as with all arts:

(a) Successful management requires creativity and the application of techniques involving extensive study and/or experience

(b) Few people possess the personal resources to be top-class managers

(c) Extensive practice is necessary before all the skills of management can be mastered.

Arguably however, management is not a 'science' in the strictly formal sense. (Note the difference between the word 'science' in this context and 'scientific management' (*see* 3) which is a particular set of propositions regarding the organisation of work, and 'management science' (*see* 32) which refers to statistical and OR techniques.) Reasons for not classifying management as a science in the academic sense are as follows:

(a) Sciences such as biology, chemistry or physics rely heavily on experimentation to prove their results. Experimentation is rarely possible in managerial situations.

(b) So many variables are potentially relevant to certain managerial problems that relations between cause and effect cannot be identified in a straightforward manner.

(c) Most management problems involve people, who often behave in unpredictable ways.

(d) Many subjective evaluations are needed to interpret interpersonal managerial relations, and certain human characteristics (personality, for instance) cannot easily be measured in numerical terms.

Nevertheless, there are benefits from treating management 'as if' it were a science. In particular, systematic logical reasoning clarifies ambiguities and helps resolve problems, and decisions are only taken after a careful analysis of relevant facts.

36. Is management a profession?

Professional bodies and the management of professionally qualified staff are discussed in 14:22. Whether management is or is not a profession is a controversial issue. Three criteria normally apply to the definition of a 'professional' activity, namely that:

(a) It should be based on an established, systematic body of knowledge, the acquisition of which requires several years' intellectual training.

(b) Certain ethical ('professional') standards must be maintained and codes of practice followed.

(c) Entry should be restricted to persons possessing predefined qualifications and experience.

While it is true that successful management is a demanding and creative activity that requires training, ability and hard work, it is equally true that no formal qualifications are necessary before a person sets up a business or is employed by an organisation as a manager. Also there exists no universally accepted set of rules governing the practice of management, and there is no professional body with the power to prevent people occupying management positions. (Doctors and lawyers, for example, can be 'struck off', and only registered chartered accountants can audit company accounts.) Anyone can hold a management job. Nevertheless, managers should take a 'professional' pride in their work, and constantly seek to improve their performances – for their own benefit and that of society as a whole.

Progress test 1

1. List the basic propositions of the human relations approach.

2. Define management.

3. What are the disadvantages of bureaucracy?

4. According to F.W. Taylor, what is the main factor that motivates workers?

5. Explain the differences between science, management science and scientific management.

6. H. Fayol said that there are five basic functions of management. What are they?

7. What are the advantages of the systems approach?

8. Explain the difference between executive and supervisory management.

2

MANAGEMENT IN ACTION

MANAGEMENT RESPONSIBILITIES

1. The practice of management

According to Peter Drucker, management is primarily concerned with the following matters:

- Setting targets (*see* 12:**17**)
- Taking risks (*see* 4:**1**)
- Devising strategies (*see* Chapter 5)
- Teambuilding (*see* 14:**22**)
- Communicating (*see* Chapter 12) and motivating (*see* 15:**20–25**)
- Relating the organisation to the environment in which it exists.

Managers have *authority* (*see* 14:**14**), *responsibility* for achieving objectives, and are accountable for their actions (*see* 6:**30**). Typically, managers must balance the interests of various groups within an organisation, resolve grievances (*see* 16:**46**), mediate between disputing employees, and persuade individuals to pursue certain courses of action. Most managerial duties involve attaining targets in conjunction with and working through other people.

2. Managerial competences

According to R.L. Katz there are three basic categories of managerial competence, as follows:

(a) *Technical competences* relating to the techniques and procedures used in a specialised function.

(b) *Human skills* concerning understanding, motivating and working with other people.

(c) *Conceptual skills* involving the co-ordination and overall integration of the organisation's activities.

The acronym POSDCORB has been used to summarise the essential management responsibilities, i.e. planning, organising, staffing, directing, controlling, reporting and budgeting. Managerial competences are discussed further in 16:**31**.

3. The views of Henry Mintzberg

Management requires the completion of many fragmented tasks. Yet, according to Mintzberg, all managerial work has certain common elements:

(a) *Interpersonal duties* which involve leading, acting as a figurehead, co-ordinating and communicating with others.

(b) *Informational responsibilities* that include collecting and analysing data, monitoring and transmitting information, command, acting as a spokesperson for others, and the control of working groups.

(c) *Decisional tasks* which require the manager to plan, organise, initiate change, allocate resources, negotiate, and handle disturbances.

At the strategic level, Mintzberg suggests, managers are involved in five major types of activity:

(a) Managing change (*see* 15:**11**) and reconciling the desirability of change with the need for organisational continuity and stability

(b) Assessing the implications of strategies

(c) Intervening to assist the process of strategy implementation

(d) Increasing their personal knowledge of their employing companies

(e) Scanning their companies' environments (*see* 5:**21**) to detect threats and opportunities.

All managerial activity, Mintzberg commented, is characterised by pace, frequent interruption, fragmentation of effort, the need for quick thinking and regular verbal communications. Importantly, all managers have to take decisions.

TAKING DECISIONS

4. Types of decision

Often, business decisions can be taken quickly without need for careful thought: the best choice might be obvious, or the consequences of a bad decision may be so trivial that only cursory attention to detail is required. For major decisions, however, a logical and systematic procedure is necessary; options must be listed and the probabilities of their success evaluated.

Decisions may be strategic (*see* 5:**1**), tactical, or operational. Operational decisions concern routine administrative matters such as deciding the lengths of production runs, when to reorder stocks, allocation of daily expenditures and so on. To the maximum possible extent, operational decisions should be taken automatically, according to predetermined criteria. Such *programmed decisions* do not require the exercise of managerial judgement, initiative or discretion.

Quality and acceptability of decisions

Sometimes, conflicts occur between the objective *quality* of a manager's decision and its *acceptability* to the subordinates who must carry it out. A certain decision may be correct, yet create unfortunate consequences for subordinates. Efficiency and acceptability do not always go hand in hand.

5. Rational decision making

The steps involved in making rational decisions are as follows:

(a) Analyse the nature of the problem and collect the information necessary to take a logical decision.

(b) Specify the objectives of the decision that needs to be taken.

(c) Break the problem down into constituent elements.

(d) Examine the resource requirements and long-term implications of various decisions.

(e) Select and implement a particular option, stating who will be responsible for undertaking necessary activities and laying down a timetable for completing the work.

Rational decision making is difficult where the objectives of the exercise are uncertain and/or where little hard information exists. In these circumstances, the 'bounded rationality' approach is frequently applied, i.e. a convenient and low-risk decision is taken in preference to a theoretically superior but less certain solution. This recognises that managers often do not have the time, information and resources to investigate issues in depth.

Rules of thumb are simple to apply and cheap to administer. Accordingly, many managers choose a 'satisficing' approach to decisions, which gives adequate rather than the best possible outcomes.

Fishbone diagrams

Otherwise known as 'cause and effect diagrams' the so-called fishbone diagram seeks to illustrate the relative importance of each cause of a problem and if possible to identify relationships between causes (*see* Figure 2.1).

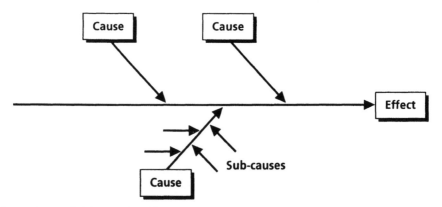

Figure 2.1 A fishbone diagram

A common approach is to examine five major factors: materials, methods, machinery, measurements and human resources (Ishikaw 1984). The factors that contribute to each of these possible causes can then be considered. Problems with fishbone diagrams are the difficulty of listing *all* potential causes of a problem, interrelations between causes, and the likelihood of multiple causes of many situations and events.

6. Brainstorming

This means churning out ideas without considering their feasibility. Every idea on an aspect of the problem mentioned by any participant is listed. However, participants are not allowed to discuss or criticise the contributions of other members, as this might inhibit creative thinking. Participants are encouraged to be as inventive and imaginative as possible, looking at problems from different angles rather than head on. Hopefully, one idea will generate others so that ideas build on themselves.

Proposals resulting from a brainstorming session are considered in a separate meeting at which the costs, benefits and feasibility of each idea are then investigated in detail and the most promising followed up.

7. Morphological analysis (MA)

This is an extension of brainstorming which seeks to discover fresh ideas by cross-referencing concepts. Consider for example a manufacturing firm that is considering an extension to its range of products. Suppose three new products, A, B and C are technically feasible and that three markets – teenage consumers, the middle-aged, and retired people – exist. To conduct a morphological analysis, management lists the products and states how each might be used in each market, thus creating $3 \times 3 = 9$ new ideas for desirable features for the intended new products. Then a third dimension could be added, consisting of (say) three ways of designing the packaging of the products, hence enabling the generation of further ideas (e.g. how best to package product C for the teenage market). This will generate $3 \times 3 \times 3 = 27$ ideas, and so on. Each idea is then critically evaluated, leaving only the best for critical investigation.

Morphological analysis adds form and structure to a brainstorming exercise. As many dimensions may be added as are deemed necessary, with a consequent proliferation of ideas. The problems with MA are that:

(a) Too many ideas might be generated – more than can be properly evaluated in the time available.

(b) Possibly, only one or two options can realistically be implemented so that the remainder of the ideas is superfluous.

8. Synergy

Synergy results from arranging the work of a group in such a way that its *collective* output is greater than the aggregate of members' individual contributions. The idea is neatly summarised by the phrase 'making two plus two equal five'.

Synergy can occur between people, between sections of a firm, or even between separate businesses, for the following reasons:

(a) Group members may spur each other on towards the achievement of a common objective.

(b) Collective effort can stimulate innovation, effort and efficiency and generally bolster group morale.

(c) There is cross-fertilisation of ideas. Individual knowledge, talents and experience are combined.

(d) Management competencies can be carried forward from one group of activities to another.

Examples of synergy occur where:

(a) It is cheaper and more efficient to undertake two activities together rather than one after another.

(b) The same distribution channel can be used for marketing several products.

(c) Spare capacity can be reduced by the integration of production processes.

(d) The results of research into one area of operations may be profitably used elsewhere.

(e) Advertising and public relations undertaken for one product will benefit others.

(f) Large discounts are available for bulk purchases.

(g) Brand identities reinforce each other.

Joint activities by two or more businesses might:

(a) Develop products and markets more quickly and inexpensively.

(b) Improve the organisation's overall cash flow position through using money generated in some areas to finance others that are currently short of cash.

(c) Enhance the collective corporate image of the firms involved.

Consequences of synergy include possibilities for lower selling prices, improved market share, higher returns on research and technical development, increased profitability and a greater return on capital employed.

9. Synectics

This involves group discussion under the direction of a leader who (purposely) is the only person who understands the true nature of the group's task. Group members are deliberately left in the dark in order to prevent the inhibition of their creativity and to stimulate the generation of completely fresh ideas. The leader directs group discussion towards consideration of a particular issue, gaining (hopefully) many useful insights into the true essence of the problem along the way.

In a sense, therefore, synectics is the opposite of brainstorming, since although it seeks to stimulate thinking, its purpose is to develop a single precise idea rather than generate a large number of options. A synectic group should normally comprise members from different functions and of varying backgrounds. The aim is to integrate the diverse talents of these individuals into a unified problem-solving whole.

10. Heuristics

A heuristic system is one that uses current experience to guide future plans, applying *ad hoc* rules of thumb in order to solve problems. Heuristic methods are common in situations where formal and systematic decision-taking procedures cannot be applied. They do not attempt to present definite solutions, but rather solutions that are tentative and subject to alteration as circumstances change. The need for heuristic methods frequently arises in business because management problems often lack structure and are subject to great uncertainty.

To illustrate the concept consider the game of chess. All chess problems can be solved with certainty using algorithms (i.e. exhaustive computational procedures that examine every aspect of the state of play) – provided powerful computing facilities and plenty of time are available. Yet a competitive chess player cannot use a computer. He or she is constrained by time and must rely on intuitive rules of thumb, based on experience, and which offer no guarantee of success. Thus, chess is like many business situations in that it is a *deterministic* game, which in practical terms must be played heuristically.

11. The Abilene paradox

This concerns the 'management of agreement'. It asserts that organisations often behave in a manner that contradicts their objectives and may even prevent their goals being achieved. J. Harvey 'discovered' the paradox during a family outing to a restaurant in Abilene, Texas. The journey was hot, long and tedious and the food was poor. A family argument ensued and it emerged that no single family member had actually wanted to go in the first place; rather, each person had assumed the rest of the family wished to make the trip and had not wanted to be seen to object.

In general, managers sometimes 'drift along' with their colleagues. Then, everyone blames everyone else when things go wrong! There are feelings of anger and irritation within the group; sub-groups emerge to represent different interests, and there is conflict and bad feeling towards everyone involved.

DECISION MAKING THROUGH COMMITTEES

12. Types of committee

A committee could be an executive body empowered to implement its own decisions, or merely provide senior management with information and advice. 'Standing committees' meet at regular predetermined intervals to consider matters relating to a particular type of issue (production or labour relations, for example) that have arisen since the last meeting. Further categories of committee exist to investigate and report on problems, to co-ordinate activities, to conduct negotiations, or to accomplish specific tasks.

13. Advantages and disadvantages of committees

Committees utilise the talents and experiences of several people, are able to examine issues in depth, and can involve all interested parties. These factors should encourage acceptance of committee decisions, for which committee members are collectively responsible. Individuals must argue their case before colleagues, and arbitrary or extreme decisions are less likely. The firm's internal communications should improve, leading to more effective co-ordination of activities.

There are, however, a number of problems associated with making decisions in a committee. It takes longer to complete work, and since committee members are usually highly paid managers, the labour cost of time spent in committees is substantial. Trivial issues might be discussed in meetings. Points may be repeated and personal arguments might develop among participants. Also, there are tendencies towards indecision in committee meetings. Compromises may emerge that satisfy nobody. Other problems are as follows:

(a) Minority groups can exert great influence on committees through their ability to hold up progress on particular issues.

(b) Collective decisions enable individuals to conceal responsibility for mistakes. It is difficult to discover precisely how a bad decision was reached.

(c) Often, committees do not have clear terms of reference.

(d) Many committees contain too many members. Committees should be large enough to include people with all the skills and experiences necessary, but not so large that decisions cannot be taken quickly. This problem frequently arises in committees containing several *ex officio* members.

(e) Committees sometimes consider matters beyond their terms of reference and which they cannot control.

(f) Junior managers may be reluctant to disagree with their seniors in a committee meeting.

(g) The committee chairperson might not be able to control debate.

14. Chairing a meeting

The chairperson of a meeting is the custodian of its rules and procedures. Chairing a meeting requires several skills, including the ability to:

(a) plan the meeting and liaise with the committee secretary to ensure the agenda is prepared and circulated

(b) become familiar with all the items on the agenda and know which members will be especially interested in each item

(c) control debate, ensuring that everyone has the opportunity to speak and that all aspects of problems are properly considered

(d) resolve disputes among members

(e) prevent speakers from wandering from the point of the item under discussion

(f) suggest compromise solutions to tricky problems

(g) summarise discussions

(h) complete the agenda within a reasonable period.

A good chairperson is neutral between the parties but always in control, possibly telling speakers to stick to the point and to wind up their contributions quickly. However, the chair should not dominate conversation, impose arbitrary solutions or fail to give the meeting sufficient time to reach decisions. Skilful chairpeople promote debate, ask probing questions of participants and draw out the maximum contribution from each member.

15. Role of the committee secretary

The committee secretary must issue a notice of the meeting's occurrence, ensure that all administrative details (room booking, circulation of documents, etc) are dealt with, and draft an agenda in conjunction with the chairperson. Agendas should begin with routine matters, moving on to more substantial issues. Each significant topic should appear as a separate item: it is bad practice to conceal major and contentious matters under a blanket agenda heading such as 'chairperson's report', since members with views on these issues will be caught unawares, not having been given sufficient time to prepare their positions. A typical order for an agenda is as follows:

apologies for absence
agreement of the minutes of the last meeting
matters arising from the minutes
chairperson's report
other items
major items for discussion and resolution
any other business
arrangements for the next meeting.

The secretary takes minutes, briefly recording what was said and noting agreed decisions. All decisions must be recorded: not just some of them. Minutes should be written up immediately after the meeting (while the memory is still fresh) and circulated to members. They must be confirmed at the next meeting as a true and fair record of the proceedings.

16. Conduct of meetings

Large and/or legally constituted meetings (the AGM of a public company, for instance) need to be conducted in a formal manner. Certain technical terms commonly arise during formal meetings. The major items are briefly explained below:

(a) *Standing orders.* The rules of procedure of a committee, e.g. size of quorum, voting procedures, specification of *ex officio* members, etc.

(b) *Ex officio member.* Someone who is a member of a committee automatically and as a matter of right.

(c) *Quorum.* The minimum number of members that must be present before decisions can be taken.

(d) *Motion.* A proposal made by a committee member. Each motion needs a proposer and a seconder. Usually, these individuals speak in favour of the motion, followed by two speakers against. Debate then ensues with the chair deciding who shall speak. If the motion is one of 'no confidence' in the chair then someone else (normally the committee secretary) temporarily takes the chair. Once a motion has been voted on and accepted it becomes a *resolution* of the committee.

(e) *Point of order.* A query regarding a possible irregularity in procedure raised by a member and put to the chair. Points of order may be brought up at any time and must be answered at once. Irregularities must be rectified immediately. If the chair overrules a point of order, then the person raising it may challenge the decision via a motion, which must be seconded.

(f) *Point of information.* A statement put to the speaker by another member through the chair. The interruption requires the permission of both the chair and the speaker, who is not obliged to accept the point.

(g) *Amendments.* Motions which seek to alter or improve other ('original') motions. A 'wrecking amendment' is one that attempts to destroy the meaning of the original motion. Most chairpeople refuse to accept wrecking amendments on the grounds that the only proper way to defeat a motion is to speak and vote against it. Amendments must be taken one at a time and each must be proposed and seconded.

(h) *Substantive motion.* A motion that has been amended by a vote of a committee. The substantive motion now replaces the original motion, which no longer exists.

(i) *Guillotine.* A time limit imposed on the discussion of a particular topic. An alternative way to terminate a discussion is for the committee to accept a motion that a vote on the issue be taken at once.

SOCIAL RESPONSIBILITY IN BUSINESS DECISIONS

17. Social responsibility

Increasingly, businesses are expected (by governments, consumer groups and community welfare organisations) to behave in socially beneficial ways, particularly in relation to the physical environment, product safety, the quality of employees' working life, and the removal of unfair discrimination in hiring and firing staff. Often, social responsibility issues arise in areas where there is no legislation, and where the correct ethical approach to a problem is unclear. Some examples are listed below.

(a) An efficient and successful business will grow at the expense of its rivals. Eventually the firm will dominate its markets. Should it cease to expand in order to avoid becoming a monopoly?

(b) Large firms contribute much revenue to the state and provide the community with goods and income from employment. Perhaps therefore their economic importance should be matched by political influence, e.g. through governments favouring big business when drafting legislation.

(c) Business decisions can affect entire communities. Should a local community be able to influence the decision making of local firms?

(d) To what extent (if any) is it reasonable to bribe representatives of client firms in order to win orders? If payment of such inducements is regarded as a normal part of a business's marketing effort, should similar bribes be offered to government officials who are capable of helping or hindering the work of the firm? If it is not considered permissible to bribe government officials in one's own country, is it reasonable to bribe government officials in other countries to secure export sales?

(e) Should a foreign company utilise child labour in host countries where this is permitted? Are social responsibility standards transferrable between nations: should a company adapt its methods to conform to local norms (e.g. by paying very low wages in underdeveloped countries) or act as a 'shining example' to rival local firms? Typically firms operating internationally adopt the norms of the host country, even if these involve standards of behaviour lower than in the head office nation. Examples are countries where there is direct discrimination against certain ethnic groups, or minimal employee health and safety requirements.

18. Approaches to corporate social responsibility

Advocates of unfettered free enterprise argue that *laissez-faire* government policies normally lead to the best possible outcomes. Businesses, they suggest, produce and trade in order to maximise their profits and, through continually striving to improve their competitive positions and productivities, necessarily increase the overall wealth and welfare of society as a whole. Free marketeers regard concerns for the environment and for equal opportunities as essentially similar to demands for products. If people want the environment to possess certain characteristics they will pay for them, and organisations will develop which, in return for payment, will manipulate the environment to satisfy the public's desires. Equal opportunities, they insist, are best achieved through the unconstrained interaction of the supply and demand for labour. If minority groups experience high rates of unemployment, all they need to do is reduce the market price of their labour. Social considerations should not concern firms. Managers are neither trained nor competent in social work, and business is not part of the social security system.

The opposing view asserts that state intervention is essential to ensure that firms do not misbehave. Large businesses possess enormous economic power. They can manipulate communities and appropriate for themselves revenues far in excess of those justified by their contributions to society. Firms are able to initiate social change, and it is only reasonable therefore that society, through its elected representatives, determine the directions of the changes that occur. Businesses, moreover, are components of a wider social system and, as such, are necessarily concerned with social issues: incomes and employment, health and safety, labour relations, occupational training, and so on. Thus, some managerial prerogatives must be surrendered for the common good.

19. Ethics

Ethics concerns the philosophical study of the moral principles that should govern human relations and conduct. It attempts to define the meaning of human well-being and to identify the factors which cause human contentment.

Ethical considerations in decision making involve subjective personal feelings about human behaviour. Note immediately that managers are born into a particular social group, are educated in a certain tradition, may subscribe to a specific religion, and absorb community values. All managers possess, therefore, some sort of moral philosophy, even if they are not aware of the fact. This philosophy helps the manager determine personal objectives, identify good and bad occurrences and evaluate the desirability of various courses of action. Numerous ethical problems can arise in managerial work. Some examples are given below.

(a) Should a manager report to the authorities an illegal act deliberately performed by his or her employing firm?

(b) Should loyalty to the organisation override loyalty to colleagues?

(c) To what extent should company affairs be regarded as confidential when company actions are deeply offensive to the individual manager?

(d) Should senior managers always back the decisions of subordinates even if these decisions turn out to be wrong?

(e) Big corporations sometimes have incomes larger than those of many nation states. How these companies use their wealth has numerous implications for the well-being of the countries in which they operate.

(f) Power and responsibility are necessarily intertwined. Typically, senior managers in big firms occupy positions where they can hurt or promote the interests of large numbers of employees, and might take decisions affecting entire communities.

Certain business practices are considered unethical throughout the world. Examples are the 'dumping' of products, i.e. selling them at less than cost price in order to drive competing firms out of business; covert involvement in the political affairs of a country; or knowingly breaking the law *vis-à-vis* consumer protection, health and safety of employees, equal opportunities, pollution of the physical environment, etc. Other forms of ethically questionable behaviour are more problematic: when the welfare of employees or the general public are endangered, *even though* this is technically lawful, and when a practice is considered acceptable in some countries but reprehensible elsewhere.

Critics of the contemporary debate on ethics in business allege that it is superficial and fails to challenge the *real* issue, i.e. the propriety of private enterprise and its effects on the distribution of wealth in society, on the dignity of labour, the overall allocation of economic resources, and the human condition as a whole. The mercenary aspects of human nature are regarded as normal. Businesses are merely expected to minimise the damaging consequences of the anti-social behaviour that sometimes results from competitive situations. If there were no private enterprise and everyone co-operated with each other – so the argument goes – then social harmony would prevail and concerns regarding 'business ethics' would be irrelevant.

20. Resolution of ethical issues

Ethical problems can be approached in either of two ways. One method is to predetermine strict moral principles and stick to them always – regardless of the circumstances of the situation. Alternatively the manager could consciously vary his or her behaviour according to the needs of each case. The former option offers consistency, and avoids managers having to wrestle with their consciences every time an ethical issue arises. However, managers following this line may become obstinate and intolerant, and will attract little sympathy if they ever have to violate their publicly stated moral codes.

The alternative, more flexible approach requires changes in the manager's moral outlook depending on the particular situation. Inconsistent decisions could result, and managers might never be really sure of the propriety of their actions. A manager's choice of approach will depend on such factors as:

(a) the culture of the society in which he or she lives

(b) his or her personal experience, education and upbringing

(c) whether the manager is intellectually innovative or tends always to accept the *status quo*.

35

21. Managerial responsibility

This means the deliberate restraint of the exercise of corporate power in order to help others. Such self-regulation can stabilise internal and external relations and ultimately benefit the organisation. Examples are monopolies that do not increase their prices; firms operating in high unemployment areas that do not pay low wages; and firms owed money that do not force credit customers into bankruptcy for not paying their bills.

Managerially responsible behaviour is necessary to secure from the wider community the co-operation needed to ensure the firm's long-run survival. Thus businesses may abstain from imposing their power not through altruism, but rather in recognition of the eventually destructive consequences of hostile actions for the wider social and commercial system.

22. Codes of Practice

A Code of Practice is a document published by a government agency, professional body, trade association or other relevant authority outlining model procedures for good practice in a particular field. Some large organisations issue their own in-house Codes of Practice on particular matters (the receipt by employees of gifts from outside companies for example). Codes give examples of excellent and bad behaviour, and recommendations regarding how things should be done. Government Codes of Practice (e.g. those issued by the Equal Opportunities Commission) are not legally binding, but will be looked at by Courts when adjudicating cases.

The obvious advantage of Codes of Practice is that they provide guidance to people who genuinely want to behave properly but who do not know what they should do in order to achieve this aim. Advice contained within a Code can be quite detailed. For example, the UK Equal Opportunities Commission Code on the avoidance of sex discrimination in employment has sections covering:

(a) The legal background, coverage of the legislation, exemptions from the Sex Discrimination Act

(b) Definitions of direct and indirect discrimination, with examples

(c) Good employment practice in relation to recruitment (wording of advertisements and so on), selection, training and promotion

(d) Terms of employment, benefits, facilities and services

(e) Grievance procedures and victimisation

(f) Dismissals, redundancies and other unfavourable treatment of employees.

The Code also contains practical guidance on formulating, implementing and monitoring equal opportunities policies. Note how a firm that visibly adheres to a recognised Code of Practice can use this fact in its corporate image advertising (companies that claim to be 'equal opportunity employers' for example).

Problems with Codes of Practice are (*i*) that their implementation is voluntary and not a statutory requirement, and (*ii*) that however well-intentioned and clearly drafted a Code might be, it can never be composed in sufficient detail to cover all possible situations.

23. Advantages to firms of acting in a socially responsible manner

It can be argued that it benefits a firm financially in the long term to behave in socially responsible ways, since only through being a good neighbour can a business acquire from the wider community the co-operation it needs for long-term survival and commercial success. Visible concern for social responsibility is useful, moreover, for a business that wishes to lobby government on matters that affect its vital interests; that seeks political influence; or which aspires to a position of leadership in the local community. Also a large organisation with a virtual monopoly of a certain market might identify itself with the moral high ground and thus avoid adverse criticism by government representatives. Examples of benefits that arise from the adoption of a socially responsible approach include the following:

(a) Projection of a 'green' image of a company is itself good for business, leading to higher sales.

(b) Energy conservation and avoidance of environmental pollution through industrial waste and spillage cuts production costs and increases corporate efficiency.

(c) Being a good employer helps the firm attract and retain high-calibre workers.

(d) Sponsorship of charitable and community events attracts valuable publicity.

Another powerful argument for business involvement in community affairs is that the more that companies contribute to the wider society the less has to be done by government, resulting perhaps in greater freedom and less state bureaucracy. If businesses do not adopt a proactive role in the wider society then social problems may emerge that government (and ultimately the taxpayer) will have to deal with. Many businesses are wealthy organisations, and managers within them are skilled and experienced administrators. Why not utilise this wealth and talent for the social benefit?

24. Arguments against firms adopting social responsibility approaches

Arguments against corporate involvement in local communities are that:

(a) It can create overdependence of the community on company handouts, which might be withdrawn at short notice.

(b) It leads to businesses assuming a disproportionately influential role in local affairs.

(c) It could undermine normal democratic processes in local government.

(d) Local services should be supplied by democratically accountable bodies and not by private firms.

(e) Social responsibility objectives may be so vague as to be meaningless.

(f) If businesses initiate social ventures that affect the general public then they should be accountable to the general public.

(g) There is no such thing as a 'free lunch' where these matters are concerned. At the end of the day any business expenditures on social improvement have to be recovered through higher prices, which detrimentally affects consumers of the goods.

(h) Individual firms which do not behave in a socially responsible manner (which pay very low wages, cut corners in relation to product safety, engage in misleading advertising, etc) obtain an unfair competitive advantage over others.

(i) Internationalisation of business has resulted in a large number of firms having to compete in world markets where rival companies are not expected to engage in any social activities at all.

(j) When dealing with social issues business executives might apply unsuitable working methods and procedures and see things from perspectives entirely inappropriate for social (rather than economic or technical) problems.

(k) Any social intervention by a business is likely to be regarded as 'good' by some people and 'bad' by others. Compact schemes for example benefit the school students who participate in them, but in so doing necessarily deny employment opportunities to other school-leavers. Equally there is no universal consensus regarding *whose* social values should be respected. And the social values of any given group or individual typically have several aspects and dimensions.

Note moreover that it is easy to *claim* that an organisation is behaving in a socially responsible manner (how many businesses would admit to being socially irresponsible?), but social responsibility is such a nebulous and unmeasurable concept that it is extremely difficult to establish whether a particular firm is exercising social responsibility or not. Often, management accepts that it should be concerned over a particular social issue; but how extensive should be the magnitude of that concern?

ENVIRONMENTAL ISSUES IN MANAGEMENT

There are two reasons for managerial involvement in environmental issues:

(a) Environmental regulations (e.g. emission standards, constraints on packaging materials, antipollution laws) impose large financial costs on firms, which have therefore a vested interest in the outcomes to environmental debates. Thus, businesses frequently lobby the government in attempts to influence environmental legislation in their favour.

(b) Many consumers regard a company's publicly stated concern for environmental protection as an important selling point for its goods. Increasingly, moreover, the business sector is held responsible for global environmental damage, notably the hole in the ozone layer, global warming, acid rain and the destruction of forests. Natural resources are being depleted faster than ever before and the world cannot sustain these losses indefinitely.

Companies can demonstrate their support for environmental conservation through incorporating 'green' messages into their advertisements, and by taking account of environmental factors in their strategies and plans (*see* 23). Other measures might include:

(a) reductions in the amounts of goods packaging, perhaps even the loose display of certain items

(b) conspicuous promotion of the energy-saving aspects of goods

(c) provision of bottle and paper banks in retail outlets

(d) adoption of technologies and working methods that reduce pollution

(e) incorporating environmental considerations into new product design.

Major problems are as follows:

(a) Market forces inevitably drive firms to pursue profit at the expense of the environment. If an individual firm adopts an environmentally sensitive posture there is no guarantee that its competitors will be equally responsible. Fears of higher costs, perhaps even of being forced out of business, can cause *all* firms to pollute the environment.

(b) The potentially harmful effects on the environment of new products is not always clear at the time of their development (the fluid used in refrigerators is a good example).

(c) Policing environmental laws and standards is expensive and frequently ineffective, as illegal waste disposal is difficult to detect.

(d) Many elements of the physical environment (such as the air that people breathe) represent 'free goods' in that no single person owns them and they may be used (and abused) at will. This fact has led to the adoption of the 'polluter must pay' principle in most industrially advanced countries, i.e. that public money should not be spent on clearing up private pollution – polluters themselves should be responsible for these costs.

(e) There is a long-run trade-off between economic growth and the sustainability of the environment.

Sustainable development

In 1987 the Brundtland Report of the World Commission on Environment and Development defined 'sustainable development' as that which 'meets the needs of the present without compromising the ability of future generations to meet their own needs', and argued the case for curtailing economic activities throughout the world in order to protect the environment. This has enormous implications for society, ranging from the choice of products made available to consumers to the adaptation of national accounting standards to enable the financial measurement of sustainable resources. Problems of implementation of sustainable development programmes are that:

(a) International action is needed to harmonise and co-ordinate national environmental policies.

(b) Governments have different perceptions of what exactly is meant by sustainability.

(c) Mass production using large amounts of natural resources is fundamental to many economies. Movements towards even partial sustainability will take many years to complete.

(d) A general slowdown in global economic development necessarily means that the world's poorer countries will not be able to catch up with industrially advanced states. This raises all sorts of ethical and political issues, as either the Third World will be condemned to continuing economic deprivation or the flow of aid from developed to developing nations will have to increase.

(e) Businesses operating within competitive markets must adopt relatively short time horizons in order to survive. Yet the economic decisions needed to secure sustainable development will span generations.

A more comprehensive set of principles is contained in the *Charter for Sustainable Development* published by the International Chamber of Commerce, which recommends companies to:

- allocate a high priority to environmental affairs
- integrate environmental policies into all aspects of the work of the enterprise
- continuously seek to improve company environmental protection programmes
- apply the same environmental policies in *all* countries in which the business operates
- educate and encourage employees to behave in an environmentally friendly manner
- conduct environmental impact assessments before undertaking new projects
- develop products that use the minimum energy and natural resources and which can be recycled or disposed of without causing environmental damage
- educate customers and distributors in the best use, storage and disposal of products
- dispose of waste in a responsible fashion
- undertake R&D intended to economise on natural resources and reduce waste and harmful emissions

- modify the methods of production and marketing of products in order to minimise their harmful impact on the environment
- encourage suppliers and sub-contractors to apply environmentally friendly policies
- prepare detailed plans for coping with environmental emergencies caused by accidents
- undertake regular environmental audits.

For information concerning European approaches to environmental protection see the M&E text *European Business*.

25. Corporate behaviour towards the environment

There exists a list of general principles, published by the leading US investment institutions, which some US companies have promised to follow when dealing with the environment. Investors in these companies are then assured that their money will not be used in certain ways. Companies undertake to:

(a) conserve energy

(b) minimise and safely dispose of waste

(c) recycle materials wherever possible

(d) protect the biosphere and eliminate air and water pollutants

(e) produce environment friendly goods and services

(f) reduce health and safety risks to employees and the local community

(g) pay full compensation to victims of environmental malpractice

(h) undertake an annual audit of how the firm's products and policies affect the environment

(i) disclose full information to employees and the general public about incidents that may harm the environment and/or damage public or employees' health

(j) make at least one member of the company's board of directors responsible for environmental matters and for implementing these principles.

INTERPERSONAL EXECUTIVE SKILLS

26. Nature of interpersonal skills

All managers must exercise interpersonal skills at least occasionally, e.g. when briefing colleagues, attending committee meetings, or discussing targets with subordinates. The main categories of interpersonal skill that managers need to study are negotiation (*see* **25**), delegation (*see* 12:**16**) and employee counselling (*see* **28**). Also important are personal organisation (*see* **28**), teamwork (*see* 14:**13**), communication (*see* Chapter 12), interviewing (*see* Chapter 16), presentation skills (*see* 32), personal assertion (*see* 30), and the management of stress (*see* 14:17).

27. Negotiation

There are three types of negotiating situation:

(a) *Conjunctive* negotiation where the parties have no alternative but to reach agreement

(b) *Distributive* negotiation over the relative shares in a fixed quantity of resources that each party will receive

(c) *Integrative* negotiation, where participants seek mutually acceptable solutions to problems.

Negotiation differs from consultation in that whereas the latter involves merely informing others of intended actions prior to taking decisions, negotiation implies willingness to *compromise* on the issues being discussed. Effective negotiation requires the following:

(a) Clear identification of *primary* demands, over which compromise is not possible, and *secondary* demands, on which concessions might be made. Note that primary demands can be relegated to secondary status during the course of a negotiation, and *vice versa*.

(b) Empathy with the feelings and motives of the other side, and careful analysis of the opposition's strengths and weaknesses.

(c) Willingness and the ability to implement negotiated decisions.

(d) Integrity in negotiations, e.g. not withdrawing offers arbitrarily, maintaining confidentiality, not introducing red herrings, etc.

(e) A professional and dispassionate approach.

(f) Sound preparation and a clear set of negotiating aims and strategies. The opponent's arguments and counter-arguments should be predicted in advance.

Frames of reference

Negotiated agreements are sometimes difficult to achieve in consequence of differences in the frames of reference of the parties to the negotiation. Frames of reference are the influences which structure a person's perceptions and interpretations of events. They involve assumptions about reality, attitudes towards what is possible, and conventions regarding correct behaviour for those involved in a dispute.

It has been argued, for example, that management and labour see industrial relations from completely different points of view, in that management tends to assume the absence of any inherent conflicts of interest in industry (the 'unitary' frame of reference), whereas unions perceive the existence of inevitable and deep-rooted conflicts (the 'pluralistic' frame of reference). In consequence, neither side can understand the basic motives of the other. Hence, negotiators need always to try to empathise with the aims of the opposition.

28. Personal organisation

Management is a varied and creative activity that absorbs large amounts of time. Measures are needed, therefore, to maximise the productive output of each working day. Such measures include:

(a) Delegation of routine fact finding and communication tasks to subordinates

(b) Minimising the frequency of interruptions to important work

(c) Careful selection of the duties requiring personal attention.

Personal workplanning involves predicting and listing all jobs needing attention, attaching priorities, and estimating the time required for each activity. Then, predetermined periods may be set aside for each category of work, e.g. dealing with correspondence, preparing reports, receiving visitors, etc. Difficult tasks should be undertaken when the individual feels most creative. A common mistake is for managers to use their most productive hours for work that is interesting but not intellectually demanding.

Activities should be ranked in order of importance, and appropriate amounts of time devoted to each job – a few extra minutes spent reading a report might be worth two or three hours in a meeting. Routine administration, tactical decision taking and day-to-day control involve duties that are scattered and prone to frequent interruption. Yet interruptions waste a great deal of time. Often interruptions arise from unwanted communications – letters, telephone calls, memoranda, etc – that disrupt more creative work. Hence some part of the working day (between 2 and 3 in the afternoon, for instance, by which time all the day's mail will have arrived) should be reserved for communication duties. If a piece of routine correspondence cannot be completed by the end of this allotted period, it should be left until the following day when it will receive first priority. Where possible, each item of correspondence should be handled only once; much time is wasted through duplicated activity resulting from repeated consideration of the same item.

29. Counselling

Counselling is important in many areas of management: performance appraisal (*see* 12:**30–35**), handling employee grievances (*see* 16:**46**), disciplinary procedures (*see* 6:**42**), coaching (*see* 16:**27**), and so on. It is the process of helping people to recognise their feelings about problems, to define those problems accurately, find solutions, or learn to live with a situation. A counselling session could involve giving advice, encouraging a change in behaviour, helping an employee accept an inevitable situation, or assisting someone in taking a difficult decision.

Counselling should occur in private, and without interruption from telephones, secretaries with messages, etc. The aim is not to impose but rather to induce people independently to learn how to overcome difficulties and take appropriate decisions. There are two approaches: directive and non-directive. With *non-directive counselling*, the counselling manager assumes that only the counsellee is capable of defining accurately his or her problems and that the most effective way of getting to the heart of a difficulty is to encourage the other party to discuss the issue at length. It presupposes that solutions to problems will not be implemented unless counsellees wholeheartedly accept their implications.

Directive counselling, conversely, involves taking the initiative and actually suggesting solutions. The possible consequences of various courses of action are outlined, and a range of actions are considered. Here the counsellor *charts a path* towards the correct decision.

Listening

Feedback is essential to good communication. It confirms that messages have been received and understood. If the communicator is entirely insensitive to feedback, then half the communication equation ceases to exist. Messages are transmitted, but their consequences are not assessed. Perceptual biases cause the communicator to misinterpret messages – irrational sentiments are disguised as logic; information that conflicts with preconceived ideas is ignored. Listening, therefore, is a crucially important management skill. Effective listening requires:

- Not interrupting the speaker except to identify points needing expansion. Note however that sitting in complete silence might unnerve and disconcert the speaker, who may assume that he or she is not getting the message across. Hence it is necessary to interject occasionally if only to reassure the speaker that he or she is being understood.
- Concentration.
- Empathy with the speaker.
- Not making judgements until after the speaker has finished speaking. This is a difficult task for a listener who disagrees fundamentally with a speaker's views.
- Regular eye contact between speaker and listener.
- Avoidance of distracting gestures.

30. Personal assertiveness

Assertiveness is not the same as aggression. The latter is intended to hurt, injure, frighten or destroy. It is hostile and harmful and results from base motives such as deprivation, greed, fear or extreme frustration which are rarely encountered in normal business situations. This contrasts with personal assertiveness, which helps individuals to exercise initiative, translate ideas into action and maximise their creative potentials. Positive, decisive attitudes – 'attacking' problems, 'defeating' obstructions, 'mastering' situations – generate states of mind that alleviate feelings of inadequacy, overdependence on others and lack of self-confidence and self-determination. Personal assertiveness enables individuals to seize initiatives and translate ideas into action, with no implications of aggressive intent. Assertiveness is an alternative to aggression (Stubbs 1985), to complete submission to the will of others, and to the avoidance of confrontation.

Advantages to personal assertion

An individual who believes not only in the correctness of a position, but also in his or her fundamental right to state that position, should not experience too many internal inhibitions when putting forward a case. The person will expect to be taken seriously and (importantly) mistakes and minor failures, passing anxieties and petty personal inadequacies, do not assume momentous significance in his or her mind. Hence the individual will not worry too much if on occasion he or she performs inadequately and, if failure occurs, will want to try again. A further benefit is greater empathy, respect and genuine concern for others; inward strength is usually accompanied by heightened awareness of the feelings of fellow human beings, since assertive attitudes equip individuals not only with the internal sense of security necessary for assertive action but also with an unselfish outlook and greater consideration for colleagues.

31. Influence skills

Influence is the effect of one person on the attitudes or behaviour of others. It may be exercised formally or informally and can operate through suggestion, persuasion, example, or threat of sanctions. Factors known to affect an individual's ability to exert influence include:

(a) the credibility of the information offered to the person or group intended to be influenced and the perceived credibility of the individual communicating the information

(b) how well a communication is organised (use of examples and illustrations to support propositions)

(c) the persuadability of the audience

(d) whether the influencer is liked by message recipients

(e) whether message recipients expect the influencer to take the lead and direct their activities.

Persuasion

Managers sometimes have to convince colleagues of the correctness of a certain position, or that they should accept a change. In these cases the facts of the situation cannot simply be allowed to speak for themselves; the expression of opinion is also required. Persuasive advocacy is facilitated by:

- Careful explanation of the case, focusing on the desired outcome while avoiding alternative interpretations of the situation.
- Emphasising points with which the audience will agree and then proceeding from the known and the agreed to issues that are more controversial. The idea behind this is that once message recipients have begun to agree they are likely to continue agreeing when the discussion is extended.
- Motivation of the audience into acceptance of a proposition by clearly indicating how the audience will benefit.
- Having prior knowledge of the audience's views on the matter to be discussed. Persuasion will be more likely the greater the audience's perception that the influencer is knowledgeable, sincere and unbiased.

32. Presentation skills

Presentations are an essential part of contemporary management life. and most managers are required to make presentations at least occasionally, e.g. in team briefings, giving instructions to several people at a time, training employees, making a formal presentation of a new proposal to senior management, making short speeches when colleagues retire, or inducting groups of recently recruited workers.

Sound preparation for a presentation is vital, and needs to cover the following:

(a) Precise determination of the objectives of the presentation. What does the presentation hope to discover? Techniques that are effective for achieving one set of presentation objectives are unlikely to succeed in other situations.

(b) Careful analysis of the potential audience. Are the members of the audience likely to be well informed on the subject? What are their values, opinions, and perspectives? How easily will they absorb the material? Are they capable of concentrating for long periods? To which arguments, examples, etc are they most likely to respond? Who will be present, and what will be their likely state of mind?

(c) Planning the task. The draft needs to contain sections for the introduction, a statement of the proposition, supporting arguments, and recommendations. A central theme should run through the entire presentation to which all comments should relate. Points to be raised should be organised into a logical sequence and delivered one by one with examples, evidence and justifications.

Addressing the audience

Presenters need to emphasise the fundamental points they wish to drive home, possibly repeating them several times during the talk. If a whiteboard, flipchart, overhead projector or other visual aid is being used the speaker must take care to continue addressing the audience and not speak in the direction of the visual aid. The entire audience should be spoken to (not just part of it), and the speaker's voice consciously modulated. Visual aids greatly enhance the quality of presentations. They clarify issues and hence reduce the number of words that need to be spoken, and they help the speaker to segment a talk into natural divisions. Although visual aids can greatly impress an audience, there is danger that the aids themselves might become the focus of the audience's attention instead of the speaker, and they can actually distract an audience. Used properly, visual aids:

- help the speaker complete the presentation faster in a logical manner
- increase the audience's rate of retention of information
- stimulate audience involvement with the discussion
- reinforce key concepts
- create an impression of the speaker's competence
- add variety to the presentation.

Visual aids are especially useful where complex diagrams or technical details are essential to the presentation. Aids should be large enough to be clearly visible to all parts of the audience; and each diagram, heading or statement should be self-contained, clear, and relevant to the discussion. Complicated figures are best put into handouts. If tables are necessary they need to be short, and the numbers within them kept to just three or four digits. An overhead projector should be turned off immediately the speaker has finished discussing the information contained in the transparency under consideration.

Progress test 2

1. Explain the difference between conjunctive and integrative negotiations.

2. Define 'ethics'.

3. What are the advantages of decision taking through committees?

4. Explain the term 'programmed decision making'.

5. What is the difference between brainstorming and synectics?

6. What are the basic categories of managerial competence?

3

BUSINESS OWNERSHIP

SOLE TRADERSHIPS AND PARTNERSHIPS

1. Sole traders

The most basic form of business ownership is the single-person firm without limited liability. This is referred to as a 'sole tradership'. Proprietors of sole traderships run them personally and are responsible for all the debts of their businesses. If the enterprise fails the owner's personal possessions are sold off to raise the money needed to settle outstanding balances. Profits accrue entirely to the proprietor. Advantages of sole traderships are:

(a) that owners have direct, personal interests in their firms and hence will insist that their businesses be as efficient as possible

(b) fast decision taking

(c) close personal relations with staff and customers

(d) that sole trader businesses are easily formed, with little formality or paperwork

(e) low overheads

(f) privacy of affairs (no accounts need be published)

(g) that they are free to diversify as they wish without needing to alter company articles and memoranda of association (*see* 11)

(h) the ability to respond quickly to changing market conditions.

2. Problems with sole traderships

The major drawback is that owners' liabilities for business debts are unlimited. Also, single-person firms are severely restricted by lack of funds for expansion and limited access to capital markets. Small businesses cannot achieve economies of large-scale production, and the absence of scale economies can result in sole traders' prices being higher than in larger enterprises.

Lack of capital could mean the sole trader is unable to afford high-quality premises, fittings, furniture, etc or to advertise adequately. Often, he or she cannot obtain trade discounts for bulk buying, or cash discounts for the immediate settlement of bills. And fear of holding unsold items for long periods may reduce the variety of goods offered. Sole traders who sell on credit may experience difficulty in recovering debts since, typically, they cannot afford lawyers, debt collectors or the implementation of elaborate debt collection procedures.

One-person businesses are chiefly found in industries where quick decisions and personal contact are essential, and where market demand is mainly local. Retailing is particularly suitable for one-person businesses. Other apposite areas are consultancy, small-scale manufacture (fashion goods, for example), the motor trade, and specialist services.

3. Partnerships

Larger businesses are possible through partnerships of two or more individuals. Each partner usually contributes capital, and will often have skills and talents not possessed by other partners. All partners are jointly liable for the debts of the business. It is common therefore for a written agreement to be drafted regulating the partnership's activities. This agreement should define authority and responsibility structures within the business; what and how much work each partner should do; how profits will be distributed, plus variations on any of the matters detailed in 5 and 6 below.

The entire partnership is bound by contracts entered into by any partner, unless the contract is beyond the commercial scope of the business or is clearly for that partner's personal benefit. Normally, management is shared between the partners, though sometimes a 'sleeping partner' will contribute capital but leave the running of the business to other partners. A sleeping partner can obtain protection against liability for the debts of the business by registering the firm as a 'limited partnership' with the Registrar of Companies. In this case the sleeping partner is legally prohibited from taking part in the management of the business, and he or she cannot write cheques or enter contracts on behalf of the firm.

4. Advantages and disadvantages of partnerships

The advantages of partnerships parallel those of sole traders: simplicity, privacy, low overheads, high motivation. Also, partnerships have wider ranges of experiences to call on when taking decisions, administrative tasks can be shared and more capital is available for expansion.

Problems may arise, however, through personal conflicts and policy disagreements between partners. Administration could be slow and inefficient. Although more than one person contributes capital, the firm might still be short of funds, and the continuity of the business is affected when partners die or retire. (The existing partnership automatically ends and a new one must be formed.) Nevertheless, partnership remains an extremely popular form of business organisation.

5. Legal formalities

The legal rules governing partnerships are set out in the Partnership Act 1890. Under this Act, no *written* agreement is needed for a partnership to exist – it is created simply through the agreement of the parties to undertake business jointly and share the profits of the enterprise. The existence of a partnership may be implied by the conduct of a group of people working together, and a partnership's life may end after a single transaction. Note, however, that an association formed to pursue social or recreational activities is not a partnership unless profits are involved. In particular, joint ownership of property is not of itself sufficient to prove that a partnership exists.

Partnerships are not limited-liability organisations and have no existence separate from their members. Thus, a contract with a partnership is a contract with all its members, who are equally liable for discharging the contract. A retiring partner is liable for debts accrued while he or she was associated with the firm, unless a special 'contract of novation' exists between the retiring partner, existing partners, creditors, and a new partner entering the firm. 'Novation' means the substitution of a new legal obligation for an old one with the consent of all parties concerned.

An important implication of joint personal liability for debts is that if some partners are insolvent when a debt is recovered from the partnership, the remaining solvent partners are responsible (to the extent of their personal estates) for all the outstanding amount. This obligation is referred to as the 'joint and several' liability of partners. Partnerships may not contain more than 20 persons (ten if the business concerns banking).

6. Partnership regulations

Although a written agreement should, in principle, be drafted, partnerships often do not bother with this. Accordingly, the 1890 Act specifies rules that apply in the absence of a written partnership document. These rules specify that:

(a) All partners shall share equally in profits and losses of the business, and take equal shares of the partnership's capital assets upon its dissolution.

(b) Partners are equally liable for the business's debts.

(c) Contributions of capital over and above those which partners initially agreed to pay should attract interest at the rate of 5 per cent.

(d) Partners shall share equally in management, and be rewarded via shares in the profit of the enterprise (no salaries are paid).

(e) New partners may not be admitted unless all the existing partners give their consent.

(f) Disputes must be settled by majority vote, unless a change in the nature of the partnership's business is envisaged, in which case a unanimous decision is required.

Any or all of these provisions can be altered via a partnership agreement. However, certain legal obligations cannot be varied or rescinded. Hence, every partner who is not a sleeping partner is an agent of the firm, binding it contractually no matter what the agreement between the partners states. Partners may therefore buy goods for the business or sell its assets, write cheques, or borrow money on behalf of the firm.

COMPANIES

7. Limited liability companies

Owners (shareholders) of a limited liability company are responsible for its debts only to the extent of their shareholding. Thus, someone who holds £10 of shares in a company will lose only £10 even if the company owes millions when liquidated. A limited liability company has its own legal personality. It can enter contracts in its own name, and can sue as an entity quite separate from its owners.

Private limited companies cannot invite the general public to subscribe to their shares or debentures (*see* 9:**22**). The overwhelming majority of limited companies are private. They exist primarily to avoid the owners being personally responsible for their companies' debts, so that the size of their share issues is not an important consideration. Many private companies have a nominal share capital of £100, of which only a small part is actually called up (*see* 9:**18**). Public limited companies (plcs) may raise capital from the general public. They are not obliged to do so but in practice the majority of public companies do in fact invite the public to subscribe.

8. Holding companies

A holding company is a company that possesses a majority shareholding in several other companies which it has either set up or acquired through purchase. Often, each subsidiary performs a specialised function that benefits the group as a whole (e.g. distribution, component manufacture, extraction of raw materials).

Subsidiary units retain their own corporate identities, brand images, etc but are controlled according to a corporate plan devised for the entire group. Operations are thus integrated on a conglomerate basis, although the continuation of individual company units makes it easier to sell off parts of the group that are no longer profitable. Some duplication of activities within the group is inevitable.

9. Advantages and disadvantages of companies

Limited companies enjoy the advantages that:

(a) Since they possess independent legal identities, their existences continue despite the deaths or retirement of shareholders.

(b) Ownership, typically, is separate from control: professional managers may be employed.

(c) Public companies can raise capital through selling shares and hence expand in order to obtain economies of scale.

The disadvantages of forming a company include the following:

(a) The legal (and expensive) requirement to have the company's annual accounts externally audited.

(b) Loss of privacy (annual accounts must be made available for public inspection at Companies House), although companies with low turnovers or employing less than 50 workers need only file very basic information.

(c) For *private* companies, the fact that shareholders (owners) who also work for the company become liable for class 1 National Insurance (NI) contributions as employees, as well as the company paying employer's NI in its role as the employing organisation.

(d) For *public* companies, the tendency towards slow decision making resulting from the separation of ownership and control.

(e) Impersonal relations between owners, managers, customers and the employees of a large company.

10. Business names

Sole traders and partnerships no longer have to register their business names (i.e. names under which they trade other than their family names), but certain restrictions on choice of a name continue and the personal name and address of the owner must always be disclosed. Current legislation is embodied within the Companies Act 1985. Under this Act, it is illegal to choose a name which implies that the business is connected with the government or a local authority or which contains any word on a list of prohibited words (unless special permission is granted), including the words Royal, British, National and Board.

Companies may select any name the Registrar does not consider obscene, offensive or illegal, provided no other company with that name has already been registered.

11. Company formation

Companies are formed (incorporated) by depositing with the Registrar of Companies certain documents, the most important of which are as follows:

(a) *The memorandum of association*, containing an 'objects clause' which specifies the purpose and range of activities of the company. If a company enters contracts in fields not covered by the objects clause (i.e. which are *ultra vires*) it may find that such contracts are not legally enforceable. The memorandum of association also contains some mundane information about the company, such as its name and address and details of its share capital.

(b) *The articles of association*, which specify the internal rules of the company in relation to shareholders' voting rights, periodicity of company meetings, etc. If articles are not deposited then courts will assume that the model articles appended to the Companies Act 1985 apply to that company.

(c) *A statement of the capital of the company*, i.e. the total value of the shares it may issue.

Public companies need at least two shareholders and a minimum of £50,000 of share capital. They must have at least two directors and a company secretary (who may also be a director). Private companies need only one shareholder, one director and a secretary (who cannot also be the sole director).

Today there exist businesses which specialise in company formation and which advertise 'off-the-peg' companies in the financial pages. These 'company registration agents' spend all their time documenting and registering companies, which they then sell for as little as £150 for a private company or £1250 for a public company.

12. Companies limited by guarantee

These are limited companies without share capital where the members guarantee that if the company ceases to trade then each guarantor will make a small contribution (usually £1) towards settlement of the company's debts. Such companies are widely used for educational and other non-profit-making organisations which, nevertheless, require limited liability.

13. Conversion of a private company into a plc

Only a plc can obtain Stock Exchange listings (*see* 9:**24**) and/or sell shares direct to the public. There are other reasons why a private company might choose to become a plc, as follows:

(a) *Prestige*. The announcement that a company is going public – accompanied by impressive press releases describing its markets, products, prospects and operations – can create impressions of success, reliability and competence that greatly enhance its image. This might be important when dealing with foreign customers.

(b) *Availability of credit from suppliers*. The higher share capital requirement of a plc (*see* **11**) encourages suppliers, landlords of business premises, etc to give more credit to plcs than to private companies.

Indeed, some companies 'go public' but then do not issue any further shares! At least one quarter of a public company's £50,000 (minimum) of allotted share capital (*see* 9:**18**) must be paid up. To meet the share capital requirement a private company with retained earnings of at least £50,000 could simply convert £50,000 of its existing book profits into 50,000 £1 shares, which are then 'issued' to current shareholders. No money actually changes hands, and no share dealing charges, taxes or stamp duties are involved. Note that (like a private company) a plc is entitled to impose restrictions or shareholders' rights to transfer shares, provided these restrictions are decided by a majority of shareholders and properly incorporated into the company's articles of association.

Next, the private company's memorandum of association is altered to state that the business is a public rather than a private company. This requires a 'special resolution' of the company's shareholders.

14. Disadvantages of converting to a plc

Becoming a plc creates a number of administrative constraints. The most serious of these perhaps is that (unlike a private company) a plc cannot purchase its own shares unless it pays for them from its distributable profits. (Private companies can redeem their shares using other components of their own capital.) Other problems created by going public are:

(a) The legal obligation to appoint an 'experienced and knowledgeable' company secretary. Section 286 of the Companies Act 1985 lists the legally and professionally qualified people (solicitors or chartered accountants, for example) regarded as suitable for appointment as secretaries of plcs, although a firm is allowed to choose from other sources. In the latter case, however, it may be called upon to justify its decision.

(b) Restrictions on loans to directors are more stringent for a plc than for a private company.

TAKEOVERS

15. Mergers and acquisitions

A merger (or 'amalgamation') is a voluntary and permanent combination of businesses whereby one or more firms integrate their operations and identities with those of another, and henceforth work under a common name and in the interests of the newly formed amalgamation.

Typically, the companies which combine jointly issue new shares in the freshly created organisation to replace existing shares in the merging organisations. This differs from a hostile 'takeover' situation whereby one business buys a majority shareholding in another company, against the wishes of the latter's management. Reasons for mergers and takeovers include:

(a) economies of scale possibly made available through more extensive operations

(b) the desire to acquire businesses already trading in certain markets and/or possessing certain specialist employees and equipment

(c) removal of competitors

(d) acquisition of land, buildings, and other fixed assets that can be profitably sold off

(e) the ability to control supplies of raw materials

(f) expert use of resources, e.g. if one firm possesses large amounts of land and buildings and the other is exceptionally skilled in property management

(g) reduction of the likelihood of company failure through spreading risks over a wider range of activities

(h) full use of production capacity and idle cash, and an increase in the ability to borrow funds

(i) additional financial and other resources, including greater capacity to undertake research

(j) tax considerations, e.g. the carry-over of past trading losses into the merged business

(k) the potential ability of a larger organisation to influence local and national governments

(l) desire to become involved with new technologies and management methods, particularly in high-risk industries.

16. Problems with takeovers and mergers

Many dangers confront newly amalgamated businesses. The following are examples.

(a) Market conditions might suddenly change following a costly acquisition.

(b) New competitors may emerge (attracted perhaps by the publicity surrounding the initial merger or takeover).

(c) Resignations of key employees in the acquired business might occur.

(d) Control difficulties created by having to manage a large and diverse organisation could arise. Note especially the need to collect, analyse and interpret enormous amounts of management information data.

(e) The activities, working methods and organisation structures of the amalgamating firms may turn out to be fundamentally incompatible.

(f) Even if the smaller of the merging businesses is more efficient than the larger, it may have little or no influence on decisions taken by the amalgamated company after the merger.

(g) A firm which takes over another and which pays for it in cash may subsequently become extremely short of liquid assets, whereas a company paying for another business in shares (e.g. two shares of the bidding company in return for one share in the target of the attempted turnover) could experience share dilution (i.e. reductions in earnings per share), to the annoyance of existing shareholders.

(h) Senior managers in one of the firms taken over might not be worth employing in the larger company hence involving the new business in dismissals and consequent employee compensation claims.

(i) Increased size can lead to *diseconomies of scale* rather than improved efficiency: bureaucracy increases and internal communications become difficult.

The financial aspects of takeovers and mergers are discussed in 9:32–40.

17. Choice of takeover target

Factors influencing the choice of takeover target include:

(a) The value of the target company's property and other assets (including its brands, goodwill and trademarks) – *see* 7:7.

(b) Share price of the target.

(c) The number of shareholders in the target company. A business with just a few dominant shareholders who are anxious to sell their shares will be easy to take over, and *vice versa*.

(d) The calibre of the target's management team, and whether existing management will recommend shareholders to accept or reject a takeover bid.

(e) The target's long-term prospects. A company experiencing short-run financial problems will pay poor dividends and in consequence the market price of its shares will fall. Yet the business might be fundamentally sound and thus represent a lucrative takeover opportunity.

18. Avoiding a takeover

A number of strategies are available to companies that wish to avoid being taken over. These include:

(a) Deliberately making a company appear unattractive to existing or potential predators

(b) Fighting particular takeover attempts directly

(c) Financing equity expansion through the issue of 'A' shares (*see* **20** below and 9:**18**).

Making the company unattractive to predators

Although it is easy to make a business unattractive to potential buyers, the actions taken will themselves damage the company in the longer term. Nevertheless, desperate managements do sometimes resort to this tactic. Specific devices include:

(a) Selling land, building and other fixed assets and using the proceeds to pay higher dividends to existing shareholders. Increased dividends might temporarily raise the market price of the company's shares, thus making it more expensive for a predator to buy a majority interest. The method is particularly appropriate if the motivation behind the attempted acquisition is the predator's desire to obtain the fixed assets of the target firm. A sale and leaseback arrangement (*see* 4:**23**) is another possibility.

(b) Locking the firm into long-term supply and customer contracts which the target knows will not appeal to the predator's business.

(c) Making large scrip issues (*see* 9:**25**) to existing shareholders in order to increase for the predator the cost and effort involved in acquiring a majority shareholding.

(d) Borrowing extensively and then rearranging the company's finances so as to be able, in effect, to use the money to pay higher dividends to current shareholders. Share prices will rise temporarily, and if the takeover goes through the predator will be left with a large burden of high-interest debt.

19. Direct action

Directors of the target company might circularise shareholders and advise them not to accept the outsider's bid. If the predator has offered to pay for target company shares using shares in the predator's company the target's circular may argue that acceptance would be against shareholders' interests, because dividends on the predator's shares could deteriorate following the acquisition. This would be due to share dilution (*see* 9:**21**), and declining overall profitability caused by the predator's inability to manage the target firm properly (through lack of experience of the industry, inadequate technical knowledge, limited access to financial resources, etc).

The existing management will enumerate its achievements – especially the company's long-run growth, its commanding positions in various markets, its success in developing new products and so on – and will explain future prospects under the existing management in an attractive manner. Other direct measures to prevent a takeover include:

(a) Encouraging a friendly outside business – quite unconnected with the predator – to purchase a large number of shares in the target company, thus making it more difficult for the predator to acquire a controlling interest. Such friendly outsiders are sometimes referred to as 'White Knight' companies.

The deal may involve an exchange of shares in the White Knight for shares in the target, or a straight cash offer to the target's shareholders – vigorously endorsed by the existing management. Equally the target might issue a large block of freshly created shares direct to the White Knight, provided this is permissible under the target's articles of association (*see* **11**). Inevitably, however, share dilution will result in the latter situation, and current shareholders might object to this occurring.

(b) Merging with another company which is more acceptable to the existing management. Of course, the predator might then attempt to take over the entire newly merged conglomeration, but this will be more difficult in consequence of the increased expenditure needed to buy a majority stake in the larger business. This practice is referred to as 'defensive merger'.

20. Issue of 'A' shares

Non-voting 'A' shares are unattractive to investors (since their prices do not rise during takeover attempts) and thus can only be issued cheaply – and even then there could be few purchasers. Nevertheless, 'A' shares sold at a discount do enable managements to raise additional equity with no possibility of their losing control. Note that the large institutional investors will not normally consider purchasing 'A' shares, which further reduces their marketability.

21. Insolvency buy-outs (IBOs)

An interesting alternative to conventional merger/takeover acquisitions is the insolvency buy-out. This involves purchasing a ready-made business from the receiver (*see* 4:27–30) of an insolvent firm. Often, production and transport facilities, premises, distribution systems and so on can be obtained through purchasing an insolvent company at a fraction of the cost either of developing them from scratch or of buying them from functioning businesses. Receivers advertise these companies in the financial press (the *Financial Times* or *Daltons Weekly*, for example). They also come up for sale through the offices of the Bailiffs of County Courts and of the High Court.

IBO businesses are sold 'as seen'. There are no warranties on the quality of the company's assets, and the purchaser is fully liable for all subsequent problems. This reduces the asking price for an IBO company, as does the fact that its receiver will be looking for a quick and convenient sale; the receiver might be having to clear up the remnants of a collapsed company's operations and his or her involvement will not be cost-effective if it merely involves collecting a few outstanding debts. Disadvantages of insolvency buy-outs include the following:

(a) In taking over the business the purchaser assumes total responsibility for honouring statutory and other guarantees given by the company on its products. Yet defects in these products might have been the *cause* of the firm's failure in the first instance! The purchaser becomes liable for service contracts, supply of spare parts, etc.

(b) The receiver will normally expect the purchaser to pay for the company in cash.

(c) Since the company is bought 'as seen' the purchaser assumes responsibility for any special dividend and/or repayment obligations to shareholders embodied in the company's memorandum and articles of association.

(d) The acquired company will have no liquid assets, and liquid capital might be urgently needed if it is to continue or recommence operations. Transfers of funds into the acquisition from another business might drain the latter of working capital (*see* 9:4).

OTHER FORMS AND ASPECTS OF BUSINESS OWNERSHIP

22. Management buy-outs (MBOs)

These occur when a business's existing owners completely withdraw from involvement in its management and arrange for its assets to be taken over by a new team, consisting primarily of employees of the firm – though perhaps with a new chief executive.

Often MBOs follow rationalisations of major companies, resulting in their discarding duplicated services or divisions. These activities may be profitable, but surplus to the parent company's requirements, e.g. because a division or subsidiary does not conveniently relate to the parent business's overall corporate plan, through shortages of cash in the parent firm, or because an acquisition has not fitted into an existing organisation. Accordingly the parent firm offers the surplus assets for sale (typically at a lower price than otherwise would be the case) to a management team drawn mainly from the current staff. This team approaches external financiers who, very often, are pleased to advance the necessary funds because MBOs carry less risk than conventional investments. The business is already operational. It has markets, established products, customers, goodwill, a sound organisation, skilled and experienced workers, and a well-developed distribution system. The new firm's opportunities for future development and improved efficiency can be clearly identified, and since its staff depend on the continuing existence of the business for their livelihoods they will want the buy-out to prosper.

Banks and venture capital companies sometimes offer special loan packages for MBOs. Note, however, that MBOs do not normally require managers to buy the division or subsidiary entirely from their own pockets; indeed, this is impossible in cases where the assets are worth tens of millions of pounds. Nevertheless, the managers involved are expected to make substantial personal financial investments in the new enterprise in order to demonstrate their commitment to the venture.

Several operational benefits accrue to MBOs:

(a) Management is free to introduce generous performance-related incentive systems. The achievement of stiff targets can be rewarded with salary levels beyond the reach of employees of a larger firm.

(b) Inefficiencies previously tolerated will be ruthlessly exposed. Those who manage the business now have a direct personal interest in the success of its operations.

(c) The new firm can concentrate exclusively on what it does best, without concern for peripheral parent company activities.

(d) Lenders and/or venture capitalists (see 9:30) might provide the specialist top-management expertise (via a non-executive seat on the board, for example) that could be lacking in the MBO team.

23. Problems with MBOs

Overoptimism is perhaps the major difficulty confronting an MBO. Growth potential is overestimated; excessive new investment occurs. Other problems include the following:

(a) Determining a purchase price for the new business (see 9:38–40). A common way of dealing with this is to put the subsidiary or division up for sale and then offer its existing management the opportunity to match the highest bid.

(b) Deciding suitable selling prices for the MBO's product(s) once its inputs, assembly, manufacturing, distribution and ancillary services are its own responsibility and not that of the parent company. Previously, certain costs would have been shared with other divisions or subsidiaries.

(c) Since a substantial part of an MBO's initial capital typically consists of loan finance it will face heavy interest charges during early trading. MBOs are thus exceptionally vulnerable to unanticipated interest-rate increases and are rarely suitable for highly geared, rapidly growing operations with high and expanding demands for working capital.

(d) Possible weaknesses in the management team. Technical ability relevant to the management of a division may not be sufficient to master the strategic complexities of running a complete business.

(e) Inherited plant and equipment might need early replacement, draining the MBO of cash. Not surprisingly, MBOs are less common in capital-intensive industries than in industries where few fixed assets are required.

(f) Conflicts of interest and employee unrest may develop as early hopes are not realised.

24. Management buy-ins

With a management buy-out, control and administration of the company remain with the existing management. This differs from the management buy-in, which involves bringing in an outside team of managers to participate in the day-to-day running of the firm. Frequently the equity needed to persuade existing management to accept the buy-in is provided by a venture capital company (see 9:30). This finance will only be available to a management team that possesses a successful track record in firms similar to the one it is seeking to enter, and which seems able to strike a satisfactory working relationship with the company's existing administration. Businesses that are underperforming for want of a stronger and more experienced management are prime targets for buy-in attempts.

Problems associated with management buy-ins include:

(a) Potential disagreements and conflicts between the current management and the outside team.

(b) The buy-in management team's lack of detailed knowledge of the company's day-to-day operations.

(c) Resentment by employees of the buy-in firm against the imposition by outsiders of new and unfamiliar working methods.

Also, companies seeking buy-in capital might not reveal the true extent of their problems, and then expect entrant managers instantly to cure intractable long-standing difficulties.

25. Continental management buy-outs

MBOs are far less common in continental Western Europe than in the UK. A number of reasons for the relatively low level of continental MBOs may be advanced:

(a) The high levels of reserves (necessary by law in certain EU member states) held within many continental companies. These reserves help firms survive recessions and hence retain divisions and subsidiaries.

(b) The absence of continental equity markets (*see* **27**) capable of financing MBOs.

(c) High salaries and attractive fringe benefits frequently paid to managers in continental companies, causing them to be unwilling to assume the risks attached to an MBO.

(d) The fact that banks are major shareholders in many continental enterprises, meaning that banks (which are normally risk-averse) will tend to discourage the carving-up of companies in which they have a significant financial interest.

(e) The tax regimes of EU countries (apart from Britain and the Netherlands) which are not generally conducive to MBOs.

There are, nevertheless, prospects for expansion in continental MBO activity – largely because of the many mergers, shakeouts and company rationalisations that are occurring in consequence of European economic integration and free trade among member states.

26. Conversion of a plc into a private company

A phenomenon essentially similar to the MBO is that of the quoted public limited company which decides to become a private company. Reasons for this might include:

(a) Resentment over Stock Exchange fees, the cost of using merchant banks, underwriters, etc

(b) High administrative costs for printing prospectuses and other share issue documents (*see* **9:25**)

(c) Market fluctuations which occasionally depress the company's share price to levels where the company becomes vulnerable to a hostile takeover.

Ownership of the reconstructed private company will be concentrated into a few pairs of hands and henceforth there will be a deliberate emphasis on financing from loan capital to avoid interference from outside investors.

The conversion process is straightforward, and the reverse of forming a plc (*see* **11**). Note, however, that the finance needed to repurchase shares currently held by outsiders has to come from distributable profits and may not lawfully be drawn from other sources.

BUSINESS ORGANISATION IN THE EUROPEAN UNION

27. Companies in Europe

Each EU country has its own company laws, practices and organisational structures, some of which differ markedly from those currently prevailing in the

UK. The major similarities and differences between continental and UK companies are as follows:

(a) All EU countries maintain the basic distinction between public (joint stock) and private companies, although registration details regarding minimum numbers of directors and shareholders, minimum share capital, auditing and documentation requirements, etc vary from state to state.

(b) Each member state has a stock exchange through which company securities can be traded, but all of these exchanges are (currently) smaller than that of the UK. The total value of shares quoted on the London Stock Exchange (i.e. its aggregate 'market capitalisation') is more than double that of the German, Italian and French Stock Exchanges combined. This is due to a number of factors:

(i) There are relatively more *family-owned* medium- and large-sized enterprises in most EU states than in Britain.

(ii) Fewer continental public companies are 'listed' on domestic stock exchanges. Instead they tend to raise equity capital via placings (*see* 9:**25**) with large investors. For example, less than 650 German companies are quoted on the Frankfurt Stock Exchange, compared with around 2,500 UK companies quoted on the London Exchange. Italy has barely 200 listed companies, the overwhelming majority of which have less than half their share capitals in the hands of the general public.

(iii) Banks in many EU states invest directly and heavily in companies (especially in Germany). Representatives of banks occupy seats on company boards and help control businesses.

(iv) There is much debenture and loan financing (*see* 9:**22**) in continental countries.

(c) It is common practice (and in some states a legal requirement) to have a two-tier board of directors (*see* 1:**29**). In several EU countries there is compulsory worker participation on supervisory boards (*see* 17:**15–16**).

(d) As in the UK, European joint-stock companies must initiate public share issues with prospectuses detailing their organisation structure, history, names of directors, balance sheets and profit and loss accounts for recent years, etc.

(e) Continental audit requirements are generally less stringent than in the UK.

28. Company structure in EU countries and the incidence of external takeovers

The meagreness of most EU share markets and hence the lack of public companies for sale has meant that relatively fewer company mergers and acquisitions have occurred in many continental countries compared with the UK; although the incidence of mergers and takeovers has increased sharply in recent years as businesses position themselves for competitive advantage in the Single Market.

Shares in medium-to-large continental companies tend to be locked into institutional investors (including banks) thus making UK-style 'dawn raids', hostile takeovers, competing bids, and all the other thrills and spills of the UK takeover market virtually unknown in other EU countries. The *advantages* of this situation are that:

(a) Companies can adopt long-term perspectives, invest, expand and develop without constantly having to be on their guard against unwelcome attempted takeovers.

(b) It provides a stable foundation upon which the macroeconomy can build and prosper.

Disadvantages are that:

(a) Absence of a free competitive market for the buying and selling of companies could mean that resources are not allocated to their most profitable uses.

(b) There is no widespread market mechanism for valuing the worth of companies.

29. Harmonisation of company law within the EU

The EU is seeking to eliminate all major differences between the company laws of member states, so that businesses will operate and compete on truly equal terms throughout the EU. Accordingly, the Council of Ministers has issued a number of Directives, draft Directives, and recommendations in this field.

Agreed directives

Directives have already been issued and/or agreed positions have been reached in the following areas:

(a) Disclosure of information by companies, financial requirements (e.g. minimum subscribed capital for public companies), contents of company accounts (including the consolidated accounts of holding companies).

(b) Minimum qualifications for company auditors.

(c) Procedures for winding up companies.

(d) Responsibilities of parent companies for the operations and liabilities of subsidiaries.

(e) Requirements that shareholders in listed EU companies disclose their shareholdings when they reach any of five thresholds (10 per cent, 20, 33 $\frac{1}{3}$, 50 and 66 $\frac{2}{3}$ per cent).

(f) The nature and extent of the information to be included in company prospectuses when selling securities to the public for the first time.

(g) The information to be provided to authorities of a member state by the branch of a company registered in another member state.

An important agreement is that from now on all member states must allow the existence of *single-person private limited companies* with simplified rules relating to AGMs and other procedural requirements.

The draft directives on European Companies

An important company law proposal has been put forward but has not been agreed, largely in consequence of dissent by the UK, namely that all EU public limited companies shall have *either*:

(*i*) a single board with a majority of non-executive directors (*see* 1:**25**) that is empowered to appoint and dismiss executive directors; *or*

(*ii*) a two-tier board comprising a 'management' (executive) board and, above that, a 'supervisory' board (*see* 1:**29**).

The proposal also stipulates that plcs employing more than 1000 people in the EU shall have employee participation in company decision making via works councils (*see* 17:**15**) with representation on company boards, or elected worker directors (*see* 17:**16**). Between one third and one half of a single or supervisory board would consist of employee representatives.

30. European Economic Interest Groups (EEIGs)

These are combinations of European businesses (companies, partnerships, or sole traders) which extend over at least two EU states. Their purpose is to pool common research and development or marketing activities, or to manage particular projects. However, an EEIG must not seek to make profits 'in its own right'.

An EEIG has a separate legal identity (established via a procedure laid down in an EU regulation of 1985), but individual members have unlimited liability for the debts of the entire group. EEIGs need not have any capital and are not required to file annual reports or accounts.

Benefits accruing to EEIGs include:

(a) Economies of scale available from combining the operations of several businesses

(b) Retention of independent status by each member organisation

(c) Provision of a vehicle through which small firms may collectively bid for large contracts

(d) The ability of a small business to enter new lines of work and unfamiliar territory

(e) Pooling of risks

(f) Groups can be set up by different forms of organisation (companies, sole traders, partnerships, etc) and different sizes of business

(g) The ease with which an EEIG can be formed and disbanded. A group can be wound up by a unanimous decision of its members, or will automatically end on expiry of a stated contract period or when the purpose for which the group was set up has been accomplished.

The contract that establishes an EEIG must specify its name (which has to include the words 'European Economic Interest Group' or their initials), address, the objects for which the grouping is formed, details of participants, and the duration of the contract (unless this is indefinite). The contract is then registered in the member state where the EEIG has its head office. Member businesses must decide how the group is to be financed and its revenue distributed. If there is no explicit agreement on this point it is assumed that all participants will contribute equal shares and receive equal revenue.

Problems with EEIGs are that they:

(a) cannot raise money from the general public

(b) must not control the activities of any member firm

(c) are taxed in line with national laws just like any other business

(d) cannot trade and seek profit on their own accounts.

CO-OPERATIVES, FRANCHISES, AND THE MNC

31. Co-operatives

These are businesses that follow the principle of one vote per member, regardless of the extent of a member's shareholdings in the firm. Workers' co-operatives (sometimes called 'producer' co-operatives) are owned by employees who elect management and divide profits among themselves. Consumer co-operatives are owned by customers. A consumer co-operative will buy and distribute goods, and often will purchase manufacturing units and sources of raw materials that contribute to finished products. A co-operative can acquire limited liability either by registering as a limited company under the Companies Act 1985 and by incorporating co-operative principles into its memorandum and articles of association, or by registering under the Industrial and Provident Societies Acts (IPSA), which defines specific requirements for the administration of co-operatives registered in this way. These IPSA rules relate to such matters as:

(a) whether members shall consist only of the co-operative's founders or whether all employees shall be members

(b) how the co-operative's surplus assets shall be distributed following its dissolution

(c) returns to members and others who lend to or otherwise invest in the co-operative.

There exist 'sponsoring agencies' which offer preprinted registration packages (akin to off-the-peg companies) to firms wishing to register as IPSA co-operatives. Registration is with the Registrar of Friendly Societies, and at least seven members are required.

32. Advantages and disadvantages of co-operatives

The advantages of co-operatives include equitable distribution of profits to workers and/or consumers, lower prices through removal of intermediate stages of production and/or distribution, and the potential for improvements in labour relations. Disadvantages are as follows:

(a) Possible lack of commitment to co-operative principles on the part of some employees.

(b) Conflicts arising between co-operative principles and the need for commercial success.

(c) Difficulties in finding new members who possess much needed technical and/or business skills and who are sufficiently interested in joining a co-operative. This might result in the business having to hire skilled workers either as non-voting employees or as sub-contractors. Hence the co-operative starts to act as a conventional employer and becomes involved in industrial relations disputes, dismissal and appeals procedures, wage bargaining, etc.

(d) Better qualified or experienced members of staff may resent having only the same management authority as junior colleagues especially when some members have contributed more capital, time and/or equipment than the rest.

33. Franchising

A franchise agreement enables a small business (with or without limited liability) to adopt a complete business format already developed by a parent organisation. Franchising is increasingly important in retail outlets for fast food, car hire, petrol stations, printing, motor repairs, and many other areas. Franchisees purchase the right to market a product or service under the franchisor's name and trade mark, and to utilise well-established business methods. The system has allowed many people to start businesses which otherwise would not have been possible through lack of finance, business knowledge and technical expertise; franchisees are sheltered under a protective umbrella of specialist skills, resources and experiences already possessed by the parent organisation.

In exchange for an initial fee plus continuing royalty payments, the franchisee obtains a well-known name supported by a variety of supplementary services which include financial loans, training in business administration, technical advice and guidelines (possibly directives) on pricing policy. If the franchisor is a manufacturer, the franchisee is usually required to purchase supplies (for example, meat for hamburgers, spare parts, ingredients for alcoholic or soft drinks) from the franchisor at prices determined by the parent firm, which also undertakes national advertising.

To succeed, a franchised product needs a steady nationwide demand, a unique image, and methods of production and presentation that can be standardised.

34. Advantages and disadvantages to franchisors

Advantages to franchisors include:

(a) Franchisees are self-employed, not employees of the parent firm. Thus, franchisees will be highly motivated to succeed in their own businesses. There are no strikes, go-slows, work-to-rules or other industrial relations problems.

(b) Expansion of retail distribution networks is cheap because franchisees carry most of the costs, and importantly, assume the risk of failure.

(c) New and unfamiliar market segments can be entered using the skills, experiences and local background knowledge of neighbourhood-based franchisees.

(d) Since large distribution networks are tied to supplies from single companies, there exist opportunities for bulk buying of raw materials at big discounts.

(e) As a franchise operation grows, trade marks, brand names and product styles become widely known to the public. The franchisor's name becomes nationally recognised.

(f) The nucleus of the franchisor's organisation remains small, and overheads are low. Large profits can result from a limited capital base. Moreover, routine administrative problems are dealt with by outlets, not central office.

The disadvantages from the franchisor's viewpoint are that it loses control over day-to-day operations and that aggregate returns are lower than if it took all proceeds from sales and not just a royalty. Other problems arise from franchisees being independent businesses rather than employees – they cannot be 'dismissed', and termination of a contract might be difficult. Typically, franchisees regard themselves as owners of their outlets (which they are not) and begrudge interference from the parent company. Also a franchisee might learn a business from top to bottom while under contract, only to set up a competing outlet on its expiry.

35. Advantages and disadvantages to franchisees

A franchise can be purchased (often with a loan arranged by the franchisor) for less than usually has to be paid for an existing business. Outlets receive advice on book-keeping, tax liability, training of staff, stock control, layout of premises and so on. Advertising, technical development and market research is dealt with by the parent company. Competition is restricted because franchisors will not franchise more than one outlet within a certain locality.

On the other hand, franchisees have no discretion over products, layouts or working methods. Unjustifiably-high raw materials prices might be charged by franchisors and, unlike ordinary businesses, franchised outlets cannot be sold without the franchisor's permission. Further problems are as follows:

(a) The brand image of the franchised product may deteriorate for reasons beyond the franchisee's control.

(b) Since royalties are invariably expressed as fixed percentages of turnover, hard-working, successful franchisees will have to pay ever-increasing sums to their franchisors. Yet, franchisees who fail lose everything.

(c) Franchise contracts cover relatively short periods, normally five years. A successful franchisee who has increased the profitability of an outlet will find that it reverts to the franchisor following expiry of the franchise contract. The franchisor will then demand higher royalties in line with the increased value of the outlet.

36. Multinational corporations

A multinational corporation (MNC) is a business that has its headquarters (domicile) in one country but which operates in many. The management of an MNC has responsibility for operations throughout the world. In consequence, its board of directors might comprise a two-tier system consisting of a strategic board which determines global policy, and one or more national boards responsible for implementing this policy in particular countries. Also, line management must be related to the geographical regions served by the corporation.

Major differences between MNCs and one-country firms are as follows:

(a) Departments dealing with individual national markets might have to give way to departments that deal with market segments defined across, rather than within, countries.

(b) Recruitment, training, appraisal and promotion procedures must be drafted on an international scale.

(c) Since they operate in many countries and market segments, opportunities for diversification are usually greater for multinationals than for other types of firm. Specific diversification issues include:

(i) choice of national markets for final products
(ii) location of production facilities
(iii) sources of raw materials
(iv) whether to produce components locally, buy them locally, import them from another of the MNC's subsidiaries in another country, or buy and import them from the rest of the world.

(d) Multinationals, because of their size, can afford to assume relatively more risk than domestic rivals. A loss in one country can be offset against profits elsewhere.

37. Organisation structures for MNCs

MNCs may select from a variety of possible forms of organisation, notably:

- International subsidiary structure
- International division structure
- Geographic structure (*see* 6:8)
- Product structure (*see* 6:6)
- Matrix structure (*see* 6:20).

Note, however, that a straightforward functional structure (*see* 6:5) is not normally appropriate for an MNC, because each functional department would need to deal with several disparate territories, all possessing unique problems and characteristics.

International subsidiary structure

Here the parent company undertakes all the organisation's main functional activities (usually including production) but sets up a number of subsidiary boards, each responsible for developing a particular market and reporting directly to head office. This is a simple and inexpensive approach to international organisation, which provides for local responses to changes in local conditions while maintaining effective central control. It is useful, moreover, for the training and development of managers within subsidiary boards.

Problems with the approach include the need for extensive liaison and co-ordination, and the tendency for subsidiary boards to mirror (perhaps inappropriately) the structure of the main company. Incorrect strategies might be imposed on subsidiaries, and local managers could lose sight of the global objectives of the organisation.

International divisional structure

Divisionalisation is discussed in 6:**18**. International divisions of MNCs furnish support services for marketing, manufacture, finance, distribution, etc to the company's operating units throughout the world. Divisions themselves may be organised along centralised or decentralised lines (*see* 6:**17**). International divisions provide the firm with a convenient device for developing a multinational strategy, and decisions on international matters are taken at the heart of the enterprise. Divisions acquire experience and expertise in international business.

Disadvantages to this form of organisation are its possible inability to handle extremely diverse international operations; the potential for conflict between domestic and international divisions; and the risk that senior management at head office will not take the international divisions seriously.

Geographic (regional) structure

This involves establishing regional divisions, each responsible for a certain part of the globe (Europe, South America, the Pacific Rim, etc). Strategies are determined at headquarters, leaving regional managements in day-to-day control. Operations can be specifically designed to suit regional conditions. Geographic structure is commonest when the countries covered by a division are in close proximity and the same product is being marketed in the area concerned. The system is clear, logical and easy to apply. There is close co-ordination between production and marketing, and local needs are taken into account. However, it becomes difficult for managers to adopt a totally international perspective on the enterprise's worldwide activities and there could be insufficient emphasis on new-product development.

Product structure

Here the firm sets up a separate division for each of its products. The system is appropriate for organisations that supply several unrelated types of product or where significant product modifications for various markets are required. Product structure is useful for management development. Each product division will be a cost centre (*see* 9:**6**) in its own right.

Problems with product structure are that the importance of marketing might not be properly recognised, and that important regions could be overlooked. Moreover, co-ordination across product divisions may be difficult.

Matrix structure

This offers a means for balancing geographic and product requirements. It is suitable for fast-changing environments and/or when complex decisions have to be made. The matrix can define groups responsible for various aspects of international operations, cutting across conventional departmental bounds. Advantages and disadvantages of matrix structure are discussed in 6:20.

Choice of structure

Final selection of the form of organisational structure for an MNC should depend on the following factors:

(a) The number, size, types and complexity of operating units in various countries.

(b) Ability levels and experience of the MNC's staff in each country, especially their capacities to think strategically and plan for the long term.

(c) Ease of communication with and control of operating units.

(d) Availability of local finance and other resources.

(e) Stability of local markets (the more uncertain the local market, the greater the need for local control).

38. Staffing problems of MNCs

An MNC must decide whether to recruit staff in host countries, or rely entirely on expatriate personnel. Locally-recruited managers possess intimate knowledge of local conditions, but might not be of the same calibre as managers brought in from outside. Equally, managers who are recruited in and are nationals of the MNC's home country might not be competent to run all the corporation's foreign operations. There may be language problems, cultural differences between regions that home country managers cannot understand, and general lack of knowledge of foreign business conditions.

Special problems apply to recruitment in underdeveloped economies, since these might not possess the education and training facilities that in advanced economies generate technically qualified and experienced management staff.

39. Advantages of MNCs

Multinational corporations can create economies of scale in production, distribution, staff utilisation, and resource procurement and allocation on a world-wide level. They have easy access to the world's capital markets and thus can finance huge investment projects with enormous productive potential. New ideas, new technologies and business methods are transmitted from industrialised to developing nations. The vast resources of an MNC enables product, processes and marketing research to be undertaken on a global scale.

Managerial staff can be trained and developed to their maximum potential. The full advantages of international specialisation can be obtained; resources are procured where they are available at lowest cost, and finished output is sold where the demand for it is greatest.

40. Disadvantages associated with MNCs

The special difficulties sometimes experienced by MNCs include:

(a) The efficiency of a foreign operation can be affected by many factors beyond the parent company's control.

(b) Communications problems might prevent the development of an effective worldwide management information system.

(c) To compare the profitability of various foreign subsidiaries it is necessary to convert local currency profits into a base currency, say sterling. But then the reported results will depend crucially on fluctuations in the rates of exchange between local currencies and the chosen base.

(d) MNCs are subject to the laws of more than one country. Host nations may require that a certain minimum percentage of an MNC's local board be their own nationals, or that some specified proportion of the share capital of an MNC's local operations be held by local residents.

(e) Host countries could impose restrictions on:

  (*i*) repatriation of profits
  (*ii*) accounting methods (to ensure that subsidiaries pay appropriate amounts of tax)
  (*iii*) the prices at which goods are exported
  (*iv*) access to local capital markets.

(f) Salary levels between countries can be enormous, leading to great resentment among locally-recruited employees against higher-paid expatriate home country staff.

Progress test 3

1. To what extent are sole traders liable for the debts of their businesses?

2. State three financial problems likely to be experienced by a partnership.

3. List three advantages and three disadvantages of a limited liability company.

4. In what circumstances might a producing firm decide to franchise the retail distribution of its output?

5. List the main problems that might be experienced following the takeover of one firm by another.

6. Explain the difference between a producer co-operative and a consumer co-operative.

7. What is a holding company?

8. Give four examples of unlawful business names.

9. Describe the main staffing problems faced by multinational corporations.

4

ENTREPRENEURSHIP AND SMALL BUSINESS MANAGEMENT

ENTREPRENEURSHIP

1. Management and entrepreneurship

Entrepreneurs organise, manage and assume the risks of businesses in order to earn profit. In the past, entrepreneurship has been associated with the ownership of businesses. Today, however, paid managerial employees frequently undertake entrepreneurial tasks. Even so, the study of entrepreneurship is important for the following reasons:

(a) Arguably, limited liability and the growth of the scale of business operations have created among managers substantial ability to manipulate resources *within* firms, but not innovative qualities and the ability to conceive and establish completely new businesses.

(b) Entrepreneurial flair and leadership ability seem to be closely linked.

(c) The adoption of entrepreneurial attitudes by the managerial employees of large organisations can frequently help these managers succeed in their work.

2. Factors encouraging entrepreneurship

An interesting observation is that in nearly every nation a sizeable proportion of leading entrepreneurs are immigrants or the first generation children of immigrants – due perhaps to the traumatic effects of the disruption of family and other ties, feelings of isolation, and *forced* self-reliance in a strange new world. Likewise, the entrepreneurial spirit is sometimes aroused in those who suffer family or other social disruptions. Separation from a social milieu (protracted military service during a war, for example), a broken home, illness or redundancy can cause individuals to rethink fundamentally the purpose of their lives and hence induce them to start businesses. Research indicates that entrepreneurial attitudes emerge wherever economic circumstances are conducive to their development. Among the factors necessary for the development of an entrepreneurial culture the following may be listed:

(a) The ability of individuals independently to procure resources for innovative activity

(b) Sympathy and support from like-minded people during times of crisis

(c) Relatively weak opposition from existing competitors and those with a vested interest in maintaining the *status quo*

(d) Perceived legitimacy of entrepreneurial attitudes, reinforced by family, friends and/or working colleagues

(e) Genuine opportunities for doing things differently and/or in entirely new ways; new products, materials, methods, systems and processes not easily handled within existing organisational frameworks

(f) Confidence in the future; belief that current effort and activities will be properly rewarded

(g) Convictions that new ideas and methods are for the social as well as individual good.

The entrepreneurial person is typically motivated as much by the prospect of creative achievement and/or high reward as by the need for security. Very often, stimuli to such feelings are culturally and societally based – certain societies have a tradition of self-reliance – manifest in desire for self-employment, to own one's own business, and to be 'one's own boss'.

3. Intrapreneurship

Within large businesses, 'organisational design' (*see* Chapter 6) is frequently regarded as the key function of management. Great effort is devoted to establishing efficient frameworks for managing *existing* systems, while the need for new and different forms of activity may be overlooked. Risk taking, coping with uncertainty, responding swiftly to changing market opportunities – these are the fundamental innovative abilities that sometimes become lost in oligarchic organisational forms.

The term 'intrapreneurship' is sometimes used to describe the existence of entrepreneurial attitudes within employees of large organisations. It can be fostered through making managers personally responsible for budgets related to their individual functions, or through treating departments as independent self-financing enterprises (which 'buy in' inputs and services from other parts of the organisation) for the purposes of budgeting and control.

Accordingly, intrapreneurship concerns the *spirit* of enterprise, even if there is complete separation of business ownership from management control. The intrapreneurial manager behaves *as if* he or she actually owns the firm. It follows that intrapreneurship is a *state of mind*, with the following distinguishing features:

(a) Perseverance and determination, manifested in willingness to work extremely hard.

(b) Willingness to take risks, though only after a careful investigation of the likelihood of success.

(c) An intuitive understanding of the operation of the marketplace, particularly in relation to the identification of new market opportunities.

(d) Unwillingness to be bound by convention, plus a dislike of bureaucracy and restrictive rules.

(e) Enthusiasm for business, emotional commitment to an organisation, the ability to inspire loyalty in subordinates and the ability to instil feelings of confidence in outside suppliers, customers and other external bodies.

4. Government policy towards new business

The success of a new business will depend on the attractiveness of its product, its cost-efficiency, interpersonal relationships within the firm, the effectiveness of its distribution network, and its owner's capacity for hard work. Unfortunately, most new businesses fail, and there are of course many reasons why this should be so (*see* 7).

Governments seek to minimise the rate of small business failure in a number of ways, particularly through:

(a) The provision of advice and information, free counselling, booklets, trade statistics, etc

(b) Subsidised training in the techniques of small business management

(c) Grants for engaging external consultants

(d) Paying owners of new businesses a personal allowance during the first year of operations

(e) Guaranteeing the repayment of parts of the loans that banks make to newly established small firms.

5. New businesses

A new business requires an idea, effort, organisation and capital. New firms may enter an existing industry using tried and tested organisation structures and policies copied from businesses already within the industry; or they might have completely new innovations. Entry to existing industries is by far the commonest mode of new business start-up. Precedents can be followed, trained and experienced labour is readily available, and existing technical methods may be emulated.

Often the people who start businesses have already worked in the relevant industry, but feel they can do better than competing firms. Frequently, however, new entrants underestimate the difficulties associated with inducing consumers to switch to a new source of supply, particularly in a static market. A firm founded on a totally new innovation has the advantage of a completely undisturbed (but untested) market and has no competitors in the short run. The new business might seek to replace entirely an existing product, method or system, or modify these in novel ways. Sometimes, a product that is widely used abroad can be introduced to a domestic economy where it has not previously been experienced.

New business development is particularly difficult when a large scale of plant is required before operations can begin. Here, start-up capital has to be substantial, so most new businesses of this type emanate from the diversification of existing firms (although it may be possible for a small business to operate initially as a supplier or as a sub-contractor to a larger unit in this case). To succeed, a new business requires:

(a) a product or service suitable for an existing or anticipated market

(b) marketing and organisational abilities

(c) adequate resources: start-up capital, premises, equipment, etc

(d) commitment and ability on the part of the owner.

SMALL BUSINESS MANAGEMENT

6. Management problems of new small businesses

Small businesses have management problems substantially different from those of larger firms. Particular difficulties result from the inability to employ specialist staff and/or to conduct comprehensive marketing research. The owner/manager of a small firm has to undertake all major management functions personally, and must deal with every administrative requirement (licensing, tax and national insurance, VAT, fire certificates, employment laws, redundancy regulations, audit requirements, etc) him or herself.

Individuals considering setting up a small business need to recognise the following realities of small business start-up and control:

(a) Many people establish their own businesses because they have been declared redundant or have otherwise become unemployed. High unemployment rates indicate a depressed local economy and general lack of consumer demand. The worst possible time to launch a new business is during a depression, since there may be insufficient customers willing or able to buy the (perhaps excellent) output of the new firm. And even if business conditions improve, larger firms may expand and take up all the extra consumer demand.

(b) Sickness, lack of stamina, or even a temporary loss of enthusiasm can cause a one-person business to fail.

(c) Numerous and diverse skills and abilities are required – plus a considerable amount of good fortune. People often underestimate the expertise necessary to make a business succeed.

(d) Eventually a small business will need to employ staff, requiring the establishment of personnel records and procedures (contracts of employment, PAYE, use of a payroll program, etc). Owners must supervise employees, exercise leadership, and motivate others to work hard.

7. Common causes of small business collapse

Failures frequently result from:

(a) lack of experience

(b) inadequate technical knowledge

(c) poor market research

(d) administrative incompetence

(e) uneven flows of work

(f) owners not preparing adequate cash flow forecasts

(g) underestimation of the set-up costs and time needed to establish a new business

(h) over-optimistic estimates of market demand

(i) inability to persuade banks and other lenders to provide short-term funds (notably through not being able to prepare and convincingly present a professional-looking business plan)

(j) failure to realise that credit customers do not always pay their bills.

Failure is less likely where small business owners:

(a) possess initiative and self-confidence, are prepared to take risks and do not feel ashamed when things go wrong

(b) are capable of devoting their full attention to a wide range of problems at the same time

(c) possess good communication skills and can inspire the confidence of others

(d) are resilient and capable of recovering from setbacks

(e) devise strategies for future activities (notably for marketing the product) and maintain careful records (especially management accounts) to monitor the firm's progress

(f) do not expand too quickly, and ensure that working capital is sufficient to support the intended growth.

8. The business plan

Business plans have three purposes: (*i*) to help proprietors examine impartially and systematically the merits of business proposals; (*ii*) to convince outside bodies (especially banks or other financiers) that ventures are worthwhile; and (*iii*) to establish criteria for assessing progress towards achieving short-to-medium-term objectives.

The plan should normally be organised as a report with the following headings:

(a) *Introduction* – the original idea behind the business. How the business will compare with others in the area. The purpose of the business.

(b) *The product or service to be offered* – production techniques, raw materials and skilled labour availabilities. Special production methods. Sources of supply of inputs, and whether components are to be bought or manufactured.

(c) *Marketing methods* – unique selling points. Comparisons with the products of competitors. Who will buy the product, and why. Size and structure of the existing market. Profiles of potential customers. Market research already undertaken. Which market segments offer the best chances of success? Customer ordering systems. Pricing strategy in relation to production costs.

(d) *Distribution* – number and nature of outlets. Availability of alternative distribution channels. Adequacy of existing distribution networks. Special distribution problems (breakages, perishability of output, need for expensive packaging, possibility of contamination) and how they will be overcome. Measures to prevent pilfering. Warehousing requirements. How many vehicles are needed and where they will be garaged?

(e) *Contingency plans* – details of what will happen if supplies are interrupted, alternative sources of raw material, effects of bad weather, strikes by distributors, etc. Listing of insurances taken out and the extent of their cover.

(f) *Competition* – extent and character of competition (including future competition). Location of competing firms and the quality of their output. Why the new business expects to be able to beat its competitors.

(g) *Personnel* – curricula vitae of the business owners and key employees, including full details of their formal qualifications, experience of the intended line of business, administrative experience and management skills.

(h) *Organisation* – proposed legal structure (partnership, limited company or whatever). Who will be in charge? Details of who will take over if the owner falls ill. Extent of administrative support. Relations with external bodies (e.g. local authorities and business advisers).

(i) *Premises* – nature of the area in which the premises will be located. Facilities available (word-processing, photocopying, etc). Description of the intended premises. Length of the proposed lease.

(j) *Legal formalities* – listings of all legal matters affecting the business: licences, fire certificates, insurance, health and safety requirements. Who is to be responsible for ensuring all legal requirements are met?

(k) *Financial matters*.

(*i*) Estimates of the capital needed for stocking up, acquiring premises and raw materials, fitting out premises, etc. How much money will be taken out of the business for living expenses. A comprehensive 12-month cash flow forecast and estimated year-end profit and loss account and balance sheet. The extent of credit to be offered, and the sensitivity of the business to late payment by key customers. How much is required for major capital expenditures? Provisions for bad debts and other contingency allowances.

(*ii*) Personal means of the proprietor(s). The extent of their personal investment in the business; their property, insurance policies and other assets that can be used as security when raising finance.

(**l**) *Objectives* – sales targets and the breakeven point. Anticipated profit margins. Key objectives for the next year, three years and five years. Outline budgets and cash flow forecasts for the next two or three years.

Plans need to be supported by market research statistics, product specifications, examples of potential buyers, results of surveys, etc. They must detail precisely *how* things will be done. Lenders want to know exactly the purposes for which money advanced will be used and how repayments will be supported.

9. Business premises

New businesses need to look ahead when selecting premises. A size and location appropriate for current needs may not be adequate in the future. Key considerations include:

(**a**) Is there sufficient parking space for customers and suppliers? Are public transport facilities available nearby?

(**b**) If customers will enter the premises to buy goods, what is the socio-economic composition of the local community and are there sufficient potential customers within the business's catchment area?

(**c**) Are lighting, heating, gas, electricity and water supplies adequate?

(**d**) How secure are the premises against burglars and vandals?

(**e**) Is an impressive-looking fascia necessary?

(**f**) How near are competing businesses?

(**g**) If the business expands, will a move to different premises become necessary and if so when?

(**h**) Are skilled workers available within easy travelling distance?

(**i**) How near are back-up services, trading associates, raw materials suppliers, etc?

(**j**) Will the business address project a poor or favourable image of the firm?

(**k**) Will the neighbourhood change in character over the next few years?

10. Leasing versus buying premises

Firms which purchase their premises retain increases in their capital value, and owned premises can be offered as security against loans. Conversely, leasehold premises require no capital outlay, and cannot be seized by creditors if the business fails.

Tenants face restrictions on their use of rented premises: structural alterations are not allowed; nor is subletting without the landlord's permission and payment of additional rent. Leases typically involve periodic rent reviews, and have to be renewed occasionally. However, it is often easier to rent than to buy, and tenants are not usually responsible for maintenance. Also, if a rented building turns out to be unsuitable – either physically or because of restrictions on traffic, noise, local authority limits on working hours, etc – then the business can cancel its lease and move to another location.

Every business requires local authority planning permission, or a 'change of use' certificate if the purpose for which the business premises are used is altered (e.g. from retailing to light engineering). However, certificates are not normally withheld unless the business would cause a nuisance or a safety or health hazard. Applications for planning permission must include details of the premises' existing and proposed use, external appearance and parking space, size, how many people the firm will employ and their working hours, the movement of vehicles to and from the premises, plus information on waste disposal methods and requirements for storing any hazardous materials.

11. Workspace premises

Local authorities and private property developers offer to small businesses 'workspace premises' whereby many small businesses share the same floor of a building. The building is 'open plan', each business occupying a defined area and sharing heating, lighting, a telephone switchboard, and perhaps even secretarial, mailing and photocopying facilities. There is a common cleaning and catering service and communal rooms for meetings and conferences. Sharing joint facilities cuts costs, and business expansion is easily accommodated by taking over adjacent workspaces. Drawbacks to workspace premises include the absence of security of tenure (they are usually let on a monthly basis), the noise and loss of privacy associated with open plan environments, and possible theft of tools and materials.

12. Financing a small business

New businesses normally begin by raising finance from founder members' resources (savings, loans from friends and relatives, sale of personal assets to raise funds) through judicious use of deferred payments for supplies, and the leasing rather than purchase of equipment. Inevitably, however, new firms will eventually need external finance. Sources of business finance are described in Chapter 9. Potential lenders will want to see the firm's business plan, plus an outline budget and detailed cash flow forecast (*see* below).

13. The outline budget

This consists of a listing of all major items of anticipated spending and sources of finance. Thus, sales revenues, loans, grants and other anticipated income for the year should be shown on one side, and expected expenditures on plant and equipment, premises, raw materials, wages, local authority rates, heating and lighting, advertising, telephone and postage, etc, on the other. Three sets of figures are needed: most optimistic, most pessimistic and most likely; each relating to various sets of possible future circumstances.

14. The cash flow forecast (CFF)

Aggregate planned income and expenditure for the year should be broken down into monthly totals showing expected receipts and payments for each month, with the closing cash balance of one month being carried forward to an opening balance for the next. The CFF is important because it takes into account the effects on monthly cash balances of credit sales and the *timing* of expenditures. Businesses frequently fail because – despite their being potentially solvent in aggregate terms – they do not realise that debtors can take extremely long periods to settle bills, whereas suppliers may have to be paid instantly and in cash. Certain quarterly payments might all fall due at the same time, possibly coinciding with other large expenditures.

Each month's figures should contain details of cash sales and stationery, etc, a realistic estimate of revenue from credit sales, business expenses (telephone, heating, stationery, etc), payments for capital equipment, wages and drawings, loan repayments and (where applicable) tax and national insurance obligations, including VAT. The methods used to calculate figures should be specified in notes appended to the document. For example, it might be assumed that one quarter of all invoices sent out during a month will be paid within that month, half during the next month, and two-thirds of the remainder in the month after that. Similarly, the CFF might assume that all materials and equipment purchases are paid for in the month following delivery.

15. Insurance

Employer's liability insurance is compulsory. Other forms of insurance are *highly* desirable, especially for business premises, plant and equipment, stock and work in progress. Commercial vehicles require separate insurance, while private vehicles used for business purposes need extra 'commercial use' policies. Further insurance might be taken out for:

(a) Consequential loss, i.e. compensation for loss of business and disruption *following* a disaster (quite apart from the loss of capital assets)

(b) Personal accident policies for owners

(c) Theft policies covering losses incurred via pilfering by staff, customers, break-in thieves, etc

(d) Goods-in-transit insurance

(e) Professional liability insurance, which covers liability arising from wrongful and/or negligent professional advice given to clients

(f) Credit insurance against defaulting customers

(g) Legal expenses insurance to cover the legal costs of disputes in which the business innocently becomes involved

(h) Public liability insurance to protect against liability to third parties killed or injured through defects in the firm's premises or through the negligence of employees

(i) Product liability cover against defects in products causing injury to customers.

Together these insurances constitute a considerable expense, and can affect substantially the business's cash flow.

16. Legal structures for small businesses

Small firms may be sole traderships, partnerships, co-operatives or limited companies. Sole traders (or partners) are entirely responsible for their own tax and NI. Tax is paid bi-annually on business profits; self-employed NI contributions are paid monthly by cheque or direct debit. When a business becomes a limited company the people running it become *employees* of the company and thus become liable to PAYE and class 1 NI contributions. Additionally, the company must also pay *employer's* NI contributions as an employer in its own right.

Payments by a limited company to its directors are deductible business expenses as far as the company is concerned and count as taxable income for the directors receiving them. Profits earned by the company attract corporation tax, but for small businesses (with annual profits below a certain threshold) the rate of corporation tax is the same as the basic rate of personal income tax, although the concession is only available for one company at a time.

17. Close companies

Companies with five or fewer shareholders (or which are controlled by any number of directors who are also shareholders) are called 'close companies'. The tax authorities might attribute the investment income of such companies to shareholders, i.e. tax officers will assume that investment income is the result of shareholders using the company as a 'money box' for the purpose of paying the low small-business rate of corporation tax (whereas if they invested similar amounts as individuals they might be liable for much higher personal rates of tax).

18. Liability for company debts

Unfortunately, many owners of small businesses believe that acquisition of limited liability indemnifies them against all personal liability for business debts. This is not necessarily the case, and the Insolvency Act 1986 has considerably strengthened creditors' ability to claim from company shareholders' personal assets in certain circumstances.

The two major situations in which personal liability arises (i.e. when a member's liability is *not* restricted to the amount of his or her shareholding) are as follows.

Wrongful trading

A court can declare that certain members are personally liable for the business's debts if it continued to trade prior to liquidation while those members knew or ought to have known that there was no reasonable prospect of avoiding the company's insolvency. Wrongful trading is not fraud (i.e. *deliberately* trading in order to obtain benefit despite knowing the business is about to fail), but is the consequence of poor judgement. The court will ask, 'What should a prudent, knowledgeable person have done in the circumstances?' If the court considers that continuation of the business for a few extra weeks or months might have enabled it to pay off a few more debts then no personal liability will arise.

Fraudulent trading

This means deliberate bad judgement, i.e. carrying on the business *intending* to put its creditors in a worse position than before. Courts may identify certain individuals as being responsible for the fraudulent trading.

Personal liability can be avoided if those involved can prove they took 'all reasonable precautions' to avoid potential problems. In practice, this might require a director to demonstrate that he or she:

(a) regularly checked the financial state of the business

(b) checked the accuracy of management control information, including accounting data

(c) planned future activities

(d) did not give preferential treatment to any one creditor (who might be connected to the director in question) at the expense of others

(e) took proper professional advice, e.g. from a qualified accountant.

19. Credit control

The cash flow problems created by credit sales cause many small firms to collapse. Several costs and difficulties are involved, including:

(a) Money may have to be borrowed at high interest rates in order to finance the business while debts are being recovered.

(b) Much time, effort and expense is devoted to writing letters, making telephone calls, issuing copy invoices, etc to customers who have not paid their bills.

(c) Inducements to customers to settle early, e.g. by giving discounts for prompt payment, are extremely expensive. For example, a firm offering a 2.5 per cent discount for payment within 30 days is actually losing 30.4 per cent $(365/30 \times 2.5 = 30.4)$ on an annual basis.

(d) The legal cost of collecting a small debt, even using the county court small claims procedure, can be prohibitive.

A small firm that sells much of its output to a handful of large companies is well advised to get to know the accounting systems of these firms so as to know when and to whom to submit invoices to ensure prompt settlement.

20. Expanding a small business

A buoyant and expanding market, rising consumer incomes, easy access to finance, low interest rates, receipt of extremely large orders and/or winning a lucrative public sector contract are among the major reasons for enlarging a small business. Other factors which encourage expansion include:

(a) Discovery of export marketing opportunities

(b) Possibilities for obtaining economies of scale (bulk-purchasing discounts, integration of production process, application of the division of labour and so on)

(c) The need to secure control over supply sources or retail outlets

(d) Availability of new market segments through modifying existing products

(e) Development of new products.

Many of the problems resulting from takeovers and mergers (*see* 3:**16**) also apply to business expansion.

21. Problems with expansion

Rapid expansion can create administrative, operational and financial difficulties that reduce overall profitability and which could cause a small business to fail. The major problems are as follows:

(a) Existing smooth-running administrative systems might be disrupted.

(b) Additional supplies of raw materials have to be purchased – perhaps for cash – and extra labour must be hired and paid immediately. However, revenue from increased sales will not be received until some time in the future.

(c) New customers may demand more credit, hence creating cash flow deficits in the short term. The cost of debt-collecting increases, and more bad debts are incurred.

(d) New premises, plant and equipment and recently hired labour might not be fully utilised, so that (expensive) surplus capacity begins to appear.

(e) General administrative costs increase. There is extra clerical work, photo-copying, more meetings, internal memoranda, etc.

(f) Industrial relations problems may emerge in a larger firm.

(g) Stockholding costs rise dramatically (warehousing, stock issue procedures, pilferage, etc).

(h) Expansion indicates to competitors that the firm is doing well. This may induce competitors to enter the market.

An expanding business needs therefore to monitor carefully the effects of growth on profitability and periodically to measure key efficiency ratios. The firm's rate of return on capital employed (*see* 9:9) must not be allowed to deteriorate during a period of growth.

22. Businesses in difficulties

A small business in serious difficulties needs an organisation system quite different from that appropriate for a prosperous and expanding firm. Rigid and narrowly defined accountability structures, instant decision taking and strict cost control are required.

The firm should draw up an emergency cash flow projection indicating priority payments and which creditors can in the short term be ignored. Slow-moving stocks should be sold at a discount in order to raise cash; surplus plant and equipment should be offered for sale at knock-down prices. The aim is to complete current orders at minimum cost yet leave the firm able to clear its debts. Additional orders should not be accepted if there is little or no chance of the work being finished. Credit sales cannot normally be allowed. Debtors should be informed of the firm's problems and asked to pay their bills, perhaps at a discount for immediate settlement. If credit orders have already been accepted it may be better to cancel these and compensate the customer than to go ahead with the work.

Sources of financial difficulty must be investigated. Is the firm overtrading? Are there bottlenecks in flows of production? How frequent are interruptions in supplies? Has the firm purchased technically complicated equipment that its staff are unable to use? A cost-cutting programme must be initiated. All capital expenditure plans should be frozen and all budgets put on to a zero-base allocation system (*see* 12:23). Essential new assets should be hired and not purchased.

23. Sale and leaseback

Failing businesses that own their premises can inject capital through 'sale and leaseback' arrangements. The firm sells its land and buildings for a capital sum equal to just below their market value, but makes the transaction contingent on the purchaser formally agreeing to lease the land and buildings back to the selling firm for a certain period at a predetermined rent. Such a deal has costs – there are legal expenses and valuation fees, capital gains tax (possibly) on the disposal, the rent charged may be relatively high, and the firm loses it security of tenure.

24. Businesses that fail

Sole traders and partners who cannot meet their debts are subject to the law of bankruptcy, whereas insolvent companies are put into 'liquidation'. Bankruptcy is governed by various Bankruptcy Acts (the latest being the Insolvency Act

1986, subsequently amended), all of which adhere to the principle that although bankrupts must use their personal assets to satisfy debts, they should then be free to start again after a 'reasonable interval'. Creditors usually become aware of a firm's shaky financial position when bills have not been paid for a long period. However, they cannot initiate bankruptcy proceedings in a county court unless one or more of the following conditions apply:

(a) A court order has been obtained ordering the debtor firm to pay a debt and this order has been presented and ignored without the firm disputing the debt.

(b) The debtor firm informs its creditors that it has had to suspend payment of its debts (this can be done through a court).

(c) Owners leave the country, or make themselves inaccessible (e.g. by locking themselves in their houses) or move demonstrably *intending* to avoid creditors.

(d) Owners fraudulently transfer their property to avoid personal liability for the debts of a failing business.

25. Bankruptcy proceedings

A creditor may petition a court for a person's bankruptcy provided (currently) at least a certain threshold amount is owed and has been outstanding for at least three months. Evidence of the existence of the debt is necessary, and the debt itself must have arisen before the petition is filed. The petition is served on the debtor and a bankruptcy hearing is arranged. Following the hearing, the court will either dismiss the petition or appoint an interim receiver, as it considers fit. In the latter case the fact is noted in government publications. The 'official receiver' (a government officer) now takes charge of the debtor's financial affairs, and becomes in effect the creditors' trustee. Note that debtors themselves may present bankruptcy petitions, i.e. they may declare *themselves* bankrupt.

26. The statement of affairs

Next, the debtor may prepare a 'statement of affairs' listing all his or her assets and liabilities, the value of the deficit and the names and addresses of creditors and the amounts due to each. The debtor must satisfy the authorities that the cause of the bankruptcy did not involve fraud or other improper behaviour on his or her part. The debtor may submit a proposal that creditors accept some proportion of what they are owed in final settlement of debts (i.e. that 'so much in the pound' be paid). A three-quarters majority of (proven) creditors is needed before such an offer may be accepted and, if accepted, must be ratified by the court following a report by the official receiver on the debtor's conduct. If the court accepts the scheme it becomes binding on all creditors and, on payment, the debtor has no further liability for the debts.

27. Deeds of arrangement

Alternatively, a 'deed of arrangement' is registered whereby the debtor's property is assigned to a trustee who administers it on behalf of the creditors. The deed must be approved by a majority of creditors, but it does not bind those who do not wish to agree. Deeds of arrangement avoid the need for public bankruptcy proceedings, since the debtor has not as yet been adjudged 'bankrupt' as such.

28. Formal bankruptcy

If the debtor is wholly unco-operative, or absconds, or a 'so much in the pound' scheme falls through, the creditors will meet with the official receiver and ask the court to declare the debtor formally bankrupt. Assuming the court agrees, it will issue an order depriving that person of his or her property and placing it with a trustee (normally an accountant who is a Registered Insolvency Practitioner approved by the Board of Trade). His or her task is to realise the bankrupt's assets as quickly as possible and to distribute the proceeds among creditors (for which duties the trustee is rewarded by an agreed percentage of the amount raised).

29. Payment of creditors

Creditors are paid according to a predetermined order specified in the Bankruptcy Acts. 'Secured' creditors (i.e. those with direct claims on specific assets, such as a bank loan secured against the firm's premises) are paid first. If the sale of the particular assets specified in the security arrangement fails to raise enough money to pay off a secured debt then the outstanding balance is pooled with the debts of unsecured creditors and the eventual 'so much in the pound' settlement applied to this amount. Next come unpaid taxes and local authority rates, followed by employees' wages, then outstanding NI contributions, and only then the firm's unsecured creditors.

30. After bankruptcy

Undischarged bankrupts are prohibited by law from obtaining credit without disclosing their bankruptcy and are not allowed to trade under any other business name (unless they simultaneously and openly reveal they are bankrupts under their previous business names). To obtain a discharge the bankrupt must apply to the court, which then informs:

(a) creditors (who may oppose the discharge)

(b) the trustee, *and*

(c) the official receiver.

The court may grant immediate discharge, or make the discharge conditional on particular events (repaying a certain amount of money, for example) and/or specify that the discharge occur only after a certain time period has elapsed. In normal circumstances a court will 'automatically' discharge a bankrupt after three years (ten if the person has been bankrupt before) provided the bankrupt has shown good faith (e.g. by conscientiously trying to settle his or her debts).

A bankrupt who conceals the existence of personal assets or who falsifies records commits a criminal offence for which he or she may be imprisoned. Failure to account for assets and/or to keep proper records is not a criminal offence, but may result in the court refusing to grant a discharge.

31. Company liquidation

A company is a separate legal entity and thus must be liquidated in its own right. All unpaid share capital (*see* 9:**18**) is called up on liquidation. Thereafter, limited liability protects shareholders from personal liability for the company's debts. As with a sole trader, liquidation proceedings can be initiated by the company itself. In this case an extraordinary resolution (requiring the support of 75 per cent of shareholders' votes) is needed and the courts are not necessarily involved. On liquidation, the company may be solvent or insolvent. If it is solvent (e.g. it was formed for a particular project which has been successfully completed), its members pay off the creditors and simply wind the company up. If it is solvent then *either*:

(a) its creditors form a committee to supervise the voluntary winding-up, *or*

(b) one or more creditors present a petition to the court for compulsory winding-up.

Note also that a shareholder may ask the court for a compulsory winding-up order.

Other circumstances in which a company may be compulsorily wound up are:

(a) if it fails to register its final accounts with the Registrar of Companies

(b) if it does not trade for more than a year

(c) when the number of its members falls below the statutory minimum (*see* 3:**11**)

(d) if a court decides that it is 'just and equitable' that the company be wound up.

Following a compulsory winding-up order the court may supervise a liquidator appointed by the company and/or its creditors, or appoint its own liquidator. Company liquidation and bankruptcy are essentially similar. The liquidator of a company is equivalent to the trustee of a bankrupt. However, instead of an interim receiver being appointed (as in the case of a sole trader or partner in a firm), a winding-up order is issued against a company. There can be no public examination of the 'company' as such, although its individual directors may be so examined. Whereas a bankrupt is 'discharged', a company is given an 'order for dissolution'.

32. Administration orders

Bankruptcy or company liquidation can sometimes be avoided through businesses obtaining an 'administration order' from the county court.

(a) *Sole traders* use administration orders to enable the court to supervise their financial affairs until they have settled their debts. This protects them from harassment by creditors, who are unable individually to enforce their specific claims without the express permission of the court. In return the sole trader promises to make a fixed monthly payment to the court, which then distributes this to creditors in proportion to the amounts outstanding.

(b) *Companies* can have administrators appointed by the court to oversee their fortunes until business improves. The company cannot be forced into liquidation while under an administrator's supervision. However, the fact that an administration order is in effect must be stated on all company documents, together with the administrator's name and reason for appointment.

Progress test 4

1. Outline four possible differences in the management problems facing small and large businesses.

2. List and describe six common causes of small business failure.

3. What sorts of information should be included in a business plan?

4. List eight factors to be considered when choosing business premises.

5. What is the purpose of a cash flow forecast? What information should it contain?

6. In what circumstances should a profitable small business choose not to expand its operations?

7. What is an administration order?

8. List the advantages of leasing (rather than buying) business premises.

5

CORPORATE STRATEGY AND PLANNING

STRATEGIC MATTERS

1. Strategic management

Strategy concerns the determination of a general direction for the enterprise and the formulation of overall business policies. Examples of strategic decisions are the choice of products a company will supply, the markets in which it is to operate, how many divisions and departments the firm is to have, whether to operate at the top or bottom end of the market, whether to acquire other businesses, and how to finance operations. Strategy embraces all aspects of business policy, planning, organisation and control. A corporate strategy is a sort of route map for guiding the overall progress of the firm.

Tactics, conversely, are the practical methods whereby strategic decisions are implemented. Examples are the choice of advertising agent, use of a particular channel of distribution, selection of production methods, deciding how much working capital to employ, whether to purchase or lease company vehicles, etc.

Policies

A 'policy' is a set of ground rules and criteria to be applied when taking decisions relating to a particular function or activity. Thus, the existence of a policy establishes boundaries that restrict the scope and nature of decisions concerning a specific issue. Examples of policies are:

- internal promotion
- only recruiting new people who possess certain levels of academic qualification
- advertising in print rather than broadcast media
- requiring at least three quotations for all purchases exceeding a particular value
- not settling suppliers' invoices until the month following delivery.

Advantages to having policies are that problems arising within the area covered by a policy do not have to be analysed each and every time they appear (decisions are simply applied in accordance with company policy); precedents are established; and delegation becomes easier. Managements develop policy guidelines to facilitate the co-ordination of diverse operations and to ensure that all decisions are compatible with the overall aims of the organisation. Coherent policies avoid confusion and lead to consistency of action in the area concerned.

2. Advantages and problems of formulating strategies

The advantages to having a strategy are as follows:

(a) Strategies provide the business with definite criteria against which to evaluate performance.

(b) The process of formulating a strategy forces the company to analyse its position and hence identify and remedy internal weaknesses.

(c) Reactions to changes in competitors' behaviour may be predetermined.

(d) The company can decide in advance how it will respond to predictable changes in customer tastes and spending patterns.

(e) Co-ordination of divisions, subsidiaries, and other component parts of the organisation is made easier. The existence of a strategy provides a focal point towards which all the firm's energies may be directed.

(f) External threats and opportunities will be identified.

(g) Important decisions are taken only after considering all the facts, not in chaotic short-run crisis situations.

(h) Long-term investments will be properly evaluated.

(i) Speculation about possible future events and circumstances may cause the firm to discover ways of influencing the future for its own benefit.

Problems with strategy formulation include the high risk of inaccuracy of long-term forecasts (*see* **16**), possible sudden and unexpected changes in environments (laws or technical regulations, for example), and the costs and time involved. In consequence, some businesses do not bother formulating strategies, preferring instead to respond to situations, opportunistically, as they arise.

There are five major steps in creating and implementing a corporate strategy:

1. Definition of mission and corporate objectives.
2. Analysis of internal and external situations.
3. Specification of alternatives.
4. Evaluation of alternatives and choice of strategy.
5. Development of plans and policies to meet strategic aims.

3. Missions

Many organisations today seek to define their 'missions'. A 'mission statement' is a concise summary of the fundamental *purpose* of the enterprise: what *exactly* it exists to do and how it wishes to relate to the outside world. Missions result from businesses' histories and traditions, their strengths, competences, opportunities and resources. Typically, mission statements focus on such matters as the markets the firm wishes to serve; desired quality levels; attitudes towards staff, shareholders, customers and the physical environment; and whether the company wishes to lead or follow competitors. The more concrete the company's mission statement, the easier it is to determine objectives, since the mission statement (which represents in effect a 'constitution' for the business) imposes constraints on policies and generally defines the parameters of the strategies the company may adopt.

4. Objectives

An objective is something the business needs to achieve in order to fulfil its mission. The clearer the organisation's objectives, the more self-evident is the choice of tactics needed to attain them. The following rules should be observed when setting objectives:

(a) Objectives should be consistent. For example, the maximisation of short-term returns usually implies frequently switching from one market or line of activity to another, and would not be consistent with an objective of attaining long-term security and steady growth.

(b) Objectives should follow a hierarchy, with the most general at the top and the most detailed and specific at the bottom.

(c) Each objective should be accompanied by statements of:

(*i*)   who is responsible for its attainment
(*ii*)   when the objective is to be achieved
(*iii*)   how the objective is to be accomplished, including a specification of the resources necessary and where and how they will be acquired.

(d) All objectives should relate directly and identifiably to the mission of the business.

(e) Criteria for deciding whether an objective has been achieved should be predetermined.

(f) Wherever possible, objectives should be stated in quantitative terms and, where extensive written instructions are required, should be written in simple English.

(g) Objectives should be reasonable: failure to achieve unrealistic objectives can lead to disillusion and a collapse in morale.

Typically, objectives relate to such matters as financial returns, rates of growth, market shares, introduction of new products, efficiency improvements, cost-cutting programmes, removal of competitors, and so on.

5. The questions to ask

In determining their strategies firms often find it useful to ask three fundamental questions:

(a) What business are we in?

(b) What business do we want to be in?

(c) What do we have to do to get where we want to be?

Careful analysis of the answers to these questions can indicate whether the firm should diversify its product range, enter new markets, change its prices, alter existing distribution channels, or make other fundamental changes.

What business are we in?

Is a motor vehicle manufacturer in the engineering business (focusing therefore on the production of engines and car bodies); or is it in the general transport business and thus needs to be interested in *all* forms of transport (air, sea, electrically powered vehicles and so on) regardless of purely technical considerations? Should a stationery firm regard itself as a paper business, or in business communications (including graphic design, photocopying machines, electronic mail equipment, etc) as a whole?

Failure to define a company's range of interests sufficiently widely makes it vulnerable to predatory competitors and to the adverse effects of technical change, since the obsolescence of a product or process or an alteration in a competitor's prices or product line may create enormous difficulties for the supplying firm.

What business do we want to be in?

Firms need to examine the profitabilities of various markets, market segments (*see* 7:6) and product lines. They should ask, 'What *else* can we do to improve our performance?'

What do we have to do to get where we want to be?

This might involve product repositioning (*see* 22), structural reorganisation, new investment, and/or a change in the capital structure of the firm (*see* 9:28).

6. The question of diversification

A company must *either*:

(a) identify the activities it performs (or could perform) really well and concentrate on these; *or*

(b) seek new opportunities in an entirely different field.

The former course assumes the firm can continue its current activities without hindrance and at peak efficiency, i.e. that no discernible threats from competitors, poor industrial relations, interruptions in supplies, or impending technological developments currently exist. For the second option, realistic opportunities must be available and the firm needs a mechanism for bringing them to light (market and/or product research, for example).

PLANNING AND PLANNING TECHNIQUES

7. Plans

Whereas strategies define the general path a business is to follow, plans state precisely *how* it intends its strategies to be realised. Strategies concern ideas, creativity and grand conceptions; plans are to do with mundane and instrumental measures for the efficient allocation of human, material, financial and other resources within the business. Plans convert into tactics and hence into operational activities such as the deployment of assets, allocation of duties, organisation of work, etc.

Planning is difficult and expensive: difficult because it requires forecasts of future environments and events; expensive since it ties up significant numbers of highly paid senior executives. There are, however, a number of advantages to formulating business plans:

(a) Important decisions are taken unhurriedly using all the data available and considering all possible options.

(b) The firm is compelled to look ahead, thus possibly avoiding foreseeable pitfalls.

(c) Departmental representatives are forced to meet and discuss common problems.

(d) The feasibility of objectives is studied in depth.

(e) Team spirit (*see* 14:**13**) is encouraged.

(f) Inefficiencies and duplicated effort may be identified.

(g) The firm will be better equipped to respond to environmental change.

(h) Activities are jointly directed towards the attainment of common objectives.

(i) Criteria are established for the effective utilisation of resources.

(j) Resource deficiencies may be identified.

(k) Participating staff should be motivated towards achieving planned objectives.

(l) All the firm's activities will be integrated and co-ordinated.

(m) Management is forced to consider its own strengths and weaknesses.

(n) Careful consideration of possible future events may uncover new and profitable opportunities.

(o) Measures to influence future events can be initiated by the company.

8. Principles of planning

Certain fundamental planning principles should always be applied, as follows:

(a) The plan should be as detailed as expenditure constraints allow.

(b) Plans should not extend too far into the future; accurate prediction of the distant future is simply impossible.

(c) *All* alternative courses of action should be considered.

(d) Side effects and implications of the actions envisaged should be examined.

(e) Instructions to individuals and departments must be incorporated into the plan.

(f) Plans should be concise and easy to understand.

As the plan is executed its effectiveness in achieving stated objectives should be monitored. Differences between actual and desired positions must be quickly identified and remedial measures introduced.

Targets embodied in plans should always be reasonable; overambitious targets can never be achieved and usually lead to low morale and cynicism among workers. Equally, targets that are too low have no operational significance.

9. Questions to ask when devising plans

A common and straightforward approach to plan formulation involves the firm asking itself appropriate questions, and planning its activities according to the replies. Examples of sets of relevant questions are as follows:

(a) What is the current rate of technical change in the industry? How might this alter? And what does the company need to do to beat its rivals in the technical field?

(b) How does the company's output differ from that of competitors, and what should it do to take full advantage of these differences when marketing its products?

(c) Is the company's access to raw materials and skilled labour assured, and if not what can be done to improve this (e.g. by offering higher wages or raw materials prices in order to secure continuing supply)?

10. Network analysis

A network is a schematic description of all the activities involved in a project and all the interconnecting links between events. Its purpose is to determine how quickly the project can be completed and to assist in scheduling, co-ordinating and controlling work. The 'critical path' of a network is the sequence of key activities that cannot be held up without postponing the completion date of the entire project. Other activities have 'float' time associated with their durations. Float is the extra time that can be taken over an activity in addition to its expected duration without affecting the completion time of the project as a whole.

The usefulness of network planning can be illustrated by considering a large construction project such as building a house. Scores of activities are involved:

a survey, soil testing, ordering supplies, hiring labour, laying foundations, inspection of work, etc. Many of these tasks will interact, some need to be completed before others can begin, while some may be undertaken at any time. The builder must calculate the expected duration of each task, and sort tasks into the order in which they have to be completed. It is then possible to work out which activities can be performed alongside others, and which must be finished before others can begin. The critical path is the shortest time between the first activity and the last, given that some activities can be completed while others are in progress. Accordingly, crucially important activities are highlighted and it becomes possible to see how the project can be speeded up through reallocating labour and other resources from some tasks to others, and how strikes, holidays, staff illnesses, non-delivery of supplies, etc might affect the project's estimated completion date.

11. Critical path analysis (CPA) and project evaluation review technique (PERT)

These are the two main approaches to network analysis. They were developed simultaneously but independently and in different locations. CPA began in 1957 with the work of James Kelly and Morgan Walker in a US chemical company; PERT was first used by the US Navy in 1958. Although conceptually similar, CPA and PERT differ in their assumptions: CPA regards individual activity times as predetermined and constant, whereas PERT uses three alternative durations for each activity – optimistic, pessimistic, and most likely.

CPA is said to be activity-oriented in that networks simply illustrate series of operations that must be performed one after the other, while PERT is event-oriented showing estimates of times needed to reach each stage in the project – having incorporated allowances for uncertainty. CPA assumes that activity times can, if necessary, be reduced provided costs are correspondingly increased (*see* 14). Thus, CPA derives the solution which incurs least cost from a choice of alternative project completion times assumed to be known with certainty. PERT, on the other hand, requires known (or guessed) probabilities of activity durations. Expected values must therefore be computed for each period.

12. An example

To illustrate CPA, consider a project that requires six activities, indicated by letters A to F in Fig. 5.1. Activity D must follow activity C, which itself must follow B; and B must follow A. Activity E starts at the same moment as A, but must be completed before activity C can begin. Likewise, F starts when A starts, and must be finished before D can commence. Activity A takes 5 weeks, B takes 2 weeks, C requires 15 weeks; activities D, E and F need 8, 15 and 6 weeks respectively. The network for this problem is given in Fig. 5.1.

The critical path is the sequence E-C-D requiring 38 weeks in total. It is impossible to complete this project in less than 15 + 15 + 8 = 38 weeks. While completing E the firm can get on with A and B which, together, take 7 weeks. Activity C cannot begin until E is finished, and E requires 15 weeks, therefore

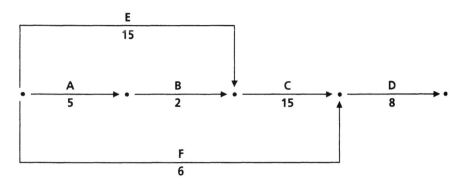

Figure 5.1 Series of operations in a network

the firm can take anything up to 8 extra weeks in completing A and B without affecting the total project duration. Activity F is not critical because it needs only 6 weeks whereas 30 weeks are available for completion of this work: there are 24 weeks' float attached to activity F. By definition, the critical path (E–C–D) has no float whatsoever. Activity A has 10 weeks' float (15 – 5) and B has 8.

A PERT solution to this problem would require the estimation of most optimistic, most pessimistic, and most likely completion times for each activity. Normally it is assumed that pessimistic predictions will be realised more often than optimistic predictions, as it seems there are many more causes of project delay than project acceleration. Then, probabilities of individual activity durations, and of the time to completion of the project as a whole, are computed.

13. Resource levelling

Resource constraints (limits on the numbers of available workers, for example) must be incorporated into the project plan, since it might not be possible to have a team do several things simultaneously. For instance, activity A might require two weeks whereas activity B, which can begin at the same time as A, may require only one. Normally, therefore, the firm would want someone to be getting on with B while A is being completed. But suppose A and B each require two workers, so that four people in total are needed for one week, and that only two are available. In this case A and B cannot be done at the same time! In consequence, it is necessary to 'level resources', i.e. to assume that B must follow A (or *vice versa*). Hence the entire network and its associated critical path will change.

14. Crash cost CPA

In CPA it is common to assume that activity times can be reduced provided the costs of operations increase. The time needed to paint a house might for example be one week if just a single worker is employed, or three days using two workers (and paying double wages). Thus, a number of alternative possible situations are simulated and the 'least cost' solution adopted, depending on the various times and relative costs involved. Note that penalty or bonus clauses in contracts specifying various completion times can drastically alter the best way of scheduling a project; it might be better to accelerate activities at higher cost (overtime payments, etc) in order to win a lucrative bonus for early completion. The absolute minimum time in which a project can be finished regardless of cost is called the crash time, and the extra expense associated with this is known as the crash cost.

15. Uses and benefits of network analysis

CPA and PERT have applications in production, marketing, installation of new equipment and introduction of new products and processes; indeed anywhere a distinct final objective can be discerned. The technique has been successfully applied to design projects; ship, bridge and motorway construction; launching new products; installation of new plant and machinery; control of sub-contract work; and movement of factory premises. Network analysis is not suitable for intellectual activities such as creative research, or for personnel or welfare work where time horizons are unclear and specific objectives difficult to describe.

Network analysis is a powerful technique of planning and control. Projects are broken down into logically ordered components, work schedules are precisely defined, progress is systematically monitored. The resources necessary for successful completion of each stage can be assessed. Crucially important tasks are identified, potential trouble spots predicted, and resources may perhaps be reallocated to hasten completion of the work. Further benefits include:

(a) Forced preplanning of tasks; co-operation and co-ordination between departments

(b) The requirement that specific targets be defined clearly and in depth

(c) Easier estimation of project completion dates and hence more accurate prediction of project costs

(d) More effective budgetary control following detailed analysis of resource requirements

(e) Identification of interrelations between activities

(f) The ability to compare actual with predicted costs as the project develops. Sources of delay and exceptional cost may be quickly isolated.

16. Corporate planning

Corporate plans determine the deployment of the company's *total* resources. They decide the technical and organisational changes necessary to achieve the goals of the enterprise. There are two basic approaches to corporate planning:

1. *Gap analysis*, whereby the planner sets targets based on what he or she believes to be attainable in the longer term and then compares these targets with forecasts of future achievement taken from projections of current activities – assuming that present circumstances continue. Divergences are then analysed, and measures implemented to bridge the gaps.

2. *'What if' analysis*, in which planners ask a series of questions to establish the various outcomes likely to result from different future environments. Outcomes are quantified in terms of expected sales, costs, expenditures, asset structures, flows of funds, and other operational variables.

Unfortunately, effective corporate planning depends in part on accurate long-term forecasts which in business are extremely difficult to achieve, for several reasons, including the following:

(a) Many variables (tax levels, business laws, interest rates, consumer incomes, etc) are determined by government and are thus beyond the firm's control.

(b) Consumer tastes can change quickly and unpredictably.

(c) New technical inventions may occur.

(d) Competitors might alter their behaviour; fresh competition could emerge.

(e) Past events upon which forecasts are based might not occur in the future.

(f) Existing suppliers, distribution options, harmonious industrial relations, etc could suddenly disappear.

(g) Technical difficulties (unreliable data, incorrect choice of statistical forecasting technique, etc) might arise.

The longer the period of the forecast, the greater the likelihood of serious error. It is wise therefore to generate several different forecasts, with a greater amount of detail the shorter the time span involved, and each forecast assuming a different scenario of events.

An effective corporate plan will facilitate the co-ordination of activities, the transfer of resources, and the organisation's capacity to cope with change. The plan will describe at the highest level of generality the resources needed for intended future operations, identifying possible new markets, applications of new technology and the likelihood of environmental disturbance. It might specify means for obtaining (say) a certain market share to be achieved within three years, a certain rate of return on capital employed, some specified percentage reduction in the labour force, greater efficiency in the use of working capital, lower aggregate expenditures, and so on.

The plan should set priorities for action, describe any changes in organisation structure that might be required, and include a timetable for its implementation. Then, the minimum criteria that need to be satisfied before the plan can be regarded as a 'success' must be specified (e.g. quantitative targets for improvements in market share, reduced costs, or increased financial return over some predetermined period).

17. Top-down versus bottom-up planning

Top-down planning involves senior management handing down specific objectives to subordinates without the latter's participation in the planning process. With bottom-up planning, conversely, departments generate their own plans for achieving broadly defined goals. Proposals from lower levels are then synthesised by a high-level planning committee.

Bottom-up planning utilises the skills and experiences of the staff who will be responsible for implementing the plans. Also, staff involvement in planning should motivate individuals towards the achievement of the targets that emerge. In practice, however, bottom-up planning is uncommon, possibly for two reasons:

(a) The inexperience and lack of expertise of junior managers in high-level policy formulation.

(b) Junior executives' unfamiliarity with the work of other departments and the overall situation of the firm.

CORPORATE ANALYSIS METHODS

18. SWOT analysis

SWOT is the acronym for 'Strengths, Weaknesses, Opportunities and Threats'. Strengths and weaknesses can be listed in relation to:

- plant, equipment, machinery and supplies
- access to finance in the short and long term
- marketing
- current products
- research and development activities
- after-sales service and customer care
- existing staff, skills and human resources
- production efficiency
- delivery and distribution
- ability to introduce new products and working methods
- suitability of premises
- quality control
- internal communications.

Opportunities and threats exist usually in the external environment. Examples of opportunities are: prospects for developing new markets and/or introducing new products, for cost-cutting programmes, exporting, taking over competitors, buying up sources of supply or distribution networks, etc. Threats can emanate from competitors, governments, risks of economic depression, changes in laws, product obsolescence or changes in public taste. Clearly, a firm will want to seize opportunities and remove threats.

19. APACS

The 'adaptive planning and control sequence' is a useful planning model that incorporates SWOT analysis. Eight steps are involved:

1. Statement of objectives

2. Appraisal of internal strengths, weaknesses, and the external environment
3. Specification of activities necessary to achieve objectives
4. Evaluation of the consequences of alternative courses of action
5. Prediction of results of actions chosen
6. The issue of orders to ensure implementation of plans
7. Assessment of results
8. If necessary, modification of the plan.

20. The 7-S system

An increasingly popular technique for analysing the quality of a firm's strategies, tactics and operational methods is the '7-S system' developed by the American McKinsey management consultancy company. It provides a systematic basis for management auditing (*see* 12:19) and a convenient checklist of the major areas where decisions may be required. The seven components of the taxonomy are as follows:

1. *Strategy* – how the company allocates its resources in order to achieve its strategic aims. Its mission and strategic policy statements.
2. *Structure* – organisation structure, line and staff relations, degree of decentralisation, authority and responsibility arrangements, etc.
3. *Systems* – the firm's management information systems, budgetary and other control mechanisms, methods for managing projects.
4. *Style* – leadership style, degree and type of supervision, interpersonal relationships within the firm.
5. *Staff* – human resource programs: recruitment, induction and training policies and the effectiveness of these. Promotion systems and the general culture of the organisation.
6. *Shared values* – group cohesiveness within the firm: morale and the extent to which employees adopt common perspectives towards issues.
7. *Skills* – the areas in which the enterprise excels: its capabilities taken as a whole.

21. Environmental scanning

This is the systematic examination of each of the firm's environments to identify opportunities and threats created by external change. Not all environmental factors can be investigated (there are too many of them) so a handful of *relevant* external variables must be selected for research. Normally, these variables concern:

(a) *Marketing* – the activities of competitors, trends in consumer taste and behaviour, changes in the size and structure of the market.

(b) *Legislation* – government attitudes to the industry, impending statutes, licensing arrangements and possibilities of increased control.

(c) *Technology* – production methods and their efficiency, new inventions, materials, processes and costs.

There are two ways of planning for environmental change. The first is to predict the external changes that might occur and then detail: (*i*) how the organisation would be affected by them, and (*ii*) how the organisation should respond. Alternatively, the planner may begin with a list of the firm's functions, followed by a listing of all environmental factors that might affect these.

22. Positioning products

The term 'market position' describes how a product is perceived and evaluated by consumers in comparison with the products of competing firms. Suppose for example that competing models of a certain type of product are rated by customers according to just two variables: reliability and price. Let there be six competing models, A to F. A survey of consumer opinion might indicate that their market positions are as shown in Fig. 5.2.

The size of each circle indicates that model's market share. Model A is the market leader. It is expensive but reasonably reliable. B and C are small followers, serving niche markets in the high-price, high-reliability zone. F is cheap but unreliable; E is about average on both counts, and so on. Examination of a perceptual map can reveal gaps in existing market provision. Clearly it is essential to select the correct variables for the axes of the diagram. Examples of possible variables are after-sales service, convenience in use, speed of operation, attractiveness of packaging, etc. Note that a product's position in consumers' minds can be shifted through modifying its characteristics, through advertising and public relations, and other promotional activities.

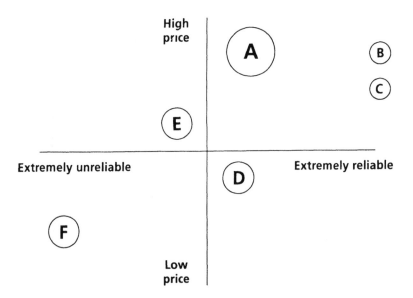

Figure 5.2 A perceptual map

23. Portfolio analysis

Companies supplying many products may be said to hold 'portfolios' of products, each possessing a particular combination of risk and return. Accordingly, products may be categorised as:

(a) *Declining products*, which contribute little to company profits because of (say) reduced demand, intensification of competition, increased production costs or low rates of market growth.

(b) *Safe products*, upon which the business depends for a steady cash flow.

(c) *Developing products*, i.e. those which are increasing their market share in rapidly expanding markets.

Normally the firm will expect a product to begin in the last category; then become 'safe', eventually moving into decline.

A large business needs a balanced portfolio of products in order to ensure (*i*) a continuous inflow of cash, (*ii*) that new products are available to take over from those in decline, and (*iii*) that all the company's activities are not exceptionally risky. The *Boston Consulting Group* suggested that companies classify their products in terms of two variables: market share and the rate of market growth. Strategies should then focus on promoting products with high shares of rapidly expanding markets. A development of this approach, the General Electric 'Business Screen' method, uses the variables 'market attractiveness' and 'organisational strength' to categorise products. Market attractiveness depends on size, growth rate, profitability and competitive intensity of the market and on how easily it can be served. Organisational strength involves the quality of the firm's product, the firm's efficiency and the effectiveness of its marketing.

Consider for example a company with three products, A, B and C as shown in Fig. 5.3. The areas of the circles indicate the relative sizes of the markets for each product, while the wedges in each circle show the firm's share of that particular market. We see that although the market for product A is large and highly attractive, the company is weak in its ability to serve this potentially lucrative segment, implying the need for further investment in this field.

Product B should probably be discarded, while product C presents a 'question mark' about how to proceed. There is a large market for product C, the firm can supply it easily, and the company already has a large market share. But the market for C is stagnant and profit margins are low.

Problems with portfolio analysis are as follows:

(a) It *describes* a firm's situation rather than telling management what it can do.

(b) Objective circumstances prevent a firm altering its product range.

(c) Market attractiveness can change suddenly, unpredictably and in consequence of factors beyond the company's control.

(d) Market share is difficult to measure because it depends on the initial definition of the market concerned: a broad definition will give the firm a relatively low market share, and *vice versa*.

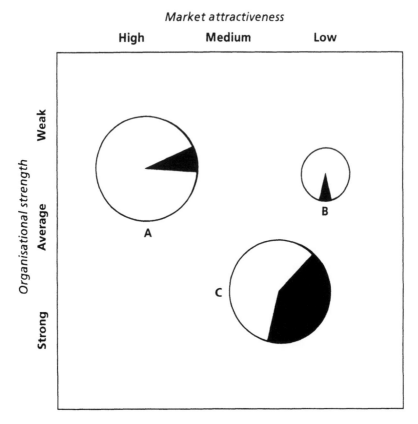

Market attractiveness

Figure 5.3

(e) Numerous factors contribute to 'organisational strength' and 'market attractiveness'. Selection of which to consider is necessarily arbitrary to some degree.

24. Competitive strategy

The theory of competitive strategy results from the work of M.E. Porter, who defines competitive strategy as 'the art of relating a company to the economic environment within which it exists'. According to Porter, five major factors determine this environment, namely:

1. Ease with which competitors can enter the industry
2. Bargaining power of customers
3. Bargaining power of suppliers
4. Ease with which substitute products can be introduced
5. Extent of competition between existing firms.

Ease of entry

New firms will find it difficult to enter the industry where:

(a) Economies of large-scale production (i.e. unit cost reductions as output increases) exist so that entrants must enter the industry on a large scale and hence assume great risk in order to gain a foothold in the market.

(b) There is much product differentiation through branding, differing designs and different product make-ups in various market segments hence requiring potential entrants to spend large sums on advertising and sales promotion.

(c) Expensive capital equipment is needed before starting production.

(d) Entrants have limited access to existing distribution channels and thus need to invest heavily in establishing their own retail outlets, dealership networks, etc.

(e) Government policy restricts entry to the industry through, for example, quality regulations, licensing arrangements and so on.

(f) Miscellaneous factors create cost advantages for existing firms: experience of the industry, favourable locations, easy access to raw materials and similar benefits.

Bargaining power of buyers

The bargaining power of a purchasing firm depends on (*i*) the number of buyers and the sizes of their orders, (*ii*) customers' knowledge of the product and competitors' prices, and (*iii*) how easily buyers can switch from one source of supply to others.

Bargaining power of suppliers

Suppliers have more power if there are few of them and if the item supplied is unique. Sometimes the client firm is 'locked into' the supplies of a certain business. This occurs where the client has designed its own production system to accommodate the special features of a certain input, so that high costs must be incurred to change the source of supply.

Availability of substitutes

Firms producing an item for which many readily available substitutes exist lose their ability to raise prices by significant amounts, since to do so would certainly cause them to lose trade.

The extent of competition

Firms can charge higher prices in industries where businesses avoid competing with each other. In such industries, companies set similar prices, and steer clear of competitive advertising.

Porter suggests the following general principles of inter-firm competition:

(a) Rivalry between firms increases as the market shares of existing firms become more equal. Severe competition is unlikely in 'market-leader, market-follower' situations.

(b) Competition intensifies as the rate of expansion of the total market slows down.

(c) Since goods which are perishable or difficult to store must be sold quickly, industries supplying such products will experience intense competition.

(d) Firms will compete most aggressively when they have much to lose from the activities of competing businesses (e.g. because of extremely large investments in plant and equipment).

(e) Competition becomes fierce when competing products acquire more and more similar characteristics, and is greatest in industries supplying homogeneous products.

A firm's competitive position depends on its market share, product quality, brand and corporate identities, distribution arrangements, and on its ability to expand or contract its operations at short notice. Successful strategies, Porter argues, must involve at least one of the following elements:

(a) *Cost leadership*, e.g. through economies of scale or especially efficient product methods.

(b) *Product differentiation*, i.e. making the firm's output appear somehow different from and superior to that of competitors.

(c) *Supplying a particular market segment*, i.e. finding a profitable niche in the market not yet serviced by competing firms.

How any one of these desirable characteristics can be achieved depends on the industry concerned: particularly on its age and the number of competing units. Thus, businesses in young industries might seek product differentiation, whereas for firms in mature industries the need to reduce costs may be seen as paramount.

A firm with many competitors might attempt to buy out as many other firms as possible in order to expand operations and hence achieve economies of scale. Conversely, businesses in declining industries may choose to divest subsidiaries and unprofitable divisions in order to focus all their efforts on small (but nevertheless profitable) market segments.

Progress test 5

1. Define the difference between a strategy and a plan.

2. List four advantages of planning.

3. Define 'competitive strategy'.

4. What are the problems associated with portfolio analysis?

5. List the major steps involved in formulating a strategy.

6. According to Porter, what factors determine a firm's competitive environment?

Part Two

MANAGEMENT FUNCTIONS

6
ORGANISATION

FUNDAMENTALS

1. Organisation theory

Organisation theory analyses the structure, functions, performance and control of organisations and how individuals and groups within them behave. To 'organise' work is to segment it into units for allocation to people and departments. The system for doing this is the 'organisation' of the firm. It involves:

- The creation of hierarchies and working groups
- Mechanisms for distributing tasks
- Arrangements for co-ordinating activities and for exercising command and control
- Establishing departments
- Centralising or decentralising activities
- Determining the extents to which individual responsibilities overlap.

Management must segment the organisation into appropriate working units and then integrate and co-ordinate the structures that emerge.

2. Nature of organisations

Organisations are social groupings constructed to achieve particular ends. They are characterised by the conscious division of labour, responsibility and authority systems, and the need for control. Normally, organisations comprise a social system plus a technical system. As social systems, organisations are affected by socio-economic and psychological forces; as technical systems they are influenced by technological and environmental change. These systems are described and discussed in the M&E text, *Organisational Behaviour*, to which the interested reader is referred.

3. Purposes of organisation structure

The essential purposes of an organisation structure are:

- to have the right people taking the right decisions at the right time
- to establish who is accountable for what and who reports to whom

- to facilitate the easy flow of information through the organisation
- to provide a working environment that encourages efficiency and the acceptance of change
- to integrate and co-ordinate activities.

The chosen structure must balance order and innovation. On the one hand, it must avoid the duplication of effort, standardise procedures, monitor the quality of work, etc. On the other hand, it should encourage initiative among the staff and generate job satisfaction in employees through presenting them with an interesting variety of disparate tasks. There is no single ideal structure that is universally applicable to all businesses. What works in one firm may not be suitable elsewhere because of differences in mission, strategies, and the calibre of personnel. In the ideal situation

- Each unit will act as a self-contained cost/profit centre
- The performance of units can be easily appraised
- Information about units is readily available (meaning they can be controlled without difficulty)
- Units are 'organic' in that each contains homogeneous elements and/or elements with a common purpose (e.g. putting all marketing activities together into a single department)
- Work passes from one unit to the next in a logical sequence
- The resource needs of each unit are clearly visible so that resources may be deployed where they are most urgently required.

4. Classical approach to organisation

This refers to a set of propositions developed by several writers (notably Henri Fayol and Max Weber, *see* Chapter 1) over a number of years. Classical theory assumes that the same basic principles can be applied to all enterprises, regardless of the particular circumstances of the organisations concerned. The major tenets of the classical approach are as follows:

(a) Individuals should be selected and trained to suit the needs of the organisation, rather than the organisation being designed to satisfy employee needs.

(b) Managerial functions should be highly specialised so that individuals develop extensive knowledge and expertise in narrowly defined areas.

(c) Organisations should have a pyramid structure.

(d) A clearly identifiable and unbroken chain of command should run from the top of the management pyramid to its base.

(e) 'Unity of command' should occur throughout the hierarchy. This means that each person should have just one boss, so that (potentially conflicting) instructions are not issued from different sources.

(f) Management by exception (MBE) should be practised. The principle of MBE is described in 12:20.

(g) Organisations should be split into departments, each possessing precisely defined boundaries.

DEPARTMENTS

Departments can be established to undertake a particular function (accounts or marketing, for example); to manage one or more of a firm's products; or to serve a certain market or region. They can also be constructed around specific people.

5. Functional departments

A *functional* department deals only with work of a certain type. Examples are production, accounts, advertising, transport, and administrative departments. Typically, functional departmentation is accompanied by a conventional line and staff structure (*see* 16) with most heads of department having executive line authority. Departments arranged on these lines can make efficient use of specialised resources. Economies of scale in the administration of a single function may be available; there is little duplication of effort; and staff become highly trained, experienced and competent in a particular field. Employees might establish useful contacts with outside providers of specialist services relevant to the function, and can research and discuss it at length with colleagues in the same field. Also, supervision may be easier within a functional department because department heads have detailed knowledge of the tasks that each subordinate performs.

Functional departmentation is logical and easy to understand, but could encourage narrow and introspective attitudes. Decision taking may be slower in firms using functional departments because issues involving more than one function must be referred upwards for resolution. And the overall responsibility for co-ordinating all major multidisciplinary projects lies with a handful of senior managers at the apex of the organisation. These managers may become overloaded with work. Moreover it may be difficult for top management to identify weaknesses in specific functions and to determine the particular functional inadequacies that caused a project to fail.

Departmental structures may become inflexible and highly resistant to change. Also, managers of certain functions might come to believe that their function is more important than others, and conflicts may result (between marketing and production, for example). Effective communication between specialists in different functional areas may be difficult to achieve. Note that certain functional services (legal or advertising services, for example) can often be purchased from external agencies and consultants cheaper than providing them in-house. Firms operating in fast-changing environments may prefer to use outsiders more often than firms whose environments are relatively stable.

6. Product departments

Product departments deal with a single product or service. Departmental staff control all activities associated with the good, including purchase of raw materials, processing, administration, and the sale and distribution of the final product. Departmental managers acquire a wide range of general managerial skills as well as expert knowledge of the problems associated with the particular product. However, duplication of activities among various product departments is likely, and departments enjoy a degree of discretionary powers they might not be competent to apply. Inefficiencies in specific administrative areas could be difficult to identify, and overall control and co-ordination of the organisation may be more complicated under this system.

The advantages of product departmentation are that:

(a) It provides an excellent means for training managers for higher-level posts.

(b) The work of the department is varied and thus possibly more interesting for employees.

(c) Since employees must necessarily acquire a wide range of skills in order to succeed in a product department, they become flexible and hence can be quickly shifted from one type of work to another.

(d) It creates opportunities for job extension (*see* 16:**21**) that may lead to improved job satisfaction and higher morale.

7. Market departments

Market departmentation can occur by geographical region or customer type. Regional sales departments are an example: local factors can then figure in decision making, and it might be cheaper to locate offices near to customers. Otherwise market departmentation could relate to customer size (e.g. by having special facilities for large buyers), retail or wholesale distribution channels, export or home markets, etc.

8. Geographical (territorial) departmentation

This is common in companies that operate over a wide geographical area. There is duplication of activities and the need for a central co-ordinating body to assume overall control. Staff become expert in the peculiarities of their particular region. Often, territorial departments are located in the regions they service. This minimises transportation and travelling costs and allows for local staff recruitment. Regional managers acquire a wide range of administrative experience that provides a sound training for higher-level positions.

9. Departmentation by person

In small family businesses, departments are often built around individual family members and, as new functional needs arise, they are allocated according to the interests of these people. Thus, for instance, one of the family might be interested in finance and advertising, so everything to do with these functions will be dealt with in that person's department. Eventually, each department controls a variety of unrelated tasks.

10. Choice of method

In selecting a method for creating departments management should consider, for each alternative, the following questions:

(a) Will the system serve the organisation's customers effectively and generate maximum concern for customer care (*see* 7:**24**)?

(b) How will marketing and production activities interrelate?

(c) Will the system help or hinder the creation and development of fresh ideas?

(d) Is the proposed system capable of rapid response to environmental change?

(e) How will each department gather useful management information (*see* 13:**7**) for incorporation in the firm's overall management information system?

(f) Can technical developments be accommodated by the intended structure?

(g) Does the proposed system enable the logical and efficient division and allocation of duties to personnel?

(h) How are employees to be motivated?

(i) Does the scheme allow for fast and efficient communication within the firm?

(j) Will the top management be able easily to co-ordinate and control all the firm's activities?

OTHER CONVENTIONAL APPROACHES

11. Human relations approach to organisation

Like the classical approach, this also insists that certain universal principles should apply to the design of organisations. According to human relations theory, however, organisations should be constructed to accommodate the social and human needs of employees rather than expecting individuals to fit into a predetermined organisational form. The approach recommends:

(a) Flexible organisation structures with overlapping responsibilities

(b) Employee participation in decision making (*see* 15:**27**)

(c) Joint determination by manager and subordinate of the latter's targets.

12. Contingency approach to organisation

The contingency school (*see* 1:**20**) asserts that organisations should be individually structured to suit the requirements of particular situations. This approach, therefore, is the antithesis of the classical proposition that authority and responsibility systems should be constant and predetermined and that universally valid organisational principles should always be applied. Factors to be considered when designing organisations include the following:

(a) The mission of the enterprise (*see* 5:3).

(b) Laws and business practices of the society in which the business exists.

(c) The competitive environment. If new firms and products regularly enter the industry the business in question needs to be able to alter its activities and organisation structure quickly and at short notice.

(d) Senior management's ability to co-ordinate and control.

(e) Employee attitudes and abilities.

(f) The calibre of the firm's management information system.

(g) Whether wide spans of control are possible.

(h) The extent to which specialisation and the division of labour lead to reductions in costs.

CONVENTIONAL PATTERNS OF AUTHORITY AND CONTROL

13. Organisation charts

These are diagrams showing patterns of authority within organisations. An example is shown in Fig. 6.1. They may be drafted for entire firms or specific departments. Charts are frequently accompanied by *organisation manuals* that include complete job descriptions and detailed information about each position indicated. The purposes of organisation charts are to:

(a) Define the accountability system of the organisation

(b) Inform individuals of their status within the management hierarchy

(c) Facilitate organisational design

(d) Enable the preparation of management succession programmes

(e) Indicate lines of communication

(f) Show each manager's span of control (*see* 14).

Problems with organisation charts are that:

(a) They can quickly become out of date, so that all the time and effort involved in their preparation is wasted.

(b) Theoretical rather than actual communication channels are illustrated.

(c) Reluctance to deviate from the system shown on the official chart can cause organisational inflexibility.

(d) Organisational relationships are often far too complex to be represented on a simple diagram.

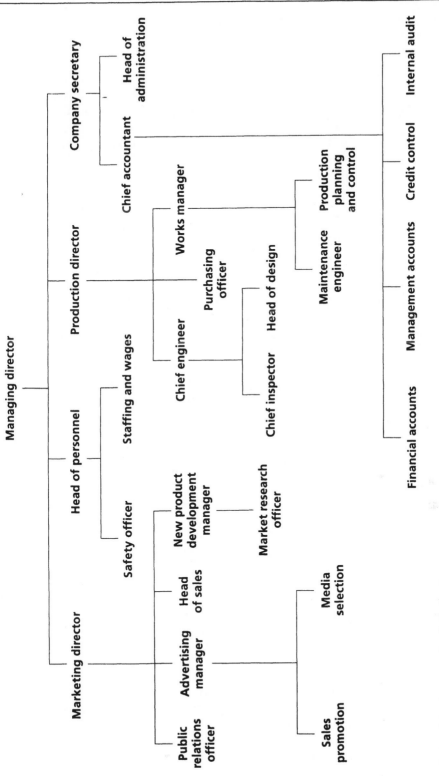

Figure 6.1 An organisation chart

115

(e) Employees may bitterly resent their jobs being ranked below those of certain other individuals.

14. Spans of control

A manager's 'span of control' is the number of immediate subordinates controlled by and reporting directly to that person. 'Narrow' spans involve perhaps just two or three subordinates; wide spans may have as many as 15 or 20 people. In practice the rule that no manager should control more than six subordinates is commonly applied in order to limit the demands placed on the time of the superior. However, wide spans are feasible when the work done by subordinates is uncomplicated, when there is good communication within the organisation, and when subordinates are well trained and enthusiastic (and thus require less detailed supervision). Note, however, that some managers are better able to control large numbers of subordinates than others.

Narrow spans create 'tall' organisation structures with many levels of authority and long chains of command. Managers are able to devote their full attention to the needs of subordinates, and duplication of effort among subordinates is less likely than in a 'flat' structure. Tall systems facilitate specialisation of functions, easy vertical communication and effective co-ordination of subordinates' work. Employees are faced with a hierarchy of positions and thus may expect regular promotion through the firm.

Flat organisations involve less direct supervision, and a greater number of subordinates experience higher-level work. Managers can communicate with junior employees without having to go through numerous intermediaries, so they remain in touch with the base of the organisation. Team spirit (*see* 14:**13**) may be higher in a flat structure.

15. Linking pin organisation

Here the manager is expected to act as a link between three levels: superiors, subordinates and peers. This requires each manager to serve on committees that bring him or her into direct contact with each level. Possible advantages to the system include better integration of activities, improved communication, and the training, development and motivation of staff. However, the organisational system becomes extremely complicated and much time has to be spent in meetings – at the expense of operational tasks.

16. Line and staff relationships

An important function of an organisation chart is to show line and staff relationships. The line organisation identifies points of contact between managers and their subordinates. Each position in the line structure has direct authority over subordinates at the next lower level. Problems that a manager cannot handle are reported to the superior specified in the chart. Likewise, work can be delegated only to immediate subordinates.

Within the line system there is an unbroken chain of command, a managerial division of labour and a clear delineation of authority. However, decisions taken at the top may have to pass through many levels before they are implemented and the system could collapse if a key person fails to pass on instructions and/or information.

The 'staff organisation' consists of specialists who advise line managers but do not themselves take final decisions. Examples of managers likely to occupy staff rather than line positions are lawyers, researchers, industrial relations specialists or technical experts. Note the distinction between a 'staff manager' and a member of a manager's 'personal staff'. The latter might be a secretary, personal assistant or other person who assists a manager (line or staff) fulfil his or her duties but who does not occupy a position in the managerial hierarchy as such.

Use of staff managers avoids line executives becoming immersed in technical detail. Staff managers can develop their specialist expertise leaving line managers free to concentrate on taking and implementing decisions. In practice, however, the distinction between 'line' and 'staff' can become extremely confused. Also, line managers may come to rely too heavily on staff advice, without asking critical questions.

Sometimes, staff managers are empowered to take and implement decisions within a restricted area. Thus for example a training officer will typically occupy a staff role, yet might be given the authority to compel employees to undertake certain staff development courses – even if their superiors would rather they did not attend. This is referred to as the 'functional authority' of a staff manager.

Conflicts between line and staff managers may occur through the latter giving esoteric and impractical advice; through line executives' jealousy of staff specialists' superior academic qualifications; or through line managers not implementing staff managers' recommendations. Equally, line managers sometimes complain of staff specialists' lack of concern for wider organisational objectives, and of their (perceived) interference with day-to-day operations.

The inverted management pyramid

This is an approach to organisation and management that seeks to turn upside down the traditional organisational pyramid that has a chief executive at the apex of the system, with senior executives underneath, middle managers below the senior management team, and so on. Critics of these orthodox hierarchies allege that customers are implicitly placed at the very bottom of the structure – beneath the lowest level of employees. Yet without customers there can be no business in the first place! Thus customers should be at the very top of the system, not at its base. Moreover, through inverting the conventional pyramid, front-line (customer contact) staff are recognised as occupying a crucially important role. Middle management supports front-line employees in the performance of their duties; senior management facilitates middle ranking executives while, at the bottom of the system, the chief executive supports the senior management team and, indirectly, everyone else within the organisation. Problems with the implementation of the concept are that:

- It is likely to be opposed by middle managers who fear losing their power and influence.

- Existing interpersonal relationships and understandings are disrupted.
- The absence of a conspicuous figure head may cause the organisation to lack strategic vision.
- It is unclear as to who is to issue directives.

Opponents of the idea of the inverted management pyramid claim that conventional hierarchies offer an efficient device for devolving authority and accountability within organisations, and that customers should not figure in an organisation chart (of whatever variety) in the first place. Rather the *raison-d'etre* of the pyramid is itself to serve customer requirements.

ALTERNATIVE FORMS OF ORGANISATION

17. Centralised versus decentralised control

Large organisations must choose whether to decentralise their operations. Decentralisation may be achieved through the creation of separate, quasi-independent subsidiary companies (each with an organisation that itself may be centralised or decentralised) or through dividing the firm into divisions. In a centralised organisation, all major decisions are taken by a central administrative body which issues binding directives to the organisation's constituent parts, the managers of which are bound by fixed rules and procedures and exercise little discretion in the course of their work. In a decentralised organisation, decisions are taken by 'local' managers with expert knowledge of immediate operational conditions, and local circumstances will be taken into account when policies are being determined. Local managers must, of course, adhere to overall directives issued from the centre, and they will be constrained by budgets and other restrictions.

The *advantages* of centralisation include the following:

(a) All major decisions can be directly related to the core objectives of the enterprise.

(b) There are no possibilities for disagreements and haggling between different decentralised units.

(c) All the firm's activities are subject to direct and immediate control.

(d) There is fast decision taking with little red tape or duplication of effort in subsidiary units.

(e) Co-ordination of activities is enhanced.

(f) Correct working methods can be imposed on all parts of the organisation.

(g) The administrative system is clear and (hopefully) uncomplicated.

Disadvantages of centralisation are:

(a) The organisation becomes inflexible and possibly unable to adapt to change.

(b) Senior managers might receive so much complex information from subordinates that important matters may be overlooked.

(c) Orders issued at the top of the organisation may be so irrelevant to the needs of component units that junior managers in charge of these units may simply ignore them.

(d) The initiative and expertise of junior managers in daily contact with 'local' operations might not be fully utilised. Local circumstances might not be considered when policies are determined.

(e) Strategic problems may be ignored through top management spending too much time on operational issues.

18. Divisionalisation

This is a common form of decentralisation. It avoids the cost and inconvenience of setting up subsidiary companies, and divisional managers are subject to closer control. Divisions may be established for different products, geographical markets, customer type (for example, retail or wholesale), function (such as purchasing, finance, etc) or method of production. Heads of division are given targets, but are left to achieve them in their own ways. Organisation within a division may itself be centralised or decentralised.

The advantages of divisionalisation (apart from the general benefits of decentralisation) lie in:

(a) its value as a training medium for the development of divisional managers for top-level posts in the parent organisation

(b) the relative ease with which divisional activities can be integrated at higher levels of control

(c) the motivation afforded to local managers who are encouraged to use individual initiative in solving local problems.

Disadvantages of divisionalisation include the extra resources required, the loss of economies of scale and specialisation, duplication of effort and the fact that divisions might regard themselves as independent bodies with objectives that differ from those of the parent organisation. Rivalries between divisions may emerge, with competing demands for attention and resources.

19. Strategic business units (SBUs)

SBUs are groupings of activities within the firm. An SBU could be an existing division or department; but the term is most frequently applied to collections of functions taken from different departments, e.g. all the firm's marketing activities might be regarded as an independent SBU, even though marketing is undertaken within a number of separate divisions. Another example would be a holding company that produced refrigerators, washing machines, electric cookers and spin dryers in various subsidiary companies creating a 'white goods SBU', with its own staff, administrative structure and resources. Member units should be compatible and collectively easy to control and appraise. It should be possible to identify the contributions to an SBU of each constituent activity.

To make sense, an SBU should:

- comprise compatible elements each possessing a direct and identifiable link with the unit as a whole
- be easy to appraise (which requires that its performance can be compared with something similar within or outside the organisation)
- contribute significantly towards the attainment of the organisation's goals.

SBUs are most appropriate for highly diversified businesses the activities of which can be grouped under distinct headings.

Advantages to the creation and use of SBUs are:

(a) They reduce the total number of administrative units that senior management has to monitor and control.

(b) Use of SBUs enables management to operate two levels of strategy: overall corporate decisions that affect the nature and direction of the enterprise; and unit level strategies relevant to specific operating environments. This facilitates the linking up of strategy development with strategy implementation.

(c) Important decisions can be taken in discrete business units.

(d) SBU organisation provides a planning framework that cuts across organisational boundaries.

(e) Units are encouraged to behave entrepreneurally.

(f) Decision making can be related to specific consumer groups and resource categories.

The main problems with SBUs are how to co-ordinate many disparate activities simultaneously and how to assess the financial and other contributions of various activities to a particular unit. SBUs are not suitable for vertically integrated companies supplying a limited range of products

20. Matrix organisation

This seeks to create project teams with members drawn from several different departments. Teams are then made responsible for particular functions. A firm's advertising team, for example, might comprise members from marketing, finance, design and sales departments; the 'health and safety at work' team could consist of representatives from the production department, personnel, quality control and (possibly) finance. In consequence, committees are assembled to oversee each of the organisation's key projects and/or operational activities.

Matrix organisation violates the classical principle of unity of command (*see* **3**) since team members have a number of different bosses, namely the heads of their 'home' departments plus the team leaders of the various committees on which they serve. Teams are intentionally multidisciplinary and cut across occupational divisions and line and staff distinctions.

The *advantages* of matrix systems are that:

(a) They are extremely flexible (teams can be established or disbanded at will).

(b) Team members develop decision-making skills.

(c) A wide range of professional competences is applied to the solution of problems.

(d) Representatives of different departments are compelled to meet and discuss common difficulties.

(e) Senior management is left free to concentrate on strategic planning.

(f) Knowledge and experience gained on one project is automatically transferred via team members to the other projects/functions to which they are attached.

(g) Managers have greater job security in consequence of their involvement in a wide range of projects or functions.

Problems with matrix organisation include:

(a) Team members may experience conflicts of loyalty between their home departments and team leaders.

(b) Managers need to be (expensively) trained in matrix organisation techniques.

(c) Decision making could be slow.

(d) Managers tend to spend much time in committees.

(e) Duplication of effort is likely.

(f) Petty 'who does what' disputes may arise within project teams.

(g) Internal communication systems become highly complicated.

21. Honeycomb organisation structures

These are based on interlocking yet quasi-independent 'cells' each of which corresponds to a certain function. The organisation deliberately recruits trained and experienced people, adding or deleting cells at will. If, for instance, the firm has a need for a transport department it simply hires an experienced and qualified transport manager plus associated support staff from outside.

A firm constructed on this principle can expand or contract operations quickly and easily by creating or disbanding cells. This contrasts with the *motherhood* approach to organisation, whereby staff are trained and developed within the business. Employees are recruited young and then put through a planned experience programme that deliberately immerses them in the company's culture and working methods. Staff undertake a wide range of duties and (hopefully) become heavily committed to the business.

22. Network structures

Networking involves employees working from home and communicating with head office via a computer link, telephone calls and occasional meetings. Employees are saved the time otherwise needed to travel to and from head office, can work the hours they please, and possibly will experience fewer interruptions during the working day. Problems with networking include the appraisal of networkers' performances, control of the quality of their output, and assessing the effort they put into completing tasks. Further difficulties arise from the potential use of the firm's equipment on projects for other employers; from copyright problems attached to new ideas, designs, programs, etc created in the networker's home; and from the need to co-ordinate at long distance the outputs of numerous network workers. Note moreover the lack of promotion opportunities typically available to network staff, who stand on the periphery of the organisation.

23. Informal organisation

Informal or 'shadow' organisations sometimes emerge alongside formal systems. They result from poor internal communications, autocratic management styles, lack of consultation with employees and the absence of formal procedures for resolving inter-departmental disputes. Informal organisation arises naturally and spontaneously as individuals begin to interact: groups begin to form to represent people with a common interest, and each informal group will develop its own perspectives and norms.

At best an informal organisation will supplement and improve the formal system. Internal communication may be greatly enhanced. Unfortunately, however, informal organisation may undermine the authority of official structures, can establish standards and objectives beyond management control, and encourage resistance to change. Management loses its grip over actual day-to-day activities. Also, informal groups can encourage excessive conformity and lack of initiative, and grapevines (*see* 12:5) may emerge. Conflicts of loyalty between a person's position in the formal system and his or her role in the informal organisation might arise.

The development of informal organisation may be prevented through adherence to the following principles:

(a) All employees should be informed of the organisation's objectives.

(b) There should be no sources of conflict between personal and organisational goals.

(c) Routine decisions taken at departmental level should not normally be overruled by higher authority. As a general rule, senior managers should back decisions taken by subordinates. Otherwise, junior managers will conceal some of their activities from superiors and a hidden, unofficial authority system will arise.

(d) No one department should dominate others to the extent that managers outside the dominant department feel they need its permission before taking decisions.

ORGANISATIONAL CULTURE AND POLITICS

24. Organisational culture

An organisation's 'culture' comprises its members' shared perceptions of issues, their customs, modes of behaviour and attitudes towards work and the enterprise. It affects the management style of the company, employees' approaches to their jobs, and opinions about what is and is not proper.

Further consequences of organisational culture might (to some extent) include:

- Communication patterns, especially in relation to vertical communications (e.g. whether these are restricted to the formal line system – see 15), and whether subordinates can openly criticise their superiors
- Approaches to remuneration management (time-based versus performance-related pay structures for instance)
- The degree of formality of company rules, regulations and procedures
- How closely employees identify with the firm
- Extent of decentralisation.

Advantages derived from a firm having a strong and distinct organisational culture include:

- The provision of a focal point for employee identification with the enterprise
- Agreement within the organisation of the basic goals need to be pursued
- Unification of effort among employees
- Potentially higher levels of staff motivation
- Easy implementation of agreed norms of behaviour.

Further benefits are that:

- There is a uniform interpretation of what constitutes correct and incorrect behaviour.
- Unanimity of purpose creates social cohesion within the firm and loyalty to the organisation. Hence staff turnover should fall.
- Employee and corporate behaviour will be predictable and consistent over time.
- There is less need for written rules and procedures.
- The organisation's unique character is clearly defined, thus contributing to the projection of a distinct corporate image.
- Internal social systems are stable.
- Employees are presented with clear information about how things should be done.

Note however that a firm's culture might itself be damaging to efficiency (a culture based on excessive bureaucracy and red tape for example) and generate inappropriate objectives. Also a strong culture might be highly resistant to change. Another problem created by the existence of a strong culture within a business is that whereas the firm's operations, objectives and working methods periodically and necessarily alter, its underlying culture might remain and be inappropriate for altered circumstances. The existing culture might be extremely difficult to change. Thus, it may be necessary to inject externally recruited staff into the organisation and/or devise incentive schemes that encourage the acceptance of different methods.

Organisational culture may be innovative, conservative, or somewhere between the two. A conservative culture is likely to generate low-risk strategies heavily reliant on what has gone, before tried and tested solutions to problems and possibly a tall management hierarchy, and authoritarian management style. Organisational culture creates norms of behaviour, attitude and perception, myths and rituals, and (importantly) feelings within employees of the value of being associated with the firm. Myths arise from exaggerated stories about past incidents, rumour and innuendo, the consequences of past mistakes (dismissal of certain employees for example), and from lack of communication and accurate information within the organisation.

Influence of culture

Positive aspects of organisational culture are that it furnishes employees with a sense of corporate identity, helps generate commitment to the attainment of organisational goals, provides employees with a frame of reference through which to evaluate issues and, by influencing individual perspectives and perceptions, stabilises interpersonal relationships within the firm. Equally, however, a culture might be highly resistant to change, encourage bureaucracy and inflexibility, and lead to short-sighted thinking within the firm. The organisation's needs and activities will regularly alter, but its underlying culture might remain constant. The continuing existence of out-of-date attitudes and perspectives among employees following changes in organisational structure and working methods is known as 'cultural lag'.

25. Types of organisational culture

Charles Handy distinguished four types of culture: power; role; task; and person. One of these might dominate the entire organisation, or different cultures may exist in various parts of the firm. The power culture stems from a single central source as in a small business that has begun to expand. Here, there are few rules and procedures and few committees. All important decisions are taken by a handful of people and precedents are followed. A role culture, in contrast, is highly bureaucratic. It operates through formal roles and procedures and there are clearly defined rules for settling disputes. Organisations dominated by a role culture offer security and predictability, but since they are rigidly structured, cannot adapt quickly to accommodate change (as can a power culture organisation).

The task culture is job- or project-oriented and manifest in matrix organisation structures (*see* 6:20). There is no single dominant leader; all group members concentrate on completing the collective task. A task culture will encourage flexibility in approach and is ideal for an environment of change. Job satisfaction is high and there is much group cohesion. A person culture might arise in an organisation which exists only to serve the people within it. Examples are partnerships, consultancy firms, and professional organisations.

According to Handy none of these cultures is better than the others. A culture arises, he argues, from historical circumstances, the existing environment technology, and the human needs of people within the organisation.

26. Formation of culture

A culture will have risen within a particular environmental context and be related to specific organisational needs. Factors contributing to the formation of a culture include:

(a) Management's stated objectives and core values. Employees who wish to progress within the organisation will tend to adopt these values in order to win the approval of their superiors.

(b) Induction systems and organisational socialisation techniques (e.g. selection methods and methods for training employees).

(c) Procedures for status symbols and fringe benefits. superannuation schemes, company housing loans, possibly the wearing of a company uniform, and so on.

Ideally the values, beliefs and expectations shared by employees should be consistent with the firm's mission, strategies and objectives. Indications that this is not the case might emerge from communications breakdowns, excessive bureaucracy, resistance to change, underperformance and poor quality output. This will require that the prevailing culture be changed.

27. Changing the corporate culture

To alter an existing culture the following measures may be required:

(a) Injection of new staff into the organisation

(b) Introduction of incentive schemes to encourage the acceptance of new approaches and working methods

(c) Emphatic managerial endorsement of new ideas, plus an increase in the flow of information between management and workers

(d) Deliberate promotion of individuals who possess flexible and appropriate cultural attitudes.

Although it is clearly important for management to understand and, if possible, determine the culture that exists within an organisation, a preoccupation with cultural matters can itself create difficulties. Employees may feel they are being manipulated and hence react in a negative manner. Also the process of culture change is never-ending so that enormous amounts of time and resources may be devoted to relatively minor cultural problems and issues.

Cultural fit

Arguably a successful enterprise needs to be able to adapt its organisational culture at will in order to fit its present environment. Within such a culture employees will communicate closely, be prepared to take risks, trust each other and work together as a team, and have high positive regard for themselves, colleagues and the company (Brown 1995). According to D. Denison (1990), flexibility in an organisation's culture:

- enables the firm to respond quickly to changing environments
- facilitates internal organisational design (departmentation, divisionalisation and so on)
- encourages the modification of employee behaviour in an appropriate manner as circumstances change.

Criticisms of this proposition (that an easily adopted organisational culture improves business performance) are that:

- Management can lose control over employees' actions (especially where risk taking is involved).
- The organisation might lack an overall sense of direction.
- Interpersonal relations may become unstable.
- A culture that is extremely hostile towards the firm's management could arise.

Culture and strategy

Culture affects the process of strategy formulation in a number of ways. It influences senior managers' perceptions of strategic issues and priorities, how they interpret information, their ethical standards, and how power is used to determine the strategic direction of the firm. Culture also impinges upon the implementation of strategy through helping individuals define their particular roles within the firm, and by providing benchmarks for attitudes, motivation and loyalty. Strategies that contradict the prevailing culture may be less likely to succeed than those in consonance with existing cultural norms. Further cultural influences on strategy formulation and business planning include:

(a) How well the company's goals are understood and supported by employees

(b) Decision making processes (participative, autocratic, etc) and the management style applied within the enterprise

(c) Whether individuals can be relied upon to be self-motivated and to implement strategic plans and decisions

(d) Attitudes towards risk

(e) How senior management perceives the very character of the organisation: as a market leader or follower, as traditional and conservative, innovative and trend setting, etc

(f) Organisational drive, vigour and vitality.

28. Organisational politics

The term 'organisational politics' is used to describe negotiations and settlements within organisations made necessary by the existence of contrasting interests and the differing perceptions of various organisation members. Political activities lead to compromises, toleration, and a stability of relationships which enables the organisation to survive.

Organisational politics typically involved the building of coalitions around issues, persuasion and advocacy, and the skilful deployment of resources and power. Control over information is a key tool in the process. Coalitions rise in consequence of bargaining among various interest groups, and a dominant coalition will emerge. Organisational politics affects which issues assume prominence within the organisation and how they are discussed and interpreted. The manner in which a problem is diagnosed may be determined primarily by the self-interests of influential individuals and coalitions. Hence organisational politics influences how decisions are taken as well as the decisions themselves. Note how certain rules, procedures and interpersonal relationships might develop outside the official management system.

A company's political power system can affect its organisation structure, even to the extent that the latter becomes unsuitable as a means for realising the enterprise's goals. Internal politics helps shape the ideas about organisation structure that are deemed acceptable and, once implemented, the organisation design most favoured by the dominant political group might perpetuate itself indefinitely. Organisational politics can affect planning (*see* Chapter 16) in the following respects:

(a) Disputes over who should undertake corporate planning activities

(b) The status of the planning function in the overall company hierarchy

(c) Possible misuse of planning mechanisms by individuals wishing to pursue their own personal objectives

(d) Resistance to planning on the grounds that it could pose a threat to vested interests within the firm and/or may expose personal weaknesses

(e) Conflicts between various functions (marketing and finance for example) regarding which department's plans are to be paramount

(f) Use of a corporate plan as a means for making redundant people who otherwise would be dismissed for underperformance.

Organisational politics are perhaps most likely to develop where:

(a) The organisation faces severe resource constraints, so that individuals and departments are compelled to fight hard for their budget allocations

(b) Environments are fast changing and uncertain

(c) There is a lack of leadership at the top of the organisation

(d) The firm does not have clear objectives

(e) Key managers have fundamentally different opinions about the basic purpose of the organisation

(f) There is little accountability and inadequate management control.

Organisational politics can damage a company in a number of respects:

(a) Certain individuals may come to act as 'gatekeepers'. An organisational gatekeeper is someone who (*i*) communicates with the outside world on behalf of an organisation (formally or informally), (*ii*) gathers information from external sources and (*iii*) through being able to withhold this information from certain of the organisation's members is able to influence the decisions it makes.

(b) Departments are encouraged to seek to make other sections dependent on them, regardless of whether these inter-relationships benefit the firm as a whole.

(c) Sectional goals might be inconsistent across the organisation and not shared by all individuals and departments.

(d) Managers may become obsessed with ideological struggle, conflict and gaining the upper hand, at the expense of getting on with their work.

(e) Bad decisions might result from the internal political bargaining process.

(f) Interpersonal relationships may deteriorate.

(g) Inaccurate information might be deliberately circulated.

(h) Decision processes can become disorganised and disorderly.

A distinction is sometimes drawn between 'legitimate' and 'illegitimate' organisational politics (Farrell and Peterson 1988; Drory and Romm 1990). The former refers to political activity regarded by organisation members as being 'within the rules', e.g. forming a coalition to block a proposal or circumventing the formal chain of command. 'Illegitimate' organisational politics, conversely, violate established norms of behaviour (whistleblowing or deliberate sabotage of other people's projects for example). 'Whistleblowing' is the practice of an employee reporting to the police or other outside authority the illegal practices or improper actions of the employing organisation. Sometimes, it occurs *via* intermediaries such as newspapers or pressure groups. If discovered the whistleblower is likely to face dismissal, and perhaps even legal action by the ex-employer.

29. Organisational development (OD)

This is the process whereby management periodically audits the suitability of existing organisation structures for its current needs, with a view to implementing change. The purposes of OD may be to alter a firm's culture; to facilitate the merger of two companies; to help repair the damage to employee morale following a round of redundancies; or to remove conflicts within the firm (e.g. between production and marketing staff). An OD exercise will examine:

(a) The effectiveness of existing communications systems

(b) Managers' and other employees' awareness of the aims of the organisation and their individual roles in achieving them

(c) The speed and efficiency of current decision-taking mechanisms

(d) The organisation's ability to respond to change.

The person or institution responsible for OD is sometimes called a 'change agent'. Often, change agents are external consultants specially engaged for the task. Outsiders are more likely to take an objective view of the situation than in-house staff, and bring to their work a wide experience of OD exercises implemented in other companies. However, they lack the detailed knowledge of the firm's operations and the long-term accountability of conventional employees.

OD could involve training and management development, creation of new departments and/or working groups, and restructuring of individual duties. Team building is a common OD technique, as it can improve the morale and social cohesiveness of the entire organisation. Often OD is implemented *via* the distribution of questionnaires designed to establish employees' opinions on the effectiveness of current working practices and on the prevailing organisational culture and core values of the firm.

INVESTIGATIONS INTO ORGANISATIONS

30. Empirical studies of organisations

In the 1940s E.L. Trist and K.W. Bamforth studied the effects on working groups in the British coal mining industry of the introduction of new mechanised methods. These new methods disturbed traditional working relationships and practices, broke up existing working groups, and caused social frictions that reduced productivity. Dislike of the new arrangements caused low morale and high rates of absenteeism.

Social and technological factors, the authors concluded, interrelate to influence task performance. Working groups are, therefore, self-contained 'socio-technical' systems in which neither the social nor the technical aspect predominates. It follows, they argued, that for any given socio-technical situation, differing working methods have differing social and psychological consequences. Hence, organisations and jobs within them need to be *designed* to suit particular circumstances.

These ideas were further developed by P.R. Lawrence and J.W. Lorsch who suggested a complete 'environmental' approach to organisation theory. Organisations emerge, they argued, to solve 'environmental problems'. Thus, organisations develop separate units (departments, divisions, functions or whatever) for dealing with the outside world. Lawrence and Lorsch studied ten American firms drawn from three industries: plastics, wood and containers. They concluded that the greater the degree of change and environmental uncertainty facing the firm:

(a) more departments and functions will be created, *and*

(b) the duties and responsibilities of each sub-unit will be more precisely defined.

This process of 'differentiation', as the authors put it, results in the various sub-units having different attitudes, patterns of interpersonal communication, formal hierarchies, and time horizons – some units react more to short-term problems than to long-run opportunities. Of the three industries, plastics was found to be the most diverse and unstable and hence the plastics firms had greater differentiation within their organisation structures. The existence of differentiation created the need for 'integration' of an organisation into a unified whole. Thus, firms in the plastics industry had many more 'integrative devices' – rules, codes of conduct, standard procedures, appointed co-ordinators, etc – than others.

Lawrence and Lorsch rejected 'universalistic' prescriptions for organisational problems. Neither the classical nor human behaviour approaches could offer organisational structures that were always suitable in all circumstances.

31. Burns and Stalker

T. Burns and G.M. Stalker investigated the attempts made by a number of Scottish firms to introduce electronics work into their existing manufacturing systems during the late 1950s. Like Lawrence and Lorsch, the authors found that the rate of change of the outside environment affected organisational effectiveness. In stable environments, structured 'mechanistic' organisational forms arose. Here, individual tasks are clearly defined; there is specialisation and the division of managerial labour, formal hierarchies, and rigid administrative routines. The emphasis is on vertical communication, with only the very senior management having overall knowledge of how the organisation works.

Firms operating within volatile environments, however, found that new and unfamiliar problems constantly arose. These firms had to respond quickly to external change. Bureaucratic organisations, according to Burns and Stalker, cannot accommodate the demands of new technology. Looser, horizontal communications systems are appropriate for these circumstances, which demand 'organistic' rather than 'mechanistic' organisational forms. Organistic structures are flexible, relatively informal, have overlapping individual responsibilities and hence a great capacity to cope with change. Many of the firms studied failed, the authors suggested, because of their inability to change from existing mechanistic structures to organistic forms.

32. Joan Woodward

Joan Woodward concluded from extensive empirical investigation that the type of technology used in production was a major factor in determining the suitability of an organisation structure for a manufacturing firm. She claimed that classical systems were best for assembly-line mass production, whereas participative organisations were appropriate for small-batch production or continuous process technologies.

According to Woodward, the more technically complex the organisation then, on average, the longer its chain of command (*see* 3), the wider the spans of control (*see* 14) of its managers, and the higher the proportion of managerial and technically qualified staff to manual labour. Note that Woodward assumed that technology is the *cause* of organisational structure and not its consequence. Also, environmental factors such as competitors' behaviour or legal constraints can significantly affect the design of organisations.

33. The work of Charles Handy

According to Charles Handy, changes in economic conditions, working practices and social attitudes have led to fundamental alterations in organisational culture and hence in approaches to organisational design, especially considering the need of so many companies to introduce flexible work patterns and to downsize the extents of their operations. Another important factor contributing to new perspectives on organisational structuring is the widespread decline of labour-intensive processes and their replacement by 'knowledge-based' production methods. Modern organisations, Handy suggests, increasingly evolve from the 'shamrock' form, through the 'federal' structure and eventually into the 'triple I' system (Handy 1989).

The shamrock organisation

This is analogous to the shamrock plant (which has three interlocking leaves) in that it comprises three distinct groups of employee, each with its own unique set of terms and conditions of employment. The first 'leaf' is a small number of core workers on permanent contracts and who run the system. They are loyal to the firm, progressive and flexible in outlook, and are handsomely rewarded for their contributions. The core is well-trained, competent and highly effective. Alongside the core is the second group in the system: the 'contractual fringe', comprising contract workers remunerated on a payments-by-results basis. The third leaf consists of casually employed part-time employees hired and fired according to the state of market demand for the firm's output. Individuals take this sort of work either because they cannot obtain full-time jobs or through preference for part-time employment. In some shamrock organisations there is a fourth leaf: the customer. Here the purchaser of the firm's goods or services undertakes certain tasks formerly carried out by employees, e.g. self-assembly furniture, self-service in supermarkets and in restaurants, and so on. The customer assumes the role of *de facto* subcontractor.

Advantages to the shamrock form of organisation include a high level of output from a limited number of workers, absence of red tape and bureaucracy and the ability to respond quickly to alterations in market conditions. Problems are the absence of feelings of loyalty towards the enterprise among many employees (whose jobs are liable to end at any time), and the organisation's heavy reliance on a handful of core workers.

The federal organisation

Small firms with 'lean' organisations might enter into close collaborative arrangements in order to acquire the resources and scope for action of large companies. Members share a common business identity, while retaining independent managements and business systems. Thus there is innovation and creativity within each shamrock organisation, while the federation as a whole develops a 'critical mass' capable of competing effectively in turbulent markets.

The triple I organisation

Eventually the organisation might progress to become a 'triple I' enterprise based on 'ideas, information and intelligence'. The triple I firm is a 'learning organisation' (*see* 15:**17**) with core workers possessing a wide range of conceptual, analytical, informational and general business skills. Managers of such firms need to be facilitators, advisors and coaches as well as decision makers *per se*.

STAKEHOLDERS

34. Stakeholders in businesses

The stakeholders in a business are the various groups which are affected – directly or indirectly – by company policies. Stakeholders may be internal or external. Examples of external stakeholders are suppliers, customers, local and national governments, trade unions, and special interest groups (consumerist or environmentalist groups, for instance). Internal stakeholders comprise employees, shareholders, creditors with security on the company's assets (bankers, for example) and departments within the firm. Each internal stakeholder will have invested something – finance, labour or other resources – in the enterprise.

The management of a business has to balance the conflicting demands of the various groups: higher wages mean lower dividends; cost cutting often results in poorer product quality. It is thus necessary for management to identify the stakeholders in an organisation, establish good relations with each group, create alliances, represent one faction to others, and so on. Management must also seek to influence stakeholders' perceptions of what the organisation should do, e.g. by persuading employees that a high pay rise may not be in the best long-term interests of the business.

Progress test 6

1. What are the purposes of an organisation chart?

2. Define the term 'span of control'.

3. List the principles of the classical organisation theory.

4. List six factors that contingency theorists might consider relevant to organisational design.

5. Define the terms:
   (a) matrix organisation structure
   (b) organisation development.

6. Explain the difference between honeycomb and motherhood approaches to organisation.

7

MARKETING

FUNDAMENTALS

1. Definitions of marketing

The Chartered Institute of Marketing defines marketing as 'the management process responsible for identifying, anticipating and satisfying customers' requirements profitably'. This is a slightly different approach to that adopted by Philip Kotler (an important writer on marketing subjects) who interprets marketing as a process of *exchange*. Marketing, he asserts, is the social and managerial process by which individuals and groups in society obtain what they need and want, and maximise their satisfaction through creating and exchanging products. Exchange occurs, he adds, when each party to a transaction has (*i*) something desired by the other side, (*ii*) can communicate, and (*iii*) can accept or reject a bid.

According to Kotler, marketing is a *social* process because it identifies society's material needs and creates institutions to satisfy them. Market exchanges are voluntary since (given a choice) consumers are not forced to purchase a particular firm's goods. Thus, suppliers are obliged to make their outputs sufficiently attractive to induce a voluntary exchange.

2. Marketing activities and the marketing mix

Marketing is a collection of activities that includes selling, advertising, public relations, sales promotions, research, new product development, package design, merchandising, the provision of after-sales service, and exporting.

The term *marketing mix* describes the combination of marketing elements used in a given situation. Appropriate mixtures vary depending on the form and industry. Major elements of the marketing mix can be listed under four headings:

(a) *Promotion* – including advertising, merchandising, public relations, and the utilisation of salespeople.

(b) *Product* – design and quality of output, assessment of consumer needs, choice of which products to offer for sale, and after-sales service.

(c) *Price* – choice of pricing strategy and prediction of competitors' responses.

(d) *Place* – selection of distribution channels and transport arrangements.

Criticism of the 4Ps approach

The concept of the marketing mix has been criticised on the grounds that its implementation encourages narrow thinking and the creation of separate and distinct 'functions' within marketing that are not well-integrated with the rest of the firm (Gronroos 1994). For example, customer service might be confined to a company's 'distribution' department whereas in fact it is so important that it should suffuse *all* aspects of the enterprise's work. Arguably the 4P approach is too simplistic and fails to capture the complex subtleties that supplier/customer relationships involve. Further allegations are that the marketing mix approach:

- is production-orientated in that it implies that the customer is someone to be manipulated and 'worked upon', rather than genuinely respected and valued as a partner
- leads to a proliferation of specialists (market researchers, media planners, sales promotions experts, etc) who lack a broad vision on the need to put the customer first
- means that many variables in addition to those quoted are crucial to the success of a firm's marketing effort; no list of variables can be exhaustive.

3. The marketing concept

Four basic approaches to marketing are possible. The first (the *'selling orientation'*) is to regard marketing as the function of finding customers for goods which the firm has already decided to supply. Here there is much emphasis on face-to-face customer contact, price cutting, heavy advertising and sales promotions. The second is the *'production orientation'* whereby management selects products that are economical to produce relative to production costs and resource availabilities, and then sets up a marketing department to distribute the goods. It is *assumed* that customers will want to purchase well-constructed mass-produced items that are made available to them at low cost. The third approach (the *'product features orientation'*) presupposes that all a firm needs to do is offer for sale high-quality sound-value products with many attractive features, provide effective after-sales service, and then the goods will 'sell themselves'.

Alternatively, the firm might seek to evaluate market opportunities before production, assess potential demand for the good, determine the product characteristics desired by consumers, predict the prices consumers are willing to pay, and then supply goods corresponding to the needs and wants of target markets more effectively than competitors. Businesses adopting the latter approach are said to apply the *'marketing concept'*.

Adherence to the marketing concept means the firm conceives and develops products that satisfy consumer wants. Note however that:

(a) Consumer demand can be and frequently is created and manipulated through advertising campaigns.

(b) Unquestioning adoption of the concept could lead to the production of items that are highly attractive to consumers but which nevertheless are expensive to supply and thus generate negligible profit.

Practical application of the concept implies the full integration of marketing with other business activities (design, production, costing, transport and distribution, corporate strategy and planning) so that the marketing department assumes extraordinary importance within the firm. Numerous conflicts with other functions could arise from this situation. The marketing department itself may be organised along product, functional or regional lines (*see* 6:4).

MARKETING AND CUSTOMER REQUIREMENTS

4. Relationship marketing

The term relationship marketing is used to describe an approach to marketing that seeks to establish long-term relationships with customers based on trust and mutual co-operation. Note how repeat orders from existing clientele are much more profitable to the firm than new business, because there is no need to spend money on advertising, visits by salespeople, etc. Relationship marketing (RM) is characterised by total commitment to customer care, openness, genuine concern for the delivery of high quality goods and services, responsiveness to customer suggestions, fair dealing, and (crucially) the willingness to sacrifice short-term advantage for long-term gain. Suppliers attempt to create and strengthen lasting bonds with their customers; they shift from attempting to maximise profits on each *individual* transaction towards the establishment of solid, dependable and, above all, permanent relationships with the people they serve. Customers are seen as *partners* in the marketing process, not as individuals to be influenced simply in order to make a onetime sale. The *practice* of relationship marketing is, of course, as old as commerce, representing as it does a truly natural approach to marketing, based on understanding and interacting with customers and empathising with their needs. Successful companies have always sought to improve customer relationships in the long term, paying greater attention to customer care, organisational learning (*see* 15:17), and relationship pricing (i.e. setting prices at levels intended to secure maximum long-term customer loyalty rather than maximise the short-run percentage mark-up on cost); in short, seeking the *integration* of the customer into the company. Implementation of RM has been facilitated, of course, by recent developments in information technology that enable firms to hold large databases containing extensive personalised details of individual consumers. This has enabled suppliers to customise and target their promotions more precisely using differentiated messages based on known *individuals* in their own right. Technological breakthroughs have occurred *vis-à-vis* database capacity, interconnectivity, enquiry language and operational efficiency.

RM techniques include the extensive provision of information on the firm and its products, personalisation of communications with customers, free gifts and samples, attractive premium offers, and the careful monitoring of the relationships formed with particular customers. More fundamentally, RM involves the establishment (where possible) of personal contacts and bonds between the customer and the firm's representatives; the eventual emergence of feelings within each party of mutual obligation, of having common goals, and of involvement with and empathy for the other side; and the integration of all the firm's activities (not just those of a marketing department) concerned with customer care. Apart from advances in information technology, other possible reasons for the development of interest in RM include:

- The rise of the consumer movement in conjunction with higher customer expectations in relation to levels of service
- Its usefulness for gaining a competitive edge over rival companies
- More extensive consumer protection legislation (e.g. on product liability, doorstep selling, unfair contract terms, etc) throughout the economically developed world
- The conspicuous example of the successes achieved by large Japanese companies that place great emphasis on long-term commitment to customers and suppliers, on total quality management, and which pay meticulous attention to customer care (which is seen not as an independent function, but as an integral and inseparable component of the firm's total configuration of activities, intimately intertwined with *all* aspects of the work of the firm)
- The huge expansion of direct marketing that has occurred in recent years.

Relationship marketing contrasts with conventional 'transactional' marketing, which has short time horizons and focuses on securing a single sale. With transactional marketing there is limited customer contact and little emphasis on customer service. Quality is seen as a matter to be dealt with by the firm's production department rather than something that should concern the entire organisation (Christopher *et al* 1991).

Markets as networks

Closer relations between suppliers and customers (especially business customers, as opposed to end consumers) has led to the proposition that many marketing situations can be analyzed in terms of the theory of networks. A marketing network comprises a supplying company and other firms with which it has built solid, reliable, long-term business relationships. The latter businesses may be customers; further organisations with which it has established links to provide mutual assistance and support (e.g. a joint venture for distributing several firms' products); the company's own input suppliers; licensees or sub-contractors; or partners in new product research and development. Within networks flows of *information* occur as well as exchanges of money and goods. Social interactions among the various parties can also influence outcomes.

5. Pricing

The price a firm may charge for its output depends on many factors, including:

(a) Consumers' perceptions of the attributes and quality of the product

(b) Total demand for the good (which depends on consumer income, the size of the market and seasonal and demographic factors)

(c) The degree of competition in the market

(d) Price elasticity of demand for the product (i.e. the extent to which a price change leads to an alteration in sales)

(e) Competitors' likely reactions to a price cut

(f) Consumers' knowledge of the availability of substitute products

(g) The product's brand image and the degree of consumer loyalty

(h) Costs of production.

A number of pricing strategies are available:

(a) *Penetration pricing*, whereby a low price is combined with aggressive advertising aimed at capturing a large percentage of the market. The firm hopes that unit production costs will fall as output is expanded. The strategy will fail, however, if competitors simultaneously reduce their prices.

(b) *Target pricing*, in which the firm predetermines a target level of profits, estimates its potential sales at varying prices, and then charges a price to generate target profits.

(c) *Skimming*, which is a high price policy suitable for top quality versions of established products. The firm must convince high income consumers that the expensive model offers distinct improvements over the standard version.

(d) *Product life-cycle pricing*. Here the price is varied according to the product's stage in its life cycle (*see* 9). Initially, a high price may be set to cover development and advertising costs. The price might then be systematically lowered to broaden the product's appeal.

(e) *Loss leading*. This means selling an item at less than its production or purchase cost in an attempt to attract custom and hence induce consumers to buy other items.

(f) *Price discrimination* involves charging different prices in different markets for the same good. It can only work if there exist barriers (consumer ignorance or high transport costs, for instance) that prevent intermediaries buying in low-price markets and reselling elsewhere.

(g) *Marginal cost pricing* means charging the customer a price that reflects the extra cost to the firm of supplying the item to that particular customer. For example, a telephone company might charge a low price for installing an inner city line, but a high price for supplying a line to a remote rural location where much additional work is required. Problems with the method include the difficulties and extra administration attached to computing marginal costs, and its unpopularity with consumers. Hence, *average cost pricing* is more common whereby all costs are aggregated and divided by expected sales to derive a common base for the final price. This is simple to apply and readily accepted by customers.

(h) *Limit pricing.* Here, existing firms in an industry collectively choose to charge lower prices than the market would bear in order to discourage the entry of new firms to the industry.

(i) *Variable (stayout) pricing* is used by firms wishing to discourage custom when they have too much business. Hence, prices are increased when order books are full, and *vice versa.*

(j) *Customary pricing* is occasionally used in inflationary situations. Price is held constant but the volume of contents of a package is reduced, in the hope that customers will not notice.

6. Market segmentation

This is the process of dividing the total market into sub-units and then modifying the product and/or the way it is packaged, advertised or otherwise promoted in order to satisfy the particular customer requirements of each market segment. Traditionally, markets have been segmented with respect to geographical location, socio-economic structure, age, sex, ethnic origin, religion, etc. Increasingly, however, attention is paid to the behavioural aspects of target segments, especially the relationship between spending patterns and the life styles (actual or desired) of various consumer groupings.

The term 'psychographics' refers to the systematic study of consumer lifestyles, attitudes, interests, opinions and prejudices as they affect purchasing behaviour. Psychographics seeks to sketch profiles of particular consumer groups and hence identify demands for certain products from key variables that characterise consumer types. For instance, an outdoor type who enjoys sport, fast cars, action-packed television programmes, etc may be attracted by products with rugged images that correspond to these conceptions.

A *differentiated* marketing strategy requires the firm to modify its products for various market segments and to operate in all sectors. Production and promotion costs are normally higher when this approach is followed. *Concentration* strategies involve focusing all attention on one or just a few market segments. *Undifferentiated* marketing means the firm offers exactly the same product using identical promotional images and methods in a wide range of markets. Differences in market segments are ignored. Products are designed and advertised in order to appeal to the widest possible range of consumers.

BRANDING

7. Branding and product policy

A product is anything a business has to sell, whether this be a physical good or a service. 'New' products could be completely fresh innovations, or modifications of existing products, or copies of other firms' products. *Branding* a product means giving it a trade name and/or logo and then seeking via advertising and other sales promotion to associate certain attractive characteristics with the branded item. Customers then *recognise* the product and, having once been satisfied by it, need not subsequently re-evaluate its worth. Thus, little fresh information about the product has to be provided to the customer after it has been branded. Note that failure to brand a product convincingly can result in the waste of much of the firm's advertising, since advertisements will promote the *generic* product category (including competitor's versions) to which the item belongs rather than the output of the firm in question.

Brands can relate to a single product or to a line (family) of related items. In the latter case an entire range of products can be jointly advertised under a single brand image. Moreover, additions to the product line are introduced easily, since no extra promotion is required: the new item is simply incorporated into the existing product range. Supermarket chains and other large retailers often sell 'own brand' products. These are attractively priced in order to cater for price-conscious customers and also to generate traffic 'in-store'.

The term *brand leverage* is sometimes applied to the practice of using a brand image established in one industry to enhance the image of a product in an entirely different field (e.g. using the brand name, logo, slogans, etc of a sports car company to market cosmetics). The practice is increasingly common and explains why businesses are sometimes taken over not for their physical assets, but simply for the names of their brands.

8. Valuation of brands

Brand names are valuable assets in their own right. They can be sold, mortgaged, assigned to others or licensed in return for a royalty or lump-sum payment. Increasingly, brand acquisition is the primary motive behind attempted take-overs, and brand values often appear as major intangible assets in the balance sheets of firms – hence affecting their gearing (*see* 9:**29**) and borrowing powers.

Ultimately the only way to value a brand is to sell it to the highest bidder. Frequently, however, there is no genuine competitive market when a brand comes up for sale, so that bilateral haggling between the seller and a single possible buyer is necessary in order to establish a price. The vendor will normally assess a brand's worth in terms of its financial value when used within the vendor's own firm. This value will depend on (*i*) the differential between the retail price of branded output and the price at which it would have to be sold unbranded, (*ii*) consumer loyalty and long-term stability of the brand, (*iii*) the impact of the brand on the business's overall corporate image, and (*iv*) how much has already been spent on developing the brand (the costs of market research and advertising, sales promotions expenses, etc). A potential brand purchaser, conversely, will wish to consider such factors as:

(a) The extent to which the brand's image can be separated from the vendor's company

(b) The brand's position as a market leader or follower

(c) Whether fresh competing brands are likely to enter the market

(d) Possible changes in consumer taste likely to affect brand performance

(e) The extent of the cash inflow expected from using the brand compared to the returns available on alternative investments.

PRODUCT LIFE CYCLE

9. The product life cycle (PLC)

Products have been likened to living organisms: they are conceived and born, they mature, decline and eventually die. A product's *introductory phase* is characterised by high expenditures (for market research, test marketing, launch costs, etc) and possibly by financial losses in the early stage. The first customers will be attracted by the novelty of the item. Typically, these customers are younger, better educated and more affluent than the rest of the population. Technical problems are likely and, realising this, many potential consumers will delay purchasing the good. No competition is experienced at this stage. Advertising is normally the most important element of the marketing mix during the introduction. The aim is to create product awareness and loyalty to the brand.

There should now follow a period of *growth*, during which conventional consumers begin to purchase the product. Competition appears, so advertisements should attempt both to reinforce customer loyalty and to broaden the product's appeal. Next, the product enters its *maturity* phase. Here the aim is to stabilise market share and make the product attractive (through improvements in design and presentation) to new market segments. Extra features might be added, quality improved, and distribution systems widened. Most consumers have by now either tried the product or decided not to buy it. Competition intensifies; appropriate strategies now include extra promotional activity, price cutting to improve market share, and finding new uses for the product.

Eventually, the market is saturated and the product enters its phase of *decline*. Public taste might have altered, or the product may be technically obsolete. Sales and profits fall. The product's life should now be terminated, otherwise increasing amounts of time, effort and resources will be devoted to the maintenance of a failing product.

10. Objections to the PLC hypothesis

The following difficulties apply to the concept of the PLC:

(a) Many products cannot be characterised in life-cycle terms (basic foodstuffs or industrial materials, for instance).

(b) The length of life of a new product cannot be reliably predicted in advance.

(c) Variations in marketing effort will affect the durations of life-cycle phases and determine the timing of transitions from one stage to the next.

(d) Competitors' behaviour may be the primary determinant of the firm's sales, regardless of the age of the product.

(e) Products do not face inevitable death within predetermined periods.

Termination of a product's life is a management decision. A product's lifespan may be extended by skilful marketing.

(f) Management can never be sure of the life-cycle phase in which a product happens to be at a particular time. How, for instance, could management know that a product is near the start and not the end of its growth phase, or that a fall in sales is a temporary event rather than the start of the product's decline?

(g) Many random factors can influence the duration of phases, turning points and levels of sales.

Note, moreover, that the expected demise of a product can become a self-fulfilling reality; management may assume wrongly that sales are about to decline, and consequently withdraw resources from the marketing of that product. Hence, in the absence of advertising, merchandising, promotional activity, etc sales do fall and the product is withdrawn!

PROMOTIONAL ACTIVITIES

11. Advertising

The EU's definition of advertising is 'the making of a representation in any form in connection with a trade, business, craft or profession in order to promote the supply of goods or services, including immovable property, rights and obligations' (EU Directive on Misleading Advertising 1984). Objectives of advertising include:

(a) Creation of consumer awareness of products, special offers and available discounts

(b) Projection of favourable corporate images

(c) Establishment of brand loyalty

(d) Development of feelings of need for specific goods

(e) Encouragement of retailers to stock certain products

(f) Reinforcement of brand images at or near points of sale.

Formulation of an advertising strategy requires the clear identification of target consumers and a definition of the product attributes they desire. Then, media are chosen to carry messages. Factors relevant to the choice of a particular medium include its:

(a) Overall coverage of target markets

(b) Capacity to penetrate specific market segments

(c) Cost in relation to the enquiries and orders it generates

(d) Frequency of appearance, e.g. daily versus weekly newspapers

(e) Atmosphere, e.g. newspapers have an atmosphere of urgency and authority

(f) Timing, e.g. most personal letters are written at weekends so advertisements requiring a written response are best placed in media that appear over the weekend.

Advertising budgets may be set in manners analogous to those outlined in 12:23. For a complete description of the advertising function see the M&E text *Advertising* by F. Jefkins.

12. Advertising agencies

Agencies plan campaigns, design advertisements, create slogans, produce artwork and television commercials, and place advertisements in suitable media. They charge commissions to the media with which advertisements are placed and thus can offer their services to client companies at very low cost; though agency work related to ancillary activities such as market research, direct mail or public relations must be paid for at negotiated rates. Advertisers do not have to use agencies, and are free to contact media directly themselves. However, agencies possess wide-ranging experience of media administration, and often they can secure bulk discounts on advertising space. Advertising which attracts agency commissions (such as that which appears in the press, on television and on posters) is referred to as 'above the line' advertising, as opposed to (non-commission bearing) 'below the line' techniques of public relations, sales promotions (*see* 17) and so on.

13. Public relations (PR)

The UK Institute of Public Relations defines PR as 'the deliberate, planned and sustained effort to establish and maintain mutual understanding between an organisation and its public'. Thus, PR concerns the creation and maintenance of goodwill. Note, however, that goodwill from some 'audiences' (consumers or governments, for instance) is more important than from others (e.g. competing firms). Hence a PR consultant will help the firm (*i*) define the various 'publics' it needs to influence, (*ii*) define the messages to which these publics will most favourably respond, and (*iii*) decide how best to reach target groups. This may involve research into how the firm and its operations and products are perceived by outsiders and into the media seen most often by the company's leading publics (e.g. which newspapers are read by the people it most needs to influence). The objectives of a PR campaign might be to:

(a) Establish a brand image

(b) Create awareness among the general public of the existence of the firm

(c) Overcome prejudice against use of the product (religious or cultural prejudices, for example)

(d) Increase the number of enquiries

(e) Improve the ratio of enquiries to sales

(f) Reduce selling costs, especially the costs of distribution and/or of using salespeople 'in the field'

(g) Achieve a higher profile in the local press and on local television

(h) Minimise the damage due to the company's image following an accident or other disaster in which the company was involved.

14. PR techniques

These include the preparation of news releases, measures to attract the attention of television and radio companies, sponsorship (*see* **20**), and exhibitions. Other PR activities involve:

(a) Lobbying local and national politicians

(b) Investor relations, i.e. the preparation of glossy brochures for presentation to current or potential shareholders

(c) Improving relations with opinion leaders and key pressure groups

(d) Staging 'events' such as visits by celebrities, publicity stunts, competitions, etc.

A crucial concern of PR is the creation of favourable corporate images. A firm's 'image' is the mental impression it projects to outsiders. This results from the identity it establishes for itself via its letterheads, logos, the fascia of its premises, the manner in which its staff respond to telephone enquiries, etc.

15. Packaging

The functions of a package are (*i*) to protect the contents, and (*ii*) to present the product to consumers in an attractive way. Factors affecting choice of a package include the cost of packaging materials, the amount of intermediate handling the goods will receive, the value of the item, whether an expensive package is necessary to enhance the image of the product, and breakage and spoilage costs (sometimes, it pays to spend less on packaging, and accept that more items will be lost or broken in transit). Packaging goods in small quantities costs more, but the mark-up on small package sizes is typically much higher than on large containers.

16. Merchandising

Merchandising is the process whereby manufacturers' representatives assist retailers (free of charge) to present products to customers in the most attractive manner. Hence, it involves:

(a) Advising on the best shelf locations for a certain type of product

(b) Provision of promotional materials (posters, leaflets, competition forms, etc)

(c) Arranging dump displays (i.e. piles of units of a product in the middle of supermarket aisles to encourage impulse purchasing)

(d) Informing retailers of forthcoming advertising campaigns and suggesting they 'stock up' in anticipation of increased demand.

17. The marketing services industry

Marketing services comprise a variety of ancillary marketing activities, mostly associated with sales promotion, direct marketing, and the creative side of advertising and public relations.

Sales promotion covers the issue of coupons, the design of competitions, special offers, distribution of free samples, etc. The objectives of sales promotion campaigns include:

(a) Stimulation of impulse purchasing

(b) Encouraging customer loyalty

(c) Attracting customers to the firm's premises

(d) Penetration of new markets

(e) Increasing the rate at which customers repeat their purchases.

Promotional techniques need to relate to the specified aims of the exercise (free samples to enter new markets, reduced-price offers to encourage repeat purchase, money-off coupons to attract customers to the premises, etc).

18. Direct marketing (DM)

Direct marketing covers direct mail, telephone selling, catalogues, and 'off-the-page' selling via cut-outs in newspaper and magazine advertisements. The DM industry consists of 'suppliers' and 'consultants'. The latter are concerned with planning and testing DM programmes, integrating DM into the client's total marketing strategy, estimating the costs of DM exercises, and evaluating alternative approaches to DM (mail-drops versus off-the-page advertisements, for example). 'Suppliers', conversely, consist of telemarketing agencies, fulfilment houses, computer bureaux, list brokers and mailing agencies.

Fulfilment houses are businesses that handle the responses to maildrops and direct mail advertisements, receive the orders from customers and despatch the goods. They also advise on probable response rates (and hence the amount of stock of the 'offered item' to hold).

Computer bureaux enter target customer names and addresses into databases, update and correct the entries, cross-tabulate names and addresses according to various characteristics, and print the results. Use of a bureau enables the client firm to avoid filling up its own computer system with the huge data files needed for DM campaigns.

Mailing agencies send out DM letters and other sales promotion literature. *List brokers* compile and sell lists of names and addresses of target consumers, for example:

(a) Readers of certain subscription magazines

(b) Members of certain clubs, organisations (the AA or various animal welfare charities, for instance)

(c) Owners of particular domestic appliances, or heavy purchasers of expensive luxury consumer items

(d) Rich and poor people in various age groups.

A *telemarketing agency* will prepare lists of telephone numbers of people likely to buy the product, and then make the calls.

19. Marketing research (MR)

The British Institute of Management defines marketing research as 'the objective gathering, recording and analysing of all facts about problems relating to the transfer and sale of goods and services from producer to consumer or user'. It is useful to make a distinction between 'market' and 'marketing' research. The former concerns the analysis of sizes and structures of markets. Hence it investigates potential consumers' ages, incomes, socio-economic backgrounds, lifestyles, and geographical locations. *Marketing* research, however, is research into any area of marketing, including consumer behaviour, the evaluation of advertising, consumer reactions to price changes, media research, appraisal of the salesforce, etc.

MR methods include sampling, the drafting and distribution of questionnaires, interviewing consumers, direct observation of consumer behaviour, analysis of statistical information, consumer audits (i.e. monitoring how and when an item is sold in a certain set of consumer outlets) and contacting representative consumers by telephone.

20. Sponsorship

Sponsorship can be expensive, but may attract much favourable publicity. Today the governing bodies of many sports and cultural pastimes have clearing houses which put potential sponsoring companies in touch with organisations in need of funds.

The disadvantages of sponsorship relate mainly to the risk of failure of the sponsored event. Moreover, a sport may fall into disrepute (through spectator hooliganism, for example) and thus tarnish the image of the sponsoring firm. Other dangers include the following.

(a) Possible 'sponsorship wars' as competitors sponsor rival teams or activities. Costs escalate as increasing amounts of money are poured into ailing sports clubs or cultural activities.

(b) Contracts with teams, orchestras, etc are normally for fixed periods. If the sponsoring company wishes to terminate the agreement on account of the sport's (or music's) waning popularity it will be required to pay compensation.

(c) Sponsored sports teams often depend critically on one or two star players. If these individuals are transferred or injured, the team's fortunes might diminish.

Drug scandals, etc involving star players may cause bad publicity for the sponsoring company.

(d) Certain sports maintain amateur status, so that financially sponsored participants may be compromised.

Various forms of sponsorship are possible. A firm might, for example, guarantee to meet a sporting club's predicted financial losses in return for free advertising facilities on the club's premises (posters, prominent displays in match programmes, loudspeaker announcements and so on). Alternative approaches might involve a joint venture (building and servicing a club restaurant, for example), or making donations for specific purposes (such as floodlights for a football club), or a general subsidy to a team or activity.

Sponsors want value for money, and thus usually demand some involvement in the management of sponsored events. Disputes might arise over such matters as:

(a) Timing of events and/or scheduling of fixtures

(b) Selection of team members

(c) To whom the team manager is ultimately responsible

(d) The extent and frequency of the recipient's reports to the sponsor

(e) Who should draft press releases and generally liaise with the media.

INFLUENCES ON CUSTOMER RELATIONSHIPS

21. Internal marketing

Philip Kotler defines internal marketing as 'the task of successfully hiring, training and motivating able employees to serve the customer well' (Kotler 1991). Thus, it is an approach to human resources management based on a marketing perspective and seeking (*i*) to help individuals understand the significance of their roles and how they contribute to the organisation (George 1990), and (*ii*) to promote, develop and sustain the ethos of customer service (for internal as well as external customers – Collins and Payne 1991). Internal marketing is based on the premise that improved relations with customers are only possible if all employees in all sections of the organisation are genuinely committed to quality and customer care. Departments within a firm can regard themselves as members of an 'internal customer chain', each link demanding high quality in the inputs it receives. Hence, *everyone* in the organisation has a customer, and each internal customer must feel satisfied before the final customer can be effectively served.

Purposes of internal marketing include:

- Facilitation of the improvement of the quality of internally provided services

- Avoidance and/or resolution of departmental or functional conflicts within the firm
- Supporting the firm's external marketing efforts
- Implementation of organisational change
- Motivation of employees
- Enhancement of the image of a particular section or activity within the firm
- Encouragement of employees themselves to purchase a company's output
- Development of teamwork
- Making employees aware of customer requirements
- 'Selling' the need for training to employees most likely to benefit from particular courses
- Instilling quality consciousness in workers' minds.

Activities appropriate for the implementation of an internal marketing programme include:

- Company newsletters and in-house magazines
- Workshops and team briefings
- Short courses
- Incentive schemes to encourage particular forms of behaviour
- Formulation of a mission statement (*see* 5:3) for the human resources function (Collins and Payne 1991)
- Segmentation of employees into various categories according to their needs and wants in a manner analogous to the segmentation of consumer markets (*see* 6); this exercise could form the basis for determining remuneration packages, working conditions, etc, for each category
- 'Test marketing' new company policies
- Implementation of company planning procedures which ensure that all employees understand the basic objectives of the enterprise.

Effective application of internal marketing techniques requires that human resources managers possess a sound knowledge of the needs and preferences of their client groups (employees, other departments, senior management, etc) and are prepared to undertake research to discover these needs and preferences if necessary. Research might include attitude surveys regarding job satisfaction, opinions concerning company policies, employee morale, and so on. Note how a firm's workers may be regarded as internal 'customers' – with the company offering jobs possessing various characteristics to each of its employees.

Benefits potentially deriving from an internal marketing programme include:

- Improved quality of work from motivated staff who are more deeply involved with the company
- Cross-fertilisation of ideas across departments
- Improvement in the organisational culture of the enterprise
- Better two-way communication between management and workers.

An additional advantage is that marketing-oriented personnel and human resources managers should be more effective in demonstrating the relevance of HRM to senior management and heads of various functions. Importantly, they will not become immersed in the bureaucratic and technical aspects of personnel management at the expense of concern for the overall purpose of the firm.

Problems likely to be experienced when implementing internal marketing programmes are:

(a) Apathy among employees, who might regard internal marketing as just another management gimmick designed to extract greater effort from workers for the same level of pay

(b) The possibility that the idea will be taken up by a few managers and sections, but not by the wider organisation

(c) Difficulties connected with measuring the effectiveness of programmes, especially the quality of intangible outputs emerging from certain departments (sometimes the calibre of the staff delivering these intangible outputs is used as a proxy for service quality).

22. Management of the salesforce

Consumer durables, bulk orders to retailers, some fashion goods, and expensive products of all kinds are sold through face-to-face contact between salesperson and customer. Inexperienced staff are normally assigned to *order-taking* functions, while *order-making* duties are usually undertaken by senior selling staff.

Recruitment

Effective salespeople are usually individuals who can identify and understand consumers' needs, and are capable of individual initiative without detailed supervision. There is, however, little evidence that academic qualifications affect selling performance, or that any one personality type is particularly effective at this type of work (though it does seem that persuasive, energetic and ambitious people are attracted to sales careers).

Remuneration

Often salespeople are paid a guaranteed minimum wage, with additional incentive elements. Time rates are popular where significant seasonal variations in demand or other factors beyond the salesperson's control are common. Note that rates of commission may be varied to encourage salespeople to concentrate on particular product lines. Alternatively, 'market-led' schemes may be implemented whereby salespeople only receive commission on high levels of sales of particular items. Hence they quickly transfer their efforts away from items that are not likely to sell.

Deployment

Staff can be deployed in geographical areas (thus minimising travelling times between home, office and customers) or be assigned to selling one (usually technically complex) product to any customer in any location. Large companies taking large orders have advantages here, since small firms dealing in low quantities must pay their sales staff similar wages to bigger firms whose staff sell larger amounts.

Appraisal

Measuring a salesperson's performance solely on the basis of value of orders received is unsatisfactory because one or two really big orders will create impressions of efficiency that are not necessarily true. Hence, sales volume should be considered relative to other factors, such as the number of orders obtained; number of calls made; how many completely new customers are secured; size of territory covered and the amount of travelling needed to contact customers. Thus, good salespeople should outperform their colleagues regardless of the particular area covered.

23. Distribution

A distribution channel is a route from the producer of a good to the final consumer. The functions of a distribution channel include the physical movement of goods, storage of goods awaiting transit and/or sale, transfer of title to goods, and their presentation to final purchasers. There are three main categories of distribution system:

(a) *Direct to consumers*, e.g. mail order or if the producer owns and controls its own retail shops. No intermediaries are involved, so prices can be lower and suppliers can ensure their goods are properly presented to consumers. The method is commonest among firms

(*i*) with large volumes of business (and thus able to justify establishing a separate sales organisation),
(*ii*) with technically complicated products, and
(*iii*) where customers are geographically concentrated and place high-value orders.

(b) *Producer to retailer*. Here the retailer bears the cost of storing goods awaiting sale. The supplier must employ salespeople to canvass retail outlets and to merchandise the product (*see* **15**). Retailers sell the goods, possibly offer credit, provide product information to customers, and ensure that goods are available in small quantities throughout the year. Franchising (*see* 3:**32**) is a special case of this method.

(c) *Producer to wholesaler*. The advantages of selling to a wholesaler include (*i*) less administration (there is no need for a salesforce, no warehousing costs, fewer deliveries, and negligible invoicing and debt collecting) and (*ii*) the transfer of the risk of product failure from the supplier to the wholesaling firm. However, final prices will be higher and wholesalers typically hold competing lines.

The *intensity* of a distribution system is the number of sales outlets it involves. Intense (many outlet) systems are appropriate where there is regular demand, where customers are widely dispersed and where little product information is needed.

24. Choice of method

In selecting a distribution system the producer should consider the following characteristics in respect of each alternative:

(a) Cost of the channel. This is affected by the size of customers' orders (discounts are necessary to secure big contracts), salespeoples' salaries and travelling expenses, costs of credit given, inventory holding costs of unsold output, and administrative costs (invoicing, debt collection, bad debts, etc).

(b) Extent of the control that can be exercised over the channel.

(c) Whether the channel improves or worsens the image of the goods (e.g. high-quality expensive output would not be congruent in a low-price cash-and-carry discount store).

(d) Geographical coverage of the channel.

(e) Reliability of distributors in relation to:

   (*i*)   product presentation and the provision of information to customers
   (*ii*) ensuring continuity of supply
   (*iii*) adequacy of customer care and after-sales services.

25. Customer care

Satisfied customers repeat their purchases and introduce new clients to the firm. Note how it is typically cheaper to obtain a repeat order than an order from a completely new customer because no additional advertising is involved. *Customer care audits* are detailed examinations of the firm's efforts in this field, including:

(a) availability of spare parts and servicing facilities

(b) length of product guarantees compared with those offered by competitors

(c) clarity of instruction manuals

(d) availability of post-purchase advice on use of the product

(e) efforts to maintain contact with the customer via maildrops, newsletters, etc in order to inform existing customers of new models, product improvements and so on

(f) the accuracy and appearance of documents sent to the customer (invoices, for example)

(g) convenience of product packaging

(h) the speed with which the firm handles customer queries and/or complaints

(i) leadtimes between the customer placing an order and delivery of the goods

(j) reliability of quoted delivery dates

(k) the ease with which customers can place orders

(l) the extent of consultation with customers prior to modifying products

(m) extent of information given about ingredients, product uses, etc

(n) the courtesy of company representatives

(o) availability of emergency help to customers

(p) the convenience to customers of the systems through which they pay for their purchases.

MARKETING INFORMATION

26. Marketing information systems

Market research provides an important input to the firm's overall marketing information system. The information that an effective marketing information system requires typically relates to:

(a) Sales by product, region, customer type and selling method

(b) Average order size and customer spend

(c) Market share and competitors' behaviour

(d) Profitability of various products and market segments

(e) Credit and discounts given

(f) Promotional costs and consequences

(g) Feedback from customers obtained through sales call reports, question-naires and market surveys

(h) Trends in sales, especially sudden market failures

(i) Changes in the composition of the buying public.

27. Marketing audits

A marketing audit is a comprehensive review of the effectiveness of the firm's current marketing activities. Audits should be completed periodically or whenever environments significantly change.

Internal audits cover such matters as the efficiency of the salesforce, the analysis of causes of differences in the performances of various marketing staff, the adequacy of existing products and the usefulness of current advertisements and other promotional techniques. Other topics for examination include:

(a) Product knowledge of employees

(b) Effects of salespeoples' commission systems

(c) Desirability of product standardisation

(d) Possibilities for doing more things in-house rather than relying on outsiders (advertising agencies, for example)

(e) Training and staff development needs

(f) Adequacy of existing marketing budgets.

External audits investigate market trends, profitability of various markets, the strengths and weaknesses of competitors, and the impact the firm's corporate image (*see* **13**) presently creates. Distribution systems should also be analysed, especially possibilities for changing or removing intermediaries.

28. Measuring service quality

Perceptions of service quality are based on the comparison of what the customer feels should be offered and what is actually provided. Hence customers' *expectations* of performance levels for various attributes of the service provider can be measured and compared with measures of customers' assessments of actual service quality. Management can then attempt to reduce the gap between expectations and perceptions. A frequently used tool for evaluating the quality of service provision is the SERVQUAL instrument developed by Parasuraman *et al* (1988) which, in its original version, was a 45-item instrument for assessing, on the one hand, customer expectations of service quality and, on the other, customer perceptions of service quality. The first section of SERVQUAL consisted of 22 questions for measuring expectations. These questions asked customers how they would expect an 'excellent' provider of the service under consideration to perform. The second part comprised 22 questions asking for customers' perceptions of how the service provider *actually* performed. A final question requested an overall assessment of service quality. The 22 items divided into five dimensions which the authors claimed were used by customers when evaluating service quality, as follows:

1. *Tangibles* such as physical facilities and equipment and the appearance of personnel.
2. *Reliability*: the ability to perform the service dependably and accurately.
3. *Responsiveness*: willingness to help customers and provide prompt service.
4. *Assurance*, involving the knowledge and courtesy of employees and whether they inspire trust and confidence.
5. *Empathy*: the extent to which the service provider is 'caring' and gives individualised attention to its customers.

Criticisms of SERVQUAL are that:

- Collapsing the analysis into just five dimensions obscures important criteria actually used by service recipients when assessing service quality.
- Arguably, an organisation should be regarded as an *integrated whole* rather than as a set of quasi-independent units.
- There are many overlaps between the five factors. Hence it is difficult to discriminate between them.
- Respondents' stated expectations of service levels might be unrealistic

and unattainable. Attempts to close the gap between expectations and perceptions could lead, therefore, to expensive activities with no hope of success.

- 'Perceptions' of a particular service provider's quality are likely to reflect the respondent's *general attitude* towards quality rather than objective facts.
- Different people interpret the concept of 'expectations' in disparate ways, e.g. as what *should* happen; or as what is likely to happen; or what is reasonable in the light of the costs of service provision; or the *minimum* acceptable level of service; and so on.

29. The marketing plan

This specifies the firm's marketing objectives and how these will be attained. The plan should include a statement of the firm's current market situation, an analysis of its marketing strengths and weaknesses, and specific targets and policies in relation to:

(a) Introductions and withdrawals of products

(b) Research and product development activities

(c) Implementation of price changes

(d) Increases in market shares in particular market segments

(e) Profit margins on various products.

Product planning

Product planning seeks to ensure that the firm always possesses a balanced portfolio of products (*see* 5:23). Thus it is necessary to monitor the demand for various product features and deploy resources to guarantee the availability of the skills and materials needed to supply appropriate items.

Sales planning

Targets are needed for sales volume, costs and profits per sale. This involves determining policies for discounts and credit allowable, sales training, and the deployment and appraisal of the salesforce (*see* 19).

Media planning

This concerns planning the firm's advertising effort, setting budgets, and evaluating advertising effectiveness in terms of cost, market penetration and coverage.

CONSUMERISM AND CONSUMER PROTECTION

30. Consumerism

Businesses are sometimes criticised for incorporating 'built-in obsolescence' into their goods, for publishing misleading advertisements, failing to test goods adequately, not marking safety instructions properly and not recalling defective products.

Consumerists demand four basic rights: information, choice, safety and redress. Lack of competition, they argue, denies consumers the ability to choose between products, while advertisements that focus on images at the expense of information foster ignorance (including ignorance of the potentially harmful effects of using certain products) among consumers. Hence, they suggest, laws are needed to guarantee basic consumer rights.

Opponents of consumerism allege that it encourages groundless petty complaints, creates unfounded fears about product safety, and that consumerist interference with commercial decisions causes inefficiency and increased production costs. If customers do not want the goods on offer – albeit with built-in obsolescence and extensive advertising – then they will not be bought! Market forces, they assert, will ensure that customer requirements are met.

31. Benefits of consumerism

Consumerists are able to draw public attention to the needs for quality, safety and reliability in products; so much so that many firms today consciously anticipate the reactions of consumer groups when drafting marketing plans. Indeed, in a sense the consumerist movement provides businesses with free market research – informing firms of customers' desires for better labelling, more effective after-sales service, reusable containers and so on. Consumerist activities, moreover, have induced several major industries to devise codes of practice covering such matters as product safety, quality control, avoidance of environmental pollution, and the establishment of independent procedures to investigate complaints.

32. EU approaches to consumer protection

The major consequence for Britain of EU Directives on consumer affairs was the passing of the Consumer Protection Act 1987 (*see* 11:8). In general, the EU approach (articulated by one of its advisory bodies, the Consumers' Consultative Committee) is to suggest that each member state provide its citizens with basic consumer rights to:

- health, protection and safety
- protection of 'economic interest'
- redress
- information and education
- representation
- 'value for money'.

The Commission has specified the following as priorities for further EU involvement in consumer affairs:

(a) Laws to require that guarantees are honoured in EU consumers' countries of residence, regardless of where the product was bought.

(b) Standardisation of the format in which credit charges are expressed, so that consumers can easily compare competing credit offers from companies in different EU states.

(c) Establishment of low-cost legal procedures for consumers seeking compensation for minor damage caused by product inadequacy.

(d) Provision of education on consumer matters to young people.

33. Consumer health and safety

The European Court of Justice determined in the *Cassis de Dijon* case of 1979 that every product legally manufactured and sold in one EU country should in principle be admitted to all other EU states. Hence national product standards should not be used to obstruct the import of goods; each member state must recognise the adequacy of the technical standards of other members. To prevent EU states from unfairly imposing technical requirements so as to discriminate against EU imports, it has been necessary since 1984 for every proposal for a new national product standard to be vetted by the product standard authorities of other EU countries, which can object to the proposal and cause its suspension if it is not strictly necessary in order to protect public health or consumers' interests.

34. EU controls over advertising

There exists an EU Directive to prohibit misleading advertising. The latter is defined as advertising that deceives or is likely to deceive the people it reaches and which, by virtue of its deceptive nature, could affect consumer behaviour or cause damage to a competing firm. The EU insists, moreover, that (*i*) the burden of proof should lie with the advertiser and not with the consumer, and (*ii*) national courts shall be empowered to halt the publication of misleading advertising.

The EU cannot, of course, control satellite broadcasts emanating from beyond its frontiers. Accordingly, the European Commission has issued a set of guidelines for advertisements broadcast via satellite, to which it invites advertisers to adhere. These guidelines request advertisements:

(a) not offend religious or political beliefs

(b) not contain material encouraging racial or sexual discrimination

(c) not engender fear in those watching the broadcast

(d) not offend prevailing standards of decency and good taste

(e) not portray behaviour that is prejudicial to health and safety.

Note the contradiction between the last of these recommendations and tobacco and alcohol advertising.

The Cross-Frontier Broadcasting Directive 1989

This guaranteed the freedom of transmission of broadcasts across national EU frontiers and established minimum rules for the regulation of broadcast advertising. Under the Directive, responsibility for the control of TV advertising lies with the authorities of the country in which an advertisement originated. The Directive

(a) set limits on the air-time devoted to commercials (no more than 15 per cent of total daily transmissions, with a maximum of 18 per cent during peak hours)

(b) banned the TV advertising of tobacco and prescription pharmaceuticals

(c) introduced guidelines for TV alcohol advertising, for advertising to children and for the sponsorship of television programmes.

THE MARKETING OF FINANCIAL SERVICES

35. Characteristics of financial services

Financial services differ from other types of product in the following respects:

(a) Financial services are *intangible*. They cannot normally be seen or handled.

(b) Usually, financial services cannot be *experienced* before they are bought. A motor car, for example, can be taken for a test drive prior to purchase but a pension plan or the benefits from an insurance policy are not consumed until a time in the future.

(c) The quality of a financial service is inextricably linked with the providing firm (rather than with physical materials used in construction or assembly). For example, a life-assurance policy purchased from a well-established company is usually regarded as of higher quality than one purchased from an unknown and newly established firm (note how insurance companies conspicuously emphasise the dates of their establishment in advertising literature).

(d) Often, the financial service provided to each customer has to be *unique*. Insurance schemes and pension plans for instance must necessarily relate to the needs of the individual consumer, depending on his or her age, sex, marital status, number of children, financial commitments and so on.

(e) Certain services *cannot be stored* (investment advice for instance), but exist only at the moment of consumption. This means the service provider cannot produce for stock during slack periods.

(f) Since financial services are intangible, consumers cannot readily *compare* the offering of one supplying organisation with the offerings of others.

(g) Financial services are (usually) expensive, *infrequently purchased*, governed by agreements containing much detail, and have many complicated technical features and attributes.

(h) Most financial services have *long product life cycles*. An insurance policy issued today is essentially similar to one issued in the last century.

(i) A financial service is purchased in *anticipation of future benefits*, e.g. using a bank account for direct debits and for paying by cheque.

36. Implications for marketing

Today, consumers expect *all* products offered for sale to be well packaged and presented, including financial services. The considerations outlined in **35** have the following implications for the marketing of financial services:

(a) Supplying institutions typically attempt to create images of *trust*, respectability, reliability and immaculate professional integrity. (Note that many customers have difficulty understanding the small print of financial service contracts.)

(b) *Potential* benefits (security in old age, higher incomes in the future, the convenience of a bank account, etc) will be emphasised in promotional literature.

(c) Sales promotions for financial services frequently illustrate how *individual* consumer needs will be satisfied by the offer of a particular supplying firm.

(d) Since it is impossible to produce for stock, service providers often devise *special schemes* to level out the pattern of demand. Hence, they might initiate maildrops offering special discounts to past customers, and try to diversify their activities. Investment analysts, for example, may diversify into mortgage and insurance consultancy; or a bank's executorship department might also work on legal trusts and company liquidation.

(e) Governments *regulate* the marketing of certain financial services, e.g. by insisting that annual percentage interest charges be prominently displayed, or that customers signing credit agreements have a statutory period in which to withdraw. The need for such controls arises for two reasons:

(*i*) Lay people cannot easily distinguish between good and bad financial service providers, nor can they necessarily determine a purchase option that best suits their financial needs. Yet, decisions taken can affect customers' financial well-being throughout their lives.

(*ii*) In view of the complexity of many financial service offers, supplying institutions may conveniently conceal the true costs of the service provided (management and 'arrangement' fees, commissions, interest rate premiums, loss of value through early liquidation, etc).

(f) Some financial services, notably banking and insurance, are perceived by consumers as a *homogeneous product*. In consequence, the individual consumer might be indifferent as to which bank or insurance company (say) he or she uses, provided it is well known. Accordingly, providers increasingly offer inducements – free gifts, zero bank charges, and so on – to attract new customers.

Progress test 7

1. Explain the marketing concept.

2. Define the term 'psychographic market segmentation'.

3. What is the 'marketing services industry'?

4. List and describe the major demands of the consumer movement.

5. How do financial services differ from other products?

6. List and describe three advantages and three problems associated with commercial sponsorship of sporting events by financial service firms.

7. How can the performances of salespeople be evaluated?

8. List the main types of distribution system.

8

INTERNATIONAL MARKETING

FUNDAMENTALS

1. Definition

L.S. Walsh (*see* the M&E text *International Marketing*) defines international marketing as:

(a) The marketing of goods and services across national frontiers *and*

(b) The marketing operations of an organisation that sells and/or produces within a given country when:

(*i*) that organisation is part of, or associated with, an enterprise which also operates in other countries; *and*
(*ii*) there is some degree of influence on or control of that organisation's marketing activities from outside the country in which it sells and/or produces.

The essential principles of marketing apply to international operations as much as they do to domestic trade, although a global outlook is required and the problems of international marketing are more extensive than for internal trade.

2. Locating export markets

There are two general approaches to this problem:

(a) Define the characteristics of consumers likely to be attracted to the firm's product and then identify countries expected to contain significant numbers of that type of consumer.

(b) Sell only to certain predetermined 'easy' markets (e.g. those with a common language or ready convertibility of local currency) and adapt output and promotional methods to suit local requirements.

Screening of countries involves the reduction of a (normally long) list of candidate countries to manageable proportions by examining life styles, tastes, income levels, demographic and socio-economic structures, cultures, consumer behaviour, competition and business methods in each potential foreign market.

3. Direct and indirect exporting

With direct exporting the exporter assumes full responsibility for transport to foreign destinations, for customs clearance, local advertising and final sale of the goods. This might be achieved via the establishment of a branch office or subsidiary in the country concerned.

Indirect exporting uses intermediaries. *Export merchants*, for example, reside in the exporter's country, acting as principals in export transactions (that is, buying and selling on their own accounts). They are wholesalers who operate in foreign markets through their own salespeople, stockists and, perhaps, retail outlets. Exporters are relieved of administrative problems, documentation, shipping, internal transport and so on, and do not carry the risks of market failure. However, they lose control over presentation of their products, and foreign sales may fall because of poor foreign retailing.

Confirming houses exist to represent foreign buyers who are not sufficiently well known for home firms to supply them on credit terms. The confirming house assumes the risk of customer default. In return it charges the buyer a commission. Export agents on the other hand charge commission to home-based firms. They sell abroad either under their own or, more usually, their client's name. Agents are not principals; risks of failure (customer default, transport breakdowns, etc) and responsibility for insurance, customs clearance and documentation lie with the exporting firm.

An alternative approach is the establishment of production and/or marketing facilities in partnership with residents of a foreign country. Such joint ventures could involve sale of licences enabling foreign firms to manufacture and sell all or part of an exporter's product, or they might involve contract manufacturing whereby local firms are used to produce products which are then distributed by the exporting company.

4. Freight forwarders

These are transport firms that specialise in transporting goods to foreign destinations. As well as actually shipping the goods at minimum cost, forwarders provide help and advice with packaging, labelling and warehousing in the recipient country. Often, forwarders can offer attractive freight rates to foreign centres because of their ability to group together numerous small shipments into one large consignment.

PRICING AND PAYMENT TERMS

5. Export price quotations

Standard definitions of common export delivery terms have been drafted by the International Chamber of Commerce. The commonest INCOTERMS, as they are known, are:

(a) *Ex Works (EXW)* which requires the customer to collect the goods from the exporter's premises.

(b) *Free on Board (FOB)*, where the buyers takes delivery when the goods are loaded on to a ship in the exporter's country.

(c) *Cost, Insurance and Freight (CIF)*, whereby the exporter pays all transport and insurance costs to a named foreign destination.

(d) *Delivered Duty Paid (DDP)* where the exporter assumes all costs and risks involved in delivering the goods to the customer's premises. Increasingly, this is the standard requirement for export sales.

6. Currency exchange risk of DDP pricing

Delivered duty paid invoicing by a UK firm exposes it to the risk that sterling may depreciate in value against the importer's currency between now and when the debt is due to be settled (e.g. 90 days hence). To be sure of how much sterling its invoices will yield the exporter can sell in advance to its own UK bank the foreign currency its customers have been invoiced to pay. The bank will quote a fixed 'forward exchange rate' for these transactions. This predetermined forward rate will apply to the conversions regardless of the actual 'spot' exchange rate in force 90 days (say) from today.

The bank requires a reward for its services and hence will quote an exchange rate for forward currency transactions which differs from the current spot exchange rate by an amount sufficient to cover the bank's exposure to risk and to make a profit.

If the exporter expects the spot exchange rate to move in favour of sterling, so that it stands to raise more sterling when it eventually comes to convert the foreign currency than it would get if the money was converted today, it may decide not to bother with forward cover.

A firm expecting to receive payments from a foreign customer over a long period can enter an 'option contract' with a UK bank whereby the exporter is given the right to sell to the bank foreign currency up to an agreed limit at a predetermined rate at any time within the next 12 months. If the spot exchange rate moves in one direction the exporter will exercise the option; if it moves in the other direction the option will not be taken up – forfeiting thereby the fee paid to the bank to purchase the option.

7. Finance of foreign trade

Payment by cheque or credit transfer is known as 'open account' settlement. UK businesses that are not prepared to accept the risks of customer default attached to open account trading may be able to use bills of exchange or letters of credit (*see* below) to finance international transactions. Alternatively, the exporter can use the services of an export 'credit factoring' company which will purchase, at a discount, invoices issued to foreign customers as the goods are supplied.

8. Letters of credit

Foreign importers who are little known in the exporter's country will experience difficulty in ordering goods because suppliers (and their bankers) will fear non-payment of accounts. Thus, importers commonly arrange for established banks (preferably in the exporter's country) to guarantee final payment. Banks which agree to do this will issue to foreign importers 'letters of credit' in which they formally assume responsibility for settling importers' debts, subject to the conditions laid down in the letters of credit.

9. Bills of exchange

A bill of exchange is a written instruction sent by an exporter to an importer ordering the importer to pay to the exporter, or anyone specified by the exporter, a certain sum of money at a specified future time (usually 90 days hence). Once a bill has been accepted by the importer (acceptance is effected by signing the bill), evidence of the debt exists. The importer returns the bill to the exporter, who now sends the goods. A bill of exchange may be held until maturity and the money then claimed from the importer, or the exporter could sell the endorsed bill to a third party (normally a bank) for something less than its face value. The bank now assumes the risk of customer default.

Of course, an importer will not be prepared to accept a bill of exchange without some assurance that the goods will be delivered. Thus documents of title, providing evidence of ownership, must at some point be exchanged. These documents (referred to collectively as 'shipping documents') will include a commercial invoice, transport receipts (e.g. a 'bill of lading' for goods sent by sea, or an air waybill), cargo insurance certificates, and possibly a 'consular invoice' (an independent confirmation that the true value of the goods matches the value stated on the commercial invoice) and possibly a certificate of origin.

Commonly, documents are forwarded through the international correspondent banking system. Thus, an exporter might hand over shipping documents and a bill of exchange to his or her own bank which then sends them to its branch (or an associated bank) in the importer's country. This branch now presents the bill of exchange to the importer for acceptance. Shipping documents are handed over and the bill is either held by the foreign branch until maturity (at which point the branch collects the money for despatch to the exporter) or the accepted bill is returned to the exporter.

AGENTS

10. Use of agents

Language difficulties and ignorance of business methods in other countries cause many firms to seek agents to represent their interests in foreign markets. Agents operate on a commission basis and may either be *brokers*, who simply bring together buyers and sellers without ever taking physical possession of the goods; or *factors* who do possess the goods until customers are found and who sometimes sell under their own names at prices they think best. A *del credere* agent is one who, in return for a higher commission, indemnifies the supplying firm against customers' bad debts. Agents differ from 'distributors' in that the latter are principals in their own right. They buy and sell the outputs of other businesses, possibly under a contract giving the distributor sole rights (subject to EU competition law, *see* 11:**13**) to retail the item in a certain geographical area.

Note that agency law differs markedly between one country and another and that in some countries agents cannot easily be dismissed. If they are they may be entitled to substantial financial compensation. (These matters are considered in 11:**31**.)

11. Choice of agent

Agents must be fully familiar with local business conditions and practices, and capable of conducting local market research. Other criteria to be adopted when choosing an agent should include the following:

(a) Whether the agent has contacts with local businesses capable of supplying specialist services to the exporting company (repair and after-sales service for example).

(b) How easily the agent can be contacted.

(c) Whether the agent will represent a competing firm and, if so, the incentives that are needed to encourage the agent to promote the exporter's products enthusiastically.

(d) How much information and feedback on matters such as consumer responses to the product, the quality of local delivery arrangements, whether local translations of operating instructions are satisfactory, etc the agent can provide.

(e) How easily the calibre of the agent's work can be evaluated.

(f) The agent's track record, how long the firm has existed and its general business reputation.

(g) How extensively the agent covers the market; how many branch offices it has and their location and whether the agent can genuinely cover an entire EU country.

(h) Whether the agent possesses sufficient resources for the task: staff, showrooms, technical competence, storage facilities, etc.

(i) The ease with which the firm can control and motivate the agent. Normally the agent will be asked to prepare quarterly sales forecasts and to explain significant deviations of actual sales from these predictions. The agent should keep a record of enquiries received, calls made, customer complaints, etc and submit details on a monthly basis.

(j) Whether the agent requires a large amount of technical training about the product and sales training for promoting it effectively.

ADVERTISING AND PROMOTION

12. International advertising

The key issue in international advertising is whether the firm should standardise its advertising messages or adapt them to meet the requirements of particular foreign markets. Some advertising messages are applicable to several countries, others are relevant to only one. Much depends on the degree of homogeneity of target consumers in various countries: their lifestyles, interests, incomes and tastes. The advantages of uniformity are that it:

(a) requires less marketing research in individual countries

(b) is relatively cheap and convenient to administer

(c) demands less creative time to devise advertisements; a single message is constructed and used in all markets.

Customisation, conversely, might be necessary in consequence of:

(a) Cultural differences between countries and/or market segments

(b) Translation difficulties between different languages

(c) Differences in the educational backgrounds of target groups in various countries

(d) Non-availability of certain media (specialist magazines, for instance) in some regions

(e) Differences in national attitudes towards advertising.

To the extent that alterations are needed they may take one or more of the following forms:

(a) Different media. For instance, listeners to commercial radio in different countries might typically belong to different socio-economic groups.

(b) Changes in symbols, e.g. using a male rather than a female model as the dominant figure in an advertisement. This might be necessary if males are the primary purchasers of the product in one market and females in another.

(c) Changes in advertisement headlines and body copy.

(d) Changes in the fundamental selling proposition. For instance, presenting a bicycle as a leisure item in one market, a fashion accessory in another, and as a commuting vehicle elsewhere.

13. Conditions for successful international transfer of advertising messages

The extent to which the same message can successfully be applied transnationally depends on whether in various countries the product:

(a) is used in the *same way*

(b) satisfies the *same consumer needs*

(c) appeals to the *same consumer type*

(d) can be sold at *similar prices*

(e) is purchased in response to the *same consumer motives* (convenience, status, impulse buying, etc)

(f) evokes mental images that can be manipulated using *pictures rather than words*

(g) can be advertised in the *same media*

(h) is *perceived* by consumers in a similar manner (e.g. technically complex electrical equipment may be seen as performing exactly the same function regardless of the customer's location) and is *evaluated using similar criteria*

(i) has just one or two universally intelligible *selling points*

(j) cannot by *law* be promoted in certain ways

(k) is purchased by consumers with *similar income levels*

(l) is typically bought by the *same family members* (wives, husbands, parents, etc)

(m) is demanded in the *same package sizes and quantities*

(n) is purchased with the *same frequency* (weekly, monthly, irregularly)

(o) appeals to the same *cultural traditions*.

14. Domestic versus foreign advertising agencies

Using a large UK-based agency for international advertising offers 'one stop shopping' to the client firm. The agency will already possess extensive stocks of research data on international markets, on foreign consumer tastes and buying habits, and on the sort of messages that are likely to succeed in various countries. And there is easy liaison with agency staff. On the other hand, a UK agency does not *necessarily* have better contacts with and information about local media than smaller foreign agencies within the countries concerned. Reasons for selecting a local foreign agency might include:

(a) Its ability to give the exporting firm a local image

(b) Potential for close and effective liaison with local distribution agents and/or other representatives

(c) Possibly a higher level of effort and commitment on the part of local agencies, which need to offer a better service in order to compete with larger and better-known multinational rivals

(d) Flair and creativity that is sometimes absent in big international agencies.

15. Production standardisation versus product differentiation.

A fundamental decision that has to be taken by firms operating internationally is whether to supply to foreign markets the firm's existing product, or modify the product to suit the needs of each foreign country. Product modification is appropriate where there exist:

(a) Significant differences in local consumer taste

(b) Intense competition in foreign markets (creating the need to differentiate a firm's output from that of foreign rivals)

(c) Special local requirements in relation to package size, technical standards, consumer protection laws and customer care facilities

(d) Differences in local climate, living conditions, literacy and technical skill level of users, customer buying habits, incomes (buyers in poor countries might need low quality products), and in the uses to which the product might be put in various markets.

Hopefully product modification will increase worldwide sales of the firm's core products through (*i*) the satisfaction of different customer needs in various regions, (*ii*) retention of existing customers by keeping the products up-to-date, and (*iii*) matching the product attributes offered by competing firms. Complementary products might be introduced to stimulate sales of existing lines, e.g. by improving the usefulness of currently produced items (gardening tools or DIY power accessories for example). The need for extensive product modification is a common impetus for firms to establish local manufacturing or assembly facilities in foreign countries, as it could well be cheaper to set up a new establishment to produce what is essentially a new product near to end consumers rather than make major changes to existing production lines and procedures at home.

The case for standardisation

A number of problems apply to product modification, notably:

(a) Extra promotional costs have to be incurred.

(b) There is duplication of effort within the business.

(c) The company may possess insufficient experience and technical know-how of different products and how to market them.

(d) Technical research and development efforts might become fragmented as increasing amounts of resources are devoted to issues pertaining to the special requirements of particular national markets.

Supplying a single unmodified product can provide several advantages: economies of scale in production, concentration of technical research into a limited area, standardisation of marketing and distribution methods, fewer staff training requirements and so on. It leads to reduced stockholding costs (because demand in any market can be met from a single inventory of the same item), facilitates the development of technical expertise in a narrow area, and allows the interchangeability of spare parts and input components between supply points in various locations. Accordingly, firms sometimes attempt to create universal products (hopefully) suitable for all markets in all regions. This might be suitable where:

(a) The essential need that the product aims to satisfy is basically the same in all national and market segments.

(b) After-sales service is easily standardised.

(c) There exists a large market across several countries and cultural differences do not necessitate adaptation.

(d) The product has a strong international brand image. Note how a particular national image can help sell an unmodified product in several markets. Japanese goods, for instance, are generally regarded as reliable, high quality and technically excellent: positive images that will help sell an overtly Japanese item in any country.

16. Trade exhibitions

These provide opportunities for meeting foreign buyers or people who influence buying decisions. Potential customers can see, feel and experience the goods. Exhibitions offer wide coverage of possible markets: enormous numbers of people can attend during a two- or three-day period. Other advantages are:

(a) the chance to size up competing firms who are also exhibiting at the venue

(b) that visitors' names and addresses can be used for subsequent maildrops

(c) the high probability of agents and distributors of the firm's category of product being among the visitors

(d) the ability to observe initial local consumer reaction to the exporting company's goods.

17. Problems with exhibiting

Many difficulties are associated with exhibiting, including the following:

(a) Most consumers visit exhibitions to browse rather than to buy. It is not easy to identify important people who influence major buying decisions within their companies.

(b) Gimmicks may be highly effective in attracting visitors to a stand, but could attract the wrong people. An audience may be greatly impressed by the music, dancing, demonstration or whatever is provided; yet not be genuinely interested in the exporter's products.

(c) It is necessary to establish criteria to determine how big a display to mount at any given exhibition.

(d) Having a large and attractive stand at an exhibition could induce competitors to do the same, thereby wiping out the benefits of exhibiting.

(e) Employees who staff an exhibition stand might treat the exercise as a holiday – paying more attention to the social aspects of their involvement with the exhibition than to finding customers.

(f) The need to dovetail exhibiting into the company's general marketing plans.

(g) Ignorance about the likely numbers and characteristics of the people who will visit the exhibition, their lengths of stay, needs and buying habits.

(h) Ensuring that the proposed stand will be well located *vis-à-vis* the layout and illumination of the exhibition centre and the anticipated traffic flow.

Not all exhibitions are worth attending, so decisions have to be taken about which to support. Criteria for such decisions should include whether the exhibition is well established (recently inaugurated exhibitions usually attract small attendances), the extent of the availability of useful information on the composition of past audiences, and how easily the leads obtained from exhibiting can be followed up.

18. International marketing research

Discovery of overseas marketing opportunities requires the assembly of information about the following:

(a) The size of various market segments, their buoyancy and prospects for expansion.

(b) Demographic structures of prospective markets in terms of age, sex composition, family structures, geographical spread of the population, etc.

(c) Market stability, local rates of inflation and economic growth.

(d) Whether local cultural norms and values might affect consumer perceptions of the firm's product, and if so the implications of this.

(e) Foreign tastes, lifestyles and spending patterns.

(f) Average local incomes and the distribution of wealth; living standards, housing, education and so on.

(g) Number of competitors, their strengths and weaknesses and modes of response to other firms' activities.

(h) Competitors' prices, product quality, credit terms, delivery periods, after-sales service, etc.

(i) How easily the firm monitors competitors' behaviour (price changes, product modifications, etc).

(j) How frequently competitors change their prices (this is a crude indicator of the stability of the local market and whether local firms do actually compete).

(k) The selling points that competitors stress in their local advertising, and why these characteristics are emphasised.

(l) Local technical product standards and labelling requirements.

(m) Local preferences regarding package size, colouring and design, weights and volumes, shapes and ease of package disposal, etc.

(n) Local taxation; investment grants for establishing subsidiaries and/or owned distribution outlets.

(o) Nature of local distribution channels.

(p) Availability of commercial services (advertising agencies, debt collectors, warehousing facilities and so on).

(q) Frequency and whereabouts of local trade fairs and exhibitions.

International market research may be undertaken by a large UK agency with international connections, or by local research firms based in foreign markets. Research companies apply the full range of MR techniques to their international work, including:

(a) consumer sampling through questionnaires and interviews (undertaken by local employees of the research company)

(b) market surveys

(c) test marketing

(d) canvassing competent local business people about a product's likely appeal

(e) interpreting foreign statistics (e.g. knowing what products are included in various statistical classifications, assessing data reliability and comparability with UK equivalents, etc)

(f) conducting local telephone surveys

(g) estimating the market shares of local competitors

(h) obtaining details of the ownership and control of competing firms

(i) assessing growth prospects in the local economy

(j) establishing why competitors choose to distribute their products through certain channels

(k) measuring local consumers' reactions to the firm's brand name and images

(l) providing sales estimates for each of several possible selling prices

(m) determining the costs and benefits of various distribution options

(n) assessing the cost effectiveness of local advertising media

(o) investigating various promotional possibilities

(p) conducting local retail audits (i.e. continuously monitoring a panel of selected local retail outlets to check the level and periodicity of sales of the client firm's product).

OTHER EXPORTING ARRANGEMENTS

19. Piggybacking and sister companies

Large firms which already operate in certain foreign markets are sometimes willing to act as agents for other businesses that wish to export to those markets. This enables them to utilise fully their sales representatives, premises, office equipment, etc in the foreign countries concerned.

Sister companies are foreign firms offering similar products and which are of similar size and structure to the one seeking a partner. They act as a foreign agent and provide information on local business methods and markets. In return the UK firm offers reciprocal facilities. Ideally the sister company should be engaged in complementary rather than competitive lines of work and face the same sorts of problems as the exporting business. The EU has consistently encouraged sister company arrangements and offers a clearing house (the Business Co-operation Centre) for this purpose.

20. Licensing

Licensing might be appropriate for a firm that possesses patented inventions, know-how (i.e. confidential but non-patentable technical knowledge) or valuable registered trademarks. No expertise in exporting is required; there are no delivery costs, no capital investments on the part of the licensor, and the risk of failure is shared with the licensee. Licensing offers rapid entry to a market, and can be undertaken by small firms. The income generated from licence royalties helps offset research and technical development costs, while the licensee firm does not itself have to invest in research and development.

Problems associated with licensing might relate to:

(a) maintenance of quality levels

(b) verification of the licensee's sales figures

(c) lower revenues compared to direct sale to the market

(d) possible failure of the licensee to exploit fully the local market

(e) acquisition by the licensee of the licensor's technical knowledge; note how the licensee might subsequently set up in competition with the licensor

(f) the need for complex contractual arrangements in certain circumstances

(g) the numerous opportunities that arise for disagreements and misunderstandings.

Licensing is most likely to succeed, perhaps, where

(a) The licensee will have to purchase input components or materials from the licensor.

(b) The licensor is already exporting directly to more markets than it can conveniently handle.

(c) It is not feasible to establish a permanent presence in a particular country.

(d) The cost of transporting goods to the local market would be excessively high.

(e) Images of locally produced items will improve sales.

21. Branches and subsidiaries

As export sales expand, the inadequacy of exporting as a means for doing foreign business might become progressively evident. The firm will (or should) have acquired detailed knowledge of foreign markets and export procedures and thus might be capable of dispensing with export intermediaries. Accordingly, the company may set up its own branches, and/or subsidiaries, possibly to oversee production operations in other countries. The difference between a branch and a subsidiary is that whereas a branch is regarded in law as a direct extension of the parent firm into a foreign country (so that the parent is legally responsible for all the branch's debts and activities), a subsidiary is seen as a separate business from the parent company. A subsidiary is responsible for its own debts and (unlike a branch) is subject to exactly the same taxes, auditing, registration and accounting regulations as any other local business.

Branches are easy to set up and to dismantle, but complicated tax situations can arise because some nations relate the amounts of tax payable by branches to the worldwide profits of their parent companies. Normally branches are concerned with the transport and storage of goods, marketing, the provision of after-sales service; and liaison with local banks, advertising agencies, suppliers and distributors, and so on. Local assembly and/or manufacture is normally undertaken by other means. In most (but not all) countries the existence of a foreign branch has to be registered with local governmental authorities. Usually the registration is straightforward, comprising the deposit of a simple form plus translated documents attesting the whereabouts and solvency of the parent company.

Advantages to operating a branch rather than a subsidiary are that:

- A branch need not have its own capital or directors
- Assets can be transferred from the parent to the branch without incurring tax liability
- No company formation or winding-up procedures are required
- Losses can be offset against the parent's profit.

Factors that might encourage the establishment of a subsidiary rather than a branch include:

- limited liability
- the ability to apply for government regional development assistance and R&D grants on the same terms as any other local business

- a local identity
- the capacity to raise capital in the subsidiary's own name and (importantly) to sell shares to outsiders
- not having to disclose the annual accounts of the parent organisation
- the ability to undertake internal reorganisations without having to report this to the foreign authorities.

Major factors to be considered when selecting the precise location of a branch or subsidiary within a country include nearness to consumers and/or centres of commercial activity, availability of government investment grants and subsidiaries, and access to local sources of raw materials and input components. Other criteria might include labour and other operating costs, the availability of high-calibre labour, and the whereabouts of the competitors.

22. Joint ventures

Joint ventures (JVs) are collaborative arrangements between unrelated parties which exchange or combine various resources while remaining separate and independent legal entities. There are two types of JV: equity and contractual. The former involves each partner taking an equity stake in the venture (e.g. through setting up a joint subsidiary with its own share capital); the latter rely on contractual agreements between the partners. Joint ventures are an example of the wider concept of the 'strategic alliance', which embraces knowledge-sharing arrangements, mutual licensing, measures to control and utilise excess capacity, etc. Usually JVs are formed to undertake a specific project that has to be completed within a set period. JVs are a flexible form of business arrangement; can be quickly entered into and shut down; enable the sharing of costs; yet are frequently just as effective a means for entering markets as more direct forms of foreign investment. Often they are used to establish bridgeheads in a foreign market prior to more substantial operations within the market by individual participants. Advantages to joint ventures include the following:

(a) Firms can expand into several foreign markets simultaneously for low capital cost.

(b) Shared cost of administration.

(c) Partners can avoid the need to purchase local premises and hire new employees.

(d) Shared risk of failure.

(e) JVs may be available in countries where outright takeovers of local firms by foreigners is not allowed.

(f) Less costly than acquisitions.

(g) Higher returns than with licensing/franchising.

(h) Firms can gain instant access to local expertise and to partners' distribution systems.

(i) Possibly better relations with national governments in consequence of having a local partner.

Problems with JVs include the possibility of disagreements over organisation and control, and over methods of operation and the long-term goals of the venture. Other disputes might arise concerning pricing policy, the confidentiality of information exchanged between members, and about how underperformance by any one of the participants is to be dealt with (e.g. whether equal compensation is to be payable to each of the parties if the project is abandoned). Further possible difficulties are listed below:

- Partners may become locked into long-term investments from which it is difficult to withdraw.
- Possible arguments over which partner is responsible for budget overspends and how these should be financed.
- Problems of co-ordination.
- Profits have to be shared with partners.
- Possible differences in management culture among participating firms.
- Completion of a JV project might overburden a company's staff.
- Need to share intellectual property.
- Difficult to integrate into an overall corporate strategy.
- Partners are not free to act independently.
- The corporate objectives of partners may conflict.
- Transfer pricing problems may arise (*see* **24**) as goods pass between partners.
- The importance of the venture to each partner might change over time.

INFLUENCES ON PRICING POLICY

23. The Maastricht Agreement 1992

This has many important implications for European business. The majority of EU member states (excluding Britain) declared their commitment to the creation of a common European currency and, independent of EU institutions, to the adoption of key elements of the European Social Charter (*see* 16:54). Adoption of a common European currency will have the following consequences:

(a) Firms will have to quote prices in a common unit, hence enabling customers easily to compare the prices of similar items sold in various EU countries.

(b) Share prices in European companies will be quoted in the same currency unit everywhere, facilitating pan-European share-trading and access to all EU stock exchanges for investors and companies wishing to raise funds.

(c) There will be a need for pan-European price-labelling, packaging and sales promotions.

(d) No currency-conversion costs will be incurred by businesses in nations within the common currency (CCA). Firms outside the CCA, conversely, will require separate prices, packaging and labelling for domestic and European markets and will face the (substantial) costs of currency conversion, forward exchange transactions (*see* **8–6**), and so on. A common currency removes *entirely* the currency-exchange risk associated with international trade.

(e) Intra-EU cash transfers will be facilitated, to the benefit of the Community's financial services industry. This in conjunction with **(b)** above could lead to wider pan-European ownership of company shares and to greater volatility in share prices as funds move freely across national EU frontiers.

24. Transfer pricing

Transfer pricing means the determination of the 'prices' at which an MNC moves goods between its subsidiaries in various countries. A crucial feature of large centralised MNCs is their ability to engage in transfer pricing at artificially high or low prices. To illustrate, consider an MNC which extracts raw materials in one country, uses them as production inputs in another, assembles the partly finished goods in a third, and finishes and sells them in a fourth. The governments of the extraction, production and assembly countries will have sales or value added taxes; while the production, assembly and finished goods countries will impose tariffs on imports of goods. Suppose the MNC values its goods at zero prior to their final sale at high prices. The government of the extraction country receives no revenue from sales taxes because the MNC's subsidiary in that country is selling its output to the same MNC's subsidiary in the production country at a price of zero. Equally the production country raises no income from import tariffs on this transaction because the raw materials are imported at zero price! The only tax the MNC pays is a sales tax in the last country in the chain. Transfer pricing at unacceptably low values has been a major problem for many developing nations. Sometimes, therefore, the government of the country in which an MNC operates will insist that a government official shall decide the price at which the MNC exports its output, and not employees of the MNC itself. Thus, the government of the host country will ensure that it receives an appropriate amount of sales tax. Similarly, importing countries might impose quantity-based instead of price-based import duties to ensure a reasonable revenue from taxes on imports of an MNC's goods.

Tax considerations aside, transfer prices need to be realistic in order that the profitabilities of various international operations may be assessed. Possible criteria for setting the transfer price include:

(a) The price at which the item could be sold on the open market (this is known as 'arms length' transfer pricing)

(b) Cost of production or acquisition

(c) Acquisition/production cost plus a profit markup (note the problem here of deciding what constitutes an appropriate profit markup)

(d) Senior management's perceptions of the value of the item to the firm's overall international operations

(e) Political negotiations between the units involved (a high or low transfer price can drastically affect the observed profitability of a subsidiary). Note the problems that arise if the 'buyer' happens to be the head office of the firm.

Normally the solution adopted is that which (seemingly) maximises profits for the company taken as a whole and which best facilitates the parent firm's control over subsidiary operations. Arm's length pricing (*see* above) is the method generally preferred by national governments and is recommended in a 1983 Code of Practice on the subject drafted by the Organisation for Economic Co-operation and Development (OECD). Note how a subsidiary that charges a high transfer price will accumulate cash, which might be invested more profitably in the selling country than elsewhere.

Problems with setting a realistic transfer price are as follows:

(a) Differences in the accounting systems used by subsidiaries in different countries.

(b) Executives in operating units deliberately manipulating the transfer price to enhance the book value of a subsidiary's profits.

(c) Disparate tax rates and investment subsidy levels in various countries.

(d) Possible absence of competition in local markets at various stages in the supply chain. Thus a 'market price' in such an area may be artificially high in consequence of the lack of local competition.

(e) There might not be any other product directly comparable to the item in question, again making it difficult to establish a market price.

(f) If a price is set at too high a level the 'selling' unit will be able to attain it. profit targets too easily (at the expense of the 'buyer') and lead perhaps to idleness and inefficiency in the selling subsidiary.

Special problems arise when goods are being transferred among the partners of a joint venture. Should the various members of the venture be regarded as 'subsidiaries' or as independent businesses required to pay a market price?

Progress test 8

1. What is a confirming house?

2. List six problems associated with conducting market research in foreign countries.

3. What are the main approaches to locating export markets?

4. What is a freight forwarder? What do freight forwarders do?

5. Explain the problems associated with transfer pricing.

6. What is the difference between a branch and a subsidiary?

7. List four advantages of licensing as a means for entering foreign markets.

8. For what reasons might an exporter decide to use a local market research company rather than an international research firm?

9

MANAGING THE FINANCE FUNCTION

FINANCIAL ACCOUNTS

1. Accounting

Accounting is the systematic recording, analysis and interpretation of financial data. The major financial accounts of a firm are its trading account, profit and loss account, balance sheet, and – if it is a manufacturing business – its manufacturing account.

A *trading account* shows the gross profit of the enterprise. Gross profit is revenue minus the cost of purchasing, assembling or directly producing the goods sold. The *profit and loss account* deducts administrative and other expenses from gross profit, giving the net profit of the firm. All the figures used to compute these accounts relate to official accounting periods and not to when receipts and payments actually happen. Thus, for instance, a gas bill for the first quarter of the year is recorded in the first quarter's accounts, even if it remains unpaid until late summer.

Manufacturing accounts are extended trading accounts, listing manufacturing costs under various categories: manufacturing wages, raw materials consumed, work-in-progress completed, factory overheads and equipment depreciation.

2. The balance sheet

This is analogous to a photograph of a firm's financial position at a particular moment in time. It is divided into two parts: assets and liabilities. Assets are the possessions of the business (premises, stock, cash, etc); liabilities show the people and institutions who own the assets or to whom they are owed. Hence, liabilities include owner's capital, bank loans, tax payable, creditors, and dividends due to shareholders. In effect, liabilities constitute the sources of the funds used to acquire assets. Therefore, since these funds are represented by an equal value of assets on the other side of the equation, assets and liabilities must by definition each add up to the same amount; hence the term 'balance' sheet. Examination of a firm's balance sheet should indicate the worth of the business and whether it is solvent.

3. Types of asset

Fixed assets are for permanent use within the business. Premises are an obvious example. They are not purchased for the purpose of resale. These assets must be written off (depreciated) over their economic lives so that the true worth of the business is known. Depreciation is regarded as a source of funds because it reduces profits and thus retains money within the business.

There are several techniques for depreciating assets, but two – 'straight-line' and 'diminishing-balance' – are most common. Straight-line depreciation writes off an asset by the same amount each period, whereas the diminishing-balance approach deducts a predetermined percentage of the net value of the asset at the end of each year, so that assets are never completely written off.

Goodwill is an intangible fixed asset. It arises when a business has been purchased for a price higher than the value of its assets. Goodwill represents the worth of the firm as a going concern – its good name, reputation, existing customers and suppliers, technical knowledge, trained personnel, the state of its order book – independent of its physical possessions. Other intangible fixed assets include ownership of patents, licences, trade marks, trading concessions and similar rights.

4. Current assets

These are short-term assets (quickly realisable) directly related to operations. Examples are stocks of finished goods awaiting sale, raw materials awaiting processing, work in progress, debtors who owe money to the firm, and cash at the bank and in hand.

Current liabilities are similarly defined, being liabilities that are repayable within the next 12 months. Longer-term loans (bank loans, mortgages and so on) are usually shown as separate items. Taxes due but awaiting payment are regarded as a short-term liability.

Working capital is current assets minus current liabilities. It represents the resources available to finance the firm's operations. It is money tied up within the business and should generally be kept to a minimum. The ratio of current assets to current liabilities is called the 'working capital ratio' or 'current ratio'. It indicates the degree of liquidity of the business, showing how many times current liabilities are covered by current assets. There is no ideal value for the current ratio. Relevant factors in determining an appropriate value are as follows:

(a) The extent to which current liabilities comprise short-term borrowing. If short-term borrowings are substantial, the current ratio needs to be higher so that creditors' demands for repayment can be quickly met.

(b) The rate of inflation. A high rate will lower the buying power of working capital, so more cash should be held at any given moment.

(c) The rate of interest. High interest rates mean large interest payments, so the current ratio should be raised accordingly.

(d) Trade fluctuations and the degree of uncertainty facing the firm. Risky environments demand higher current ratios.

Since some current assets take longer to liquidate than others it is desirable to have a ratio which measures a firm's capacity to settle immediately its current liabilities. The 'acid test ratio' (also called the 'liquidity ratio') achieves this. It incorporates only those current assets which can be instantly turned into purchasing power. Thus, stocks of raw materials and work in progress which take some time to convert into cash are ignored. The liquidity ratio retains 'debtors' as a current asset, which is based on the optimistic assumption that all debtors will settle their outstanding balances on time. The value of the liquidity ratio should be about one, meaning that current liabilities are fully covered. Values exceeding one are undesirable because surplus liquid funds should always be invested in alternative and profitable uses.

The treasury function

Management of a company's financial resources is sometimes referred to as the treasury function, which involves *inter-alia*:

- Minimisation of working capital via prompt collection of debts, efficient use of prompt payment discounts, etc.
- Investment of short-term balances in the highest interest-earning accounts
- Management of foreign exchange risks
- Minimisation of the costs of borrowing through cash flow forecasting, use of financial futures, selection of the best borrowing instruments and so on
- Minimisation of banking costs. This might involve the periodic analysis of the costs and benefits of various banking services, reviews of the quality of bank services and the selective use of invitations to tender for the company's banking business.

MANAGEMENT ACCOUNTS

5. Management accounting

This is concerned more with the accounting information needed for operational decision making than with financial accounts per se. It involves:

- The design and operation of management information systems
- Budgetary planning and control
- Data processing
- Costing and cost control (*see* **6–7** below and 12:**28**)
- Investment appraisal (*see* **8**)
- Breakeven analysis (*see* **7**).

6. Measurement of costs

Costs are divided into two categories: direct costs and overheads. *Direct costs* are the costs of materials, labour and other direct expenses. *Overheads* are costs that are not attributable to specific products. They relate to the upkeep of the environment in which production takes place. Examples are maintenance of buildings, rent of premises, lighting and heating, secretarial and administration services, costs of cleaning and so on. Unlike most direct costs, overheads usually do not vary with respect to the volume of production, though in practice the categorisation of particular costs as fixed or variable can be difficult. Rent is clearly fixed, electricity used to power a machine is variable, but electricity used for lighting the premises which is switched on for longer periods during busy spells is partially fixed and partially variable. The sum of direct costs for materials, labour and other expenses is sometimes called the prime cost of a product. Thus, final production cost comprises prime cost plus overheads.

There are problems associated with the allocation of overheads to individual items, since firms typically manufacture several products. Fixed costs must therefore be split up among the various products according to some predetermined criterion. Many firms define *cost centres* to which all the costs of producing particular goods (or services) may be apportioned. Cost centres can be departments, sections of departments, processes or production lines. All direct costs are easily attributable to appropriate cost centres. Overheads, however, are not. Deciding how to allocate overheads is difficult, and varying the criteria used can alter dramatically the estimated costs (and hence price) of an individual product.

The term 'costing' is applied to the prediction, measurement and categorisation of costs and their allocation to individual products or activities. Cost prediction using prespecified norms is known as 'standard costing'. This is defined in 12:28.

7. Marginal costs

The marginal cost of a product is the additional cost of producing one extra unit of output. The difference between a product's sale price and its marginal cost is called its *contribution*, indicating how much the additional unit contributes towards overheads. As output expands, aggregate contributions from marginal units will eventually absorb all overheads. The *break-even point* is the level of output where total fixed costs have been absorbed.

A typical break-even chart is sketched in Fig. 9.1. At zero output, fixed cost is zero. Total cost comprises fixed cost plus variable cost as shown. Break-even occurs where the total cost line intersects the line for total value of sales. The latter has a constant slope because the example shown assumes a uniform sale price. The principle is unchanged if the total cost and sales lines are curved rather than straight. This occurs following relaxation of the assumption that variable cost is identical for each unit produced. Economies of scale at higher outputs might be possible which enable unit variable costs to fall. In this case the total cost line will exhibit decreasing marginal costs. Similarly, high sales might be achievable only at reduced unit selling prices, so that the value of sales also becomes a curve.

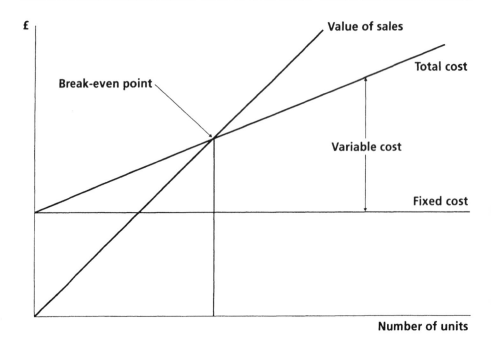

Figure 9.1 Break-even chart

8. Investment appraisal

This concerns the assessment of the profitabilities of capital projects so that the desirabilities of various projects may be compared. The major methods of investment appraisal are as follows.

Computation of net present value (NPV)

Here the analyst calculates how much money would need to be deposited today in the best available interest-bearing financial asset in order to create an eventual compound interest return equivalent to the expected profits from a physical investment such as a machine. If this amount is less than the cost of (say) the machine then the machine will not be purchased.

Calculation of the internal rate of return (yield) of a physical asset

This involves calculating the rate of return on the asset itself (in terms of the profits it is expected to generate) and comparing this with external rates, usually the current rate of interest. If this computed rate exceeds the actual market interest rate then an investment in the machine is preferable because it will yield higher returns than investing an equivalent amount in an interest-earning deposit.

Unfortunately, the internal rate of return (IRR) method sometimes generates confusing and/or incorrect results. Errors can be rectified by making adjustments, but the calculations become complicated. For further details the reader is referred to the M&E text *Investment Appraisal* by G. Mott.

Calculation of the payback period

Here, possible investments are ranked in terms of the periods needed to recoup capital costs, and an appropriate decision rule is adopted (e.g. 'accept all projects that pay back initial costs within three years'). Risks are minimised because longer-term investments, which put resources at risk for protracted periods, are rejected.

The payback method recognises that successful investments will induce imitative behaviour by competitors. Also, rapid reimbursement of early expenditures enables firms to avoid raising finance from external sources. Disadvantages of the method are that:

(a) Longer-term projects with low returns in early years are rejected even though, eventually, they could be financially worthwhile.

(b) Projects with low annual returns typically involve less risk than high expected return capital investments. Thus, paradoxically, the firm might be encouraged to assume greater, not lower, risks.

Computation of the average rates of expected returns on projects for a predetermined period (e.g. three years)

Projects with the highest expected average returns are chosen. The following difficulties are attached to this method:

(a) It is assumed that an average return of, say, 25 per cent over five years is better than one of 15 per cent over twelve, even though in practice, this is not always the case. The risks associated with intended projects should also be considered.

(b) It ignores the fact that a project which generates a large early return followed by lower revenues later on will provide *immediate* income that can be reinvested quickly even if the computed average return over the longer period is low.

RATIO ANALYSIS

9. Financial ratios

The *working capital ratio* is considered in 4 above. Other important financial ratios are as follows.

Return on capital employed

Gross capital employed is defined as fixed assets plus current assets. Net capital employed comprises fixed assets plus current assets less current liabilities. Proprietors' capital employed means net capital employed less long-term loans owing by the firm. Problems arise in measuring asset values (cost or market valuations, for example) and choosing which assets to include in computations. For instance, some firms regard cash and other idle assets as irrelevant when assessing performance, because idle assets are not involved in profit creation. And how should goodwill be treated?

Further problems arise when defining profit. Earnings retained within the business for future investment may be thought of as a profit which has not been distributed; or alternatively as a working asset used to generate further revenues.

The return on capital employed is an overall measure of efficiency and as such is commonly used to compare firms and industries. Often, low-risk firms in stable industries have lower-than-average values for this ratio.

Earnings per share

This is computed as annual after-tax profit divided by the total number of a certain category of the company's shares (usually ordinary shares, see 18).

The price-earnings (P/E) ratio

Division of the market price of a share by earnings per share gives the 'price-earnings ratio' which shows how many years it would take an investor to recoup his or her capital outlay if current earnings continue and all these earnings are paid out as dividends. The following should be noted when interpreting price-earnings ratios:

(a) Profitable, fast-growing companies which plough back most of their earnings into new investment have low declared profits, but might be greatly valued by investors. Hence the share price and P/E ratio of such a company will be high.

(b) Declared profits can be affected by windfall income, sale of capital assets, etc and thus give a misleading picture of the strength of the firm.

(c) A company's P/E ratio can change dramatically on rumours of a takeover bid, even though the firm's operational capacity has not altered.

Dividend yield

Proportionate dividend returns to an investor are shown by the ratio of dividend per share to the share's market price.

Dividend cover

The ratio of earnings per share to dividend per share shows the extent to which the firm is paying out its earnings to shareholders in the form of dividends, rather than retaining profits within the business.

Miscellaneous financial ratios

These include:

(a) Ratio of bad debts to sales. This indicates the risk of selling on credit.

(b) Ratio of capital employed to fixed assets. The extent to which physically realisable plant and equipment, premises and vehicles are available to settle outstanding debts is shown in this ratio. A high value means there are few assets that can be sold off in the event of liquidation.

(c) Ratio of net worth to indebtedness. Net worth is the amount of issued share capital plus all financial reserves which belong to shareholders. Hence, the ratio shows shareholders' interests as a proportion of the interests of debenture holders and other creditors.

Stockholding

Excessive stockholding is revealed in the 'stock turnover ratio':

$$\frac{Cost\ of\ sales}{Average\ stock}$$

where cost of sales is the value of opening stock plus stock purchases during an accounting period less stock at close. This ratio shows the speed of inventory turnover. If, for instance, the accounting period is one year and the ratio has a value of 2, then on average a unit of stock is held for six months. Values lower than 2 mean that stock is held longer than six months and *vice versa*. High values are appropriate for firms facing irregular market demand where sudden changes in taste can lead to heavy, unexpected sales.

Debt collecting

The ratio:

$$\frac{Value\ of\ debtors}{Annual\ sales} \times 12$$

shows the average period, in calendar months, required to collect debts.

SOURCES OF FINANCE

10. Short-term finance

Time elapses between the purchase of raw materials, hire of labour, leasing of equipment, etc and the sale of final goods. Finance is necessary to bridge the gap. In general, the source of business finance should be related to the purpose for which it is intended. Short-term finance should be used to bridge short-term deficits; long-term finance should be used for purchasing long-lived capital assets. Thus for example a machine expected to last six years should be bought using a six-year loan (during which period the machine is generating the profits needed to finance repayments); a ten-year asset should be purchased with a ten-year loan, and so on. This will balance the company's cash outflows in relation to interest and capital repayments against the earnings created over similar periods by the equipment purchased. The major sources of short-term finance are described below.

11. Overdrafts

Interest on overdrafts is lower than for longer-term fixed-period loans (since the bank's money is only at risk for a short while), and is only charged on daily balances outstanding. The overdraft may be paid off whenever the firm pleases and at that moment all interest liabilities cease. Thus, overdrafts are especially suitable for financing increases in working capital (e.g. extending credit to customers, building up the firm's work-in-progress stocks) because such trans-actions quickly generate the returns needed to repay the amount borrowed. Problems with overdrafts include:

(a) Interest rates may rise dramatically and unexpectedly in consequence of government anti-inflation policy.

(b) Technically, overdrafts are repayable on demand.

(c) The low cost and flexibility of overdrafts tempt many firms to use them (inappropriately) for the purpose of purchasing major capital assets, hence creating long-term liabilities financed by short-term borrowing which may have to be repaid quickly.

12. Fixed-term loans

With a fixed-term loan, the firm agrees to borrow a predetermined sum for a fixed period at a constant rate of interest. Usually, the lender will impose a contractual restriction on the borrowing company's ability to borrow from other institutions. This is to avoid complications regarding which assets are security for which loan. Often, loans incorporate interest rate swap agreements (*see* **32**). Also, many loans offer 'capital repayment holidays' whereby only the interest is payable during the first two or three years of the loan.

Further features of fixed-term loans are as follows:

(a) Lenders will normally insist that such loans be secured against tangible assets, including the borrower's personal property if insufficient business assets exist.

(b) Since the loan is for a fixed term, it is not repayable at will as is the case with overdrafts. Usually, however, these loans can be repaid early without penalty if the borrower so desires, subject to the lender's permission.

(c) An arrangement fee is payable to the lending bank.

Advantages of fixed-term loans are as follows:

(a) Cash flow forecasting in the borrowing firm becomes easier. The borrower knows precisely the interest and capital repayments necessary and when they are required.

(b) There is intense competition among providers of fixed-term loans, resulting in wide consumer choice in relation to the specific features of the loans on offer.

(c) These loans can be arranged for specific projects, so that sometimes the assets acquired with the money borrowed can *themselves* be used as security for the loan. Accordingly the lender need not take a charge (security) against the firm's total assets.

(d) Loans can be related to the specific purposes to which they are applied. Thus, a five-year loan can be used to purchase an item with an expected life of five years; a shorter-period loan might be obtained to finance additional working capital required for a self-liquidating project, and so on.

Problems with fixed-term loans are that interest will be higher than on overdrafts (reflecting the fact that the bank's money is put at risk for a longer interval), and the fact that the lender's arrangement fee could be as high as 1 per cent of the value of the loan (subject to negotiation and an upper ceiling).

The more the firm wishes to borrow, the greater the amount of information it will have to provide to the lender. A detailed balance sheet and cash flow projection will be expected, plus a business plan (*see* 4:8) and, for large sums, regular (perhaps even monthly) management control data on the progress of the business's projects. Additionally, the bank may impose a requirement that the profits remaining within the business after its owners have taken personal drawings must exceed the annual interest payable by a specified minimum ratio (two to one, for example).

13. Leasing

While not a direct source of finance *per se*, leasing provides an alternative to medium-term credit since it releases funds that would otherwise be used to purchase capital. Rentals are predetermined and do not change with interest rates, and modern equipment will be leased – there is no temptation to continue using obsolete equipment for fear of heavy capital outlay.

With 'operating leasing' the leasing company expects to lease the same equipment to many customers in succession and is itself responsible for its maintenance and repair. Under a 'finance lease', conversely, the leased item is used by a single firm until the end of the item's useful life. Hence, its capital cost plus the leasing company's profit are payable by the lessee in equal instalments, with the lessee being responsible for repairs. The advantages of leasing are that:

(a) No security has to be offered to the leasing company (as is normally the case with a loan).

(b) The overall cost of leasing can be lower than borrowing money and interest to purchase equipment outright.

(c) The firm's gearing ratio (*see* **29**) is not affected.

Leasing rather than buying is an attractive proposition for a loss-making or low-profit business, since a firm in this position does not have end-of-year profit balances against which it can set its depreciation ('writing-down') allowances. Depreciation reduces the book value of the firm's profits and hence its liability for tax.

With leasing, however, the leasing company purchases the asset and hence claims the depreciation allowance available on that type of item. The financial benefit is then passed back to the lessee in the form of reduced monthly rentals. Moreover, monthly rentals are themselves a tax-deductible business expense as far as the lessee is concerned.

14. Factoring and invoice discounting

Factoring involves the outright sale (at a discount) of debts owed to the company to an outside body in exchange for cash. The factor takes over the administration of the client company's invoices, collects the money and (importantly) assumes the risk of customer default. How much is paid for the invoices is subject to negotiation but will depend ultimately on the magnitudes of debt involved, the degree of risk, and the extent of the paperwork needed to collect payment. The cost of the factor's services typically breaks down into four components:

(a) A service charge of perhaps 1 or 2 per cent of the value of sales to cover the cost of administering invoices.

(b) A financing charge (equivalent to loan interest) on the money turned over to the company by the factor. This will normally be 3 to 5 per cent above bank base rate and is payable on the period between the company's receipt of cash from the factor and the dates when creditors settle their bills.

(c) A premium of about 1 per cent to cover the cost of bad debts.

(d) Extra charges for legal fees incurred by the factor while collecting money owed against invoices.

Advantages to factoring include the following:

(a) Regular cash inflows are assured. Hence the company can settle its own bills promptly (possibly obtaining cash discounts from suppliers) and hence will acquire a high credit rating.

(b) Other lines of credit are left open.

(c) Low administrative costs for managing the firm's sales ledger, and no debt collecting.

(d) The method is simple and convenient.

(e) Gearing (*see* 29) is not affected.

(f) Factors are expert in debt-collecting techniques and may be able to persuade recalcitrant debtors to settle their outstanding balances more convincingly than could the company's own accounts staff.

(g) Many factors offer ancillary services to their clients, e.g. information on customers' credit status; industry norms for prices and terms and conditions of sale; news about which regions and/or industries are experiencing recession (evidenced by exceptionally late payments by firms in these industries/regions), and so on.

With invoice discounting, the company receives a cash payment (effectively a loan) from the invoice discounter against the value of the invoices issued to customers, but retains responsibility for debt collection and for an agreed proportion of bad debts.

Factoring and invoice discounting can avoid disruptions in cash flow caused by customers delaying payment for their credit purchases. They are sources of finance in the sense that cash is rapidly injected into the business following the sale of goods, thus enabling the firm to avoid having to wait for payment or borrow from other sources.

Problems with factoring and invoice discounting

Factoring and invoice discounting, while convenient, can be expensive compared to the interest payable on loans. Also, the client company is usually expected to sign a 12-month agreement with the factor or discounter so that it becomes locked into using factoring/discounting services.

A problem with factoring is the client company's loss of contact with its customers where debt settlement is concerned. Either the factor will collect debts under its own name – which might irritate the client's customers – or under the client's own letterhead. In the latter case, however, it will still pursue long-outstanding debts vigorously – in the client's name – regardless of possible damaging effects on customer relations.

Factors and invoice discounters are not usually interested in contracts with very small businesses. While it is possible to arrange factoring/discounting for smaller firms, the fees charged will be high relative to the turnovers of such enterprises.

15. Trade credit

Delaying settlement of debts enables firms to use internally the funds that would otherwise be remitted to suppliers. Trade credit is free, no interest charges are involved. However, suppliers will eventually refuse credit and demand cash on delivery. Also, the discounts that are sometimes available for prompt payment will be lost.

16. Security against loans

Banks and other lenders normally require security for substantial loans. From the lender's point of view the ideal security should be quickly realisable, have a stable value, and fully cover the amount borrowed. Among the commonest assets used as security are those listed below.

(a) *Equities*. Shares in public rather than private companies are preferred because these have a known current market value. Banks will not normally advance up to the full quoted value of shares because market share prices fluctuate.

(b) *Life assurance policies*. Individuals can assign to their banks all benefits accruing under a life assurance policy. If the borrower defaults the bank will liquidate the policy at its surrender value, which will be the maximum sum advanced.

(c) *Land.* Note the substantial legal and administrative costs attached to valuing and conveyancing land.

(d) *Guarantees.* These occur when one person assumes responsibility for debts incurred by another. The most stringent form of guarantee is an 'indemnity', whereby the guarantor is responsible for settling a debt regardless of the circumstances of the default.

(e) *Debentures.* A loan to a limited company may be secured by issuing to the bank a debenture (*see* **22**) charged against the company's assets. In consequence, the bank becomes a priority creditor should the business be liquidated.

(f) *Hypothecation.* To hypothecate a loan the borrowing company gives its bank the right to claim the goods that it purchased with the money borrowed should the loan not be repaid. The goods will be retained until the debt is settled. Meanwhile, the bank has neither possession nor control of the goods – it must rely on the customer's willingness to hand them over, undamaged, following default. Hypothecation is rarely used nowadays.

LONG-TERM CAPITAL

17. Nature of long-term finance

Long-term finance mainly comprises funds raised through the sale of shares and debentures (*see* **22**).

What is a share?

When a business becomes a limited company its ownership passes to new owners – shareholders – each of whom (literally) buys shares of the business and hence is entitled to corresponding proportions of its trading profits and/or capital gains. Shareholders lose their investment if the company is liquidated and if there are no funds remaining after its employees, creditors and the tax authorities have been paid and all outstanding mortgages, fixed and floating charges, and other secured lending have been settled.

The returns paid to shareholders are known as *dividends*. Since the company's profits belong to shareholders it is up to them to decide how much dividend on shares the company will pay (as opposed to retaining profits within the business for further investment). This they do in a free vote at the Annual General Meeting of the company.

18. Share capital

The 'nominal' (or 'authorised') capital of a company is the maximum amount its articles of association (*see* **3:18**) specify that it can raise through selling shares. This may differ from 'issued' (or 'allotted') capital, which is the proportion of nominal capital actually sold. Payment for shares is 'called up' from shareholders in instalments. 'Paid up' capital is that part of issued capital that has been called and for which payment has actually been received. Shareholders who fail to respond to calls are liable to forfeit their shares.

Today the commonest type of share is the 'ordinary' share. Ordinary shareholders carry the risk of the business and receive dividends only if profits are made. And if the company collapses they are repaid their investment only after all the firm's other debts and obligations have been settled. Normally each ordinary share carries one vote, although non-voting ordinary shares (called 'A' shares) may be issued.

19. Preference shares

Holders of preference shares are entitled to a fixed percentage rate of dividend, which is paid before ordinary shareholders receive any return. Should the company be liquidated, preference shareholders' capital is redeemed before that of ordinary shareholders. Preference shares may be cumulative or non-cumulative. Cumulative shareholders are entitled to dividends in respect of past years when no profits were made and no dividends paid.

'Participating' preference shares carry, in addition to the fixed rate of dividend, the right to a share in any profits left over after other dividends have been declared. Occasionally, firms issue 'redeemable' preference shares which, subject to the terms of the contract, holders may redeem or the company may buy back at some future time if they decide to exercise the option. Preference shares are less common today than in the past because of changes in UK company law which have made them less tax efficient for issuing companies. Of course, combinations and variations of categories are possible. The 'preferred ordinary share', for example, is entitled to dividends after preference shares, but before ordinary shares.

The term *mezzanine finance* is sometimes used to describe preference shares, because they are half way between equity and loan capital. This term (which means 'middle layer') might also be applied to any form of long-term finance which is not fully secured against the company's assets, but which ranks for payment before ordinary shares in the event of the company's liquidation. Suppliers of mezzanine finance face substantial risk without having votes in the business; accordingly they demand higher returns on their investments.

20. Deferred shares

These are usually issued as a component of a firm's initial share capital when the company begins or when it is taken over. They carry heavy voting rights relative to their nominal values and, because of this, are sometimes called management shares. Deferred shareholders receive all profits after other classes of share have received dividends, and have the right to all surplus assets on liquidation following settlement of the company's debts and reimbursement of other shareholders.

21. Share dilution

As more shares are issued, profits have to be distributed to increasing numbers of shareholders so that if earnings remain stable the dividend payable to each shareholder must decrease. This process is known as *share dilution*.

22. Debentures

A debenture is a loan to a company secured against its assets. Most debentures are fixed-term (five years, for example) and carry a fixed rate of interest. Debenture holders are creditors to the firm, not shareholders, and have no voting rights. The issuing firm is legally obliged to pay debenture interest in full on the date it is due. If necessary, the firm must be liquidated and its assets sold off to raise the money required to meet this commitment.

Convertibles

These are fixed interest stocks (usually debentures) which carry the right of conversion into ordinary shares at a prespecified time in the future. They are issued at lower interest rates than standard debentures because investors are attracted to the possibilities of large capital gains on conversion. Convertibles are commonly used to finance takeovers because they avoid share dilution (*see* **21**).

RAISING MONEY ON THE STOCK EXCHANGE

23. What is the Stock Exchange?

The Stock Exchange is a market place for shares. It is privately owned and has nothing to do with the government. The owners (members) of the Exchange will not allow the shares of any company to be traded using its (now fully computerised) facilities: only approved shares can be transacted via the Exchange. The process of obtaining approval is known as 'obtaining a quotation'. Once a company has a quotation, the current prices of its shares are 'listed' each day by the Exchange and hence published in national newspapers.

To encourage investors to purchase shares via the Stock Exchange rather than through some other medium the Exchange provides a measure of protection to investors who use its facilities. This involves:

(a) A compensation scheme for investors who lose money in consequence of Exchange members not meeting their obligations

(b) The imposition on members of rules to prevent them unfairly manipulating share prices or otherwise exploiting the public

(c) Requiring quoted companies to disclose crucial management information both to the Exchange and to investors (news of takeover bids, capital restructuring, sale of assets, etc).

24. Obtaining a quotation

Normally, a company must have traded profitably for at least five years and have a share capital of at least £500,000 before it will be considered for a full Stock Exchange quotation, and the Exchange will carefully investigate the company's affairs prior to giving a listing. Once it is listed, at least 25 per cent of all its share issues (*see* **25**) must thereafter be made available to the public.

The shares of quoted companies are readily sold through the Exchange, and this marketability enhances the attraction to investors of quoted securities. Thus, listed companies should find it easier than others to sell their shares to the investing public. Other benefits associated with a quotation include:

(a) An improved public image through having the company's name mentioned in the *Financial Times* and other national newspapers

(b) The fact that quoted securities are generally acceptable as payment for takeovers

(c) A quick and convenient mechanism for assessing the worth of the company through the interplay of market forces

(d) Reduced dependence on banks and other lenders for business finance.

The disadvantages of becoming a quoted company include the subsequent administrative costs of new issues (*see* **25**), and possible loss of control (outsiders may freely purchase shares in the business).

25. Raising capital by share issue

Public limited companies wishing to raise money by share issue will normally do so through the 'new issues market', which consists of institutions that specialise in the sale of new shares, although other methods are available (*see* below). First the company will (normally) consult a merchant bank for advice on the timing of the issue, an appropriate issue price and how best to underwrite the flotation. Underwriters are institutions that guarantee to buy (at a predetermined price below that of the official issue) any shares not purchased by the public.

Share issues may proceed in any one of several ways:

(a) *Issue by prospectus.* A 'prospectus' is published in several newspapers detailing the company's past record, recent accounts, its senior management, and the purposes for which the money is intended. Members of the public are invited to subscribe for shares at a single stated price.

(b) *Rights issue.* This means selling extra shares to existing shareholders. New shares are offered (usually at an attractive price made possible by the low administrative cost to the company of raising capital in this manner) in proportion to shareholders' present holdings, e.g. one new share for every five held.

(c) *Issue by tender.* The procedure here is the same as issue by prospectus, except that investors are invited to bid for the shares above some specified minimum price. Shares are then allocated to the highest bidders. Any shares not allocated (because there are not enough bidders above the minimum stated price) go to underwriters.

(d) *Offer for sale.* This method is identical to issue by prospectus, but initially all the shares are taken up by an 'issuing house', i.e. a financial institution – which may or may not be a merchant bank that specialises in floating new issues. The issuing house subsequently offers the shares to the general public.

(e) *Placing.* An issuing house places the shares with investment trusts, insurance companies, pension funds and other large institutional investors rather than advertising them to the general public.

(f) *Scrip issues.* A scrip issue (sometimes called a 'bonus' issue) is a 'free' issue of shares to existing shareholders to account for the increase in the value of the company that has occurred in consequence of it ploughing back large parts of its profits into land and buildings, new machinery and equipment, etc. Dividends in a company pursuing this sort of policy will necessarily have been lower than was possible, although the worth of the business will have been mounting.

By definition, the extra assets purchased with retained earnings *belong* to shareholders, who are thus allocated bonus shares to acknowledge their property rights over the additional value of the company. Note, however, that the firm's profits must henceforth be distributed over a greater number of shares so that future dividends per share will have to be lower.

26. Unlisted securities markets (USMs)

Many European stock exchanges have unlisted securities markets which enable smaller companies to raise capital by selling shares to the general public and (importantly) thereafter have their shares valued and traded in an orderly and regulated way.

Entry to a USM is normally much cheaper than obtaining a full quotation (there are lower costs for underwriting, publishing advertisements, banker's fees, etc); less documentation is required; only a small part of total share capital has to be sold to the public; recently established businesses may join; and in most countries no minimum size of firm is specified.

Problems with unlisted securities markets are:

(a) Despite the reduced administrative burden, the cost of raising money on a USM can be high compared with alternative possibilities (sometimes 5 to 10 per cent of the value of the finance eventually obtained).

(b) In having their shares traded on the free market, companies must accept that share prices become subject to market forces. A general collapse in share prices could enable an unwelcome outsider to obtain a substantial interest in a company at minimal cost.

(c) The fact that a USM listing makes a company's shares readily marketable (and hence more attractive to shareholders) itself means the company becomes available to takeover predators.

(d) Investors on a USM might not place appropriate values on small yet dynamic companies new to the market.

(e) A company which issues new shares through a USM may then find itself under great pressure to pay substantial dividends to shareholders, even if the company really needs to retain its profits for internal use.

27. Over-the-counter share dealings

There exists an 'over-the-counter' (OTC) market in non-quoted shares, managed by share dealers (who are licensed by the Stock Exchange but are not full members) on an *ad-hoc* basis. Note that investors who buy shares on the OTC market are not covered by the Stock Exchange investment protection scheme (*see* 23). OTC share issues are normally advertised through 'investment reports' consisting of glossy brochures that describe the company and its prospects in the best possible light. The report will outline the firm's history, operations, earnings potential, etc.

To participate in the OTC market the firm must apply to a licensed dealer active in the field and ask for an 'OTC listing'. The dealer, if interested, will then analyse the company and predict a suitable selling price for its shares. Normally the dealer will engage an accountant or specialist management consultant to undertake this task. The consultant will audit the internal efficiency of the applicant firm and evaluate its strategies, markets, strengths, weaknesses, opportunities, barriers to expansion and so on. Fees for this service are passed back to the applicant company.

Next the dealer will approach directly potential purchasers of the applicant's shares, and will include details of these shares together with brief details of the company's prospects in a newsletter distributed periodically to investors currently using the dealing firm. Fees for the dealer's arrangement, publicity and other services normally come to between 2 and 3.5 per cent of the total value of new shares 'floated' in this manner.

Buyers of OTC shares typically comprise investment institutions (insurance companies, pension funds, investment trusts, etc), employees and trade associates of companies using the market, and private investors.

28. Choice of capital structure

Companies can finance expansion through selling shares, issuing debentures or obtaining other interest-bearing loans, or through retaining the bulk of their earnings. Shares have the advantage that dividends need not be paid in loss-making periods. However, outsiders gain votes as shares are issued so that existing majority shareholders may lose control. Debenture financing involves no loss of control since debenture holders have no votes. But the risk of liquidation is higher because debenture interest must be paid in full, on time, regardless of current financial circumstances. Overdrafts may be called in by the company's bank.

The alternative is to plough back profits. No interest is payable and there is no risk of outside takeover. However, whereas the value of the company goes up as profits are reinvested in new plant and equipment, the market price of the company's shares could fall, since profit retentions necessarily reduce the amount available for dividends. Investors are looking for high dividends, and the demand for the shares of a low dividend company might be weak. Thus, paradoxically, increases in a firm's physical assets land and buildings, equipment, vehicles, work in progress, etc might be accompanied in the short term by declining share prices. In the longer run, shareholders are entitled to receive bonus shares (*see* **25**) to cover increases in company asset values. In the short term, however, dangers exist that outsiders might be able to buy a controlling interest in the firm for less than the monetary value of the company's physical assets.

Public companies must consider carefully, therefore, the relative proportions of debentures, shares and retained earnings they should include in their capital structures. Debenture financing is appropriate for steady, low-risk industries, whereas shares are better for riskier, high-return environments where profits fluctuate and money for interest payments may not be available in some years. Companies whose shares are highly valued in relation to capital employed and which are earning high returns are likely to retain substantial parts of their profits.

29. Gearing

The ratio of a company's borrowing to its total share capital is known as its 'gearing'. This term is also used, loosely, to describe the ratio of borrowing to assets in sole traderships and partnerships.

Companies that borrow heavily relative to their share capital are said to be highly geared, and *vice versa*. Lenders typically impose on borrowing companies a contractual restriction on the latter's ability to borrow from other sources, i.e. borrowers' gearing ratios are limited to agreed maximum values. This ensures that the lender has first claim on a borrowing company's assets if it goes into liquidation, and there will be no other lenders with secured claims on the failed business's funds.

30. Venture capital

With venture capital financing, an outside body (a merchant bank, for example) takes shares in a business in order to inject capital, then takes an agreed proportion of the profits for a prespecified period, and sells the shares back to the company at a predetermined future date at a price agreed in the initial contract. Venture capitalists are looking to invest in sound businesses that wish to expand rapidly.

Problems with venture capital are as follows:

(a) The high cost (possibly in excess of 30 per cent) of capital raised in this manner.

(b) Borrowers must regularly submit detailed reports, containing much confidential information, on the progress of their business.

(c) Lenders typically impose contractual restrictions on borrowing firms' gearing (*see* **29**) and minimum values for net assets (*see* **9**) and the maintenance of financial reserves (this is to enable venture capitalists to recoup their initial investments if borrowing companies go into liquidation).

(d) If the firm fails to achieve certain specified targets the contract may provide for the venture capitalist taking control of the company. The venture capitalist is a shareholder in the business, and as such may be keen to liquidate it (in order to sell off the firm's assets to raise money to redeem share capital) at the first sign of financial difficulty.

31. Financial engineering

This is a continental term sometimes used to describe the processes whereby large companies seek to obtain long-term funds at short-term rates of interest (which are lower than rates on long-term loans). Financial engineering techniques include:

(a) *Multi-option facilities.* Here a consortium of banks and/or other lending institutions guarantee the company immediate access to low-cost funds during a predetermined period. This is possible because, at any moment in time, certain members of the consortium will possess idle balances that may be used for short-term lending. Thus, funds can be made available on a continuous basis. A consecutive series of such short-term loans from various lenders represents long-term finance as far as the borrowing company is concerned.

(b) *Forfaiting.* A company engaged on a long-term and expensive project with a large customer can have the latter accept a bundle of bills of exchange (*see* 8:9), each maturing on a different date. The first bill could be payable after six months, the second after 18 months, the third after three years etc, up to the last bill maturing on completion of the project. These accepted bills may now be discounted *en bloc* with the company's own bankers.

(c) *Issue of commercial paper.* Since 1986, large quoted UK companies with net assets (i.e. fixed plus current assets less current liabilities) of at least £50 million have been legally entitled to issue unsecured promissory notes, known as 'sterling commercial paper'. Purchasers buy this at a discount and redeem it on maturity at its face value.

(d) *Financial futures.* These are options, purchased today, to borrow money at predetermined future dates for specified periods at rates of interest fixed in advance in the option contract (which is known as a 'forward rate agreement'). Large businesses can buy a variety of futures, using the ones they eventually need and reselling the others.

Swap agreements are contracts whereby lenders and borrowers consent to exchange one set of repayment and interest-rate obligations for another. Swaps are only available on long-term loans.

FINANCIAL ASPECTS OF MERGERS AND TAKEOVERS

32. Financing a takeover

Acquisitions can be paid for with cash; shares or debentures in the predator company; or a mixture of these.

Payment in securities

The main advantage to target shareholders of being paid in securities rather than in cash is that no capital gains tax is payable on securities, whereas acceptance of cash represents a taxable 'disposal' for capital gains purposes. The securities offered could include ordinary or preference shares, fixed-interest stock, or convertibles (*see* **22**).

This type of bid can be 'underwritten' through the predator arranging for a third party (a merchant bank, for example) to guarantee that it will buy at a certain minimum price the shares distributed to target shareholders. In consequence, those who accept the predator's offer are assured they can quickly convert the shares into cash (albeit at an underwritten price somewhat below their face value). The third-party financier charges the predator a fee for this facility.

To enhance the appeal of a 'shares for shares' offer the predator needs to convince target shareholders that shares in the predator company have genuine value, particularly if the offer is not underwritten in the manner previously described. This will be difficult if the predator's dividend payment record is poor, and/or the predator has few tangible assets. Convertibles, straight debentures, or a cash plus preference shares offer might carry greater credibility in these circumstances, especially if the share capital of the resulting larger business will be severely diluted in consequence of the acquisition.

33. Payment in cash

Predators that do not possess the cash needed to pay for intended acquisitions must borrow the necessary funds. Sometimes the loan is secured, in effect, against the assets of the target business. Such acquisitions are commonly referred to as 'leverage buy-outs'.

Theoretically, a tiny business could purchase a huge corporation in this way. However, the predator firm will have to convince the third-party lender of its competence and determination to see the deal through, of its integrity, and of its overall managerial experience and ability. What happens if the takeover fails and the borrowing predator collapses without repaying the money? The assets against which the loan were provisionally secured will not be available, and the predator's own assets may be insufficient to cover the loan!

34. The leverage buy-out and the junk bond

Security offered for these purposes may be in the form of debenture stock issued against the predator's (currently inadequate) assets. Such debentures are often called 'junk bonds' because at the time they are issued they are not backed by assets sufficient to cover the loan. The term 'junk bond' is now a generic. It is used to describe any loan stock secured against dubious or intangible assets. Indeed, junk bonds have sometimes been secured against other junk bonds!

In fact, attempted leverage buy-outs can make a profit even if the bids are unsuccessful. Suppose for example that the predator launches a hostile takeover bid and buys up (say) 20 per cent of the target's voting share capital. Assume that the bid is opposed by the target's board of directors, and that current major shareholders do their best to resist the takeover (*see* **18–19**). The predator might now offer to sell its 20 per cent stake in the company back to these shareholders, but at a significantly higher price – in return for a promise by the predator to abandon the attempted takeover. Big profits have been made in this way. It is sometimes referred to as 'greenmail'.

35. Reluctant bids

All a predator requires is a 51 per cent stake in a target firm. For quoted companies, however, Stock Exchange rules require that once a bidder has acquired a 30 per cent shareholding he or she must offer to buy *all* remaining shares in the company at a price not lower than the highest price paid during the previous 12 months. Bids which result from this requirement are sometimes called 'reluctant bids'.

Stock Exchange rules in relation to takeovers and mergers are spelt out in the *City Code on Takeovers and Mergers*, which is not a legally binding document, but rather a set of recommendations compiled by representatives of leading city institutions. Specific provisions of the code are that:

(a) Directors of a company receiving a takeover offer (this company is referred to as the 'biddee') should inform shareholders immediately, and should disclose any shareholdings that the directors might have in the company that is making the bid.

(b) Shareholders in the biddee company must be given adequate time to consider their decision, and be provided with all the relevant facts.

(c) The board of the biddee company must not frustrate the bid through withholding vital information.

(d) There should be no discrimination between various classes of shareholder.

'Dawn raids' whereby a big shareholding in a target company is acquired from large investment institutions on a single day are restricted to 15 per cent of the shares of the company involved. And this must be followed by a week's pause to allow other shareholders to consider their position.

Any purchase of more than 1 per cent of a large company's share capital should be disclosed to existing shareholders, and the use of third parties to purchase shares 'in secret' – avoiding thereby the disclosure of the name of the bidding company – is explicitly forbidden. This latter recommendation (and since the *City Code* is non-statutory its rules have only the status of recommendations) followed cases where, for example, not only did a bidding company get other companies to buy shares in a biddee company on its behalf, but it actually offered to these third-party companies a financial indemnity against any loss in market value of the biddee company's shares that might occur during the period of the takeover bid.

36. The reverse takeover

This is a low-cost means for converting a private company into a quoted plc. The private company finds an existing quoted plc which is effectively defunct, say because of a natural decline in its commercial fortunes (e.g. through technological obsolescence of its products, loss of markets, inefficient high-cost working practices, etc) or in consequence of bad management, or simply through lack of interest in the business by its majority shareholders. Shares in these companies are effectively worthless, and are sometimes referred to as 'penny shares'. There is in fact a market in penny shares: investors buy them speculatively in the hope that the companies concerned will be used for a reverse takeover, or that new managements will revive their fortunes, or that their technological environments will change.

Next, the majority shareholder of the private company purchases a majority shareholding in the defunct quoted plc, which now 'takes over' the private company, paying for the latter using shares in itself. In effect, an entirely new business has been created – incorporating the original private company – but which is already quoted on the Stock Exchange. Exactly the same procedure applies if the predator firm is an unquoted public company rather than a private company in the first place.

37. Advantages and drawbacks of the reverse takeover

This procedure avoids the costs and inconveniences of obtaining a quotation through normal channels, and circumvents the need to disclose detailed information about the firm's prospects and operations to the Stock Exchange Council. A problem is that the Stock Exchange is likely to suspend the new company's quotation if its new field of operations significantly alters as a result of the takeover. However, the suspension will only be temporary provided the Stock Exchange is given all relevant information and the firm demonstrates that the deal is entirely honest and fair. Another potential difficulty is that shareholding in the plc that is the subject of the reverse takeover may be widely dispersed. The City Code requirement that the predator bid for all these shares at a common price (see 35) could mean that the cost of the acquisition turns out higher than first anticipated.

VALUATION OF TAKEOVER TARGETS

38. Valuation of quoted companies

Price-earnings ratios (see 9) are frequently used as a starting point for valuing companies for which market share prices are available (i.e. quoted or USM companies or companies whose shares are traded on the OTC market – see 27).

The P/E ratio indicates how quickly the predator will recoup its initial outlay if the target firm continues to earn profits and distribute them at its current rate. However, the market share price quoted could be an unreliable indicator of the true worth of the business. Random market fluctuations can distort market values, and the company may have lucrative investment plans and projects not known to the general public. Also, a company that has recently raised additional capital through share issue may have done so at low prices in order to attract investors.

Note moreover that the predator might be expecting the target's earnings to increase significantly in consequence of the takeover, so that an assessment of the anticipated improvement needs to be incorporated into the calculation. Further difficulties are as follows:

(a) Windfall income and/or undisclosed changes in accounting valuation methods may have affected recent figures for the target company's earnings.

(b) High profits might be incurred in high-risk environments. The target firm might simply have been extremely lucky. Yet the risks associated with its operations might cause future earnings to collapse.

(c) Low-dividend payouts in a company controlled by a small group of investors could be due to the owners extracting money from the business through other avenues, rather than to low profits or through the company ploughing back its profits into new investment.

39. Valuation of unquoted companies

One way of valuing a private or unquoted public company is to examine the price-earnings ratios of *quoted* companies with similar operations and facing comparable risks in the same industry as the unquoted firm. These ratios are averaged (provided the individual components are not too dissimilar) and – given that the target firm's current earnings are already known – a market price for the target may be inferred.

The problem is that the comparator companies may have profit retention policies and growth potentials entirely different from those of the target business. In particular, rapidly expanding firms that temporarily plough back most of their earnings into new investment will have high P/E ratios. In consequence, the use of an average P/E ratio that includes such businesses to calculate a value for a takeover target which is not growing as rapidly, can result in the overvaluation of the target company.

40. Asset valuation

Balance sheet figures do not necessarily provide accurate valuations of the objective worth of a company's assets. Balance sheets are prepared according to standard accounting conventions in relation to depreciation rates, historical costs versus market values, stock valuations, the treatment of intangibles (ownership of intellectual property), etc. In valuing a company it is necessary therefore to prepare what is in effect a 'Doomsday Book' of all the company's assets, liabilities, and current and intended activities. The list should include details of the firm's:

(a) property (and all the potential uses to which it can be put)

(b) existing and planned projects

(c) vehicles, equipment, furniture and machinery, taking account of the age, condition, replacement costs and second-hand value of each item

(d) leases on premises, including allowances for impending rent reviews and/or the effects of dilapidations clauses

(e) fixtures and fittings

(f) consumables (stationery, for instance)

(g) stocks of finished goods and work in progress

(h) pension rights obligations, share options, etc in respect of staff

(i) potential capital gains tax liabilities on the revaluation of assets which might have to accompany the sale of the business.

Also required are data on remuneration cost per employee computed on an hourly basis (i.e. the employee's wages plus fringe benefits plus any other income divided by his or her annual hours after deducting holiday entitlement and past average sick leave).

Tax losses can crucially affect the takeover value of the business, since current trading losses can normally be carried forward and offset against future profits – provided these profits relate to the same trade. This is not the case, however, if the nature of the business changes substantially following the takeover. Past trading losses can represent a considerable 'hidden asset' within a target firm. If a target company has tax losses which for technical reasons cannot be passed on to its new owners then, assuming the losses benefit existing shareholders when the business changes hands, the price paid for the company needs to be adjusted downwards by a corresponding amount.

Progress test 9

1. What are the purposes of business accounting?

2. List the possible sources of business finance, distinguishing between short and long term, and give an example of how each type of finance may be used.

3. Define the following:

(a) Participating preference share.

(b) Deferred share.

(c) Payback period.

(d) Internal rate of return.

4. List four types of security that a bank might accept against a business loan.

5. List five examples of fixed and variable costs.

6. What is venture capital?

10

OPERATIONS MANAGEMENT

THE SCOPE OF OPERATIONS MANAGEMENT

1. Definition

Operations management (OM) concerns the transformation of material resource inputs into outputs of goods and services. It is normally associated with manufacturing; but might equally involve, for example, transport operations, warehousing, or the deployment of physical items such as shelving, refrigerated cabinets and checkout tills in a retail outlet. OM is particularly associated with techniques of production and labour incentive schemes.

2. Production

To 'produce' goods is to convert raw materials and/or components into finished items. Production can occur to a client's precise specifications (*job* production), or in repetitive *batches*, or *continuously* on conveyor belts and assembly lines.

With job production (shipbuilding or house construction, for example) there is little scope for standardisation of parts or integration of processes. Also, workers may need to be skilled in several different areas. The firm cannot plan its output until customers have placed orders so it is not possible to produce for stock. Consequently, firms engaged in job production might experience long idle periods (during which overheads are still being incurred) between jobs.

Batch production involves finite and predetermined production runs. Sales might be regular, but of insufficient volume to justify uninterrupted production. This mode of production occurs where a product's design or specification is altered regularly. Goods may be produced for stock. Continuous (flow) production is mass production appropriate for standardised, homogeneous products. Typically it is capital-intensive and uses robots (*see* 5) on totally-automated production lines. The economics of mass production require that plant, equipment and labour be fully utilised all the time in order to reduce overheads per unit of output. Hence, the firm must be prepared to accumulate large amounts of stock whenever sales fall.

The method adopted affects the extent of the division of labour applied (and hence the monotony of operatives' work), the availability of scale economies, costs, and the levels of skill and training required in workers.

3. Production departments

These employ a wide range of categories of staff: operatives, researchers, storekeepers, designers, quality controllers, engineers and scientists, etc. Much of the firm's fixed capital will be deployed here. The duties of a production department might include:

- Work scheduling
- Determination of production methods
- Work study and work measurement
- Costing (*see* 9:**6** and 12:**28**)
- Factory and workplace layout
- Product design, research and development
- Maintenance, inspection and quality control
- Stores and stock control
- (possibly) Purchase of raw materials
- Security.

4. Automation

Automation may be fixed or flexible. Fixed automation involves processing and/or assembly via predetermined sequences of operations that cannot be altered by virtue of the nature of the equipment. Flexible automation allows for changes in the order and character of operations, thus enabling outputs to be varied periodically. When installing a flexible automation system the aim is to minimise the set-up periods required to alter equipment, goods transit arrangements, etc. Increasingly, computers and robots are used for such purposes, leading to complete 'flexible manufacturing systems'.

5. Robotics and flexible manufacturing systems (FMSs)

A flexible manufacturing system consists of a collection of computer-controlled machine tools and transport and handling systems, all integrated via the use of a master computer. Most FMS arrangements rely heavily on robots for routine production. The advantages of using robots for manufacturing are as follows:

(a) Closed-loop machine and assembly schemes (*see* 12:**13**) are operated more easily through robotic systems; leading to lower work-in-progress inventories and less need for (costly) manual intervention.

(b) Shiftwork creates fewer problems because not many people are needed to operate unpopular shifts (10 pm to 6 am, for instance).

(c) The ratio of managers to human operatives rises dramatically, so that each manager has fewer operatives to control.

(d) Robots do not demand higher bonuses for more intensive working.

(e) Training and other staff development costs fall.

Recently produced robots incorporate reprogrammable computers that can quickly change the nature of the robot's activities. Hence, the same robot may be used for several different purposes: assembly-line work (grasping, machining and moving goods from a fixed position), materials handling (shunting goods from one location to another), clearing up the workplace, spray-painting, stamping or otherwise identifying stock items, etc.

6. Advantages of flexible manufacturing

The essential advantage of flexible manufacturing is that it enables new production specifications to be implemented immediately, thus allowing frequent and rapid modifications to output for different orders (necessary to satisfy the needs of various markets and consumer categories). Further benefits include:

(a) Lower stockholding made possible through more precise work scheduling

(b) Reductions in machining times

(c) Less need for control by (highly paid) managers and increased possibilities for tight central administration

(d) Enhanced potential for the integration of marketing and production functions.

7. Manufacturing automation protocol (MAP)

A 'protocol' in the manufacturing context is a set of rules and procedures for exchanging information and instructions between different types of computer system. Accordingly, the term describes the linking-up of the offices, assembly lines and processes in different locations in order to increase the efficiency of closed-loop manufacturing operations (*see* 12:**13**). MAP is an example of 'open systems' computing (*see* 13:**13**).

8. Optimised production technology (OPT)

OPT is more of an *approach* to production management than a specific procedure. It seeks to minimise work in progress by isolating and, where possible, removing bottlenecks in materials flows. Importantly, it does *not* assume that peak efficiency is attained by keeping every machine, worker and process fully employed all the time. The steps involved in installing an OPT system are as follows:

(a) Identify bottlenecks, e.g. the time taken to set up machines or to adjust tolerances, delivery holdups, stockouts, etc.

(b) Devise work schedules to guarantee that the equipment or processes associated with bottlenecks are fully supplied at all times – even if this means plant, equipment and labour standing idle further back in the chain of production.

(c) Integrate the entire system under a single, coherent production plan.

9. Operations planning

This has two aspects: (*i*) 'preproduction programming' which concerns product design (*see* **28**) and the specification of dimensions, material inputs and quality standards, and (*ii*) 'process engineering', i.e. choice of production methods, the design of tools and equipment, work scheduling and project management. Production plans are implemented by *production controllers* who seek to minimise manufacturing delays by regulating flows of work. This requires the collection of information about work awaiting completion; available machinery, labour and materials; work priorities and constraints. Interruptions may result from non- or late delivery of materials, from machine breakdowns, staff sickness, strikes, staff lateness due to public transport difficulties, computer malfunctions or stock shortages.

10. Maintenance

Maintenance is the work undertaken (*i*) to ensure that plant, equipment, buildings, etc are fully operational, and/or (*ii*) to deal with breakdowns in the minimum possible time. *Preventative* maintenance seeks to avert breakdowns before they occur; *corrective* maintenance involves repairing faults that are reducing a system's output or overall level of efficiency; *running* (routine) maintenance necessitates taking plant or equipment out of service for routine overhaul; while *breakdown* maintenance means rectifying equipment failures, e.g. through replacing faulty components.

The term *planned maintenance* describes the process of drafting a predetermined programme for the upkeep of equipment and/or buildings. Items are serviced at specified intervals, or whenever certain danger signals appear. The aim is to prevent unanticipated breakdowns through ensuring that equipment or buildings are kept in a satisfactory state of repair. This requires careful record keeping *vis-á-vis* equipment condition and age, identification of the reasons for equipment failure, and predictions of equipment operating life. Items must be regularly inspected for indications of excessive wear, materials fatigue or other signs of poor condition. Planned maintenance is not appropriate for situations where the time to breakdown is unreliable and the cost of periodic maintenance outweighs that of *ad-hoc* repair.

11. Project management

There are two types of project: self-contained projects (construction projects, for instance); and those which are elements of other projects or of an ongoing programme. In either case the duties of the project manager are to assess the feasibility of the project, negotiate supply contracts with third parties, commence and complete operations, and arrange support services.

Project managers co-ordinate activities, motivate employees and plan tasks. They must unify effort, forecast workloads, determine priorities and schedule jobs. Priorities have to be established, critical activities identified, and potential difficulties exposed. Specific project management duties include:

(a) conducting feasibility studies

(b) estimating costs and activity start and completion times

(c) putting work out for tender and procuring supplies

(d) work scheduling and deriving critical paths

(e) negotiating the best possible supply prices with subcontractors

(f) quality management (*see* **31–35**)

(g) 'progress chasing', i.e. ensuring that inputs are delivered on schedule and that project activities are completed on time

(h) monitoring and appraising the performances of members of the project team and reporting on these

(i) negotiating penalty clauses with suppliers *vis-á-vis* late delivery of supplies

(j) advising on insurance, licensing requirements, planning permission, etc, wherever required

(k) detailed costing of the project.

12. Research and development (R&D)

Industrial research concerns the acquisition of technical knowledge about products, processes, materials and working methods. 'Pure' research is exploratory and general: immediately applicable results are neither expected nor required. 'Applied' research, conversely, investigates specific practical questions.

Whereas pure research is usually funded by the state or an entire industry, applied work is typically initiated and paid for by the individual firm. The aim of applied research is quick improvement of a particular situation. Applied work, moreover, may itself provide the stimulus for major theoretical breakthroughs.

Research costs include salaries, equipment and facilities (laboratories, for example), and the consequences of resources possibly being tied up for long periods with no financial return. Note moreover that once a large amount of money has been invested in a project which so far has yielded zero returns, the firm might continue to fund the research in (possibly hopeless) attempts to recoup its initial outlay. Also, results eventually obtained might contribute enormously to the advancement of science, yet generate no profit for the sponsoring firm! Further problems might include:

(a) Research staff becoming more committed to their research than to the achievement of organisational objectives

(b) High turnover among researchers as individuals seek more challenging research opportunities in other firms

(c) Deciding when to abandon unproductive projects

(d) Conflicts between researchers and line managers over research objectives and timetables

(e) Evaluating the effectiveness of R&D. This requires the analysis of the financial returns (cost savings, increased sales, etc) attributable to R&D activities; the identification of product improvements directly due to R&D; and the comparison of the consequences of the firm's R&D effort with those of competitors. Sometimes it is better to copy and improve competitors' products (provided they are not protected by patent) rather than spend large amounts on new product research.

13. Manufacturing strategy

This follows from the determination of the issues discussed in Chapter 5. It requires decisions on how the manufacturing function can be best organised and administered in order to assist the firm attain its mission. Elements of a manufacturing strategy will include decisions on:

(a) The technology to be used in manufacturing

(b) Major investments in plant and equipment

(c) The nature of quality control and quality assurance procedures (*see* **35**)

(d) Human resource development, especially training in technical and managerial skills

(e) How to integrate market research with new product development and to relate manufacturing activities to the marketing concept (*see* **7:3**)

(f) Integration of CADCAM, etc into the firm's overall mangement information system

(g) Whether to make or buy input components (*see* **15**)

(h) Conformance quality (*see* **31**) and design quality (both of which have implications for production costs and hence the selling price of output)

(i) Delivery/reliability/price trade-offs

(j) The extent of after-sales customer servicing.

PURCHASING

14. The purchasing function

The purchasing function covers the procurement of raw materials, components, capital equipment, office furniture, stationery, etc; the negotiation with suppliers of input quality levels and the prices of purchased goods; and the monitoring of sources of supply.

Other duties might include (*i*) record keeping (especially of stocks of goods and of the time lags that occur between placing orders and receiving supplies), (*ii*) inspection of goods received, and (*iii*) handling disputes with supplying companies.

Purchasing departments can be organised according to types of material purchased, or by particular areas of operation. In the former case, each purchasing officer buys just one variety of product, and thus develops intimate knowledge of the good and its suppliers. Otherwise, purchasing officers supply all the requirements of a specific department or production line, covering many different product categories.

15. Make or buy decisions

A major decision is which inputs to purchase and which to produce within the firm. A business that produces its own components enjoys complete control over their specification, design, quality and time of delivery. Also, all the profits from manufacture go to the producer and not an outside company. However, external suppliers normally produce far more units than those delivered to individual purchasing companies, and thus may experience substantial economies of scale (and in consequence lower costs and supply prices).

16. Centralised versus decentralised purchasing procedures

In a decentralised system, each department is responsible for obtaining its own supplies. The method is quick and convenient but does not allow bulk purchases; and higher prices may be paid through ignorance of alternative sources. Centralised procedures enable the employment of specialised buying staff who can pinpoint the best available products, prices, and the quickest delivery periods. Also, economies of scale in administrative processes may be available in centralised systems. Further advantages of centralisation are as follows:

(a) Standard contracts, forms and clerical procedures can be applied to all purchase transactions.

(b) Suppliers may be willing to offer low prices in order to secure a large order from a central purchasing department.

(c) It enables the implementation of 'just-in-time' purchasing systems (*see* 23).

(d) The purchasing department can establish long-term relationships with supplying firms and encourage suppliers to improve the quality of their products.

(e) Purchasing, stock and work-in-progress control systems can be fully integrated.

17. Purchasing policies

Supplies can be obtained in a number of ways, including:

(a) *Purchase by contract.* Here, contracts are issued to certain firms to supply all requirements for specific goods for predetermined periods (one year, for example). This enables the purchasing firm to avoid carrying large amounts of stock, provided deliveries are steady and reliable. Contracts bear fixed prices, so the firm cannot seek cheaper sources while existing contracts are in force. The method is suitable where price fluctuations are not expected.

(b) *Purchase by quotation.* With this method, every significant contract is put out for tender. The technique prevents the establishment of long-term relationships with suppliers who, in the course of time, might be willing to offer special discounts to a major customer.

(c) *Speculative purchasing.* If input prices fluctuate significantly, large-scale purchases when prices are exceptionally low might be worthwhile. Note that surplus stock might be sold on the open market at a profit when market prices increase. Additional stockholding costs are incurred with this method.

18. Stock levels

The variables affecting how much inventory a firm should hold include rates of stock usage, time lags between placing orders and their delivery, warehousing costs, and natural deterioration of materials held for long periods. Also relevant are the interest payments or profits forgone through holding stock instead of other investments, and the clerical and other administrative costs of placing orders for stock replenishment.

Stock ties up working capital. Thus, a business should hold the minimum stock of raw materials, work-in-progress and finished goods that it possibly can – subject of course to being able to meet the needs of user departments and final customers. This fact accounts for the introduction of 'just-in-time' inventory management systems (*see* **20**) in many companies.

19. ABC analysis

ABC analysis is the process of classifying items (stock items, defective products, customers, salespeople, etc) into three distinct categories, A, B and C. Class A items are those which are the most important, e.g. if 15 per cent of a firm's inputs account for 70 per cent of its inventories, or if 10 per cent of a salesforce accounts for the great bulk of sales. Class B items are fairly important. Class C is for unimportant items – which may be numerous but which collectively have little effect. The aim is to identify the crucial A items and apply appropriate policies, which normally will be different from policies relevant for categories B and C. For example, if (say) 5 per cent of inventory items account for 80 per cent of aggregate inventory value then great care should be devoted to the purchase, delivery and scheduling of these goods.

JUST-IN-TIME METHODS

20. Just-in-time (JIT) procedures

To operate a 'just-in-time' production control system, work is planned so that each production unit delivers to the next unit precisely the input it requires in order to proceed with the next stage of manufacture (or processing) and delivers the input just in time for the work to begin. In consequence, few if any stocks of inputs are carried, and there is no bunching of production lines or queues anywhere in the system.

Production workers themselves are expected to operate the system, which – if it succeeds – will result in the need to carry much less work in progress than before (sometimes as much as four times less than previously). Each worker assumes personal responsibility for quality and production control. Workers are organised into 'cells' which organise their own work and are put in charge of the repair and maintenance of the equipment they use, of quality control, and the timing of movements of work from one cell to another. Hence they acquire much experience of operational decision making and routine production control.

21. Requirements of JIT systems

The method requires precise scheduling of raw materials procurement, production processing and despatch. And there has to be a predictable daily demand throughout the entire sequence of manufacture, with minimal change over time and extremely reliable equipment. Moreover, successful application of JIT methods implies the need to simplify products and rationalise product lines to avoid having to carry numerous different components and other input stocks. Further prerequisites for an effective JIT system include:

(a) High standards of equipment maintenance to prevent breakdowns, plus immediate attention to machine failures that do occur

(b) Flexible and well-trained operatives capable of undertaking work anywhere currently required

(c) An efficient monitoring scheme for identifying problems as they arise.

22. Kanban systems

Kanban is the Japanese word for 'card'. Japanese factories adopted the practice of having production units indicate their need for supplies by passing a card to the preceding workstation. Although cards are no longer used, the essentials of the system remain, with perhaps a flag or empty space on a floor indicating the need for fresh supplies. The system requires that each section take just a few hours' worth of work in progress at a time, hence reducing average inventory. Sections pass on to the next stage in production *precisely* the amount requested and no more. Hence there are many set-ups for production runs and the minimisation of set-up time is a key requirement for the success of a Kanban system.

23. Just-in-time purchasing

This rests on the philosophy of frequent, regular, small deliveries combined with long-term contracts with supplying firms. Hence, purchasing staff spend little time looking for the best deal for each order and instead devote their attention to helping suppliers improve the design and quality of inputs.

24. Autonomation

The term *autonomation* is used to describe the 'autonomous control' of defective production. Clearly, JIT systems collapse if defective items are transferred between units. Hence, automatic stopping mechanisms (mechanical or simply the observation by a worker that something is abnormal) are built into production/assembly lines to prevent large outputs of defective goods.

25. Materials requirements planning (MRP)

This means scheduling the manufacture of dependent items (components, sub-assemblies and so on) that have varying lead times and inventory requirements, in order to satisfy customers' orders on time but with minimum holdings of work-in-progress stocks. MRP synchronises the ordering and delivery of manufacturing processes. It requires accurate forecasting of the demand for the final products and precise timetabling of activities. Sophisticated versions of such (computerised) systems are called 'manufacturing resource planning' methods. These integrate MRP with the total management information system (*see* 13:6) of the firm.

DESIGN AND STANDARDISATION

26. Standardisation

Benefits resulting from the standardisation of products include possibilities for longer production runs, lower manufacturing and packaging costs, easier movement of goods and cheaper stockholding (since fewer types of component need be held). Component parts become interchangeable and can be used for several purposes. Other advantages include:

(a) Fuller use of existing machines and labour, easier work planning and scheduling

(b) Quicker inspection, better quality control

(c) More specialisation and division of labour

(d) Simplification of clerical records.

Note, however, that product standardisation may be highly undesirable from a marketing point of view.

27. Value analysis

This is a technique for reducing production costs through the systematic study of the *function* of a manufactured item. In this context, the function of a product is the characteristic that makes it operate properly (e.g. lift a weight, transport an item, heat a room, or whatever). Production engineers ask the question 'what is this item intended to do?' and then ask 'is there a cheaper way of achieving this purpose?' The consequence of the analysis might be the abandonment of a particular component and its replacement with a cheaper substitute, or its redesign, or a change in the process of manufacture.

Products consisting of many components are more likely to benefit from value analysis than single-unit items, since multicomponent products offer greater scope for cost reduction through removal of unnecessary functions. Typically the value analyst will look for improvements or financial saving in areas such as product reliability, ease of maintenance, combination of functions, packaging and cost of installation. Techniques for achieving this include:

(a) Finding *additional* uses for components

(b) *Adapting* items to satisfy further requirements

(c) *Augmenting* components to extend their range of application

(d) *Reducing* the contents of an item (less packaging, for instance)

(e) *Combining* inputs.

28. Design

Two considerations determine a product's design: the need for efficiency in manufacture and its appeal to customers. The design process can be broken down into sections:

(a) Specification of the function of the product

(b) Determination of consumer tastes and preferences

(c) Assessment of materials required

(d) Evaluation of available alternatives.

Designers can control many variables: quality of the finished product, machining tolerances, processing time and aesthetic properties. Equally, however, they are constrained by several restrictions, including cost limits, non-availability of certain materials, market acceptability of the resulting product and technical manufacturing requirements. A good design will:

(a) minimise materials and labour inputs

(b) maximise the efficiency of production

(c) reduce machining and processing expenses

(d) be functional, yet attractive to customers.

29. Computer-aided design

Computer-aided design (CAD) is an increasingly common feature of design processes. It offers vastly improved control over images, showing three-dimensional objects in perspective and allowing the elongation and/or rotation of lines about a selected axis. This saves the designer enormous amounts of time when investigating alternative design structures. Also, modern CAD programs incorporate facilities for performing calculations on stored data. Hence, weights, volumes, surface areas, etc can be computed for numerous design possibilities and their effects on production cost instantly determined.

30. CADCAM

Computer-aided design and computer-assisted manufacture (CADCAM) techniques involve not only design and manufacture but also testing, inspection, assembly, packaging and despatch. All processes are fully integrated, with raw materials inputs, machining specifications, workshop instructions, tolerances, etc being generated from initial design input data. CADCAM originated with the automation of production lines and associated measurement and analysis of machine tool movements. As firms with automated production acquired computing facilities they began to create data files recording all known machine tool movements and their effects. Special programs were then written to quantify and control production line work.

With CADCAM, information is transmitted instantly between design machining and assembly stages of production. Since there are no time delays or intervening agents there are few possibilities for breakdowns in communication, misunderstandings or misinterpretation between departments. Integrated computerised systems require fewer staff and are faster, more reliable and more accurate than those based on manual labour. Duplication of effort is avoided and costs are reduced. Control of a CADCAM system does not rely on periodical data collection. Information on activity at any given moment in time is available, and the implications of particular events can be immediately assessed. Recent versions of CADCAM systems are sometimes referred to as 'computer-integrated manufacture' (CIM).

QUALITY MANAGEMENT

31. Definition of quality

The term 'high quality' is meaningless without a yardstick against which the words 'high' or 'low' may be assessed. Indeed, 'quality' can mean different things to different people, including:

(a) how well an item satisfies a customer's particular requirements

(b) quantity in relation to price

(c) product reliability and longevity

(d) technical features

(e) range of characteristics

(f) aesthetic appeal

(g) how closely a manufactured product adheres to a design specification

(h) an item's fitness for the purpose for which it is intended.

It follows that the concept of quality needs to be carefully defined in each given situation. A cheap and mass-produced disposable item can be of exceptionally good quality provided it does its job. Accordingly, it is conventional to distinguish two aspects of quality, namely:

(a) *Conformance quality*, i.e. the degree to which an item satisfies its technical specification

(b) *Design quality*, i.e. all the attributes that customers perceive as contributing to the worth of the product.

32. Inspection and statistical quality control

Substandard production results from random variations in processes, or from systematic deficiencies which can be due to operator or management inadequacy or to environmental problems.

Statistical quality control seeks to identify defective production that has been created by assignable deficiencies in materials, equipment or working systems and to distinguish this output from defectives which result from chance. Thus, inspection staff might select random samples of output, compute the probability that each sample will in normal circumstances contain less than a certain number of defectives (e.g. that no more than five in a hundred items should be defective), and interfere with the production process only if the number of defective items in the samples inspected exceeds the predetermined limit. The aim is to ensure that items do not pass to the next stage in the production process if an unacceptably high proportion of them are substandard.

33. Centralised versus decentralised inspection

Inspection can be centralised or decentralised. With centralised inspection, goods are sent to a central testing department containing specialised test equipment and its own administrative staff. There is easy supervision of testing procedures, but there is also the need to transport goods to the central inspection area. Handling costs increase, and there are risks of damage while goods are in transit.

Decentralised (floor) inspection, conversely, involves inspectors testing materials *in situ* as they are received or produced. Problems can be identified where and when they occur. Inspectors, departmental supervisors and operatives meet regularly; quality difficulties are discussed; work flows are not interrupted. Floor inspection is best for heavy or bulky items or where output from one process is needed quickly for input to another. Central inspection is appropriate if the equipment used in testing is itself heavy or otherwise immobile. It is often the case that really accurate measurement is possible only if sophisticated testing apparatus that cannot be moved from the test area is used.

34. Contemporary approaches to quality management

The modern approach to quality management is to regard production and inspection not as independent functions but rather as integral and interrelated components of the total quality system, with operatives *themselves* assuming responsibility for quality control. Excellence is taken for granted, so that independent inspections are seen not as a means for improving quality, but as an insult to the firm's workers.

Similar concepts can be applied to the purchase of outside supplies. Indeed, it is arguable that the very act of laying down precise acceptance criteria itself implies that some defective input is acceptable provided certain predetermined minimum standards are satisfied. In this case inspection becomes a *source* of low quality!

35. Quality assurance (QA)

Quality assurance concerns the total system needed to assure customers that certain minimum quality standards will be met within the supplying firm. Formal QA standards have been drafted by various bodies (including the British Standards Institution's BS 5750) which specify that supplying firms implement definite procedures for ensuring that appropriate 'quality environments' are maintained, e.g. that the tools used on certain jobs be of a particular type, and that only qualified and certificated staff be employed on certain projects. Often, QA is implemented through checklists issued to various departments asking them to scrutinise their procedures and confirm that certain measures have been undertaken. Typically, a checklist question will ask, 'What have you done to ensure that . . .?', and then ask the respondent to detail the measures applied.

A QA system might invite supplying firms to improve as well as provide contracted items, and to initiate themselves alterations in the appearance, design or durability of requisitioned products. The quality of a good involves its fitness for the purpose for which it is intended as well as its physical conditions on despatch. Suppliers need therefore to know the purposes of the articles they are invited to produce, and the operational circumstances of their use. Hence, a clear statement of purpose – leaving technical details (including perhaps the choice of input materials) to the discretion of the supplying firm – might have greater long-term value than precise and detailed specifications of weights, sizes, machine tolerances, etc.

ISO 9000

BS 5750 is the UK version of the international quality assurance standard ISO 9000, which itself is based in large part on BS 5750. The latter is a detailed and extensive document with several parts and appendices. It requires the supplier to demonstrate its ability to design and supply products in predetermined ways.

Apart from design procedures, the specification covers the supplier's own procurement systems: its inspection and testing methods, the means by which customers may verify its claimed quality systems, how customers can check the supplier's records and other documents relating to quality procedures and how customers may confirm the nature and extent of quality-related training given to the supplier's staff. The aim of BS 5750 is to provide suppliers with a means for obtaining BSI certificated approval that their quality management systems are up to scratch. Customers may then have confidence in a company's ability (*i*) to deliver goods of a prespecified quality and (*ii*) to maintain the quality of its output at a consistent level. This should increase the saleability of the firm's outputs. Further advantages to BS 5750 certification are that it:

- demonstrates the company's commitment to quality
- requires the standardisation of quality procedures throughout the organisation
- facilitates the identification of problem areas
- improves the image of the firm
- may increase operational efficiency
- leads to greater awareness of customer needs
- can cause staff to be better motivated.

Problems with BS 5750 include the following:

(a) The financial cost to a business of altering its (perhaps perfectly reasonable) quality control methods to meet BS 5750 may be colossal in relation to the overall improvement in quality that results.

(b) So called 'consultants' may attest that, in their opinion, certain firms within which they have installed QA systems now satisfy BS 5750 standards, and issue documents to that effect. Unsuspecting members of the public might confuse such attestation with that formally recognised by BSI.

(c) Firms seeking BS 5750 accreditation themselves determine the level of quality of output. BS 5750 applies to the procedures for maintaining a certain quality level, even if the quality of the final output is intentionally low.

(d) Maintenance of a new system based on BS 5750 can be expensive and time consuming.

(e) Procedures might become bureaucratic and inflexible.

(f) Staff affected by implementation may react negatively to change.

TOTAL QUALITY MANAGEMENT (TQM)

Total quality management (TQM) means the implementation of strategies, tactics and operational methods for integrating practical quality control techniques (statistical quality control, inspection, QA, etc) with organisational cultures conducive to the continuous improvement of quality. It focuses on the totality of the system rather than its individual parts, seeking to identify the causes of failure rather than the simple fact that failures have occurred. Causes of failure could involve cultural inadequacies, poor teamwork, bad leadership, lack of individual commitment and motivation, and other psycho-social problems as well as technical operator and/or equipment inadequacies.

36. Implications of TQM for employee relations

TQM has implications for employee relations because (along with JIT) it demands a far higher standard of management than previously and, critically, a style of management that evokes full and committed cooperation from labour.

TQM requires from *management*:

- Commitment to the provision of long-term security of employment for workers
- Provision of training to enable employees to complete a multiplicity of tasks
- Trust in workers' abilities to deal with quality issues
- Day-to-day involvement and face-to-face communication with the workforce.

It requires from *employees*:

- Acceptance of collective responsibility for the success of the business
- Flexible attitudes and a willingness to undertake a wide range of duties
- Willingness to contribute to problem-solving.

Further implications of TQM are that:

- Even the totally unskilled worker requires training, i.e. instruction in the need for quality and how the organisation is seeking to achieve it.
- Employees working in different departments need to know about each others' problems.
- Piece rate wage payment systems are to be avoided, as they encourage the production of substandard output.

37. Implementation of TQM

Typically the steps involved in implementing a total quality management system are as follows:

(a) Senior management itself becomes fully aware of the concepts and techniques of quality management.

(b) Steering committees are formed and pilot projects identified.

(c) *All* employees are introduced to the basics of TQM and informed of top management's commitment.

(d) Training programmes are devised and effected.

(e) Suppliers are brought into the company's TQM planning.

(f) New methods relating to continuous improvement, prevention of defective output, reduction in variation, etc, are introduced.

(g) The system is monitored and audited.

Clearly, the above demand that employees be intimately involved in the implementation process and that their knowledge and capabilities be respected.

In particular, employees need to be recognised as **(a)** problem solvers, **(b)** the people who actually implement solutions, and **(c)** improvers of current working methods. TQM also requires first class leadership, with managers who are able to instil a sense of purpose and commitment to TQM procedures. Employees simply cannot be passive bystanders in the TQM process.

Policy requirements for involving employees in TQM include the following:

(a) Management should consciously regard employees as if they were the firm's customers. Hence, management must attempt to discover employees' needs, perspectives and situations. Managers become mentors and facilitators rather than authority figures.

(b) Managers need to regard basic-grade workers as having valuable contributions to make to the quality management process. This may require a sea-change in attitude in some enterprises.

(c) Workers have to be educated to believe that they *should* seek continuously to improve working practices. This means convincing the workforce that employee suggestions and contributions are highly valued.

(d) Each worker needs to be shown how his or her actions affect the attainment of the firm's quality objectives.

Effective implementation of TQM requires:

- Integration of genuine concern for quality into the culture of the *entire* enterprise (not just parts of it)
- The design of business systems to reinforce the quality philosophy
- The constant search for new and better ways of doing things
- Research into quality issues in relation to existing products as well as research connected with product innovation
- Incorporation of quality targets into strategic objectives
- Commitment from top management
- Flexible employee attitudes towards the acceptance of change.

38. Quality Circles

A Quality Circle is a departmental workers' discussion group that meets regularly to consider, analyse, investigate and resolve production and quality problems. The group is trained in problem solving technique and, importantly, is given resources and (limited) authority to implement decisions. Circles concentrate on mundane, practical (rather than organisational) problems, and solve them using ideas and methods developed by the workers themselves. Advantages of Quality Circles include possible higher motivation of employees as they become involved in company decision taking, and the application of workers' experiences, knowledge and operational skills to the solution of problems. And since Circle decisions are taken by those responsible for their implication they are almost certain to be carried out.

Problems with Quality Circles include feelings of apathy as the novelty of the experience begins to fade, perceptions among workers that they are undertaking managerial responsibilities without managerial pay, and frustration at not being able to discuss wider company policies. Frictions may arise within the group over how best to tackle particular difficulties.

Kaizen systems are more extensive than Quality Circles. They seek to achieve *continual improvement* in processes through the direct involvement of workers in a cycle of 'planning, doing, checking and actioning'. Accordingly, Kaizen systems are regarded as an integral part of company operations overall, concerned not just with operational problem solving but also with suggesting improvements to all aspects of working life.

39. Taguchi methods

Genichi Taguchi is a Japanese expert on quality management whose approach to the subject has profoundly influenced contemporary thinking about quality issues. Poor quality, he argues, imposes several 'costs' on society, including customer dissatisfaction, unreliability, product repair and replacement costs, the need for inspection, loss of customer goodwill and, in consequence, reductions in market share. He concludes that losses can be minimised through the following policies:

(a) Paying *less* attention to measuring deviations from specification, and *more* attention to analysing and removing factors that cause variability in output.

(b) 'Off-line quality control', i.e. designing goods so they can be produced with the minimum item-to-item variation in the product and its performance.

(c) Experimentation to determine the critical product parameters that generate variability in production.

(d) Clear identification of controllable quality variables (material inputs, machining tolerances and so on) as opposed to those beyond the manufacturer's command. The latter variables are referred to as 'noise'!

INDUSTRIAL ENGINEERING

40. Nature of industrial engineering

The term 'industrial engineering' refers to those aspects of operations management which seek to improve the quantity and speed of production. Industrial engineering covers the following activities:

(a) *Work study*, which consists of 'method study' (*see* 42) to eliminate unnecessary tasks and avoid the duplication of effort, and 'work measurement' (*see* 43), i.e. the assessment of the times needed to complete tasks (including relaxation and contingency requirements).

(b) *Motion study*, concerning the analysis of fatigue caused by human body motions and the positioning of tools and control panels.

(c) *Ergonomics*, i.e. the improvement of the relationship between the employee and the working environment. Practical applications include workplace layout, lighting, heating and ventilation, acoustics, design of instruments and controls, and design of office furniture.

(d) *Factory layout.* Machinery and equipment can be arranged by product or process. Product layout involves grouping together in one location all the equipment needed to manufacture an item from start to finish. The close proximity of different stages in the production process cuts waiting time between processes, reduces material-handling costs, and quickly identifies production-line breakdowns. Process layout places alongside each other machines and equipment concerned with a certain type of work. Skills develop within specialised areas, and labour trained on one machine can quickly be put on to others when breakdowns occur. The term *group technology* is used to describe the practice of arranging processes, products or equipment into related 'families' in order to minimise the distances that materials and operatives must travel to fulfil their functions. Criteria for defining groups might involve similarities in size or shape of manufactured items; in product attributes; in machining requirements; or in the workforce skills needed to produce various types of output.

41. Advantages and problems of industrial engineering

Advantages of industrial engineering include better use of resources, fewer wasted materials, less handling of components, smoother production flows and lower costs of labour.

Problems typically arise from the human side of the implementation of exercises, notably:

(a) Fear of redundancy among employees

(b) Line managers resenting the contributions of industrial engineering analysts, whom they may perceive as a threat to their authority

(c) Group resistance to change (*see* 15:**12–14**)

(d) Communication breakdowns between managers and workers (*see* Chapter 12)

(e) Possible lack of consultation with employees over changes in working practices

(f) Inadequate procedures for resolving disputes and grievances (*see* Chapter 16)

(g) Imprecise objectives for industrial engineering projects.

42. Method study

Method study aims to improve working practices. A common approach to method study problems has emerged, known as the 'six-step' procedure. The steps are as follows:

1. Selection of tasks for the study – specification of the objectives of the exercise and careful definition of the nature of the problem that has to be solved.
2. Recording of methods currently in use – analysis of shortcomings of the existing system and tabulation of current procedures.
3. Examination of methods – resolution of the work studied into its constituent parts, identification of duplicated efforts and potential simplifications and elimination of unnecessary tasks or combination of tasks.
4. Development of new and better ways of doing work – deciding which procedures to keep and which to abandon, as well as improving current practices.
5. Installation of new methods – consultation with interested parties and alignment of new methods with the overall management structure of the firm.
6. Maintenance of the new system – monitoring results, keeping records and comparing results with previous performance.

43. Work measurement

Work measurement is the systematic and detailed study of operations and movements in work situations. The aim is to establish how long jobs should take in normal circumstances, allowing for the need for rest between activities. These 'standard' times then become yardsticks against which actual performance can be assessed.

In measuring work, management is usually concerned with estimating the times needed by competent, experienced workers for completion of specific tasks at predetermined levels of performance. The International Labour Office (ILO) has a 'rating standard' centred on a performance level of 100 for brisk activity by an average experienced worker on piecework; and ranging from level 50 for slow, clumsy work to a maximum 150 for outstanding performance requiring intense effort and concentration. Many problems are associated with the timing of workers, for example:

(a) Different people need varying periods to complete identical tasks, depending on their skills and experiences.

(b) It would be unfair to use times achieved by outstandingly proficient workers as standards for everyone else.

(c) Workers who know they are being observed are liable to slow down.

The latter difficulty has caused time study officers to apply ratings when measuring workers' efforts. Ratings are subjective assessments of workers' performances. Normal working speed is rated at level 100 in accordance with the previously mentioned ILO scale whereas ratings on workers suspected of going slow are adjusted downwards. Observed times are multiplied by ratings to derive 'basic' times on which workers' remuneration depends.

44. Organisation and methods (O&M)

This is the application of work study to clerical administrative procedures: form design, office layout and planning, document creation and retrieval, and the efficient use of office machines. The aims are to simplify work, avoid duplicated effort, eliminate unnecessary paperwork, and generally speed the flow of documents within an organisation. Achieving these objectives might involve the detailed study of organisation charts, updating job descriptions, preparing flowcharts, and revising work manuals. O&M exercises typically proceed through asking the following questions:

(a) What presently is being done?

(b) What is the purpose of the activity?

(c) Who performs each operation and can the work be deskilled?

(d) Where and when are operations performed?

(e) How are operations completed?

Then, flowcharts are drafted to show the movements of documents between workstations and to record the work done at each point in the flow. Careful study of a flowchart can reveal unnecessary delays, bottlenecks, sources of error and duplication of activities. In consequence, new procedures can be introduced with improved communication between departments, tighter management control, fewer documents, fewer errors and more even flow of work.

45. Office organisation

Offices have three purposes: they are places of work, social environments and representations of the firm's corporate image to the outside world. As places of work, offices are centres of administrative activity, concerned particularly with the acquisition, recording, analysis and distribution of information. Office services may be centralised or decentralised. The former involves grouping together office staff into large central units that service individual sections. Supervision is easier and communications are simplified. In a decentralised system, conversely, departmental managers can control and directly monitor all clerical work done for them. Moreover, clerical workers employed in specific functional departments become familiar with the particular requirements of those departments.

46. Re-engineering

This means the radical redesign of business processes, normally via the use of the latest information technology, in order to enhance their performance. Conventional approaches to efficiency improvement sometimes fail because they focus on automating and speeding up existing systems and processes, merely perpetuating old ways of performing operations rather than addressing fundamental deficiencies and replacing out-of-date systems as a whole. Often, moreover, firms seeking efficiency gains do little more than tinker with the prevailing organisation structure in the naive belief that this alone will lead to the desired result. Problems with simple organisation restructuring are:

(a) The revised structure is likely to become out-of-date very soon after it is implemented.

(b) Frequent alterations in company structure destabilises the organisation and demoralises workers.

(c) Existing employees are likely to be thrust into new and unfamiliar roles for which they lack experience and/or training.

(d) Significant time periods are needed for people to adjust to each restructuring.

Re-engineering, conversely, involves challenging underlying assumptions and changing the basic rules and philosophies concerning the ways a business is managed. Examples of re-engineering include:

- Abolition of job descriptions and departmental boundaries
- Widespread use of empowerment (*see* 15:27)
- Integration of a large number of operations
- Finding new ways of achieving specific outcomes
- Creating organisation structures based on desired results rather than the functional duties needed to attain them, e.g. by having one person overseeing several types of task and assuming full responsibility for reaching a specific objective
- Involving users of the outputs to processes in the design and execution of those processes. For example. departments that work on raw materials could be made partially responsible for selecting and controlling suppliers of the raw materials.
- Centralisation of control procedures using computers
- Having decisions taken on the spot. where work is performed. Note how this implies the removal of some layers in the management hierarchy and hence a 'flattening' of the organisation.

Typically, business process re-engineering attempts to simplify radically the basic low-level operations of a company (e.g. all the operations that go into satisfying a customer order). This could involve collapsing departmental boundaries, integrating computerised management systems, shortening lines of communication and removing marginally useful procedures.

PAYMENTS METHODS

47. Remuneration systems

The purpose of a remuneration system is to attract, retain and motivate good calibre workers. To achieve this, a system should:

(a) be mutually acceptable to management and employees

(b) be clear, understandable and simple to operate

(c) relate wages to the quantity and quality of work done

(d) offer a guaranteed minimum below which income cannot fall

(e) not confront the worker with unattainable objectives in order to earn a reasonable wage

(f) be cheap to operate and not absorb excessive amounts of clerical time

(g) not present the firm with unexpectedly overlarge wage bills

(h) enable beginners and the less competent to earn reasonable amounts

(i) not result in too many overlapping grades and differentials.

Note, however, that wage levels are ultimately determined by the supply and demand for labour. Any system will fail if it does not recognise this fundamental reality.

48. Time rates

Time rate systems pay workers a predetermined wage per period (hour, day, week or month) regardless of how much they produce. Earnings are steady and predictable. The system is cheap and simple to administer. Time rates are particularly suitable where excessive working speed could produce accidents. Successful application of time rates requires uninterrupted workflows, and implicit agreement by employees to work reasonably hard. A possible disadvantage of time rates is lack of incentive, thus necessitating close and detailed supervision.

49. Piece rates

Here workers are paid according to how much they produce regardless of the time taken. This provides employees with incentives and reduces the need for detailed supervision. Workers determine their own earnings and are encouraged to initiate improvements in work techniques. However, output quality could diminish and accidents may result from employees working too quickly. Since wage payments are determined by workers themselves, the firm will experience an uneven distribution of wage costs through an accounting year depending on how much work employees decide to do at various times.

Measured day work is an alternative to straight piece work. It is a fixed-time rate system, based on work study (*see* 43), where expected standards of performance are determined by work measurement techniques. Instead of receiving so much per item the worker is required to produce a certain number of items per week (say), for which he or she is paid a predetermined fixed weekly wage.

50. Bonus schemes

Bonus systems seek to stimulate effort and output, but are unlikely to succeed unless:

(a) work can be measured

(b) the pace of work is subject to control by the worker

(c) labour is a major and vital component of the production process

(d) workers do not experience delays caused by factors beyond their control, including poor performance by other employees.

51. Profit sharing

Profit-sharing schemes supplement employees' wages with extra payments according to profits earned in previous trading periods. Profits are shared among workers according to their basic wage, length of service, or some other criterion. The aim is to encourage loyalty and long-term commitment to the company. Problems with profit sharing are that:

(a) Payments are not immediately connected to individual effort.

(b) Intervals between profit distributions are usually quite long, so workers may not be able to relate the amounts they receive with work done during the preceding period.

(c) If profit shares are paid in the form of equities in the business the recipients may resent being expected to finance the business as well as work for it as employees!

Progress test 10

1. State three major characteristics of production departments which make them different from other types of functional business department.

2. Define the following: (a) job production, (b) operations planning, (c) Kaizen system.

3. Outline briefly the work of a typical design department.

4. List the advantages of centralised inspection procedures.

5. What are the major factors likely to cause the failure of a Quality Circle?

6. State the disadvantages of piece-rate payments systems.

11

LEGAL ASPECTS OF MANAGEMENT

FUNDAMENTALS

1. Sources of law

'Common law' is law that has existed for as long as society can remember. It was originally based on custom but through the centuries became unified via recorded court decisions. 'Statute law' is law made by Parliament. This can itself give rise to legal disputes over the meaning of words and phrases contained in statutes, and the courts may be called upon to determine the correct interpretation.

There are important differences between 'criminal' and 'civil' law. A crime is a wrong that is followed by *criminal* proceedings, after which the wrongdoer is punished by fine or imprisonment. Criminal proceedings involve a 'prosecutor' and an 'accused' person. *Civil* wrongs (e.g. breaches of contracts or torts – *see* below) are followed by civil litigation through which one party, the 'plaintiff', seeks a court decision against a defendant. The former is said to 'sue' the latter for damages; there is no question of police, fines or imprisonment being involved. The situation is merely that of a disagreement between individuals which has to be resolved by a court which acts as an impartial outsider.

2. European Union law

This is binding on all EU member states, including Britain. There are three types of legislative measure:

(a) *Regulations*, which are laws that apply immediately and equally in all member states.

(b) *Directives*. These specify a necessary outcome (e.g. to achieve equal pay for work of equal value done by men and women) but allow the government of each member country to introduce its own particular legislation to achieve the desired objective. Every Directive states a time period within which member states must attain the result required by the Directive. If this does not occur within the designated period an individual may seek to enforce the Directive through his or her national courts.

(c) *Decisions* of the European Court of Justice. These have the same effect as Regulations.

Additionally, the European Commission issues *Recommendations* which are not legally binding, but express the Commission's considered opinions about how certain matters should be treated.

Commission *Notices* are also important, especially in relation to competition law. These are pronouncements of the European Commission on various matters, such as:

- the legality or otherwise of exclusive dealing contracts with commercial agents
- co-operative joint ventures
- the activities of motor vehicle intermediaries
- exclusive purchasing and distribution agreements

Although a Notice can be withdrawn, and despite the fact that the Commission is not legally bound by the terms of a Notice it has issued, it is unlikely that the Commission could fine a company in relation to a restrictive agreement covered by a Notice.

3. Contract and tort

Apart from breaches of statutory obligations, the main causes of legal difficulty in business arise from 'torts' and disputes over contracts. A 'contract' is an agreement between two or more people which is intended by them to have legal consequences. For a contract to exist it must possess the following essentials:

(a) An offer by one party and acceptance by at least one other

(b) The intention to create legal relations

(c) 'Consideration' (a return promise, e.g. to pay money for goods), or 'form' such as a written deed specifying each party's rights and obligations

(d) Each party must have the capacity to contract (e.g. a promise by a five year old child to purchase a Rolls Royce motor car has no legal standing)

(e) Consent to the terms of the agreement

(f) The agreement must be legal and be technically capable of being completed.

Contracts need not be in writing. For details of contract and other aspects of business law see the M&E text *Business Law*, by P.W.D. Redmond and R.G. Lawson.

Torts

A tort is a 'civil wrong' (rather than a 'crime' for which a person can be prosecuted) which is not a breach of contract and the remedy for which is a claim for damages or a court injunction compelling someone to do or cease doing something. Negligence (*see* **32**) is a commonly alleged business tort. Libel and slander are other examples.

4. Laws affecting business management

Apart from the general laws of contract, tort, and statutory provisions relating to company formation and other forms of business ownership (*see* Chapter 3), the main laws that affect management are laws that seek to protect consumers (including laws on fair competition), laws protecting employees, laws relating to credit, the law of agency, industrial relations laws and the law of negligence.

CONSUMER PROTECTION

5. Misrepresentation and the sale of goods

Under the Sale and Supply of Goods Act 1994, goods sold to customers must be of 'satisfactory quality' in relation to fitness for purpose, appearance and finish, freedom from minor defects, and safety and durability. If the goods on offer are defective then defects must be pointed out or be clearly visible at the time of sale. A supplying firm is not lawfully able to impose a condition on a sale saying that the supplier does not accept responsibility for the goods' quality, suitability or delivery as required by the Act.

Where goods are delivered to a buyer who has not previously examined them, the buyer must be given a reasonable opportunity to inspect the item(s) prior to their acceptance The Act defines goods of 'satisfactory quality' as those meeting the standard that a reasonable person would regard as satisfactory taking account of the supplier's description of the goods, the price, and all other relevant circumstances.

The Misrepresentation Act 1967 sought to prevent retailers making false statements about merchandise prior to its sale. Anyone who has been misled can apply, under the Act, for compensation equal to the value of the loss incurred through relying on false information. Misrepresentation may occur innocently or fraudulently. The former involves statements that are genuinely believed to be true. Fraudulent misrepresentation involves false statements which are recklessly or knowingly given. Sellers are assumed to possess expert knowledge about the quality and features of the goods they supply.

6. Miscellaneous consumer legislation

The Unfair Contract Terms Act 1977 deals with the use of disclaimers and exemption clauses, restricting them to certain specified circumstances. Thus a notice displayed by (say) a supermarket containing the general statement 'anyone who enters these premises does so at their own risk' has no legal validity because such a statement seeks to avoid responsibility for death or injury to employees or customers that might arise through the firm's negligence, failure to implement statutory conditions, or other fault.

The Supply of Goods and Services Act 1982 codifies consumers' rights in contracts that involve not only supply of goods but also their installation. In consequence of the Act, the services (such as installation) supplied with physical goods must be carried out with reasonable skill and care to ensure that the goods supplied fulfil the purpose for which they are intended, and the services must be completed within a reasonable time. Under the Weights and Measures Act 1985 it is a criminal offence for suppliers not to specify the quantities of most prepacked goods on the packet, tin or bottle in which they are contained.

7. The Data Protection Act 1984

This Act is intended to regulate the use of personal data. It covers information stored in mainframe, mini- and micro-computers, wordprocessors, punched-card systems or any other automatic data retrieval mechanism. 'Personal' data is defined as information which relates to living people who can be identified from that information. Sole traders are regarded as living individuals, but companies are not. Holders of personal data (including customer accounts, staff records, details of clients) must register with the Data Protection Registrar and provide brief details of why the data is held and to whom it may be disclosed.

An important feature of the Act is its provision that the people on whom information is collected may request from data holders details of the information held on them, and that inaccurate information be removed or corrected.

8. The Consumer Protection Act 1987

This abandoned the need for plaintiffs to prove the supplier's negligence when pursuing defective product claims. However, the Act does not go as far as to render suppliers absolutely responsible for defects in their products. Instead, a supplier is generally liable, but not if he or she can demonstrate that the 'state of scientific and technical knowledge' at the time the product went into circulation was *not* such that a supplier could be reasonably expected to have known about the defect the product contains.

Under the Act, a 'producer' is not only the manufacturer of a finished article, or its raw materials (or the extractor of raw materials) or the manufacturer of component parts, but may also include any firm or person who imports, processes, distributes or otherwise supplies (e.g. by hiring or lending) the product. A 'product' is defined as any good (including electricity) or part of another good or raw material. Producers are liable for their products, as is any person putting a *name, trade mark, or distinguishing mark* (such as a business logo) on the product.

Consumer safety

The Act makes it illegal not only to supply unsafe goods, but also to:

(a) possess them (e.g. by holding them in stock)

(b) provide inadequate instructions for their use thereby causing accidents

(c) fail to provide proper warning of dangerous aspects of the goods

(d) fail to apply all reasonable measures (having regard to cost and the likelihood of improvements) for improving the safety of goods.

Retailers have a special protection under the Act. They are not liable for the defective goods they sell provided:

(a) they did not know the goods were unsafe, *and*

(b) that such ignorance was reasonable in the particular circumstances.

Note that tobacco is explicitly excluded from the Act.

Other provisions

Under the Act it is a criminal offence (punishable by fine) to mislead consumers over product prices. The Act also strengthens the provisions of the Trade Descriptions Act 1968, which established the general principle that it is illegal to advertise goods in such a way as to give incorrect, misleading or false information about them.

9. The Consumer Credit Act 1974

Retail businesses that formally 'lend' money (normally at interest) to their customers, e.g. through 'budget accounts', via a finance company, credit card charge accounts, personal loan accounts, payment by instalment agreements, etc are subject to the Consumer Credit Act 1974 and thus require a licence (from the Office of Fair Trading) to grant credit. Licences are only given to 'fit people', and trading without a licence is a criminal offence. However, the licensing provisions of the Act only apply to credit agreements between certain threshold values. The Act forbids the charging of 'extortionate' interest and lays down many rules about how credit may be advertised.

Exemptions

The Act applies only to credit transactions within a certain range of values (very small and large credit agreements are excluded). Also excluded are:

(a) borrowing by limited companies

(b) mortgages

(c) accounts that must be totally cleared each month (e.g. debts accrued on an American Express card)

(d) loan arrangements involving fewer than five repayments.

Purchase agreements

If money is lent for a *specific* purpose (e.g. to buy a television set) the lender can be held equally liable with the supplier of the goods for any defects in them. This is why credit card companies such as Access or Barclaycard may be liable for the quality of the goods purchased using a credit card facility (although they are not liable for goods bought with cash drawn on a credit card).

Hire-purchase

Under the Act, a hirer has the right to terminate a hire-purchase agreement at any time once the installation charges plus half the total purchase price have been paid. If less than half the price has been paid the hirer can be required to make up the balance to 50 per cent before cancelling the agreement, or face a penalty. Hirers who settle early are entitled to a rebate on credit charges accrued under the deal.

Once one third of the purchase price has been remitted the owner cannot repossess the good without a court order. Note that these rules apply only to hire-purchase and not to credit sales.

10. Debt collecting

The law on debt collecting is governed by the Administration of Justice Act 1970 plus the precedents established by a number of test cases brought under this Act. It is illegal to use or threaten violence or even to harass unduly people who are in debt. Courts have imposed rules that it is unlawful to send several persons to collect a debt, or a person with a large dog, or to approach members of a debtor's family with threatening suggestions. Debt collectors may not pass themselves off as court officials, or threaten criminal (as opposed to civil) proceedings. It is unlawful to discuss a person's debts with his or her neighbours or to post notices about these debts in shop windows near to where the customer lives. Nor can a debt collector park a vehicle conspicuously marked 'Debt Collector' outside a customer's home.

Recovery of small debts occurs through the 'small claims procedure' of the County court, the formality of which is less than for full County court proceedings. Also, costs cannot be awarded to the winning side in a small claim action in normal circumstances (although minor administrative costs are recoverable). If a claim is successful it is up to the claimant (and not the court) to enforce the judgment. This may be done through one or more of the following methods:

(a) An *attachment of earnings order*. The court instructs the debtor's employer to pay his or her wages to the party owed the money.

(b) An *attachment of debts (garnishee) order*. Third parties who owe money to the debtor are instructed to pay these amounts direct to the court.

(c) A *warrant of execution*. The court instructs a bailiff to seize and sell sufficient of the debtor's personal assets to settle the outstanding balance.

(d) A *writ of equitable execution*. Rents and other income from land and property due to the debtor are paid to a court-appointed receiver.

(e) A *charging order*. This prevents the debtor selling land or securities until a debt has been settled.

(f) *Initiation of bankruptcy proceedings. See* 4:25.

11. Reservation of title clauses

In certain (somewhat complicated) circumstances it is possible to incorporate a clause (sometimes called a *Romalpa* clause after the court case that established the precedent in these respects) in a contract of sale whereby goods supplied to the customer remain the property of the supplying firm until they are paid for. Thus, should the customer sell the goods to a third party before reneging on the debt the supplier can approach the third party and reclaim the items, which in law still belong to the supplier.

LAWS ON COMPETITION

12. Fair trading

The Fair Trading Act 1973 established the Office of Fair Trading (OFT), the role of which is to encourage industries to devise their own codes of practice for fair treatment of customers, and to provide rulings for complaints received from the public that concern important matters of principle. For example, the OFT determined that the pre-1979 practice of newspapers and television companies only being prepared to pay commissions to advertising agencies 'recognised' by their representative trade associations was illegal. The 1973 Act also set up the *Monopolies and Mergers Commission* which is empowered to investigate mergers and any monopoly situation where at least 25 per cent of a market is controlled by a single supplier or group of suppliers.

The Restrictive Trade Practices Act 1976 required that all agreements between businesses to fix prices, regulate supplies, etc be registered with the OFT. Such agreements are presumed void unless the parties to them can prove they are beneficial to the public at large. Most UK law on restrictive practices is now subsumed into EU competition law.

13. Treaty of Rome provisions

Article 85 of the Treaty of Rome prohibits trade practices which prevent, restrict or distort competition. Agreements by firms to carve up the European market among themselves are void and thus unenforceable in the courts of member states. Article 86 prohibits firms which already occupy a dominant position in an EU market from abusing that position. A dominant position is defined as a position of economic strength which enables an enterprise to prevent effective competition by being able to operate independently of its competitors and customers. The Treaty of Rome defines the following as abuse of a dominant position:

(a) Imposition of unfair prices for purchase of raw materials or sale of final goods.

(b) Restrictions on production.

(c) Restrictions on distribution, e.g. through gaining control over the supply of raw materials and then cutting off supplies to competing businesses.

(d) Holding back technological development.

(e) Charging different prices to different customers.

Companies can be fined up to 10 per cent of their worldwide turnover for breaching EU competition law.

14. Enforcement of Articles 85 and 86

Any person or organisation suffering in consequence of a breach of Articles 85 or 86 may sue for compensation through their own country's courts. Otherwise, complaints against companies are heard by the European Commission, which can issue a formal warning and – if this is ignored – may approach the European Court and ask that fines (of up to 10 per cent of turnover) be imposed on the errant organisation.

Nevertheless, the Commission is anxious to encourage co-operation among businesses and thus will not regard as violations of Articles 85 or 86 any agreement for the following purposes:

(a) exchanges of opinion

(b) joint market research

(c) joint collection of trade and market statistics

(d) co-operation on the preparation of accounts or on matters relating to tax

(e) provision of trade credit

(f) joint-debt collecting.

15. Position of small firms

A wide range of practices common among small firms could be caught by EU competition law, notably:

(a) Exclusive dealership arrangements

(b) Joint ventures with other businesses

(c) Licensing of intellectual property rights

(d) Franchising.

Community law extends, moreover, to any 'concerted practice' that prevents, restricts or distorts competition. A concerted practice is a situation where businesses do not enter a formal agreement but where their collective actions imply collusion.

In recognition of the fact that co-operation between small firms will not distort competition appreciably, the Commission has issued a Notice on Minor Agreements exempting from Articles 85 and 86 all situations where:

(a) the goods or services covered by an agreement represent less than 5 per cent of the total market for these goods or services; *and (additionally)*

(b) the aggregate turnover of the parties to the agreement is less than a certain threshold (currently 200 million ECU).

An agreement that breaks EU competition rules is regarded in law as null and void and thus unenforceable.

16. Block exemptions

Even if the criteria outlined in **14** and **15** are not satisfied the Commission may exempt agreements that:

(a) contribute to improving the methods of producing or distributing goods or to the promotion of technical or economic progress; *and*

(b) give consumers a fair share of resulting benefits; *and*

(c) will not significantly reduce competition across the entire Single European Market.

Applications for exemption must be submitted to the Commission *unless* the following are involved in which case an automatic 'block exemption' applies and no formal application is needed (provided of course that points **(a)** to **(c)** immediately above are met):

(a) Exclusive distribution or purchasing agreements

(b) Patent and (unpatented) know-how licensing

(c) Research and development agreements

(d) Motor vehicle agreements

(e) Franchising (*see* 3:**33**).

EMPLOYMENT PROTECTION

17. Laws on employment

The most important of these is the Employment Protection (Consolidation) Act (EPCA) 1978. This covers employees who have worked continuously for at least two years. To be continuous, the employment must not contain gaps caused, say, by the worker leaving the firm and then being re-employed. Short-term contracts issued one after the other will build up continuity in the same way as a single contract for a longer term.

Under the Act, employees have the right not to be unfairly dismissed; that is, not to be dismissed for reasons other than gross misconduct, demonstrably inadequate performance, genuine redundancy, or some other *substantial* reason. In cases of genuine redundancy, employing firms must follow a statutory procedure, and some financial compensation must be offered. Firms must give adequate warning of intended redundancies and must consult with the recognised union (i.e. the union they normally deal with) before redundancies are implemented. Firms are required to seek alternative work for those threatened with redundancy, and the staff involved are entitled to paid time off work to look for other jobs. Criteria used in selecting employees for redundancy must be objective and fair.

Other important rights conferred by the EPCA 1978 include:

(a) The right to a written contract of employment within eight weeks of starting work

(b) Maternity pay for pregnant employees plus the right to reinstatement after the birth of the child (details of these matters are given in the M&E text *Human Resources Management*)

(c) Entitlement to a written statement of reasons for dismissal

(d) Minimum periods of notice, defined as one week for each year of continuous service up to a maximum of 12

(e) The right to time off for public duties, such as service as a Local Councillor, Justice of the Peace, or School Governor.

Employees who believe they have been unfairly dismissed or otherwise denied any of the rights embodied in the EPCA 1978 may complain to an industrial tribunal (*see* **19**). All complaints received by industrial tribunals are referred first to ACAS (the Advisory Conciliation and Arbitration Service), an officer of which will try to assist parties to settle the dispute through discussion and compromise. If settlement is not forthcoming, the dispute goes before a tribunal which can order the reinstatement of a dismissed employee, or compensation.

18. Laws against discrimination

The Equal Pay Act 1970 requires that men and women receive equal pay for work of equal value. All the terms and conditions of a woman's (or a man's) contract of employment must not be less favourable than that which would be issued to a member of the opposite sex. It is illegal to lay down separate rates of pay for men and women.

The Sex Discrimination Act 1975 sought to ensure that men, women and married persons be treated equally in employment situations. Thus, employers are not allowed to discriminate against women in:

(a) selection procedures

(b) terms on which employment is offered

(c) access to opportunities for training or promotion

(d) fringe benefits

(e) deciding which workers shall be made redundant.

Sex discrimination can be direct or indirect. The former means treating people unfavourably simply because of their sex; for example, segregating women employees into separate departments and paying them lower wages. Indirect discrimination occurs when an employer applies a test or condition that puts one of the sexes at an unfair advantage. An example here would be a condition that all job applicants be over six feet three inches tall for work where the employee's height is not important. There are, however, exemptions available under the Act. These relate to:

(a) employment mainly outside Great Britain

(b) employment in religious organisations that operate a sex bar

(c) employment in the armed services.

Also, jobs where sex is a 'genuine occupational qualification' are exempt. Examples would be actors playing male or female roles; jobs in single-sex schools, hospitals or other institutions; and jobs where decency or privacy require employment of a particular sex.

Since 1 January 1984, any person has been able to claim equal pay relative to a member of the opposite sex employed by the same firm who does work of *equal value*, as determined by a job evaluation study (*see* 14:7). Hence, a woman (say) need not identify a man who is doing identical work for the firm on higher wages, she merely has to demonstrate that her job is *worth* the same in terms of its 'demands'. Such demands might relate to the effort, skill, responsibility assumed, working conditions or decision-taking capacities required for effective performance.

The Race Relations Act 1976 offers similar rights to ethnic minorities. As with the Sex Discrimination Act there are exemptions including work where membership of a particular race is a genuine occupational qualification. Complaints against discrimination are heard by industrial tribunals.

19. Industrial tribunals

Employees who believe they have been unfairly dismissed under the EPCA 1978 (*see* 17), or subject to sexual or racial discrimination, or who wish to register complaints under a variety of other employment laws and regulations may initiate actions in industrial tribunals. These are independent courts consisting of three persons: two lay members (one from each side of industry – employers' organisations and trade unions) plus a legally qualified chairperson. Procedure in tribunals is meant to be informal relative to other courts (members wear ordinary clothes, not wigs and gowns). Witnesses can be called to give evidence (on oath) and may be subpoenaed by the tribunal if they refuse to attend.

If it is unclear whether the tribunal is entitled to hear the case (e.g. if the employer claims the worker has not completed two years' continuous service in an unfair dismissal case) then a 'preliminary hearing' may be called to investigate this matter. Also, if having quickly examined the basic facts of the case the tribunal feels that the position of one of the parties is legally unsound – say because a dismissal was obviously unfair, or because a disgruntled worker has initiated a case frivolously or vexatiously simply to annoy the employer – then a 'pre-hearing assessment' will be convened to establish agreed facts and, if appropriate, warn one of the parties that its case will probably fail. If the party receiving the warning wishes to proceed it may do so (before a different tribunal) but, if it loses, it could be ordered to pay the costs of the hearing (normally, each side must bear its own costs).

20. Laws on wages

These are now embodied in the Wages Act 1986. Under the Act it is generally illegal to deduct money from an employee's pay or for the firm to require the employee to pay back money received in wages except in the following circumstances:

(a) Deductions for income tax and NI or if a court has ordered that part of a person's wages be paid to a third party (e.g. to settle a fine or money owing under a court judgment).

(b) Payments requested in writing by the employee, such as trade union or sports clubs subscriptions.

(c) Agreed deductions for lateness or poor work, provided the agreement is incorporated into the employee's contract of employment.

(d) Accidental overpayment of previous wages or expenses.

(e) For *retail employees* (i.e. anyone handling cash transactions with customers – bus conductors, for example) deductions to make good cash shortages (e.g. money missing from the cash till) or stock deficiencies.

Deductions must not exceed 10 per cent of the wages due on any one pay day (except the last pay day before the employee leaves the firm) and the deduction must be made within 12 months of the detection of the shortage or deficiency. Employee complaints about these matters are dealt with by industrial tribunals.

INDUSTRIAL RELATIONS LAW

21. Laws concerning trade unions

The main laws regulating trade union activities are as follows:

The Trade Union and Labour Relations Acts 1974 and 1976

These restored to employees complete immunity from civil action in relation to industrial disputes (some aspects of immunity had been removed in 1971). Hence, workers involved in *bona fide* trade disputes cannot be sued by their employers for damages arising from their breach of contract of employment (or inducing or threatening a breach of contract), subject to the provisions of subsequent legislation.

The Employment Act 1980

This stated that although picketing of workplaces is lawful, employees may only picket their own place of work. Secondary picketing was declared unlawful, and workers engaging in it can be sued for damages by the affected firm. Note, however, the difficulty of defining 'secondary action', particularly where subsidiary companies are involved. Moreover, secondary action is still lawful if it is taken against an employing firm's customers or suppliers in order to 'further a dispute'.

The Employment Act 1982

The main consequence of this Act was to increase compensation payable to workers unfairly dismissed for joining or refusing to join a trade union. It removed trade union immunities for unlawful acts committed outside a 'trade dispute' while simultaneously narrowing the definition of what a trade dispute involves.

The Trade Union Act 1984

This placed trade unions under the obligation to ensure that every voting member of their 'principal executive committees' has been elected by the union's membership, and that all such elected committee members are re-elected every five years. The Act also removed immunity from unions and their officials in cases where they induce a breach of contract or interfere with a contract without having balloted their members in advance.

The Employment Act 1988

Under this Act, *any* industrial action to enforce or maintain a closed shop became unlawful. The Act also established new rights for trade unionists; notably the rights (*i*) not to be unjustifiably disciplined by a union for not supporting a strike, (*ii*) not to be instructed to strike without a ballot of all union members, and (*iii*) to inspect the union's accounting records. It also became unlawful for a union to use its funds to compensate a member for the consequences of his or her unlawful conduct during a dispute, e.g. by paying a member's fine, or even promising to do so. And the statutory procedures for electing members to important union committees were generally tightened. In particular, every candidate must be able to prepare an address and have this delivered to all members, and postal ballots must be used wherever 'reasonably practicable'. The Act provided for the creation of a new government official, the *Commissioner for the Rights of Trade Union Members*, whose task will be to assist individual trade unionists claim their legal rights.

The Employment Act 1989

This removed most legal restrictions on the employment of women in 'traditional' male industries (coal mining, for instance) and increased from six months to two years the period of employment that must elapse before a worker is automatically entitled to a detailed written statement of the reasons for his or her dismissal. Numerous restrictions on the hours of work of young people (including current prohibitions on young people working night-shifts) were withdrawn. Also, employees who apply to industrial tribunals may now be required to pay a deposit of up to £150 if a pre-hearing review of an intended case considers the application to have no reasonable prospect of success or to be frivolous, vexatious or unreasonable.

The Employment Act 1990

This made it unlawful to refuse to employ someone because he or she is or is not a member of a trade union (i.e. it outlawed the pre-entry closed shop). Other major provisions of the Act were that:

(a) Immunity of union members from civil actions in respect of industrial disputes does not apply in cases where 'secondary action' has occurred, except in the course of peaceful and *lawful* picketing.

(b) Unions became liable for the torts of *all* their officials, including local workplace representatives (shop stewards) unless they formally repudiated their officials' actions in a prescribed manner.

(c) The rule that it is 'fair' (*see* 17) to dismiss striking workers only if *all* strikers are dismissed and not just some of them was rescinded in circumstances of 'unofficial' industrial action. Hence an employer may now sack selected unofficial strikers in order to make an example of them. Any person involved in subsequent industrial action in support of someone dismissed on these grounds is not immune from civil liability and may thus be sued for damages by employers and other interested parties.

The Trade Union Reform and Employment Rights Act 1993

This provided for seven days' notice to be given to an employer of a union's intention to take industrial action or to ballot its members on industrial action. Additionally the Act provided that:

(a) Members of the public be given the right to apply for a court order restraining a union from taking *unlawful* industrial action.

(b) Any employee working more than eight hours a week be entitled to a written statement of his or her main terms and conditions of employment within two months of starting a job.

(c) Employees be free to join *any* trade union of their choice (i.e. unions will not be able to decide among themselves which workers shall belong to which union).

(d) 'Check-off' arrangements whereby union subscriptions are deducted at source from a worker's wages be confirmed by the employee in writing and renewed every three years.

(e) Pregnant employees be entitled to 14 weeks' maternity leave irrespective of length of service.

HEALTH AND SAFETY

22. The law on health and safety at work

This is governed primarily by the Health and Safety at Work (HASAW) Act 1974, although certain other statutes and some elements of common law are also involved. Under the 1974 Act, firms have a general duty to ensure so far as is 'reasonably practical' the health and safety at work of all employees. Breach of this duty can lead to a *criminal* (rather than civil) prosecution. Plant, machinery and other equipment must be safe and well maintained, and all arrangements for handling, storing and transporting articles and substances must be safe and free of health hazards.

Although the Act requires employees to take 'reasonable care' to ensure they neither endanger themselves nor others at work, it is ultimately the responsibility of the employing firm to insist that safety policies be implemented. For example, if protective clothing is necessary then not only must the company provide it free of charge, but must also ensure that it is worn – if necessary by disciplining recalcitrant workers.

The Act is administered through a Health and Safety Commission which is a watchdog body that delegates its powers to a Health and Safety Executive (HSE). The latter issues codes of practice which, while not legally binding or enforceable, are looked at by courts when adjudicating cases.

23. Safety representatives

In consequence of the Act, if a firm recognises a trade union then if the union so wishes it may appoint 'safety representatives' at the place of work. The roles of the safety representative are (i) to investigate accidents and dangerous occurrences, (ii) to inspect the workplace every three months (or following serious accidents or near accidents), (iii) to liaise with outside inspectors, and (iv) to make representations to management on safety matters.

Representatives are entitled to copies of any relevant information (accident reports, for example) that the employer is statutorily obliged to maintain. Departmental managers are entitled to accompany the representative during inspections. Notice of an inspection need not be given if an accident or dangerous incident has just occurred. Safety representatives are legally entitled to 'reasonable' facilities for undertaking inspections, and to paid time off to carry out safety duties and attend union safety training courses.

24. Safety committees

If two or more union safety representatives so insist, the firm is legally obliged to establish a 'safety committee' within three months of a request in writing. The role of the committee is to consider:

(a) welfare, health and safety matters affecting employees

(b) trends in accidents within the firm

(c) the causes of specific incidents

(d) safety training and the development and implementation of safety rules.

There have to be equal numbers of union and management representatives on the committee, and the management side should possess sufficient authority to implement committee decisions. Note that safety representatives are *not* accountable to the committee, only to union members. Nor does the existence of a safety committee (which might include medical doctors, nurses and other expert members *ex officio*) imply that safety issues should not be subject to collective bargaining between management and unions.

Many firms employ a specialist safety officer to represent them on safety matters. Full-time safety officers (unlike union safety representatives) are not protected against criminal liability if they fail in their duties.

Management of health and safety

A number of EU Regulations on the management of health and safety at work came into force in 1993 requiring employers to undertake 'risk assessment exercises' intended to identify potential dangers to the health and safety of employees or anyone else likely to be affected by the firm's operations. The Management of Health and Safety at Work Regulations 1992 in particular required that the risk assessment be completed by competent people (who may be outside consultants) and that, for firms with five or more workers, a permanent record of the exercise be maintained. In addition the firm is obliged to:

(a) Devise and implement specific procedures for dealing with emergencies

(b) Draw up a plan for putting into effect preventative and protective measures

(c) Train employees in safety matters and ensure that workers are capable of avoiding risks. Employees (including temporary workers) must be informed of risks in *language they can understand.*

(d) Take into account working conditions and local workplace hazards when selecting equipment

(e) Identify unavoidable risks in relation to handling operations, having regard to the shape, size and weight of the load and the ergonomic characteristics of the workplace (humidity, space available, etc).

25. Safety policies

Any firm employing more than four workers is legally obliged to prepare a written statement of its health and safety policy and bring this to all employees' attention. The statement should contain a general declaration of policy, a description of the firm's safety organisation (e.g. names of company safety officers and union safety representatives, information about the safety committee), and details of specific alarm systems, procedures for reporting accidents, facilities for safety training, etc.

26. External inspections

HSE (and other) government inspectors visit firms periodically to ensure they are complying with various legal requirements. Inspections also occur following complaints by workers or members of the public and after serious accidents. If an inspector finds that an offence has been committed then he or she may either (*i*) inform the employer on the spot of the unsatisfactory item and later ensure that remedial action has been taken, or (*ii*) serve an 'improvement notice' compelling positive action within 21 days, or a 'prohibition notice' forcing the firm to cease a risky activity, or (*iii*) prosecute the firm before magistrates. Appeals against improvement or prohibition notices are heard by industrial tribunals. Typically, appeals are based on the grounds that it is 'not reasonably practical' to comply with the notice, e.g. if the risk of injury were extremely small and the cost of complying with the order heavy.

27. Safety training

Section 2 of the HASAW Act 1974 requires employers to provide such training and instruction to workers as is necessary to ensure their health and safety. Two types of safety training are necessary: training in rules and procedures, and policy training for managers. The former should include information on hazards in specific jobs, the firm's safety policies, location and use of fire appliances, etc. Policy training needs to cover the law on health and safety, codes of practice relevant to the industry, plus training on the organisation of safety committees, inspection requirements and so on.

28. Vicarious liability

This occurs when one person is held liable for someone else's tort even though the former has not committed any wrongful act. For example, a principal may be responsible for the torts of his or her agent; and employing firms are normally responsible for the torts of their employees provided:

(a) the employee is acting under a contract of service (and is not therefore an 'independent contractor')

(b) the tort is committed 'in the course of employment' (including cases where the wrongful act is implicitly authorised by the employer or is 'incidental' to the course of employment).

For further information on these matters see the M&E text *Employment Law*, by C. Carr and P. Kay.

29. Miscellaneous legislation

The Employers' Liability (Defective Equipment) Act 1969 provides that when a worker is injured because of a defect in the equipment provided by his or her employer and the defect is the fault of a third party (the equipment's manufacturer, for instance), then the injury is deemed to be also attributable to the negligence of the employer even if no actual negligence has occurred. The employer can, of course, sue the third party for any loss suffered.

Under the Employers' Liability (Compulsory Insurance) Act 1969, every employer must insure against liability for bodily injury or disease sustained by employees in the course of their work, and a copy of the insurance certificate must be displayed on the premises. Other important legislation is provided under the Occupiers' Liability Acts 1957 and 1984 which require the occupier of the premises to take 'such care as in all circumstances is reasonable to see that visitors will be reasonably safe in using the premises for the purpose for which they are invited by the occupier to be there'. Visitors are defined as persons on the premises for the benefit of the occupier (customers, for example), guests and those entering under contract. Note that under the Unfair Contract Terms Act

1977, notices warning of dangers or hazards will not necessarily relieve an occupier from liability for injury to visitors – notices proclaiming that 'persons entering these premises do so at their own risk' have no legal effect.

The Disabled Persons Employment Acts 1944 and 1958 seek to help disabled people secure employment through requiring employers of more than 20 persons (unless the employer's business involves certain types of physically demanding work) to employ a quota of 3 per cent registered disabled people.

AGENCY AND NEGLIGENCE

30. Agency

Agents undertake tasks on behalf of clients, usually by putting them in touch with third parties. However, the agent then drops out of resulting contracts – which are just between the client and the third party. For instance, a commercial estate agent will put the owner of a property in touch with suitable tenants, but the contract that ensues is between landlord and tenant only, so that if the tenant fails to pay the rent the agent is *not* liable for the resulting debt. The rules of agency are as follows:

(a) The agent cannot act for a third party as well as the client without disclosing the fact to everyone concerned.

(b) Agents are obliged to maintain strict confidentiality regarding their clients' affairs, and to transmit to them all relevant information.

(c) If an agent does not pass on money deposited with the agent but owing to a third party, the client is still liable for the third-party debt.

(d) The client is liable for damages to third parties for wrongs committed by an agent 'in the course of his or her authority'.

(e) Clients are obliged to indemnify their agents for expenses incurred while reasonably exercising their duties.

31. The EU Agency Directive 1986

This harmonised agency law throughout the EU (although it only became fully effective from January 1994). Under the Directive, any individual or company acting as an agent (excluding bankruptcy receivers and insolvency practitioners – *see* 4:30; partners, employees or officers of firms; or commodity dealers) has the right to receive the following on termination of an agency agreement:

(a) Full payment of any transaction predominantly attributable to the agent's work during the period of the agency, even if the transaction is concluded after the agency has been terminated.

(b) A lump sum not exceeding the agent's average commission for one year. To complete this average the agent's earnings over the last five years are considered (or less if the agency has not been in force for five years). The lump sum could be payable if the agency has ended because of the death of the agent.

(c) Damages for losses (e.g. loss of goodwill – *see* 9:3 in appropriate circumstances.

EU proposals on agency agreements

The European Commission is seeking to amend EU competition law (*see* **13**) so as to ban *exclusive* agency agreements that involve more than 200 million ECU and/or which cover at least 5 per cent of the relevant market. An exclusive agency agreement is one that gives the agent a sole right to sell the principal's output in an exclusive territory, even though the agent is legally regarded as an auxiliary organ of the principal's firm. The proposals make a distinction between 'integrated' and 'non-integrated' agents. For *integrated agents*, the principal may:

(a) grant the agent the sole right to sell in a certain territory

(b) require the agent not to handle competing products during the course of the agreement

(c) prevent the agent selling outside a specified territory

(d) impose a ban on the agent competing with the principal for up to two years following expiry of the agency contract.

These restrictions will not be allowed for non-integrated agents, who will be regarded in law as independent traders. To be classed as a non-integrated agent the agent must:

(a) not assume the financial risk or primary responsibility for transactions

(b) be remunerated via commission paid (only) by the principal

(c) have at least one third of his or her turnover attributable to a single principal

(d) not possess obligations that compete with the principal's business (e.g. through carrying competing products).

Application of contractual restrictions to non-integrated agents who do not satisfy the above criteria could result in the principal being fined by the Commission. The restrictions themselves would automatically be deemed unenforceable and void. Also, third parties damaged by the restrictive agreement would be able to sue either the principal or the agent for compensation.

32. Negligence

Negligence can relate to physical acts or to the provision of advice and verbal statements. It is the omission to do something which a reasonable ordinary person would do, or doing something that a prudent and reasonable person would not do. For negligence to occur there must be:

(a) a duty of care owed by the defendant to the plaintiff, e.g. not to act in a way that causes injury

(b) a breach of that duty; *and*

(c) resulting damage.

Contributory negligence

Sometimes industrial and other accidents happen in consequence of more than one person's negligence, e.g. if an employee was injured by an inadequately guarded machine when the employee was 'larking about' at the time of the accident. In such cases the courts will divide responsibility for damages between the parties; for instance, 60 per cent to one party and 40 per cent to the other.

Professional negligence

Here the duty of care arises in relation to one party's *reliance* on the advice of another. Moreover, professional people owe a duty of care not only to their clients, but also to third parties who they know are relying on their skill. The key considerations here are whether the advice (*i*) is given casually without any intention of it being relied upon or in circumstances in which it would be unreasonable for anyone to rely on the advice, and (*ii*) comes from a person who claims expert knowledge of a certain matter.

Progress test 11

1. What is the purpose of the Misrepresentation Act 1967?

2. Describe the implications of the Unfair Contract Terms Act 1977.

3. In what circumstances does the Sex Discrimination Act not apply to employees?

4. What are the major provisions of the Employment Act 1988?

5. What types of court order are available to firms seeking payment of long-outstanding debts?

6. What is a 'block exemption'?

7. Define 'negligence'.

12

COMMUNICATION AND MANAGEMENT CONTROL

THE CHALLENGE OF COMMUNICATION

1. Communications systems

Communication concerns the exchange of information, opinion and sentiment. A *communications system* links together the constituent parts of a firm's organisational structure, and provides for the creation, distribution, interpretation and execution of instructions. It transmits news of management's intentions to employees, and provides feedback to management on employee responses to its proposals.

The need to transmit and receive information is common to all organisations. Management has to pass instructions to the workforce, to explain its policies and objectives, and to tell workers if their jobs are threatened. Specific needs for downwards communication from management to employees relate to such matters as:

- how and when work is to be completed
- employees' duties and obligations
- management's plans and intentions
- changes in organisation structure
- health and safety procedures
- performance standards and company objectives.

Employees need to communicate with management in relation to:

- queries regarding management's instructions and stated intentions
- whether they are able to complete their work effectively, given the resources available
- suggestions for improving working methods and processes
- problems experienced at work.

Sound employee communications are essential for the smooth running of an enterprise for a number of reasons:

(a) Individuals need to be able to behave and take decisions in accordance with company policy. Effective co-ordination of the firm's activities is impossible without management/employee communications.

(b) Change can only be implemented successfully if the reasons for the change plus its implications for workers are communicated to and accepted by the people likely to be affected.

(c) Employees' basic perceptions of their work and of the company are substantially determined by the quality of its employee communications.

(d) Workers have the chance to respond to communications from management by providing the latter with valuable feedback.

2. The communication process

Information is *encoded* for transmission via a *message* that is received and *decoded* by another party. Encoding involves the choice of an appropriate form of words for the message. Decoding requires the *interpretation* of the message. *Noise* is any form of interference with messages that has the effect of producing extra and distracting information, e.g. technical jargon or overlong and unclear sentences.

Messages that flow up and down the organisation are called vertical communications. The formal channels for these are usually illustrated in a firm's organisation chart. Vertical communications systems are important for ensuring that policy decisions are implemented. Horizontal communications occur among employees of equivalent rank, and matters discussed are not referred to higher authority. The horizontal communications system does not involve the flow of authority. Rather it concerns the exchange of news and opinion among equals.

3. Communication decisions

Three major communication decisions are necessary, as follows:

(a) *When to communicate.* Managers commonly assume that colleagues and subordinates have been informed of particular issues and problems when, in fact, they have not. Communication of every piece of information that might be relevant to an individual is not feasible; otherwise the firm would devote all its time, energy and resources to transmitting messages, most of which are of little practical use. Thus, choices have to be made.

(b) *How to communicate.* Media for transferring messages include letters and memoranda, telephone conversations, meetings, posters and noticeboards, house journals, and written reports (*see* 9). Informal channels may also be important, especially 'grapevines' (*see* 5).

(c) *With whom to communicate.* Choice of recipient depends on the purpose of the message transmitted. Correct choice of message recipient will ensure that instructions issued will be carried out because those responsible for their implementation will know precisely what they have to do.

4. Breakdowns in communication

Many factors cause communication problems. Common examples are as follows:

(a) Managers assuming that colleagues have been informed of issues when in fact they have not.

(b) Information being sent to the wrong people, or incorrect and/or inadequate messages being transmitted.

(c) Failure to pass on important messages.

(d) Distortion of messages as they pass through the system. The meaning of a message might be slightly (or substantially) altered at each stage in the process.

(e) Delays in processing information.

(f) Communication overload, i.e. managers receiving so many messages that most are disregarded.

(g) Inappropriate wording of messages, e.g. using language that 'goes over the heads' of message recipients, or using vague and meaningless words and sentences.

(h) Failure to emphasise important points.

(i) Subordinates feeling embarrassed about approaching their bosses with important information.

(j) Managers hearing only what they want to hear and disregarding all critical comment.

Inadequate employee communication can impose a number of costs on a company, including:

- Bad decision-making consequent to individuals not receiving the correct information
- Misunderstandings among sections leading to costly mistakes
- Incorrect perceptions of company and personal objectives
- The possible emergence of grapevines (*see* **6**)
- Conflicts and industrial disputes resulting from misunderstandings (as opposed to irreconcilable divergences of views)
- Lack of employee commitment to the employing organisation
- Poorer quality output in consequence of workers not understanding the importance of their role in the quality management process
- Employee resistance to change and the possible development of 'them and us' attitudes
- Non-implementation of plans and policies
- Inconsistent activities and lack of co-ordination.

Note, moreover, that a management's failure to communicate with workers may be interpreted by the latter as management not regarding them as people worthy or capable of receiving and understanding information.

One-way and two-way communication

One-way communication (which does not involve any feedback from the recipient) is appropriate for topics that are routine, straightforward and uncontroversial. However, one-way communication is *not* adequate for matters affecting employee welfare or that concern issues about which employees can express useful opinions. Two-way communication (which gives the recipient(s) an opportunity to respond and react) is time-consuming and demands patience and personal skill, but should be used for subjects which are complicated, unexpected, of personal concern to the receivers, or involve matters about which they could make a worthwhile contribution. A better decision may be reached, and it will be accepted more readily.

Autocratic one-way communication is particularly unsuitable for IT-driven computerised workplaces where important decisions have to be taken by lower echelons and where objectives are not attainable without the active *commitment* of employees.

5. The grapevine

Formal communication channels might be circumvented through the emergence within an organisation of an informal 'grapevine', i.e. a loose collection of unofficial communication passages which operates alongside the official system. Grapevines are common where employees know each other well and exchange information casually without the knowledge or permission of higher authority. They spread gossip and rumours, especially concerning matters pertaining to employee welfare.

Although the grapevine is strictly unofficial, people holding key positions within it (namely those who spread the most information) may find that their status in the official system is enhanced in consequence of their grapevine activities. Even without deliberate malice, grapevines frequently misrepresent issues because the facts behind situations are exaggerated or otherwise altered. There is no mechanism for checking the validity of the information transmitted, or for refuting falsehoods. Grapevines tend to distort reality, and can be used to initiate unsavoury rumours.

The most efficient way to suppress a grapevine is for management to present clear, accurate and comprehensive information to employees. Note, however, that management may decide consciously to allow a grapevine to survive because it provides a fast and effective means for distributing news. Also, views which management might not want to be made known officially can be made known through the grapevine.

Management by walking around

Objective setting, appraisal, accountability systems, etc., are fine for establishing procedures and monitoring progress, but too often they fail to provide the detailed and accurate information on day-to-day operations and (most important) on staff morale necessary for effective control. Management by walking around (MBWA) is a simple solution to the problem of gathering information about actual behaviour within an organisation. The manager looks and listens, talks to employees and becomes personally involved with happenings at the workplace level. More specifically, MBWA concerns:

- reviewing and appraising sources of information

- looking for new and better contacts
- learning how people (senior managers as well as junior employees) *feel* about the organisation and each other
- finding out how the staff perceive customers, and assessing whether they recognise a personal responsibility for customer care.

MBWA brings managers into daily contact with quality and productivity problems. Managers observe at first hand which jobs are easy and which difficult. Further *advantages* of MBWA are that managers cannot avoid recognising employees' difficulties; that it provides valuable feedback on the success of recently introduced equipment and methods; that it demonstrates management's commitment to genuine employee communication; and that it is likely to result in actual changes designed to overcome workers' problems. It is especially useful for obtaining the 'gut reactions' of employees to management's proposals.

Visits should not be at fixed times or dates, or employees might 'prepare' for the visit so that an unrepresentative impression is generated. The system should operate at all levels within the organisation and a variety of managers need to be involved – not just a handful of interested individuals. *Problems* with MBWA include the following:

- Managers might engage in the practice simply to waste time.
- Workers could learn how to manipulate the system in order to present to their bosses favourable but untrue images of their work.
- Visits could become little more than friendly social chit-chats that add nothing to the company's efficiency.
- Managers are taken away from possibly more important duties.
- In a large company a senior manager cannot visit *all* sections on a regular basis.

PERSONAL SKILLS OF WRITTEN COMMUNICATION AND REPORT WRITING

6. Writing instructions

Written instructions describe, explain and/or specify quantities or relations. They do not (normally) have to evaluate, justify, persuade or recommend. Readers need to *understand* the instructions, but do not have to remember them, because they have a written document to which they can refer. Clarity of exposition and logical *ordering* of material are thus fundamentally important.

Specific instructions are normally prefaced by an action: 'Unscrew the top from the bottle', 'Take a piece of metal four inches long', 'Carefully remove the contents', etc. Writers of instructions should ask themselves the following questions:

(a) Who will use them? How competent, knowledgeable and motivated are the intended readers?

(b) What precisely is necessary for the reader to be able to do something, and how quickly? Is it essential that the reader be able to understand the thing before operating it? For example, one does not have to know how a petrol engine works in order to change a spark plug.

7. Rules for writing instructions

Every query that a reader might raise must be predicted and the answers incorporated into the instructions, which should be in simple English and not use vocabulary and/or technical terms unfamiliar to the typical reader. Additionally the writer should:

(a) arrange the instructions in the exact order in which operations should be completed, and organise the information in the form of a list

(b) write each instruction in the most basic manner possible

(c) be comprehensive, ensuring that all necessary steps are included

(d) write in the imperative (as in this list) and in the second person

(e) use plenty of headings

(f) avoid ambiguous and uncommon words (few readers will bother looking up the correct meaning of a word in a dictionary)

(g) insert at the end of the list of instructions a checklist of things to look for if the operation has gone wrong

(h) have someone who has not previously performed the task work through the instructions, without help, and then have a second person do the same.

8. Letter writing

Letters should always be written in the first person, and be as brief as possible – if a letter is more than two pages long it is sometimes better to present it as a report (*see* below) accompanied by a short covering letter. The quality of routine letter writing can be improved by following a number of simple rules:

(a) Define the purpose of the letter, i.e. determine what the reader is supposed to do, think or feel after reading it.

(b) Prepare a list of points to go into the letter, and then arrange these in a logical order.

(c) Go straight to the point of the letter in the first paragraph. State relevant information at the outset. Follow this with paragraphs for:

- (*i*)   supporting details
- (*ii*) evidence and views
- (*iii*) conclusions
- (*iv*) actions required
- (*v*)   a closure, thanking the reader for his or her attention.

(d) Aim for a clear, simple, polite and direct style that avoids pompous phrases.

Memoranda are used instead of letters for interdepartmental communication within organisations. They are usually shorter and more direct than letters. There is no need for a salutation ('Dear Sirs') at the start or 'Yours faithfully' at the finish. Otherwise, memos should be structured in the same order as letters, but with headings and sub-headings within the text. A memorandum provides a permanent record of a communication. Their disadvantage is the tendency of many managers to write too many of them and to distribute copies to too many people.

9. Reports

A report is a presentation of facts, opinions and recommendations for action. Information contained in a report should be concise, accurate and logically organised. All reports should contain statements of their terms of reference and brief summaries of major conclusions. The following tasks are involved in writing reports:

(a) *Collection of material* – obtaining information, conducting research, checking the accuracy of facts and distinguishing facts from opinions.

(b) *Selection of material* to be included in the report.

(c) *Ordering sections* – classification of material, placing sections in a logical order, and deciding headings and sub-headings.

(d) *Writing the report* – choosing a style appropriate to the audience for which the report is intended, and choice of illustrations, tables, graphs and diagrams.

There is no single correct way in which to structure a report, though most begin with a title page and brief summary, followed by a table of contents, introduction, text of the main body of the report, conclusions, recommendations, and finally appendices containing tables, technical calculations, references, etc.

10. Rules for writing reports

The style of a report should aim to *inform* rather than impress. It should be clear, concise and comprehensive. Writers of reports should adhere to the following rules:

(a) Put the title (which should fully describe the contents of the report), together with the author's name, departmental address, date of submission and circulation list on a separate covering page.

(b) Begin the report with a one- or two-paragraph summary of its major findings.

(c) Start the introduction with a clear statement of why the report is necessary, its objectives and terms of reference.

(d) Write the report bearing in mind the needs of those who are to read it; asking what they need to know, what sort of illustrations, examples and supplementary data will help them understand the report, etc.

(e) Keep within the report's terms of reference.

CONTROL

11. Management control

Control links inputs to outputs, monitors activities and provides feedback to those in command. Actual performance is compared with targets, and remedial action implemented wherever required. An effective control system will be:

(a) clear and fully understood by all concerned

(b) easily adjusted as circumstances alter

(c) based on accurate information

(d) associated with reasonable and logically determined targets

(e) cheap to administer and requiring the minimum amount of detailed supervision.

12. Feedforward and feedback

Feedback informs controllers of the consequences of their decisions. Note that since feedback is necessarily retrospective, it can arrive too late to remedy a deficiency. Feedforward, conversely, involves the prediction of problems and the implementation today of measures intended to overcome them. Thus, whereas feedback systems concentrate on initiating remedial actions at the output stage, feedforward schemes are pre-emptive and centre on decision making in the input period. If inputs differ from activities necessary to overcome predicted difficulties, they are altered in appropriate ways.

13. Closed- and open-loop feedback mechanisms

With a closed-loop system, information on current performance automatically adjusts operations in an attempt to rectify divergences between planned and actual activity. For example, the speed of a production line might automatically and instantly adjust itself according to the number of defectives it produces, or inventories might be automatically replenished as stock-usage rates increase. Open-loop systems, in contrast, require human intervention. They remain constant unless someone takes the initiative to implement an alteration.

14. Co-ordination

This means the unification of the efforts of all the individuals working for an organisation. Efficient co-ordination requires sound information gathering and reporting procedures, effective appraisal systems, and a procedure for rapid intervention to deal with shortcomings. Co-ordination involves motivating other people, work scheduling, resolving interpersonal conflicts and dealing with grievances. The main techniques for co-ordinating organisations are:

(a) Appointment of a full-time liaison manager whose major duty is to co-ordinate the work of many departments. Normally a senior person with the authority to impose decisions undertakes this role.

(b) Creation of a permanent task force to co-ordinate activities. Each member of the task force represents a particular department.

(c) Use of an *ad hoc* co-ordinator seconded from a top management position for a short period.

15. Control methods

The following control methods are commonly applied by organisations:

- Delegation (*see* **16**)
- Management by objectives (*see* **17**)
- Management auditing (*see* **19**)
- Management by exception (*see* **20**)
- Budgeting (*see* **21**)
- Performance appraisal (*see* **30**)
- Ratio analysis (*see* **29**)
- Standard costing (*see* **28**)

16. Delegation

Delegation is necessary when a manager's workload becomes excessive and/or he or she is confronted by technical problems of a specialist nature. It means the assignment by a manager to subordinates of authority to undertake certain tasks, while retaining ultimate responsibility for their satisfactory completion.

Delegation is a valuable means for training subordinates for higher-level duties, since work of increasing difficulty can be delegated, thus gradually improving a subordinate's capacity to act independently. The principles of delegation are as follows:

(a) Subordinates must be given all the resources and information necessary to implement their decisions.

(b) Those selected to receive delegated work must be competent to complete it satisfactorily.

(c) Delegation should be planned carefully, and not regarded as a quick way for senior managers to jettison distasteful tasks.

(d) Managers should recognise that subordinates will make occasional mistakes when attempting higher-level assignments.

(e) Subordinates should not be subjected to continuous supervision as they complete delegated work (as this stifles initiative).

(f) Managers should back the decisions taken by subordinates while they are completing delegated assignments, even if managers do not wholeheartedly agree with them.

(g) Care is needed in the selection of duties for delegation; it would be ludicrous if, for example, a senior manager delegated responsibility for purchasing new factory premises while personally continuing to order the office furniture. Duties particularly appropriate for delegation are fact-finding assignments, preparation of rough drafts for reports, investigation of the feasibilities of various approaches to problems, or straightforward analysis of routine information.

17. Management by objectives (MBO)

With MBO managers and subordinates jointly agree subordinates' goals (preferably in quantitative terms) and then systematically monitor progress achieved towards their attainment. MBO starts at the apex of the organisation: the firm's corporate plan determines divisional and departmental objectives, which are then broken down into targets for sections and individuals.

Advantages of MBO include the following:

(a) The involvement of subordinates in setting personal objectives encourages their co-operation and motivation towards achieving targets.

(b) Management is forced to clarify its aims and to state the criteria used in their formulation. Superiors and subordinates are obliged to communicate.

(c) The causes of successes achieved in attaining objectives can be identified and analysed.

(d) Employees are compelled to consider their roles and how best to achieve their targets.

(e) Performance appraisal (*see* **30**) becomes possible.

(f) MBO can be related to training and management development programmes.

(g) Subordinates' personal achievements are recognised.

18. Problems with MBO

The *disadvantages* of MBO are listed below.

(a) Devising MBO programmes is extremely time consuming. A system whereby managers simply impose targets on subordinates without consultation might be more efficient.

(b) Targets might become out of date immediately following their determination.

(c) Certain targets cannot be specified numerically (advisory work, for instance).

(d) Possible overemphasis on the achievement of immediate short-term goals at the expense of longer-term objectives.

(e) Difficulties created through subordinates not being given the resources or authority necessary for completion of tasks allocated to them.

Action plans

Objectives must be clearly stated and fully understood by subordinates. Hence, the resources needed to attain targets should be specified in MBO *action plans*. A convenient way to begin an action plan is with the words 'your performance will be considered satisfactory if . . .', and then filling in the rest of the sentence. Employees' performances should be reviewed regularly in order that shortcomings be quickly identified and remedied. If targets are impossibly high they must be amended.

19. Management auditing

A management audit is a systematic analysis of the effectiveness of an organisation's policies and administrative procedures. As well as periodic audits (every three or four years, for instance), *ad hoc* audits are necessary whenever the business environment significantly changes. The purpose of an audit is to reorganise resources – material, financial and human – and redirect effort towards the more efficient attainment of organisational objectives. Minor audits, taking one department at a time, might be completed between major analyses.

Two types of audit are needed: internal and external. External audits examine the general environments – legal (the effects of changes in employment law, for example), economic, market opportunities, behaviour of competitors, etc – surrounding the organisation. Internal audits investigate operational systems within the enterprise. A typical audit will examine such things as:

(a) management style and communications

(b) whether organisation charts and job specifications are clear and up to date

(c) whether organisational and departmental objectives are understood by all department members

(d) possible duplication of activities

(e) operational efficiency within sections

(f) plant and/or office layout

(g) output quality.

20. Management by exception (MBE)

This is the practice whereby subordinates submit to their superiors only brief condensed reports on normal operations but extensive reports on deviations from past average performance or targets set by higher management. Once established, standards should be monitored by picking out significant deviations from predetermined norms. Exceptionally good or bad results are analysed in detail and explanations supplied, but the day-to-day functioning of the organisation within reasonable divergences from normal practice is not questioned.

MBE enables senior managers to devote their full attention to major policy issues and avoid becoming immersed in routine administration. However, MBE does have *disadvantages*, as follows:

(a) Delays occur between the moment a problem arises, the moment it is noticed, and the time remedial action is implemented.

(b) Since 'acceptable deviations' from target performance are tolerated without investigation, it is possible for a particular activity to be perpetually above or below standard by a relatively small amount without the fact ever being reported.

(c) The administrative work involved in preparing summary statistics to ascertain whether operations are within acceptable limits can itself be extensive.

BUDGETARY CONTROL

21. Budgeting

Budgets constrain expenditures. Also they indicate how much particular activities should cost. Upper spending limits are specified for each department for predetermined future periods, and the amounts given to departments are then broken down into subsidiary budgets relating to specific tasks. Hence, for example, the marketing department's budget might be split into components for advertising, marketing research, distribution, sales promotions and so on.

Some firms produce both short-term budgets which cannot be altered, and long-term budgets that vary as circumstances change. Two factors determine the budget period: the amount of accurate information on expected expenditures, and the degree of uncertainty in the commercial environment in which the firm exists.

22. Advantages and disadvantages of budgets

In preparing budgets, management is compelled to relate resource requirements to corporate objectives; and the meetings, discussions, joint decision making and general co-ordination of activities necessitated by budget planning encourage co-operation and common approaches to achieving company aims. Budgets impose financial discipline on those responsible for their administration. Spendthrift departments are identified and can be penalised by reductions in future allocations, while cost increases which cause rapid exhaustion of existing budgets can be isolated and their effects on the organisation as a whole assessed.

There are, however, a number of difficulties attached to budget formulation. The major problems are listed below.

(a) Heads of department often ask for larger budgets than are actually necessary, in anticipation of having their budgets cut. The determination of sensible budgets becomes haphazard in these circumstances.

(b) Managers sometimes deliberately overspend in order to strengthen their arguments for increased allocations in future periods.

(c) It is difficult to distinguish between a budget which has been exceeded because of genuine additional spending requirements and one exceeded through administrative incompetence.

(d) Attempts to keep within budget limits may cause managers to cut costs excessively, thus depriving the firm of essential investments in new equipment, machines and administrative facilities.

(e) Some budgets are overspent, others do not use all the funds available. Thus, a mechanism (referred to as 'virement') is necessary for transferring unused balances to areas which require extra funds. So why bother with budgets in the first instance? Note that the preparation of detailed budgets is time consuming and expensive.

(f) If a budget remains unspent towards the end of a financial year, departmental managers might indulge in wasteful spending simply to exhaust the outstanding balance.

(g) Budgets can hide inefficiencies. Naturally, managers will seek to spend all the money they receive even if the expenditure is not objectively necessary.

23. Budget allocation methods

Often, budget allocations are linked to an appropriate performance index. Advertising budgets, for instance, are commonly related to the volume of sales – it is assumed that increasing sales require additional advertising in order to sustain and continue the sales expansion. This approach is cheap, simple and convenient, and is 'market led' in that resources are automatically channelled towards products with obvious market appeal that are likely to do well in the future. However, it ignores the possibility that extra advertising might be most needed when sales are falling. Otherwise the main methods for determining budgets are as follows:

(a) *Rolling budgets.* The budget allocated for the next 12 months is set equal to actual expenditures during the previous 12 months, updated on a month by month basis.

(b) *Competitive parity.* The firm estimates and copies the budgets allocated to various functions by major competitors.

(c) *The profit-level approach.* Departmental budgets are automatically increased when profits are high and *vice versa*.

(d) *The responsibility (operational) approach.* Individuals are asked how much they need in order to achieve predetermined objectives. Resources are then distributed and the individuals assume personal responsibility for administering the resulting budgets.

(e) *The zero-base approach.* This attempts to overcome the problem of managers deliberately overspending to increase future allocations. There is no presumption whatsoever that the amount given during one budgetary period will be repeated. Indeed, each departmental budget is initially set at zero, assuming thereby that no funds at all will be made available in the future. Hence, heads of department must argue for a new allocation at the start of each and every period. Intended activities have to be respecified and their expected costs re-estimated. Managers are forced to review periodically their plans and working methods, thus encouraging the identification of high-cost activities. The drawback to zero-base budgeting is the enormous amounts of time managers must devote to periodic assessments of costs and to the repeated presentation of budget proposals.

Another technique is the simultaneous specification of not one but several different budgets for the same department or activity. The budget applied will depend on the particular circumstances prevailing at the moment of implementation. Here, the firm recognises the impossibility of foreseeing all future circumstances and so makes allowance for a range of contingencies.

24. Installation of budget systems

Most budgetary control systems begin by considering carefully the sales forecasts embodied in a firm's marketing plan. These indicate anticipated revenues from the sale of target numbers of units of output at certain prices allowing for the effects of bulk order discounts and/or special promotions (money-off coupons, etc) and associated costs.

The expected costs of creating the level of output envisaged in the sales forecasts will be set out in the firm's production, overheads and capital expenditure budgets (*see* **26** below).

25. Principal limiting factors

These are the major constraints which limit an organisation's activities (and hence its ability to spend). Usually the dominant constraint is expected sales revenue since this determines how much money will (or should) be available to purchase the inputs needed to produce the goods. Other possible limiting factors (sometimes called 'principal budget factors') are shortages of labour, scarcities of raw materials or restricted machine capacities. Budget systems normally proceed by first preparing those budgets most critically affected by the principal limiting factors. Thus, for example, a business that faces acute shortages of skilled labour will draft its labour utilisation budget (*see* below) *before* considering anything else.

26. The production budget

This specifies the expected cost of creating a certain volume of output, allowing for the cost of overtime working, for warehousing and other inventory costs and for raw materials and finished component purchases. Usually, separate sub-budgets are established for the acquisition of significant inputs. For example, a raw-materials budget might be established to plan the purchase and delivery of raw materials and to ensure that storage facilities are available when they arrive.

The labour utilisation budget

The purpose of this budget is to itemise the costs of employing and deploying labour, including training costs, recruitment expenses, overtime costs, plus estimated losses caused by employee sickness and other sources of absenteeism.

Plant utilisation budgets

These state the planned costs of operating various categories of plant and equipment. (The technical difference between 'plant' and 'equipment' is that plant is fixed in location, whereas equipment can be moved around.) Maintenance costs are usually included here.

Overheads budget

For budgeting purposes overhead items are broken down into categories for production, marketing and administration, and for generic items such as rent. Often, research and development expenditures are classed as a general overhead and thus incorporated into this budget rather than treated as an operating expense.

The capital expenditure budget

Acquisitions of major items of capital plant and equipment benefit the firm for several years (or more). Thus, even though capital assets might be paid for in a lump sum, only a proportion of their total cost should be set against the capital expenditure budget for a particular period.

27. Budget reporting and control

Additional budgets may be prepared for administrative costs such as general management, legal services, audit fees, etc, and for whatever particular functions (personnel, packaging, distribution, special production processes) are relevant to the firm.

All budgets which are measured in monetary units are drawn together in a *master budget* showing all anticipated operating and capital expenditures grouped together under appropriate headings. Thereafter, differences between actual and budget figures must be measured periodically (e.g. weekly, monthly or quarterly) and incorporated into *budget reports*. The following rules should be applied to budgetary reporting procedures:

(a) Problems should be reported to the managers who are empowered and in a position to take corrective action.

(b) Reports should be clear, precise and easy to understand.

(c) Statements of the causes of divergences and the measures needed to rectify them should, whenever possible, be included with reports.

(d) Figures quoted in reports should be directly comparable between one period and the next. Data definitions and the time intervals to which information refers should be stated.

(e) Reporting procedures should be regularly reviewed to avoid duplication of information.

28. Standard costing

This applies the work study concept of standard performance to the estimation of production costs. Expected values for material usage, labour time, machine expenses, etc are computed and subsequently compared with the actual cost of making a product. Expectations (standards) may be specified in terms either of past performance or anticipated future possibilities. Differences between predicted and realised costs are called variances; they highlight deviations of actual performances from prior assessments of how long an item should take to produce, how much raw material it should require, and the value of the overheads it should (theoretically) absorb. Careful analysis of variances will reveal sources of inefficiency.

29. Ratio analysis

This permits the comparison of relative performance figures (rather than absolute amounts) over time. Each department must choose the ratios most relevant to its needs. A credit control department for instance will be interested in the ratio of bad debts to sales, while production managers will want to measure (among others) ratios of costs to outputs and average inventory to purchases. Normal values for key ratios may be predetermined, and acceptable deviations specified. Management by exception procedures can then be applied.

Ratios should be relevant to the purpose for which they are intended, and should be computed consistently: data definitions should not be altered without good cause. If a change in the basis of computation is inevitable, ratios calculated using different criteria should not be compared. Important financial management ratios are considered in Chapter 9.

PERFORMANCE APPRAISAL

30. Nature of performance appraisal (PA)

This concerns the analysis by a manager of a subordinate's successes and failures experienced during a certain review period (typically the previous six or twelve months). Manager and subordinate meet to discuss the former's assessment of the latter's performance.

The purposes of PA are to improve employee performance and to minimise bias and unfair practices in assessment procedures: employees are told the criteria to be used in the course of the appraisal, and may even be able to challenge them. PA is used to estimate employees' suitability for promotion or training, and possibly to compute performance-related pay. The advantages of PA include the following:

(a) Managers are compelled openly to discuss their assessments of subordinates' work with the individuals concerned and are thus forced to base their evaluations on rational criteria.

(b) Employees may be motivated to increased effort in order to improve the result of an impending appraisal.

(c) Incorrect statements of facts relating to subordinates' work and/or allegations of sub-standard performance can be disputed by subordinates.

(d) Management obtains valuable feedback about the implementation of policies, thus contributing to the firm's management information system (*see* 13:6).

(e) Employees become aware of what precisely is expected from them and of their status in the eyes of higher authority.

(f) Appraisal interviews might expose useful information concerning previously unknown skills and special competences possessed by subordinates. These data can be incorporated in the firm's human resources plan (*see* 16:3) and used for staff development and management succession programmes.

(g) Employees can inform managers of barriers that have prevented them improving their performances.

Appraisals are normally categorised into three types: performance reviews, potential reviews and reward reviews.

31. Performance reviews

These examine recent activities and the *reasons* for success and failure. 'Critical incidents', i.e. specific cases of outstandingly good or bad performance, are isolated and discussed.

Reviews can take the form of either a free report in which the manager presents a general assessment of the subordinate's performance (with the manager deciding the evaluation criteria to be applied and without going into detail over specific issues), or a checklist of predetermined headings.

32. Free reports

These are in effect essays about subordinates' abilities. The appraiser may be instructed to include certain topics in the report (e.g. the subordinate's technical competence, willingness to cooperate, etc); otherwise the precise format is left to the manager completing the appraisal. Problems with free reports include the following:

(a) Possible overemphasis of recent events at the expense of considering the employee's overall average performance.

(b) Favouritism and the application of different criteria to the evaluation of different employees.

(c) Managers not keeping comprehensive records on subordinates' work.

(d) The inability of many managers to translate their thoughts into lucid written English.

(e) Managers may be extremely reluctant to comment on subordinates' activities preferring to treat them as professional colleagues rather than inferiors upon whom they are entitled to pass judgement.

(f) Few managers have received any training in the concepts and techniques of performance appraisal.

33. Checklists

Checklist headings could include: punctuality, job knowledge, accuracy of work, attitude, etc. Assessors might then award a grade (e.g. marks out of ten; or 'A', 'B', 'C', etc) for each attribute, or be asked to place a tick alongside one of a number of statements about the appraisee's ability in a certain area. For example, if 'initiative' is one of the checklist headings the alternatives offered might appear as follows:

Initiative	Tick as appropriate
Requires very little supervision	_____
Requires supervision only occasionally	_____
Sometimes needs to be told what to do	_____
Frequently needs to be told what to do	_____

The advantages of checklists are that they are easy to understand, quickly completed, and logical criteria are predetermined.

Disadvantages include the possibilities that:

(a) Haste and carelessness in filling in a checklist may lead to unfair assessments.

(b) The characteristics specified in the checklist might not be entirely relevant to the particular job under consideration.

(c) Appraisers may rate every subordinate as 'fair' (which is a somewhat meaningless term) or average (a 'B minus' grade or a mark of six out of ten, for instance) for all categories. To avoid this, some appraisal systems insist that only a specified proportion (e.g. 25 per cent) of evaluations be placed in central categories.

34. Behaviour expectation scales

Choice and measurement of appraisal criteria are perhaps the greatest problems in any appraisal system. A vast range of variables is potentially relevant to any particular job, and deciding which to include is extremely problematic. Moreover, attempts to *quantify* certain employee characteristics (e.g. creativity, co-operation, enthusiasm, disposition, etc) are necessarily difficult.

The behaviour expectation scale method – sometimes referred to as the 'behaviourally anchored rating scale' (BARS) method – attempts to circumvent these problems by requiring assessors to select some aspect of a subordinate's behaviour that is considered indicative of his or her performance in a particular dimension of a job. For example, the superior of an employee being appraised under the heading *ability to cope with stress* would be asked to complete a form which begins with the words, 'I would expect this employee to behave in the following way:' followed by a list of statements from which the appraiser must choose. Among the statements might be:

(a) Rarely exhibits symptoms of stress

(b) Occasionally becomes frustrated

(c) Shows irritability when subordinates underperform

(d) Acts erratically under stress

(e) Flies off the handle when provoked

and so on. Associated with each statement is a certain number of points indicating the relative desirability of the indicated behaviour, so that 'occasional frustration' might score seven points, while 'flying off the handle' (which is much worse) scores three. These scale values are said to be *anchored* against the typical employee behaviour that each statement represents.

The problems with BARS systems are (*i*) their complexity and the time they require to devise and administer, (*ii*) the selection and definition of appropriate job dimensions, (*iii*) the specification of examples of good and bad behaviour, and (*iv*) deciding how many points to award to each statement.

35. Potential reviews

These consider the employee's capacity to advance through the organisation. Workers are informed of their future prospects, and of the training and experience they need in order to achieve promotion. Results from potential reviews provide inputs into the firm's staff development, recruitment and management succession programmes. The problems with potential reviews are as follows:

(a) Managers sometimes assess their subordinates' potentials more in terms of successes achieved in subordinates' *current* jobs than on their capacity for higher-level duties.

(b) A negative outcome to a potential review may damage an employee's morale (rather than stimulate additional effort to overcome deficiencies).

(c) Fears that an employee may resign following a negative review might cause a manager not to discuss the results of the exercise with the worker. Hence the employee does not become aware that he or she has no chance of promotion.

(d) A positive review might lead a subordinate to expect rapid promotion even if there actually exist few opportunities for advancement. The employee then feels aggrieved when promotion is not forthcoming.

36. Reward reviews and performance-related pay

Performance reviews may provide an input into the determination of employees' pay increases. It is conventional, however, to conduct salary assessments well after performance and potential reviews have been completed, for two reasons:

(a) PA seeks to improve efficiency. If salary is discussed it inevitably dominates the conversation to the detriment of fresh ideas for enhancing productivity.

(b) Salary levels are determined in part by market forces and union pressures independent of employees' abilities.

Progress test 12

1. Distinguish between vertical and horizontal communication.

2. List four possible barriers to communication.

3. Distinguish between feedforward and feedback.

4. Define the term 'zero-base budgeting'. What are the advantages and disadvantages of this approach?

5. Explain the difficulties involved in preparing a performance appraisal checklist.

6. Define 'standard costing'.

13

DECISION SUPPORT AND INFORMATION TECHNOLOGY MANAGEMENT

INFORMATION TECHNOLOGY

1. Nature of information technology

Information technology (IT) is the acquisition, processing, storage and dissemination of information using computers. IT has revolutionised office work, and is about to revolutionise telecommunications (i.e. the transmission of information via radio waves or electric cables). Integration is the core concept in the application of IT to administrative duties. Computers may be linked and networks created. A network shares common information; each of its components having direct access to the processing capacities of other users.

The facts needed to produce information (sales, receipts, invoices, values, expense claims, stock issues, etc) are termed 'data', and the process which transforms raw data into information (i.e. useful items or summaries of data) is known as data processing (DP). Raw data are the *input* to the system; information the *output*. The processes that convert input into output involve sorting, storing, amending, performing calculations on, adding, deleting or retrieving data. These processes should be as precise, accurate and inexpensive as possible. Information outputs must be relevant to users' requirements, easily understood by them, up to date and easily available.

IT strategy

Strategies (*see* Chapter 5) for managing IT systems need to encompass the total resources of the organisation, having particular regard to the following matters:

(a) Staffing. Selecting recruits best equipped to handle IT-based management systems. Determining training requirements. Deciding how those competent in IT are to be rewarded and their salary differentiated with other categories of staff.

(b) Determining the extent of modifications to existing products, administrative arrangements and working methods required to obtain maximum benefit from an IT-driven organisation.

(c) Altering organisational structures, including spans of control, delegation arrangements, number of levels of authority, etc in order to make the best use of the latest IT.

(d) Integrating IT into all aspects of the firm's operations.

(e) Deciding whether to develop a unique system in house or to purchase a standard commercial system (*see* **12**).

Determination of an IT strategy is one of the most important of all senior management functions, due to the ever-increasing complexity of modern business and the enormous efficiency improvements that the effective utilisation of IT can create. Further stimuli to the development of an IT strategy might include:

(a) rival firms gaining competitive advantage

(b) information overload within the organisation

(c) environmental turbulence accompanied by an increased need to gather and analyse information from external sources

(d) organisational restructuring and/or being taken over by another firm

(e) ferocious competition in markets both at home and abroad.

Products have to be supplied quickly, economically and at a high level of quality; and only by using modern technologies can most companies keep up with rival firms. Judicious use of IT can lead to a first-rate administrative system, effective decision making, efficient use of resources, and high productivity levels within the firm. IT helps businesses cope with complexity, uncertainty, and the explosion in the volume of information (internal and external) that has become available to companies in recent decades. As organisations become more sophisticated, so too must the techniques and procedures of organisational control – techniques that in today's world are invariably based on IT.

Information technology can be an important source of competitive advantage through:

(a) linking the firm to its customers and suppliers

(b) improving operational efficiency

(c) helping management devise and implement high calibre strategies

(d) creating a fresh entry barrier for firms outside the industry

(e) making it difficult for business customers to switch to alternative suppliers that have incompatible IT systems

(f) facilitating business re-engineering (*see* **10:46**)

(g) improving quality management. Note how modern TQM systems rely heavily on computerised production and IT.

(h) enabling the firm to respond quickly to environmental change

(i) facilitating the monitoring of key performance indicators

(j) enabling the firm to service niche markets via product differentiation and flexible manufacturing (*see* 10:**5**)

(k) monitoring suppliers and reducing procurement costs

(l) integrating marketing with production

(m) improving management control.

Rapid conveyance of control information facilitates fast and effective decision taking. The quality of decisions should improve because computerised systems enable operations research models and solution techniques to be applied, and advanced methods of planning and co-ordination to be implemented. Decisions are taken on the basis of more comprehensive information and the likely consequences of a wide range of alternative courses of action can be explored.

2. IT and human resources management

Those who operate IT-driven administrative and production systems typically require a higher level of education and training than the traditional manufacturing worker. At the same time, however, the need for conventional craft skills has diminished. Labour flexibility within a computerised working situation requires *technologies* rather than crafts people. In particular, the range and quality of the information potentially available to everyone in the organisation is greatly increased. Hence, traditional dividing lines between occupational categories break down, and the demarcation of jobs can become irrelevant: vertically as well as horizontally. Other important possible consequences of computerisation with implications for human resources management include the following:

(a) Deskilling of tasks in certain parts of the enterprise while new types of skill are required elsewhere, leading perhaps to resentments and conflicts between various categories of worker.

(b) Total integration of all phases of production, office administration and internal communications, causing more frequent and perhaps closer interactions among employees in different sections of the firm and between various levels in the managerial hierarchy.

The competencies needed to succeed within a computerised work environment are general in nature and not necessarily related to particular occupations. Hence there is much scope for job rotation, undermining thereby employees' specific control over what were previously highly specialised jobs that could not easily be given to other categories of worker.

3. Possible HRM problems

IT staff (and computer literate employees generally) frequently occupy key positions in organisations whereby they can cause great disruption through taking industrial action. This could induce management to treat computing personnel more favourably than other categories, and to try and arrange the division and pattern of work so as to ensure that not too much disruptive potential lies in a few pairs of hands.

To the extent that computer staff are treated differently to other types of worker, a number of sources of conflict may arise, as follows:

(a) Sometimes, computer literate staff with specialist qualifications have the same status, earn similar salaries, and occupy the same grades as line managers who – although they contribute a great deal to the organisation's work – are not as well certificated academically and have not had to spend several years studying for professional examinations. Accordingly, those who operate the computerised system might treat with disdain the work of line managers and resent the fact that computing staff and line managers are graded and paid equally. Conversely, line managers may begrudge the computer worker's self-assumed intellectual status.

(b) Those who manage the computerised system might expect to be able to exercise discretion and judgement in the course of their work, but at the same time must comply with the bureaucratic rules and demands of the wider organisation. They are subject to the authority of senior administrators, yet usually are not fully involved in the formulation of the administrative processes that determine the rules.

(c) Other categories of employee (including line managers) might form a coalition against computing staff whose level of education and social status they resent and whom they do not feel should be taking significant decisions on behalf of the company.

4. Implications for organisational structure

Often the introduction of a new IT system necessitates the rearrangement of the departmental structure of the firm. Computerisation tends to encourage centralisation of administrative procedures. Data is summarised and distributed automatically, circulating around a central control unit which can receive and monitor management information continuously. Requirements for local data interpretation and decision taking might diminish. Less delegation from senior to junior managers is likely in a computerised system because higher management obtains better, faster and more comprehensive information. Consequently senior managers exercise much tighter personal control. Indeed the great bulk of senior managerial work in some industries can, in principle, be conducted from a computer terminal.

5. Organisation of IT staff

The basic issue here is whether to concentrate IT resources into one or more centralised units, or to disperse IT expertise throughout the firm. Some firms have 'information centres' to support sectional IT activities (especially end-user computing). Each centre gives specialist advice to a number of departments, has access to sophisticated software, and may undertake more difficult computing tasks. The problem is that the centres could lack detailed knowledge of sectional IT requirements and become 'marginalised' within the organisation. Other alternatives are the creation of a single centralised department to oversee all IT activities, or widespread dispersion of responsibility for IT throughout the firm.

Centralisation

Advantages to the creation of a centralised department include:

(a) Rapid responses to systems failures

(b) Cost savings made possible through the avoidance of duplicated activities

(c) Better security

(d) Clear responsibility for IT activities

(e) Tight control over the system

(f) Accumulation of technical expertise within the central unit, together with the application of sophisticated support facilities and software

(g) The ability to recruit highly qualified IT staff, whose talents can be fully utilised in a centralised IT department (a career ladder will exist within the unit)

(h) Improved productivity of IT procedures

(i) The fact that staff can be quickly redeployed within the department.

However, centralisation can lead to a splitting off of IT development from the rest of the organisation, and costs may run out of control as IT specialists pursue their particular interests. 'Chinese walls' might be erected between IT and other functions, with IT not being regarded as an integral part of the management structure of the firm. Further problems with centralisation are:

(a) Inflexible attitudes and administrative bureaucracy may emerge.

(b) The centralised unit might lose touch with the goals of major IT user departments.

(c) Long delays may occur before user departments experiencing difficulties can be serviced.

(d) It can be difficult to allocate the costs of the centralised unit to user departments. Should these costs be regarded as a general overhead to be spread across the entire firm (thus penalising sections that do not use the unit's services), or should IT-intensive departments pay more than the rest?

(e) If the central unit fails the company's entire IT system will collapse.

Decentralisation

Factors encouraging dispersion of responsibility for IT (via the creation of Information Centres for example) include:

(a) Massive increases in the power of desktop computers

(b) The development of high-quality end-user computing software

(c) Growing computer literacy among middle managers

(d) The large variations in the IT needs of certain departments.

Dispersion results in IT specialists being closer to end-users and (hopefully) more in tune with their everyday needs. Users are involved with devising and operating the system and should in consequence be better motivated towards making it succeed. Further advantages are that:

(a) Systems that emerge should be immediately relevant to the business's operational requirements (rather than being selected for their purely technical excellence).

(b) Systems are more likely to be flexible and responsive to changing circumstances.

(c) Computer awareness is encouraged throughout the organisation.

(d) End-user computing is facilitated (*see* **16**).

(e) Creativity is stimulated.

(f) Information is processed close to where it is to be used.

(g) Decentralised units can tailor their activities to the specific requirements of particular functions and/or departments.

(h) IT costs are directly related to user sections.

(i) IT is more closely integrated into the organisation system of the enterprise.

Problems with dispersion include communication difficulties, computer illiteracy among certain types of staff, and duplication of effort. Costs may be higher and (importantly) not as visible as when the IT function is concentrated into a single unit. Other difficulties are that:

(a) Working methods in various units may become incompatible and lead to poor co-ordination.

(b) Dispersed facilities might not be able to cope with complex and technically sophisticated IT problems.

(c) The role and status of IT specialists might be unclear.

(d) Arguments between dispersed IT staff and functional line managers might develop.

6. Facilities management

This involves an arrangement whereby an outside organisation takes over a company's entire computing function, managing it on the client's behalf, and possibly using the latter's equipment and employees. In effect the client obtains a ready-made computing department at low overhead cost and does not have to train its own executives in computer management. Facilities management providers typically work for several companies at the same time. The client will (usually) pay:

(a) an annual lump-sum fee

(b) rental charges on equipment (when the client does not directly own the system)

(c) equipment maintenance costs

(d) an hourly charge while the system is in use, covering the wages of computing staff plus general support services.

Usually, responsibility for providing data in a form acceptable for input to the system lies with the client company.

Problems with using a facilities manager are that the client (*i*) becomes entirely dependent on the former's services, and (*ii*) loses control over computing costs. Also the facilities manager might use the client firm's system to complete work for other clients.

MANAGEMENT INFORMATION AND DECISION SUPPORT

7. Management information systems

Efficient management information systems (MIS) enable management to plan, co-ordinate, organise and control. They provide the information needed for strategic planning and for day-to-day operations. Strategic information requirements include data on business ratios (return on capital employed, ratios of debt to equity capital, interest payable on borrowed money, etc), on current trends in external capital markets, the firm's liquidity position, aggregate cash flow forecasts, market research data and so on. Tactical information needs might involve ratios of profits to working capital, stock to current assets, sales to output; rates of return on specific investment profits; information on production bottlenecks, capacity constraints, etc.

An important MIS function is to highlight potential difficulties with debtors and suppliers. What, for example, is the average delay between delivery of goods and the issue of invoices? How quickly do customers settle their accounts? What are the effects of offering discounts for prompt payment? What is the ratio of creditors to purchases? How long, on average, do suppliers take to deliver goods, and to what extent can payments to suppliers be delayed?

Other categories of information that an MIS should supply include the following:

(a) Market information:

    (*i*)   effectiveness of sales personnel

    (*ii*) responsiveness of sales to price changes

    (*iii*) market trends

    (*iv*) behaviour of competitors

    (*v*) adequacy of distribution channels.

(b) Financial information:

    (*i*) whether budgets are being adhered to

    (*ii*) length of trading cycles

    (*iii*) adequacy of cash inflows

    (*iv*) need for external financing.

(c) Work-in-progress information:

    (*i*) ratios of work in progress to production, stock to sales, etc

    (*ii*) identification of slow-moving stock

    (*iii*) frequency and causes of stockouts

    (*iv*) stockholding costs

    (*v*) causes of machine breakdown and other interruptions in production.

8. Installation of an MIS

To install an MIS it is necessary to consider when, how and to whom information has to be transmitted, and how best to summarise data in a form that enables its fast and accurate evaluation prior to taking decisions. In practice, however, difficulties emerge, including the following:

(a) Relevant information might not reach the right people. Managers commonly assume that colleagues and subordinates have been informed of particular facts when, actually, they have not.

(b) Breaks in the chain of command. Information should flow vertically through the enterprise from its top to its bottom via the channels illustrated in its organisation chart. Often, information 'bottlenecks' occur at supervisory and middle management levels since supervisors and middle managers not only receive information from above (and have to decide whether to act on it) but also collect feedback from lower levels.

(c) Horizontal flows of information among colleagues of equal rank may be interrupted if certain individuals deliberately conceal information or – through incompetence – do not pass it on.

(d) The *culture* of the organisation may be resistant to change. This could create special problems if the MIS cuts across existing departmental boundaries, challenges informal information transmission systems, or creates 'information gatekeepers' (i.e. individuals who handle large amounts of information and become powerful through being able to withhold vital information from colleagues they dislike).

The effectiveness of an MIS should be evaluated against its capacity to assist in taking decisions; particularly through enabling the comparison of various possibilities in new and meaningful ways. Note that there is little point in confronting, for example, a sales manager with an array of figures on market trends, promotional costs, survey results and so on if he or she cannot understand what they mean. In this context the skill of the manager lies in recognising what summary data are relevant and useful, and the format in which they are required.

9. Implications for organisation and control

The implications of computerisation for the management of organisations are as follows:

(a) The volume of data handled is not constrained by the availability of clerical labour.

(b) Activities may be monitored continuously rather than (say) at the end of each month.

(c) Tendency towards centralisation of administrative procedures. Data circulate around a central control which receives and instantly responds to management information.

(d) Less delegation from senior to junior executives, since higher management obtains better, faster and more comprehensive information.

(e) Ability of senior management to exert tight personal control. A large amount of senior managerial work can now be done from a computer terminal.

(f) Improved quality of decisions and the possible application of advanced management methods to administrative tasks.

Note how the various levels of management typically require the information they receive to be formatted in different ways. First-line managers, for instance, usually need clearly defined and frequently present information on such matters as inventory levels, staff and equipment availability, work completion plans, etc. Executive managers require information that enables them to take a general view of the efficiency of an entire department or function; while top management needs information which is useful for taking wide-ranging strategic decisions. Information for senior management will normally include external information and involve summaries of complex and extensive issues.

10. Decision support

Effective control requires the collection, summary and evaluation of data prior to taking decisions. A decision support system (DSS) comprises an integrated collection of computing tools for solving problems and taking decisions. Key elements of a DSS are a database containing factual information, a spreadsheet, possibly an expert system (*see* **14**), modelling and graphics programs, and programs for data manipulation and statistical analysis. DSS software provides a framework for breaking problems down into constituent parts plus a means for specifying decision criteria. 'What if' and other sensitivity analyses then become possible.

Managers using DS systems are able to call up and instantly summarise huge quantities of data, may formulate models for analysing likely consequences of various courses of action and can select the criteria on which final decisions will be based. Accordingly, the managers involved need to know the models and software available; their assumptions, uses and limitations; and hypothesis testing and elementary operations research.

Relations with the MIS

The management information system collates, stores and retrieves data. It provides the data inputs to the DSS and does not involve the exercise of managerial discretion *per se*. DS systems, conversely, focus on the manipulation of information and the structuring of decision making tasks. Extensive managerial knowledge and judgement is needed to make effective use of a DSS.

DECISION SUPPORT FACILITIES

11. Commercial software

'Software' is all the instructions (in the form of programs) that enable the computer to function. System software (also called 'operating' software) comprises programs which take over the running of the computer once they are loaded. Application software performs tasks (such as word-processing or stock control) and is used within a particular operating system. Few firms, especially small firms, employ people to write company-specific application programs as there now exist a wide variety of readymade packages, and many standard commercial programs contain menu-driven procedures which enable them to be adapted to meet particular users' requirements.

If greater specialisation is needed, 'custom built' software may be commissioned from professional software designers. However, the high cost of this relative to the straight purchase of existing programs encourages firms to alter their internal routines to make them compatible with available software programs rather than vice versa. Changing an existing administrative system is often cheaper than commissioning 'designer' software, and has the added advantage that well-established commercial programs are usually error-free whereas custom-built software can contain many errors (requiring the personal attention of the individual who wrote the program), some of which might not be revealed for several months (or even years) following installation.

12. Choice of package

In choosing a package for a certain application the firm should examine the following factors:

(a) The program's ability to handle the volume of data entries (e.g. the number of customers' names and addresses held on file) necessary for the business's purposes.

(b) Speed of operation.

(c) Quality of output, especially if the output consists of written documents that will be seen by outsiders.

(d) Ease of use. Ideally, a program should be capable of operation by an inexperienced person.

(e) Flexibility. Good packages allow the user to modify, via menus, the basic structures of their operations and output. Note, however, that a package purchased to run on one system (IBM compatible, for example) will not normally run on another – a different version of the same package will be required.

(f) Availability of support services from the program manufacturer. Many software suppliers offer free advice (over the telephone) on the use of their programs (including the correction of errors found in the program itself) for three or six months from the date of purchase.

(g) Whether the program is user-friendly, how much training (if any) is required prior to its use, and any problems or drawbacks associated with its operation.

13. Open systems

An 'open' computer system is one that interconnects computers from different manufacturers, enabling them to communicate and work together. Open system interconnection (OSI) has applications in CADCAM (*see* 10:**30**), MAP (*see* 10:**7**) and (importantly) in electronic trading. A major example of the latter is the 'electronic data interchange' (EDI) system increasingly used for export/import transactions. EDI enables the fully-integrated electronic-mail exchange of documents between exporters, customers, banks, goods carriers, insurers, agents and distributors, dock and harbour authorities, customs and excise departments, freight forwarders and so on.

OSI systems offer greatly reduced clerical costs, faster delivery and payments cycles, and fewer errors in transmitted documents.

14. Artificial intelligence and expert systems

The term artificial intelligence (AI) means the simulation of human thought processes in order to select the best mode of behaviour, e.g. taking a decision or responding to a situation. Expert systems are a major application of AI.

Expert systems attempt to mimic the human expert, applying the same knowledge and procedures to problem solving as would a highly-skilled professional person (e.g. a medical doctor examining a patient). The facts and diagnostic processes contained in the package enable it to answer questions in a seemingly intelligent fashion. Packages themselves are divided into two parts: a 'shell' which is a program to process information in a logical way, and a database containing the information and rules about how it must be interpreted. The shell manipulates the database according to a preset pattern, and various combinations of questions may be asked of the data. Questions are asked in the form, 'What if . . ., and . . ., and if something else happens?' The answers should correspond to those of an expert instructor. Hence the package can be used to *diagnose* simulated problems, and in so doing develop the user's personal knowledge of the subject and suggest how best to investigate logically the problems that it involves.

15. Applications of expert systems

Expert systems have been applied to the training of telecommunications engineers (for fault diagnosis on printed circuit boards), to training operatives how to adjust complex electronic equipment, and to training betting-shop managers how to settle complicated bets (such as 'What are the odds if the number of runners in a horse race exceeds 12 and the race is a handicap and the chosen horse is placed third and . . .'). New applications of expert systems to business are constantly being discovered. For example, cheap packages are now available to prepare shortlists of job applicants to invite for interview following the receipt of numerous completed applications. Users simply type-in key information taken directly from each candidate's application form and then specify various criteria (typing/shorthand speeds, possession of certain educational qualifications, number of years' experience of a particular kind of work, etc) deemed crucial for successful performance in the job. Criteria can be altered at will and hence different sets of shortlisted applicants generated according to the various sets of candidate characteristics.

16. End-user computing

Use of expert systems is an example of 'end-user computing', i.e. the imaginative manipulation of computer packages and systems by employees who have no special qualifications or expertise in computing or IT. End-user computing is becoming an important subject in its own right, and software and systems are increasingly being designed to give the non-specialist package-user maximum discretion in determining the nature of the outputs of systems. It has, moreover, a number of implications for organisation and management, including the following:

(a) Opportunities for greatly increased productivity among whitecollar workers, who will be able to choose *how* they complete IT-related tasks. This should make their jobs more interesting and provide numerous possibilities for job enrichment (*see* 15:**21**).

(b) A levelling out of the performance levels of the best and worst employees, since the computer will do a lot of the employee's basic work.

(c) Faster decision making.

(d) The need for staff who are capable of assessing the reliability of outputs from expert systems that contain information on topics with which they are not familiar.

(e) Less demand for expert staff managers (*see* 15:**21**).

(f) Greater access of employees to a wide range of the firm's databases. Note how this can create data security problems and possibilities for the deliberate disruption of systems.

(g) The need to involve users in the initial design of a system.

(h) Employees are presented with:

- new alternatives regarding how work can be completed
- more interesting tasks, challenges and responsibilities
- a wider range of duties to be completed
- the need to take an increased number of decisions
- fresh possibilities for restructuring the working day.

Introduction of end-user computing is often accompanied by the 'downsizing' of systems, i.e. the increased use of small but powerful personal computing systems and applications, made possible by the enormous expansion in the capacity of the typical PC that has occurred in recent years. Downsizing implies greater systems flexibility, decentralisation of costs, and improved responsiveness to local needs. On the other hand it can involve a substantial capital outlay, weaken central control, and impose additional workloads on staff in user departments.

Strategic issues related to end-user computing are as follows:

(a) Definition of the role of end-user computing in attaining corporate objectives.

(b) The extent of central management control over end-user computing activities.

(c) Who is to select hardware and software (i.e. the degree of user involvement in the process).

(d) How the system is to be developed, how quickly and by whom (users or specialist IT staff).

Advantages and problems of end-user computing

Advantages of end-user computing are:

(a) Individuals are able to develop their IT skills.

(b) Each section of the firm can use IT at a level of sophistication appropriate for its particular requirements.

(c) The approach encourages creativity and innovation among employees.

Problems with end-user computing include duplication of activities, higher costs, the possible emergence of inconsistencies in working methods, and perhaps a general lowering of the quality of the firm's overall IT activities. Users might not define problems in an appropriate manner, with consequent waste of computing time and resources. Training needs are extensive (and costly) and money has to be spent on technical support (either from a centralised unit or from outside consultants). Note moreover that some individuals might be extremely reluctant to become involved in the system, creating extra work for other people. Further difficulties are that:

(a) End users might not be competent to select the decision support tools that are objectively the best to apply in complex circumstances.

(b) Users might concentrate on short-term issues at the expense of long-term systems development.

(c) Bad IT working practices may be passed on from department to department.

SYSTEMS PLANNING AND DESIGN

17. Systems analysis

A 'system' is a set of procedures for achieving a stated objective. A payroll system, for example, has procedures which convert pay rates, overtime records, PAYE and national insurance contributions into payslips and direct debits into employees' bank accounts. Business systems comprise hardware, software, operating methods and people. The task of systems analysis is to organise their interactions to produce desired outcomes. It need not involve computers, but if a system is not computerised then the speed, accuracy, reliability, and huge data storage and manipulative abilities of computers are lost.

Analysts examine the information requirements of each of the firm's departments and identity interrelations between them. A 'master file' is created for each key activity, fed by appropriate subsidiary files. The stock control master, for instance, is fed with facts on stock issues, receipts of supplies, requisitions, etc, and generates information on stock shortages, holding and acquisition costs, and replenishment dates for various inventories. This output constitutes input to the purchasing master, which contains suppliers' names and addresses, delivery periods, prices and so on.

18. Systems analysis methods

The procedure for conducting a systems analysis is as follows:

(a) State the purpose of the organisation and its major objectives (only then will the division of the intended system into functional units make sense).

(b) Specify output requirements, including the formats of documents (invoices, credit notes, stock requisitions, etc).

(c) List the reporting procedures that will govern the new system (i.e. what information is needed by which manager, where and when).

(d) Investigate existing procedures regarding data collection and retention, people-machine interfaces, interpersonal communications structures, and so on.

(e) Design a new system, i.e. determine the processes necessary to satisfy users' requirements.

19. Systems design

The aim of systems design is to create an integrated information and control system that is easily implemented and co-ordinated, and which can be adapted and expanded to meet future needs.

First the business must identify *sub-systems* of functions to be computerised (payroll, stock control, etc) and decide which to tackle first (usually that which is easiest and/or for which reliable commercial software exists). For each sub-system, management next prepares a statement of:

(a) its purpose and longer-term objectives

(b) anticipated costs and benefits

(c) expected technical problems and possible causes of difficulty

(d) staff training requirements

(e) form of new documents required

(f) how the sub-system relates to the wider system and how, specifically, it meets certain aspects of the overall system's needs

(g) how the sub-system will be monitored when operating

(h) the extent to which it can be modified and adapted to satisfy anticipated future requirements

(i) who shall be responsible for implementing each sub-system and by when

(j) which sub-systems are 'crucial' in the sense that failure to implement them successfully will lead to the collapse of the entire scheme

(k) necessary changes in the firm's organisation structure

(l) the final information outputs to be produced and the summary control information (e.g. monthly or semi-annual sales figures, quarterly profit and loss accounts, or weekly inventory levels) expected of the system. Raw-data requirements, file structures and processing methods may then be determined.

20. Systems planning and logical systems design

Logical systems design is 'back-end' systems analysis. An agreed format for the *output* of the sub-system is specified, and the analyst then works back through the various stages of the system, specifying the inputs and procedures needed to produce the predetermined format. In other words, the analyst asks the question: 'What input data is required, how should it be stored and manipulated, how many files are needed and of what type, in order to generate the information?'. The analyst then develops a system configuration to meet these needs.

Systems planning means determining the order in which a business's functions are to be computerised. It is an important activity with crucial implications for the organisational structure of the firm. Also, effective systems planning ensures there will be no mismatches between printers, keyboards, processing units, output terminals and so on. The firm must identify priority areas for computerisation and then organise procedures for meeting these priorities in the most efficient way.

21. System maintenance

The details of the company's computerised system should be embodied in a written manual containing operating instructions, rules of procedure, copies of all standard documents and lists of the actions to take if various malfunctions occur. This manual is necessary for ensuring continuity following staff changes, absences due to holidays or sickness and for the training of employees. Systems should be reviewed periodically and the following questions asked.

(a) Has the system operated within its budget, and if not, why not?

(b) How well has the system satisfied the objectives originally set?

(c) Have environmental circumstances altered so as to require changes in the system (new accounting standards or procedures, for example)?

(d) Can areas for improved efficiency be identified?

(e) Have users expressed dissatisfaction with either the system's procedures or with the adequacy of its outputs?

(f) Has the firm's corporate strategy (see Chapter 5) altered since the last review and if so how does this affect the system?

(g) Is each sub-system satisfactorily fitting in to the total configuration?

Progress test 13

1. List five problems associated with computerised control systems.

2. What are the implications of computerisation for the organisational structure of a firm?

3. Outline the essential personal qualities that functional line managers need to possess for successful operation of a computerised control system.

4. Define the term 'decision support system'.

5. Explain the differences between a systems analysis and a systems plan.

6. What is 'telecommunications'?

Part Three

THE HUMAN SIDE OF MANAGEMENT

14

THE NATURE OF WORK

TYPES OF WORK

1. Definition

Work is the effort directed towards the attainment of a goal. It involves the completion of tasks and the assumption of responsibilities. Whether work is enjoyable, or little more than a means for achieving a material end, depends on a number of factors, including:

(a) Individual inclinations towards work

(b) Whether a job provides creative opportunities and possibilities to undertake varied and interesting duties

(c) The culture of the society in which the employee lives (ancient Greece, for example, relegated work to slaves)

(d) Childhood socialisation and upbringing.

2. Problems created by certain kinds of work

People with jobs have income, status, and a means for interacting socially with others. The latter can represent an important motivating factor: pay and physical working conditions are not *necessarily* the critical determinants of employee morale.

Monotonous work, however, creates special problems, notably the following:

(a) *Alienation*, i.e. the feeling that work is not a relevant or important part of the employee's life. It is associated with feelings of discontent, isolation and futility. Alienated workers see themselves as powerless and dominated. It is most likely to occur on automated assembly lines where workers undertake just a single task and where contacts with other people are infrequent.

(b) *Frustration*. This occurs when employees feel unable to control their work in ways that enable them to achieve personal objectives, e.g. if they cannot regulate the pace of work or are compelled to undertake what to them are meaningless tasks. Other possible causes of frustration are lack of involvement in decision making and the absence of procedures for having grievances redressed. Workers react to frustration either positively – by attempting to overcome the problems causing dissatisfaction – or negatively. Examples of negative reactions are aggression (quarrels with colleagues, hostility towards management); apathy (lateness, absenteeism); unwillingness to assume responsibility; poor quality work; high propensity for accidents, and high rates of labour turnover. Frustration might be reduced through employee participation in decision making, training and staff development, improved communications and job design (*see* 15:26).

(c) *Boredom*, which is caused either by continuous repetition of a simple task or by the social environment in which work is completed. (Workers may feel bored through being socially isolated rather than through the monotony of the work.) Complicated tasks need concentration. Workers performing complex jobs typically become absorbed by them and do not experience boredom.

3. Choice of occupation

Children are prepared for work via vocational education, careers guidance, school-to-work transition programmes, work induction and special training schemes. Their first information about work results from listening to parents' conversations about jobs. Then, as they grow up they do increasing amounts of school 'work'. At school, attitudes supporting the desire for occupational success are consciously developed. Scholastic achievement is rewarded and success in competitive sports encouraged. Discipline patterns in schools, moreover, are often intended to train young people to fit into patterns of supervision and authority in employment.

Schools and parents play a crucial role in determining a child's self-identity and, in consequence, guide the child towards a particular type of occupation. Other important factors affecting the job a school-leaver takes might include:

(a) the nature of local industry

(b) unemployment rates and the availability of jobs, in particular occupations

(c) the person's age (and hence level of qualifications) on leaving school or college

(d) societal constraints on entry to particular occupations (sex or race discrimination, for example).

4. Careers

A career is a predictable series of related jobs that progressively increase in status, reward and responsibility. Careers can occur within a single organisation, or by moving between organisations. Whether an individual has a successful career depends on several factors, including luck, personal circumstances, individual competence, creativity and willingness to take risks and seize opportunities. Other considerations are whether the individual:

(a) can observe the work and behaviour of higher-level managers at first hand

(b) experiences the departments, assignments and types of work most relevant to furthering a career

(c) identifies career alternatives (possibly via career counselling)

(d) appreciates his or her personal strengths and weaknesses.

Career planning is especially difficult when both parties to a relationship have interesting and well-paid jobs, since a promotion for one of the partners that necessitates geographical relocation may involve the other partner abandoning his or her own career. Some companies recognise this problem and consciously avoid the geographical transfer of people in such a situation, or they try to find appropriate work for the relocated person's other half either within the company or elsewhere.

Empirical research into career planning and development is discussed in the M&E text *Organisational Behaviour*, to which the interested reader is referred.

5. Part-time work

The large increase in casual and/or part-time work that has occurred in Britain over the last quarter century has brought with it new problems of human resource planning (*see* 16:4), utilisation, appraisal and control. Casual and part-time workers may be preferred to full-time staff for three main reasons: (*i*) lower cost (full-timers are often not fully utilised throughout the year, whereas casuals work on specific assignments); (*ii*) the ease with which the size of the labour force can be varied; and (*iii*) the fact that casuals and part-timers are typically not covered by employment legislation (*see* 11:17).

6. Core and peripheral ('flexible') workers

'Core' workers are full-time permanent employees who plan, take decisions and organise the work of casuals. They have security of tenure, are superannuated, and enjoy a variety of fringe benefits. 'Peripheral' workers, conversely, are hired as and when required on short-term and/or part-time contracts. They exercise little discretion over how they perform their duties. Peripherals might include job sharers, agency employees, homeworkers and self-employed contractors as well as casuals and part-timers.

Special problems apply to the management of flexible workforces, possibly including:

(a) Low morale among peripherals, who do not feel they really 'belong' to the organisation

(b) High labour turnover and hence the loss of good-quality peripheral staff

(c) Poor communications with and between peripherals

(d) Deciding how to appraise the performances of casual and part-time workers

(e) Securing adequate representation of peripheral employees in management/union negotiations, on health and safety committees, etc

(f) Preventing permanent full-time workers resenting the presence of peripherals, whom they might regard as a threat to their jobs

(g) Controlling the quality of recruitment of casually-employed staff

(h) Arranging for the supervision of peripheral employees and deciding whether this should be done by other peripherals in a higher grade or by core workers. Note that flexible workers are not usually capable of handling crises or sudden influxes of extra work since they lack the resources, information, experience and authority necessary – leading perhaps to overwork among core staff.

To overcome these problems, firms employing large numbers of flexible workers sometimes apply the following measures:

(a) Guarantees of re-entry to a job after a break in continuity of service.

(b) Introduction of formal job-sharing arrangements. (Note, however, the 'two Monday mornings' syndrome this might create.)

(c) Having peripherals choose how and when they complete their duties (through homeworking, for example).

(d) Offering working conditions comparable to those of permanent core workers, including full recognition of peripheral employees' contribution.

(e) Incorporating grievance procedures, right of appeal against dismissal, etc into peripherals' contracts of employment.

(f) Paying peripheral workers to attend training courses and general discussions about the firm's objectives.

(g) Making peripherals responsible for the quality of their outputs, and generally broadening the scope for their jobs.

7. Job evaluation

A job comprises a collection of characteristics and obligations including skill requirements, responsibilities, working conditions, and possibly certain abilities such as the ability to withstand stress or the capacity to lead, co-ordinate, plan, control and organise. Job evaluation seeks to establish a rational basis for assessing the worth of a job and then to position it within the hierarchy of jobs existing in a particular organisation. The advantages of job evaluation include the following:

(a) Wages are directly related to workers' contribution, so that employees may be fairly paid.

(b) Inequitable job structures are avoided. Common criteria are used to determine employees' wages.

(c) All jobs of equivalent value in terms of skill requirements, responsibilities, etc will be equally graded regardless of the department or section in which the work is performed.

(d) Once a job hierarchy has been established, promotion systems that specify the qualifications needed for advancement from one level to the next can be implemented.

8. Job evaluation methods

Job evaluation assesses the characteristics of jobs rather than the personal qualities of the individuals who undertake them. Traditionally, three methods have been applied to job evaluation; two of these, however, today create legal difficulties. The ones with legal problems are as follows:

(a) *The ranking system*, whereby management (or a ranking committee that includes employee representatives) makes an overall assessment of each job, taking account of all its aspects. It is a subjective, impressionistic evaluation which does not attempt to quantify the relative significance of particular elements of a job. Ranking is quick, easy and cheap to apply, but it does not evaluate the individual *demands* of a position. The 'whole' job is compared against other whole jobs and is ranked according to its perceived importance. At least three 'benchmark' jobs are defined at the top, bottom and in the middle of the hierarchy. Jobs are then slotted into the hierarchy according to their relationships to the benchmark jobs and to each other.

(b) *The grading system.* Here management predetermines a number of grades into which all jobs are fitted. The lowest grade is usually reserved for unskilled workers, the highest for senior management. Job specifications are examined (perhaps by a committee) and assigned to an appropriate grade. Typically, there are no more than six or seven grades, otherwise grades become meaningless. Too few grades, on the other hand, create large differences in skill and other requirements within each grade. Management has to write grade as well as job descriptions to operationalise the system.

Ranking and grading methods are 'non-analytical'. Under EC law (which is binding on the UK), however, jobs must be evaluated *analytically*: 'felt fair' general assessments of jobs – making subjective evaluations without attempting to quantify their main components – have been declared unlawful in test cases concerning equal opportunities legislation.

Today, therefore, the commonest approach is to apply a 'points system' whereby all the factors deemed relevant to all the jobs under consideration are listed. Management then ascribes an appropriate number of points to each factor for each job. Examples of factors include numerical ability, responsibility for cash or equipment, training requirements, technical expertise, physical strength needed, and the extent of supervision of others. Weightings may be introduced depending on the degree of importance of a particular factor in a certain job. Points are then aggregated and jobs allocated to appropriate grades.

Problems with job evaluation include the following:

(a) Employees may overstate the qualities necessary to complete their jobs, while supervisors may lack personal experience of subordinates' work and thus be unable to apply objective evaluations.

(b) Complex jobs with multifaceted characteristics are difficult to evaluate.

(c) Ultimately, wage rates depend on market forces. Changes in the supply and demand for certain categories of labour can cause the results of an expensive job-evaluation exercise to become irrelevant.

(d) Often, job-grading decisions are taken following negotiations with trade unions; haggling occurs and compromises are reached. What is the point, therefore, of attempting formal evaluations in the first instance?

(e) In consequence of an evaluation study certain employees may be adjudged overpaid in relation to their contribution. Typically, such individuals are 'red circled', i.e. they continue to receive their existing salaries but, when they leave the organisation, their replacements are engaged on a lower grade. However, new holders of these posts may bitterly resent being paid less money than their predecessors.

(f) The implications of equal-opportunities legislation for job evaluation are extremely complicated, since under the 1984 amendments to the Equal Pay Act any person is entitled to the same remuneration and conditions of service as a member of the opposite sex who is doing similar work, or *work of a similar value*, as judged under a *job evaluation* exercise. Interested readers are referred to the M&E text *Human Resources Management* for a discussion of this issue.

WORKING IN GROUPS

9. Formation of groups

Groups form either through management decision or naturally and without encouragement from outside. Through working together, people establish customs and norms that affect relationships, working methods and attitudes towards the employing firm. The more a person wishes to belong to a group the more he or she will want to comply with its standards: feelings of attachment become greater and the power of the group to compel obedience is enhanced.

Groups may be primary or secondary, formal or informal. A primary group consists of members who come into direct contact. Secondary groups are larger, less personal, and lack immediate direct contact between members. Examples of primary groups are small departments within a firm, project teams, families, sports teams or other direct contact recreational associations. Secondary groups might be factories, communities, long assembly lines where there is little interpersonal communication, or geographical divisions of a company.

Formal groups are deliberately created by management which selects group members, leaders and methods of doing work. They are characterised by a high degree of managerial involvement in co-ordinating, controlling and defining the nature of the activities they undertake. Informal groups are established by people who feel they have something in common. Members organise themselves and develop a sense of affinity to each other and to a common cause. Often, it is an informal group that actually determines how much work is done.

Note that informal groups could form specifically to oppose the wishes of management.

10. Group norms and cohesion

A group norm is a shared feeling about how an issue should be interpreted or a task completed; or a common attitude, perception or belief. Norms could relate to working methods, quality of output, how various people should be addressed, status of individual members, etc.

Norms are particularly important in determining workers' attitudes towards change, since norms can create or overcome resistance to new methods, and they greatly contribute to 'group cohesion', i.e. the degree to which members are willing to co-operate and work in unison. Cohesion enhances group morale and productivity and causes stability in group behaviour. Equally, however, pressure for conformity can stifle initiative.

The following factors encourage group cohesion:

(a) The more frequently and closely group members interact.

(b) The extent to which members regard the external environment as hostile (and thus see the group as a protection against external threats).

(c) Homogeneity of group members in terms of background, age, education, outlook, ethnic or social origin, etc.

(d) Whether members perceive entry to the group as a special privilege afforded only to selected people.

(e) Members' enthusiasm for group objectives.

(f) The similarity of the tasks upon which individual group members are engaged.

(g) The existence of group bonuses.

Note that high group cohesion need not be associated with high productivity, low rates of absenteeism, enthusiasm for work and other desirable characteristics, but rather with the reverse. Cohesive groups can conspire to restrict output, perhaps even to disrupt the organisation's work.

11. Design of working groups

Working in groups is not always more efficient than working alone. Frequent disturbances from colleagues and the need to consult before taking action can retard progress and constantly irritate the individual worker. Nevertheless, much work must of necessity be completed in groups. Thus it becomes necessary to construct groups in such a manner that productivity, employee commitment and job satisfaction increase. The following principles apply to the design of efficient working groups:

(a) Group sizes should be reasonably small. This reduces the amount of time necessary for supervision and the co-ordination of group activities, and decision taking will be faster. Also, large groups encourage the emergence of sub-groups and factions differing in terms of status, length of service, opinions on social and work issues, etc.

(b) Group leaders should be selected according to their compatibility with particular groups.

(c) Participation of group members in making decisions that affect the group should be encouraged, since this (usually) improves morale and stimulates co-operation and the emergence of new ideas.

(d) Group cohesion (*see* **10** above) should be developed. Cohesion is enhanced if members frequently interact and depend on each other for support and reward.

(e) Group objectives should be made known to all members, and defined clearly and precisely.

(f) Group membership should be as homogeneous as possible, with members having similar attitudes, self-identities and outlooks.

12. Group structure

Working groups can adopt one of three organisational structures: the hierarchy, the network or the team. Hierarchies typically exhibit a pyramid form of authority and decision making, with a distinct chain of command from the apex of the organisation to its base.

A 'network', in contrast, consists of a number of workers (or collections of workers) who operate autonomously but nevertheless consciously seek to co-ordinate their activities. Each person takes independent decisions and there is no coherent chain of command. Rather, members are (usually) of equal rank and are accountable to a single central control.

13. Teams

All teams are groups, but not every group behaves as a team. The defining characteristic of a team is that its members co-operate and *voluntarily* co-ordinate their work in order to achieve group objectives. Team members are highly interdependent, and each individual must to some extent interpret the nature of his or her particular role. In a team, each person feels inwardly responsible for promoting the interests of the working group and personally accountable for its actions.

Within a team there will be a high degree of group cohesion, much interaction, mutual support and shared perceptions of issues. Team members will be willing to interchange roles, share workloads and generally help each other out. A working group can develop into a team and *vice versa* – a team can lose its coherence and begin to operate as if it were a network (with other members working independently and in emotional isolation from other participants), or as a hierarchy within which individuals will not initiate activity unless they are instructed to do so by a direct superior.

Team spirit can be encouraged through group leaders encouraging members' suggestions for altering working methods, inviting discussion on issues affecting the group, explaining to members their precise duties and responsibilities, and vigorously defending the group in the outside world. The leader should welcome initiative, new ideas and independent attempts to solve problems, consult regularly with individual members and be ready to alter working structures and arrangements following consultations.

Poor teamwork is most likely where working conditions are bad; where there is an inequitable distribution of tasks and responsibilities (especially of unpleasant and/or exceptionally demanding duties); where numerous pay differentials arise, and where there is little job security. Staff lose confidence in the team's ability to achieve its objectives, comment is interpreted as criticism, the quality of work declines, staff lack effort and petty grievances arise.

14. Authority and power

Authority is the right to control, to give orders, to determine subordinates' workloads and take official decisions on behalf of a group. A manager is *appointed* to a position of authority.

Power – the ability to initiate group activity – is not the same as authority. An individual need not be appointed to a formal managerial role in order to exercise power. The extent of an individual's power can depend on his or her ability to coerce others into obedience through threats of punitive action. Other determinants of power are:

(a) personal charisma

(b) group members' willingness to accept direction

(c) the extent to which group members identify with the values of the person involved

(d) the person's ability to satisfy group members' needs

(e) whether group members perceive the person to possess expert knowledge of the activities on which the group is engaged

(f) the extent to which members feel that a person's leadership position is legitimate, say because of seniority within the group.

Powerful people normally enjoy their work more than others and, because of their ability to affect the behaviour of others, can act in innovative ways. And they are fortunate in that whereas formal authority usually carries with it responsibility for decisions and, ultimately, for the performance of the group, power without authority does not require the individual to take the consequences when things go wrong.

CONFLICT

15. Conflict at work

Conflict has positive aspects: it spurs initiative, creates energy and stimulates new ideas. Unfortunately, it can also cause the misdirection of efforts against workmates instead of towards the achievement of the organisation's goals. Two types of conflict are common in work situations: conflicts with authority and conflicts between functions (manifest sometimes in interpersonal disputes). Conflicts may be resolved by senior management imposing solutions, or through compromise. Imposed solutions might encourage retaliation and discourage interchange of ideas. However, outcomes are reasonably certain, whereas compromises rarely satisfy all parties to a dispute. Conflicts are best resolved by relating their particular circumstances to the objectives of the firm. The best solution for the attainment of these objectives should be the solution chosen to settle the dispute.

16. Causes and effects of conflict

Conflict may be caused by the following difficulties:

(a) unclear authority structures

(b) conflicts of interest

(c) personal disputes

(d) differences in the perception of group and organisational objectives

(e) 'who should do what?' arguments

(f) competition for resources

(g) poor co-ordination of activities within the firm.

Communication problems (*see* Chapter 12) frequently emerge from conflict situations. Other consequences are inflexible and insensitive attitudes and excessively formal personal relationships among employees. Some of these problems may be overcome through:

(a) regular job rotation

(b) job design (*see* 15:26)

(c) improving team spirit (*see* 13 above)

(d) group bonuses

(e) improving the flow of information through the organisation

(f) arranging work so that it cuts across departmental and occupational boundaries

(g) employee counselling (*see* 2:29).

STRESS

17. Stress at work

People react to stress physiologically and psychologically. On encountering a stressful situation the individual will experience a release of hormones which drain blood from the skin and the digestive system; glucose and fat are released into the blood, and breathing becomes faster. Continued exposure to a stressful environment causes tiredness, irritability, physical upsets such as headaches and rashes, and possibly alterations in personality and behaviour – such as excessive drinking or outward aggression.

Stress can be caused by:

(a) bad personal relationships

(b) inadequate communication

(c) frustration and the feeling that promotion opportunities have been unfairly blocked

(d) feelings of personal inadequacy and insecurity

(e) conflicting demands by superiors who impose different, incompatible objectives

(f) unclear self-identity.

Physical manifestations of stress include restlessness, hyperactivity, impatience, high blood pressure, headaches, weight loss and skin complaints. Stress might cause other illnesses which result from its effects – excessive smoking, poor diet and so on. Severe exhaustion, cramp and backache can occur in extreme cases.

Generalised anxiety is a common symptom of stress. It affects the ability to concentrate and relax, creates irritability and generates feelings of malaise and unease.

18. Management of stress

Stress can be managed in the following ways:

(a) deliberate avoidance of situations likely to cause stress (meetings with certain people, for example)

(b) relaxation techniques

(c) delegation of work to subordinates

(d) better design of jobs (*see* 15:**26**) to remove stress-creating elements

(e) training in stress management

(f) provision of in-house counselling services

(g) identification by management of employees unable to cope with stress (via performance appraisal, for example) and putting these workers on to non-stressful duties

(h) clear identification of job priorities and the setting of reasonably attainable objectives

(i) breaking up the working day in order to include non-stressful activities.

PROFESSIONAL WORK

19. Nature of professional work

The traditional definition of a professional worker is of someone who belongs to an institute or association the purposes of which are:

(a) to maintain or improve members' occupational status; *and*

(b) to enhance members' standards of performance through training and a system of certification usually (but not always) involving a series of examinations.

Today, however, the concept of 'professional' encompasses a variety of categories of employee. Teachers and nurses, for example, typically regard themselves as 'professional' employees.

20. Professional bodies

Professional bodies have existences beyond the control of employing firms. Their functions are as follows:

(a) Examining, training and education; the production of syllabuses and teaching materials; and the provision of short courses.

(b) Establishment of standards of professional conduct, backed up by disciplinary procedures and the threat of sanctions against those who break the association's rules.

(c) Distribution of information on new developments, practices and other items of interest to members.

(d) Enhancement of the status of the profession via public relations exercises, contributions to debates on topical issues affecting the profession, and generally acting as a pressure group to further members' interests.

(e) Conducting salary surveys among members and publishing summaries of the results.

21. What is a profession?

The characteristics of a profession are as follows:

(a) Practitioners take a genuine pride in the quality of their work, and feel loyalty towards the profession as well as to employing firms.

(b) The knowledge needed to master the profession is non-trivial and can only be obtained through several years' training and experience, evidenced by passing examinations.

(c) There is a 'community of knowledge' among members who often want to impress professional peers with their ability to undertake higher levels of professional work.

(d) Knowledge obtained during training should distinguish members from other people working in the same field.

22. Management of professionally-qualified staff

Special problems apply to the management of professionally-qualified staff, as follows:

(a) Professionals' talents and qualifications might not be fully utilised by employing organisations, causing resentment among these workers.

(b) Line managers may insist that professionals alter their working methods in order to fit in with bureaucratic organisation structures.

(c) Senior managers might not be competent to appraise the performances of professionally-qualified subordinates.

(d) Separation of professional employees from the normal line of command may undermine the authority of the central administration.

(e) A highly-qualified professional might resent being paid less than line managers on the same grade who have not had to pass professional examinations.

(f) Large organisations often employ members of several different professional associations, who may compete with each other for the favour of senior management. Lawyers, for example, may feel they deserve higher status than (say) accountants.

(g) Often, professionals are engaged on specialist activities and thus fail to acquire the breadth of general management experience attained by colleagues in line management. Hence they cannot advance to the top of their employing organisations.

To resolve these problems, large businesses sometimes apply the following measures:

(a) Provision of management training to professional employees.

(b) The establishment of 'staff' positions (*see* 6:16) for professionals.

(c) Matrix organisation and widespread use of project teams.

(d) Creation of 'federal organisation' structures wherein individual professionals are given personal autonomy over how they do their work, but which have separate administrations to perform routine management tasks.

(e) The setting-up of quasi-independent 'professional support units' that concentrate entirely on the provision of a particular professional service. The legal department of a commercial bank is an example.

Progress test 14

1. (a) What are the essential differences between formal and informal groups?
   (b) Why should management care whether informal groups emerge?

2. Define the following terms:
   (a) secondary group
   (b) group norm
   (c) group cohesion.

3. Explain how the following might contribute to group cohesion:
   (a) the external environment
   (b) homogeneity of members
   (c) internal communication structures.

4. What are the differences between authority and power?

5. List three factors that management should consider when designing working groups.

6. In what circumstances might employees become bored with their work?

7. List four consequences of frustration at work.

8. What are the major factors involved in an individual's choice of occupation?

9. List four cases of stress in work situations and three ways in which stress can be controlled in individuals.

10. List six problems likely to be encountered in the management of professionally qualified staff.

15

LEADERSHIP, MOTIVATION AND MANAGEMENT STYLE

LEADERSHIP

1. Management style

The term 'management style' has two (related) meanings. One is the demeanour that a manager adopts when dealing with subordinates; the other is the collective approach of the management of an entire organisation to questions of leadership, participation, employee appraisal and control. In the former context the particular style chosen will depend on personal inclinations, training and experience, and on environmental factors. It will affect managers' relations with their subordinates, group productivity, and patterns of interaction among employees. In the macro-organisational sense, management style helps determine formal structure, line and staff relationships, whether the firm uses project teams, the frequency and character of committee meetings, and so on.

2. Leadership

Leadership is the process whereby one person influences the thoughts and behaviour of others. Between the extremes of complete autocracy on the one hand and a totally permissive approach on the other there exists a continuum of possible leadership styles. *Autocratic* leadership involves issuing detailed instructions and the close supervision of subordinates' work. Relationships between managers and their subordinates are highly formal, and sanctions are imposed if subordinates underperform. Workers are not expected to exercise initiative; indeed, this might be actively discouraged. The advantages of autocratic leadership are that it is extremely likely that work will actually be completed on time; task requirements and interpersonal relations are clearly-defined; and there is fast decision making. However, employees' enterprise is suppressed and their knowledge and experience are not applied to the maximum extent. If the leader is absent it is unlikely that work will be completed.

Permissive leaders, conversely, specify broadly-defined overall objectives and leave subordinates to achieve these as they think best. There is much communication with subordinates, and extensive employee participation in management decisions. Subordinates' job satisfaction, skills and capacities to undertake more demanding duties should increase. Disadvantages include slow decision making, possible lack of positive direction, and the fact that certain people are not capable of contributing to decision taking or of working without close supervision.

3. Leadership theory

'Trait' theories of leadership (which exert little influence today) asserted that leadership ability is innate. Certain people, it was alleged, are born with personality traits (decisiveness, assertiveness, initiative, self-assurance, etc) which make them fit to be leaders. The problem here is the enormous range of traits potentially affecting leadership ability, and the impossibility of measuring the existence and extent within individuals of many of these.

The human relations approach (*see* 1:**14**), conversely, suggests that effective leadership can be learned; it is not necessarily innate. Participative styles are advocated. The role of the leader is to suggest rather than impose solutions. Much of the human relations theory of leadership derives from the work of Douglas McGregor (1906–64) who outlined two alternative sets of assumptions concerning human nature that a manager might adopt. He labelled these 'theory X' and 'theory Y'.

4. Theory X and theory Y

Managers who subscribe to theory X assumptions believe that the typical worker lacks ambition, is self-centred, indifferent to the welfare of the organisation, and will avoid effort whenever possible. Employees are assumed not to want responsibility; to prefer being told precisely what to do; and to welcome the security offered by strict managerial control. It follows that inducements, sanctions and close supervision are necessary to make employees work hard.

Theory Y, in contrast, asserts that individuals (normally) do not require coercion to make them work; they can be relied upon to exercise self-direction and self-control and to put maximum effort into their activities. Indeed, people actively seek rather than avoid responsibility.

McGregor condemned the theory X suppositions. Work, he argued, is natural to the human species, and those who perform it will devote their full attention, effort and interest to completing their tasks. This approach has been criticised on the grounds that it is excessively altruistic, overestimates the enthusiasm of employees, and ignores many fundamental realities of work (e.g. the unavoidable existence of conflicts of interest in industry, the inevitability of boring and unpleasant tasks, etc).

5. Contingency theories

These insist that no single leadership style is universally applicable to all situations because each set of circumstances is to some extent unique. Thus, leaders must adjust their approaches as situations change. Hence an effective leader is one who accurately identifies the factors which determine the essential character of a situation. Examples of such factors are:

(a) Relationships between the leader and the group, in particular the degree of confidence of the group in the leader's abilities

(b) The nature of the tasks undertaken by subordinates: whether the tasks are easy or difficult, routine or varied

(c) The degree of authority vested in the leader

(d) Whether members of a workgroup have similar backgrounds and abilities.

The advantages of the contingency approach are that it compels managers to analyse systematically the nature of each situation, and that leaders can be allocated to groups most receptive to their styles of command. However, substantial training and expertise are needed to implement the contingency approach effectively. And because a certain style is adopted in one situation but different styles in others, management may appear inconsistent in its general approach.

6. Empirical studies of leadership behaviour

Many practical investigations into leadership behaviour have been undertaken. These are discussed fully in the M&E text *Organisational Behaviour*, to which the interested reader is referred.

7. The work of John Adair

According to John Adair, effective leaders simultaneously satisfy three sets of interdependent needs, as follows:

(a) *Task needs*. These relate to the work that has to be completed. A leader must be seen to strive to achieve group objectives, or he or she will lose the confidence of the group. Failure to satisfy task needs results in frustration and disenchantment among group members, in criticism of the leader, and in the eventual collapse of the group. Task needs may be satisfied through planning, allocating duties, giving targets to individuals, setting standards, and the systematic appraisal of members' performances.

(b) *Group needs* relate to team spirit (*see* 14:13) and morale. The group must be held together through effective communication (*see* Chapter 12), discipline and other measures (*see* 10:12–13) for enhancing team work. Discipline, i.e. the means for ensuring that work is carried out and that rules, norms of behaviour and instructions are obeyed, is improved if there are clear instructions and each group member knows precisely what he or she is required to do. Leaders enforce discipline in order to prevent harm being done to the efforts of the group. Leaders should set a good example, not break rules themselves, and not exercise favouritism or impose unreasonable obligations on others.

(c) *Individual needs* of group members. The leader should seek to discover what each member wants from the group and how these needs can be satisfied and harmonised with task and group requirements. Examples of measures for meeting individual needs are coaching (*see* 16:27), counselling (*see* 2:29), motivating and staff development.

The three needs interconnect because an action in one area affects others. Hence, leaders must seek consciously to relate the satisfaction of individual and/or group needs to the achievement of group tasks. Leadership training, Adair argues, should be directed towards increasing a person's sensitivity to the three sets of needs, particularly through training in how to define objectives, team briefing, organisation of work, practical motivation, planning and control. Adair's is a contingency approach in that it requires leaders to alter the mix of effort devoted to satisfying various needs according to the overall situation.

8. Choice of personal leadership style

Autocratic approaches might be suitable when subordinates' work is repetitive and/or unpleasant. Permissive styles could be appropriate where subordinates are skilled, highly motivated and/or where complex work is involved. Other relevant factors include:

(a) whether the leader is respected by subordinates

(b) extent and quality of interpersonal communication within the firm

(c) the remuneration system adopted (*see* 10:**46**)

(d) experience and capability of the leader

(e) degree of homogeneity of employees within the working group.

9. Transactional and transformational leadership

A *transactional* leader is one who organises subordinates' work efficiently, sets reasonable objectives, and provides subordinates with all the help, advice and resources necessary to achieve their goals. *Transformational* leaders, on the other hand, are those who are able to convert subordinates' fundamental attitudes in order to increase their commitment to the employing organisation. Such leaders have charisma, vision, self-understanding and empathy with subordinates' needs.

Charismatic leaders are seen by subordinates as possessing extraordinary abilities, and can inspire great loyalty and enthusiasm within a working group. The determinants of charisma include subordinates' backgrounds and attitudes towards authority, relationships between the leader and the group, the situation to hand, and the extent to which the leader shares a common interest with group members. Other relevant factors are:

(a) subordinates' trust in the leader's competence, knowledge and commitment to achieving group objectives

(b) the leader's interpersonal and influencing skills

(c) subordinates' prior commitment to the organisation.

Effective transformational leadership requires recognition of the need for change, willingness to behave unconventionally, direct communication with subordinates and the establishment of an emotional bond with members of the team.

Self-leadership and self-managed teams

Arguably there is little need for formal leadership in the modern workplace situation, which is increasingly likely to involve working in a team. According to this view, employees are quite capable of motivating themselves to perform unattractive as well as appealing tasks (Manz and Sims 1987) and to determine which group members are best qualified to complete particular duties. Advantages to self-managed teams include lower supervision costs, higher levels of employee interest in the work of the organisation as a whole, and hopefully the optimum use of human resources.

According to S. Kerr and J.M. Jermier, the need for leadership can be mitigated in many workplace situations by a number of factors, as follows:

(a) *Organisational characteristics* such as cohesive work groups that remove the need for supportive leadership, and the formalisation of working procedures (which results in group members not needing to ask a leader how to perform duties).

(b) *Job characteristics*, e.g. routine duties, feedback within a task and/or interesting and satisfying work.

(c) *Employee characteristics*. It is unlikely that workers who are experienced, trained, willing and able will need to be led. Professionally qualified employees are normally capable of looking after themselves.

To the extent that work groups do not need to be led, the particular style of leadership applied by the group's formal supervisor is largely irrelevant, explaining perhaps the very mixed results that have been obtained from many empirical studies in the leadership behaviour field.

MANAGEMENT OF CHANGE

10. Need for change

The need for change arises from the discovery of new materials and processes, the entry of new competitors to a market, shifts in consumer tastes, and from alterations in the cultural, political, economic and legal frameworks within which a firm exists. Management must be able to respond to change; to harness its energy and quickly adapt to new situations. Change may occur in one or more of the following directions:

(a) *Technical*, affecting products, working methods, work location or the speed and/or quantity of production. Organisations which themselves initiate technical change have the advantage of being able to control its consequences to some extent.

(b) *Environmental*, concerning the legal system, social and cultural conventions, the state of the local and national economy, consumer attitudes, and the country's tax regime.

(c) *Demographic*, including changes in the age structure of the population, family size, regional distribution of the workforce, membership of various religions, etc.

11. Managing change

There are two basic approaches to the management of change. One is to forecast all environmental changes relevant to the firm that might occur and then predict how the organisation will be affected by them. The other is to list all the firm's major functions and follow this by an analysis of all the environmental factors that might affect these functions.

Once the need for a change has been discovered its implications must be evaluated. This requires the definition of the alterations in operational methods, staffing levels and the employee attitudes and perspectives necessary to implement alterations. New equipment and systems may be required. Jobs might have to be redesigned and the organisation restructured.

12. Employee attitudes towards change

Workers may fear change because of its potential for the disruption of existing work groups and interpersonal relations, and the feelings of insecurity and threats to individual status and financial reward that it creates. The employee is forced to realise that skills and experience acquired over many years may have no further value, and that retraining might be needed to cope with new methods. Such fears might be overcome through the following devices:

(a) Maintaining existing work groups intact wherever possible.

(b) Employee participation in decisions concerning the practical implementation of change.

(c) Improved communication with workers, regularly informing them of intended alterations.

(d) Human resource planning (HRP), i.e. predicting the consequences for labour of changes to working practices and redeploying workers to alternative functions. HRP is discussed in 16:3.

(e) Creation of financial reserves specifically earmarked to pay for the retraining of employees adversely affected by new methods. The reserve could also be used to encourage natural wastage, e.g. through the early retirement of older workers.

(f) Careful explanation to employees of the benefits of change and of the technical superiority of new systems.

(g) Preparation of detailed records on each employee's qualifications, attributes and experiences, thus enabling management to assess a worker's suitability for alternative duties.

(h) Encouraging flexible attitudes in employees through training programmes and through arranging work in such a manner that the skills and experience acquired in one job can be quickly and easily transferred to others.

(i) Application of wage payment systems that encourage the adoption of new and better working methods.

13. Overcoming resistance to change

Kurt Lewin suggested three steps for overcoming resistance to change:

1. *Unfreezing* – getting rid of existing practices and ideas that stand in the way of change. This will require a high level of communication with employees to convince them that change is necessary. Often workers experience the so-called SARAH effect (Shock, Anger, Rejection, Acceptance, Help) at this stage as they are forced to confront the inadequacies of present arrangements.
2. *Changing* – teaching employees to think and perform differently.
3. *Refreezing* – establishing new norms and standard practices.

There are a number of alternative ways in which the programme might be implemented. Kotter and Schlesinger outline four possible approaches:

1. *Education and communication.* This approach aims to make employees fully aware of all aspects of the situation and to convince them that change is necessary.
2. *Participation and involvement.* Hopefully, participation by employees in deciding exactly how to implement change will stimulate their commitment to new methods.
3. *Negotiation and agreement.* This is appropriate where several distinct interest groups may be discerned, some of which may be adversely affected by intended changes.
4. *Manipulation.* Here, management carefully selects the information about a proposed change that is to be given to workers in order to present the change in the most favourable manner. There is a danger, however, that employees may recognise management's manipulation of data and bitterly resent the fact that they are being manipulated.

14. Change agents

A change agent is a person who fosters change within an organisation. Usually (but not necessarily) the change agent is an external management consultant who specialises in this type of work. Outsiders might be more objective and dispassionate than internal employees of the company, but will lack the detailed knowledge of day-to-day operations that the latter usually possess. Also, internal staff know exactly where to look for information, and they are fully accountable for their actions in the long term. (Outsiders move on as soon as an assignment is completed.) On the other hand, in-house staff may lack the necessary insights, creativity and management skills, and will not be exposed to penetrating independent criticism.

External consultants should have extensive experience of implementing change in other organisations, so that the firm in question will benefit from other companies' work. Outside consultants have no vested interests in the welfare of particular departments and are not concerned with internal organisational politics. They have up-to-the-minute knowledge of the latest techniques, and need not be afraid of asking questions of *anyone* in the organisation. Note how internal staff can benefit simply by observing a top-class external consultant at work.

The change agent may advise on job and organisation design, on improving the firm's communication systems, or on the need for retraining and management development.

15. Management systems and resistance to change

Rosabeth Moss Kanter (b. 1943) examined 115 examples of successful innovation occurring within American companies, concluding that certain management attitudes and practices invariably inhibited the introduction of change. Examples of these attitudes and practices were:

(a) suspicion of new ideas or suggestions emanating from the base of the organisation

(b) management through committees

(c) allowing one department to criticise and interfere with another's proposals

(d) assuming that high-ranking employees know more about the organisation than low-ranking employees

(e) assigning unpleasant tasks (dismissal of employees, for example) to subordinates

(f) not involving subordinates in decisions to restructure the organisation

(g) exercising tight supervision and control

(h) perceiving subordinates' problems as indications of their failure, and treating a subordinate's discussion of a problem as an admission of his or her incompetence

(i) telling subordinates that they are not indispensable

(j) regularly criticising subordinates but only rarely praising them.

16. Chaos

Arguably, disorder and confusion are endemic to business situations, so that management theory and practice should focus on the best means for responding to uncertainty and change. Scientists have been interested in the theory of chaos for generations, seeking to understand the effects on macro-systems of micro events (e.g. a butterfly flapping its wings in northern Siberia can generate a chain of events leading to a hurricane in the USA). The number of possible combinations of micro events and potential outcomes was so immense that new thinking on the nature of 'prediction' and 'uncertainty' was required, taking into account the fundamental instability of nature. These ideas have begun to influence management theory as the pace of organisational and environmental change has accelerated to unprecedented levels.

The 'chaos approach' challenges the conventional scientific emphasis on seeking to discover relationships between cause and effect, since the conventional approach assumes regular mechanistic 'laws of the universe'. Rather it is necessary to recognise that every event affects every other event in some way or other, so that there are no clear and direct chains of causality: the consequence of a change in one variable causes something else, which affects other things which themselves have implications for numerous further variables, including that which altered in the first instance. Thus, nature is a continuous feedback system with inputs and outputs mutually interacting. 'Laws of nature' exist, but are far too complex to be explained in terms of straightforward cause-and-effect relationships. Consider for example the determination of the shape of a snowflake as it drifts towards the ground. The surrounding air quality, temperature and other environmental conditions affect the snowflake, which itself is simultaneously influencing the environment (by lowering its temperature, changing the humidity, etc), which affects the form of the snowflake, and so on.

A state of equilibrium (balance) in a business situation can be upset by seemingly trivial events (staff transfers, personal disagreements, changes in procedures, etc) that have knock-on effects which interact and multiply in an extremely complicated manner. Chaos theory has been offered as an explanation for unexpected turmoils on stock exchanges and foreign exchange markets, the instability of world oil and other commodity prices, and the sudden collapse of organisational structures. The chaos approach has many implications for management, including the following:

(a) Managements cannot control long-term future activities because future environments are totally unpredictable (in consequence of the complexity of cause/effect linkages).

(b) Stable environments can suddenly explode into unstable environments for no seemingly apparent reason, and vice-versa. Hence it is necessary to recognise that 'anything can happen' and plan accordingly.

(c) Organisations can appear to be stable and then suddenly become highly unstable.

(d) Unstable organisations need not be unsuccessful.

(e) Dynamic forces are constantly pulling a business in different directions. Examples of such forces are market conditions, regulatory frameworks, decentralisation of decision making, and human desires for excitement or for a quiet life. An organisation that moves towards stability is likely to ossify and lose its innovative edge. Equally, however, movements towards extreme instability can lead the organisation to collapse.

(f) Firms must be flexible and responsive to environmental change. They need to have effective information-gathering systems and to focus on short-term rather than long-term activities.

(g) Long-term planning is basically useless, as it is not possible to predict future environments.

(h) Mission statements should be regularly updated.

(i) Statistical forecasts will typically be wrong. Simulation and scenario building is preferable as a means for taking decisions.

To cope with chaotic situations firms need to be able to learn from past and current activities, systematically review the lessons learned from recent experience, and hence develop rapid and flexible responses to fast-changing environments.

17. The learning organisation

The term 'learning organisation' is sometimes applied to companies operating in turbulent environments that require transformations in working methods and which – in order to facilitate the introduction of new systems – train and develop their employees on a continuous basis. Hence the very essence of the business – its products, markets, processes and orientations – is likely to alter totally from period to period. Learning organisations discover the key characteristics of their environments and are thus better able to plan ahead. The learning organisation will attempt to identify interactions between the firm's sub-systems that facilitate or inhibit the management of change and is better able to cope with environmental and other change because it can accommodate unpredictability. It is not encumbered with rigid and out-of-date plans and procedures.

Nature of organisational learning

To learn means to absorb knowledge, acquire skills and/or assume fresh attitudes. Learning results in permanent changes in ability or behaviour, as opposed to short-term changes which are soon reversed. Organisational learning means all the processes whereby freshly discovered solutions to administrative problems pass into the firm's 'managerial memory', hence becoming integral parts of the organisation's mechanism for reacting to future events. A consequence is that decision-making procedures are continuously modified and adapted in the light of experience.

18. Single loop and double loop learning

According to Chris Argyris, organisations can be extremely bad at learning, unless the learning is simple and routine. Hence an organisation quickly loses the benefits of experience and reverts to its old bad habits. 'Single loop' learning, according to Argyris, is the learning necessary for an employee to be able to apply existing methods to the completion of a job. This is contrasted with 'double loop' learning that challenges and redefines the basic requirements of the job and how it should be undertaken. Single loop learning typically involves the setting of standards and the investigation of deviations from targets. Double loop learning means questioning whether the standards and objectives are appropriate in the first instance.

Implementing DLL

DLL inevitably occurs within organisations as they experience crises, fail to attain targets, and experience environmental change. Learning about mistakes in these situations however is costly and inefficient; decisions are taken too late to be effective, and all the benefits of forward planning are lost. Rather the organisation needs to:

(a) educate its managers in the methods of learning by doing

(b) formulate its objectives and standards in such a way that they can be evaluated on a continuous basis and the basic assumptions that underlie them can be empirically tested

(c) seek to learn in advance of environmental turbulence or, if this is not possible, adapt its behaviour systematically through trial and error as situations develop. The first loop in the double loop system is the discovery of facts, acting upon them and evaluating the consequences. Knowledge gained is formal, systematic and explicit. The second loop involves the development of skills and 'know-how' resulting from the first loop and hence a change in fundamental perspectives on the matter under consideration. This feeds back into the interpretation of the facts embodied in the first loop and the actions taken thereafter. Hence, both behaviour and understanding of events and environments will change.

Training, employee relations and staff development

Companies operating in fast-changing environments require regular transformations in working methods and (in order to facilitate the introduction of new systems) must train and develop their employees on a continuous basis. Note however that a learning organisation is far more than a firm which spends large amounts on training. Rather, it requires the unqualified acceptance of change at all levels within the business, including basic grade operatives. Implications of the learning organisation for training, employee relations and staff development are as follows:

(a) Current policies should be open to question and challenged by all grades of employee. Indeed, management should welcome and actively support such questioning.

(b) Individuals should not necessarily be penalised for experimenting on their own initiative and making mistakes.

(c) There is a need for heavy emphasis on employee communication, with management diffusing information on current environmental trends throughout the organisation.

(d) Employee appraisal and reward systems need not be linked to the attainment of existing goals but rather to finding new and profitable fields of activity.

(e) Workers must possess an understanding of customer requirements.

(f) Employees need to 'learn how to learn', taking their example from top management.

Note how an organisation is, at base, a group of individuals, so that the manner whereby groups within it learn is affected by social, interpersonal and other intangible factors as well as information systems and other formal learning facilities.

Problems of implementation

Creating a learning organisation is difficult, for a number of reasons:

(a) Employees at all levels within the organisation must want to learn. Thus, the establishment of a learning organisation is a bottom-up process that may not fit in with the culture of a pre-existing bureaucratic and hierarchical system.

(b) Inadequate information gathering and internal communication systems.

(c) Organisational politics (see below) that might impede widespread acceptance of the idea.

MOTIVATION

19. Definition

Motivation results from the drives, needs and aspirations that determine behaviour. Theories of motivation depend primarily on the concept of human need, since attempts to satisfy needs seemingly affect most aspects of human activity.

Motivation theories come in two forms – 'content' theories, which ask the question 'What are the needs that motivate people to behave in certain ways?' and 'process' theories which seek to explain specific actions, concentrating on the thought processes that people experience prior to behaving in a particular manner. Process theories are embodied in the work of V.H. Vroom and of Porter and Lawler (see 24). Equity theory (see 24) also belongs to the process school. Content theories are exemplified by the work of A.H. Maslow (see 20), D. McGregor (see 4) and F. Herzberg (see 22).

20. Maslow's need hierarchy

According to the American psychologist A.H. Maslow (1908–70), individuals are motivated by five levels of need. When a person has satisfied the first level he or she then moves on to satisfy the second level, then the third and fourth levels, etc. The five categories of need, in the order in which Maslow supposed the individual would seek to gratify them, are as follows:

(a) *Physiological needs* – food, clothing, heat, shelter and similar basic survival requirements: wages from employment enable the individual to satisfy these needs.

(b) *Security needs* – job tenure, home security and protection against reduced living standards. Purchase of life, house and medical insurance and collective activities through trade unions are examples of attempts to achieve security.

(c) *Social needs* – the needs for affection, to belong to a community and to feel wanted. Attempts to satisfy social needs result in social, cultural, sporting and recreational groups, and at work in trade unions and formal and informal communication systems.

(d) *Esteem needs* – desires for physical possessions, for recognition by others (evidenced perhaps by the acquisition of status symbols), for authority over others, plus internal psychological demands for self-respect and self-assurance.

(e) *Self-actualisation needs* – the search for personal fulfilment. Having satisfied all other needs the individual will want to accomplish everything he or she is capable of achieving; to develop individual skills, talents and aptitudes. Few people ever reach this final stage.

21. Criticisms of Maslow's theory

Maslow has been criticised on the following grounds:

(a) The theory is suppositional and not based on reliable empirical evidence.

(b) Although the theory classifies and describes human needs, it does not examine their basic sources.

(c) Some of the needs listed in the Maslow hierarchy might not be considered important by certain people. Many needs are *socially* and *culturally* determined and thus vary between communities.

(d) Individuals may demand the satisfaction of higher-level needs even though lower needs have not been satisfied. Thus for example an unemployed person on a low income may feel a need for esteem just as acutely as he or she feels the need for clothing, shelter or security.

Modifications to Maslow's approach are discussed in the M&E text *Organisational Behaviour*, which deals with motivation theory extensively.

22. The work of F. Herzberg

Herzberg argued that two entirely separate sets of factors influence human behaviour. One relates to the need to avoid pain and obtain the basic necessities of life; the other is the need to develop personal capacities and potentials. Herzberg questioned professionally-qualified employees (engineers and accountants) about the events at work which increased or reduced their satisfaction. Factors generating dissatisfaction were: inadequate pay, bad personal relations with colleagues, poor supervision, unpleasant physical working conditions and absence of fringe benefits. These are called 'hygiene' or 'maintenance' factors (from the analogy that hygiene does not improve health, but does prevent illness): when catered for they do not actually increase a worker's job satisfaction but their deficiency creates dissatisfaction.

The factors responsible for creating satisfaction (*motivators* in Herzberg's language) were:

(a) sense of achievement on completing work

(b) recognition from others within the organisation

(c) responsibility assumed

(d) varied work, involving an assortment of interesting tasks

(e) prospects for promotion.

Motivators encouraged better quality work, hygiene factors did not: a worker might resign because a hygiene element was inadequate, yet would not work harder because the factor was satisfactory. Likewise the absence of suitable motivators would not cause employees to resign, but an increase in the strengths of motivating factors would significantly improve effort and performance.

Herzberg's theory is sometimes called the 'two-factor' theory (the two factors being motivation and hygiene). Its most startling conclusion, perhaps, was that pay is a hygiene rather than motivating factor. Note, however, that Herzberg was concerned with the attitudes towards work of qualified professional and managerial staff and not with shop-floor workers who might be much more concerned with prospects of immediate financial reward.

Achievement needs

According to David McClelland (1961), the need to achieve is a primary motivating factor. Other important needs, he suggested, are the needs for power and affiliation. Achievement-oriented people were said to (*i*) prefer tasks for which they had sole responsibility, (*ii*) avoid risk, and (*iii*) monitor continuously the effects of their actions. 'Need achievers', as McClelland called them, worked extremely hard and constantly sought to improve their performances. Power seekers, conversely, were motivated by the prospect of controlling subordinates. Affiliators wanted pleasant relationships with colleagues and to help other individuals. McClelland used the term nAff to characterise an individual's need for friendly relations with others. People with a high nAff had strong desires for approval by peers and in consequence tended to adopt conformist attitudes when working in groups. The term nPow was applied to describe an individual's need to control, to influence people and be responsible for them.

Arguably, individuals with high achievement needs often make good entrepreneurs running their own businesses, or managers of self-contained units within large companies. Note however that need achievers are not *necessarily* effective managers. They are concerned with their personal advancement, but may not be capable of encouraging others to succeed (a vital management skill).

23. Money as a motivating factor

F.W. Taylor (*see* 1:3) argued that high wages provided primary motivation for effort. Other writers, Herzberg for example, disagreed with this view. The arguments in favour of money being a dominant motivator are its ability to purchase a wide variety of goods and services, and the fact that high wages indicate occupational competence and offer a yardstick for evaluating individual success. On the other hand, group and social influences are known to exert great pressure on workplace behaviour, and many people who already possess far more money than they objectively need still work extremely hard! Also, the concept of a 'high wage' is itself subjectively determined. A certain wage may be seen as excellent by one person but mediocre by others.

24. Process theories

Equity theory asserts that individuals continuously compare their own rewards with those of other employees whom they regard as expending similar amounts of effort. If workers perceive their reward/effort ratios to be out of balance (a state of mind referred to as 'cognitive dissonance') then discontent and low motivation are common. Only when employees believe their returns are comparable to those of others (relative to the effort involved) will a state of 'distributive justice' be thought to exist, resulting in high motivation.

V.H. Vroom also emphasised the importance of employees' expectations about whether their efforts would receive just rewards. His 'expectancy theory' states that an individual's behaviour is affected by:

(a) what the person wants to happen

(b) that person's estimate of the probabilities of various events occurring, including the desired outcome

(c) the strength of a person's belief that a certain outcome will satisfy his or her needs.

Predictions of what will happen in the future are usually based on what has happened in the past. Thus, situations not previously experienced (for example, new working practices, job changes, environmental alterations) give rise to uncertainty and may in consequence reduce employees' motivation. Accordingly, employees need to be able to identify clear connections between effort and reward. Otherwise they will not be motivated.

L.W. Porter and E.E. Lawler further explored the relationship between expectations, effort and income. The effort an employee puts into his or her work depends, they argued, on two factors: the extent to which the rewards from the work will satisfy the individual's needs for security, esteem, independence or personal self-development; and that person's expectation of high effort leading to high reward.

25. Job design

This means the variation of the duties, responsibilities, degree of authority, working methods, etc attached to a job in order to make it more interesting and to increase the personal involvement and commitment of the worker. Jobs may be 'enlarged' or 'enriched' The term 'job extension' embraces both these categories.

Job enlargement involves broadening the scope of a job through giving the worker a more varied selection of duties. Note how this contradicts the recommendations of scientific management (*see* 1:3–4) which insists that jobs be broken down into small, specialised and easy-to-perform units. In fact, the application of the scientific approach frequently resulted in boredom, alienation (*see* 14:2) and apathy among workers that actually reduced productivity. Job enlargement seeks to motivate the worker through reversing the process of specialisation.

Job enrichment, conversely, means the allocation of more difficult tasks to the worker. Jobs are made more demanding; extra decision-making duties are assigned; use of additional skills and greater effort is expected from the worker. Typically, job enrichment occurs as part of a staff development programme or during extreme shortages of skilled labour.

Job extension may be achieved through the following practical devices:

(a) Combining existing single tasks into a composite whole.

(b) Requiring that workers be responsible for controlling the quality of their work.

(c) Allowing employees discretion over how they achieve objectives.

(d) Involving people with colleagues and, where appropriate, final customers.

The underlying principle is that the wider the variety of tasks undertaken, the more the employee will realise the significance of the job in the wider organisation, and hence the more productive will be the worker. Of course, some jobs are more easily extended than others. Assembly lines in automated factories may offer few opportunities for interesting work. In this case, higher pay and/or greater worker participation could be primary motivators.

In situations where job enlargement is not possible, an alternative is to put workers through sequences of different jobs. Each job is boring, but monotony is relieved through regular job rotation.

26. Participation in decision making

Employee involvement in management decision making has long been recognised as an important motivating factor. Limited forms of worker participation are increasingly common; they occur through workers' committees, advisory groups, Quality Circles (*see* 10:36) and through formal joint consultation.

The *advantages* of participation are that:

(a) Unworkable decisions are less likely because those responsible for their implementation have the opportunity to point out potential difficulties.

(b) It encourages responsible attitudes among workers.

(c) Workers feel involved with and committed to the organisation.

(d) Management receives valuable feedback from employees about day-to-day operations.

(e) It encourages flexible attitudes among employees and reduces resistance to change.

(f) The knowledge and expertise of junior staff are applied to decision-making processes.

(g) It assists staff development.

(h) Workers are more likely to abide by jointly-agreed decisions.

Arguments *against* employee participation in management decision making include the following:

(a) It might interfere with managerial prerogative (i.e. the right of management – which represents the interests of the enterprise's owners – to manage).

(b) Decision making becomes slow and possibly inefficient.

(c) Employees might not be competent to comprehend the complex issues sometimes involved in managerial decision making.

(d) Certain decisions necessarily require the discussion of confidential information that cannot be disclosed to workers.

(e) Employees might not take participation seriously, and may adopt short-sighted and selfish perspectives.

Practical aspects of employee participation in the management of EU companies are discussed in 17:17.

27. Empowerment

An employee's feeling of being in control and of significantly contributing to an organisation's development can be greatly enhanced by 'empowering' that person to complete tasks and attain targets independently, without constantly having to refer back to management for permission to take certain actions. The employee is trusted to take sensible decisions. Hence, for example, salespeople might be empowered to offer special discounts to prospective customers, production operatives can be empowered to decide the speed of an assembly line, and work teams may be empowered to determine the extent and intensity of the use of robots within a section of a firm. The aim is to enable employees who actually have to deal with problems to implement solutions quickly and without recourse to supervisors and/or higher levels of management. This is increasingly necessary as large and bureaucratic organisations 'delayer' management hierarchies in the search for administrative efficiency and lower costs. Removal of one or more entire layers of the management pyramid is a fast and sometimes highly effective means for streamlining management communication and control.

Empowerment differs from 'delegation' in that whereas the latter is the devolution of duties from boss to subordinate (albeit with the authority to implement decisions), empowerment is a general approach to operational management, requiring not just the passing down of power and responsibility through a hierarchy but also that the individual workers actively contribute to improving the performance of tasks. Benefits to empowerment include:

- The encouragement of individual creativity and initiative, commitment to the enterprise and team spirit
- Decision taking at the most suitable levels
- Facilitation of performance management
- Faster and more flexible responses to customer requirements
- Higher levels of self-confidence and motivation among employees
- Better relations between management and front-line (customer contact) employees
- A 'meetings of minds' *vis-à-vis* customers and the firm's staff regarding what constitutes product quality (Schneider *et al* 1980)
- Receipt of valuable ideas for new products from front-line employees
- Provision of an early warning system regarding customer dissatisfaction
- Immediate correction of mistakes.

Problems with empowerment are that greater care has to be exercised when hiring employees, who then need more training than in conventional circumstances. Staff might take bad decisions, and customers may be treated differently leading to resentments among those not receiving favours. The entire organisation might need to be redesigned in order to make empowerment operationally effective.

Bowen and Lawler (1992) suggest that four conditions need to apply in order for empowerment to succeed, namely that employees receive:

- Information concerning the organisation's performance
- Power to make decisions that genuinely influence the direction and performance of the organisation
- Knowledge enabling them to understand and contribute to organisational performance
- Rewards that are based on the organisation's performance.

Progress test 15

1. Why should organisations consciously plan for change?

2. Define the term 'change agent'.

3. (a) List the five levels of the Maslow need hierarchy.
   (b) Define the term 'self-actualisation' and give four examples of how it might be achieved.

4. According to Herzberg, was financial reward a motivator or a hygiene factor?

5. State Vroom's expectancy theory of motivation.

6. Distinguish between job enlargement and job enrichment.

7. List four disadvantages of employee participation in management decision making.

8. Define leadership.

9. What are the main problems with the trait theory of leadership?

16

PERSONNEL MANAGEMENT

NATURE AND SCOPE OF PERSONNEL MANAGEMENT

1. Definition

The UK Institute of Personnel Development defines personnel management as 'that part of management concerned with people at work and their relationships within an enterprise'. Specific personnel department responsibilities include the following:

(a) *Forecasting future labour requirements.* Estimating the firm's demand for labour, matching this with available supply and identifying likely shortfalls or surpluses.

(b) *Employee appraisal (see* 12:**30–36**).

(c) *Recruitment.* Preparing job specifications, drafting job advertisements and selecting advertising media, interviewing candidates and assessing appropriate salary levels for new employees.

(d) *Training.* Induction of recruits, identification of training needs, initiation of training courses and management development.

(e) *Health and safety.* Informing employees of their rights and duties, identification of hazards, accident prevention and provision of first-aid facilities.

(f) *Welfare.* Giving advice on workers' personal problems and administration of pension schemes.

(g) *Consultation and negotiation.* Suggesting new ideas for improving productivity. Liaison with trade unions, collective bargaining and industrial relations.

(h) *Dismissal.* Selecting workers for redundancy, calculating redundancy payments, ensuring that employees are not unfairly dismissed, dealing with appeals against unfair dismissal and subsequent litigation.

2. Roles of the personnel officer

The personnel officer has two roles: *service* and *advisory*. Service tasks include drafting job advertisments, salary administration, human resource planning (*see* 3 below), implementation of statutory employment regulations, and the administration of grievance and dismissal procedures. Advisory duties involve the personnel officer giving expert counsel to line executives on personnel matters, e.g. terms and conditions of employment, job evaluation (*see* 14:7), recommendations for promotion or wage increases, and issues relating to industrial relations. The personnel officer guides and recommends, but final decisions are taken by line managers. Personnel officers, therefore, occupy 'staff' positions (*see* 6:16) in organisational hierarchies; yet they have 'functional' responsibilities (*see* 6:16).

3. Personnel management and human resources management

Personnel management is an important element of the broader subject of human resources management, although in practice the two terms are frequently used interchangeably – emphasising the fact that the people employed in a company are resources which are at least as important as financial or material resources and must be given careful and expert attention.

Employees will not submit passively to manipulation or dictatorial control by management but more and more expect and demand some influence in the way they are employed. Research in the behavioural sciences shows that an appropriate response by management will benefit the company.

Personnel management techniques in, for example, appraisal, training and job evaluation can only be successfully applied with the consent and support of the employees.

The following relationships and differences between human resources management (HRM) and personnel management may be distinguished:

(a) Personnel management is practical, utilitarian and instrumental, and mostly concerned with administration and the *implementation* of policies. Human resources management, conversely, has *strategic* dimensions and involves the total deployment of human resources within the firm. Thus, for example, HRM will consider such matters as:

(*i*) the aggregate size of the organisation's labour force in the context of an overall corporate plan (how many divisions and subsidiaries the company is to have, design of the organisation, etc)
(*ii*) how much to spend on training the workforce, given strategic decisions on target quality levels, product prices, volume of production and so on
(*iii*) the desirability of establishing relations with trade unions from the viewpoint of the effective management control of the entire organisation
(*iv*) human asset accounting, i.e. the systematic measurement and analysis of the costs and *financial* benefits of alternative personnel policies (e.g. the monetary consequences of staff development exercises, the effects of various salary structures, etc) and the valuation of the human worth of the enterprise's employees.

The strategic approach to HRM involves the integration of personnel and other HRM considerations into the firm's overall corporate planning and strategy formulation procedures. It is proactive, seeking constantly to discover new ways of utilising the labour force in a more productive manner thus giving the business a competitive edge. Practical manifestations of the adoption of a strategic approach to HRM might include:

(*i*) incorporation of a brief summary of the firm's basic HRM policy into its mission statement

(*ii*) explicit consideration of the consequences for employees of each of the firm's strategies and major new projects

(*iii*) designing organisation structures to suit the needs of employees rather than conditioning the latter to fit in with the existing form of organisation

(*iv*) having the head of HRM on the firm's board of directors.

More than ever before, human resource managers are expected to contribute to productivity and quality improvement, the stimulation of creative thinking, leadership and the development of corporate skills.

(b) HRM is concerned with the wider implications of the management of change and not just with the effects of change on working practices. It seeks proactively to encourage flexible attitudes and the acceptance of new methods.

(c) Aspects of HRM constitute major inputs into organisational development exercises.

(d) Personnel management is (necessarily) reactive and diagnostic. It *responds* to changes in employment law, labour market conditions, trade union actions, government Codes of Practice and other environmental influences. HRM, on the other hand, is *prescriptive* and concerned with strategies, the initiation of new activities and the development of fresh ideas.

(e) HRM determines general policies for employment relationships within the enterprise. Thus, it needs to establish within the organisation a *culture* that is conducive to employee commitment and co-operation. Personnel management, on the other hand, has been criticised for being primarily concerned with imposing *compliance* with company rules and procedures among employees, rather than with loyalty and commitment to the firm.

(f) Personnel management has short-term perspectives; HRM has long-term perspectives, seeking to *integrate* all the human aspects of the organisation into a coherent whole and to establish high-level employee goals.

(g) The HRM approach emphasises the needs:

(*i*) for direct communication with employees rather than their collective representation

(*ii*) to develop an organisational culture conducive to the adoption of flexible working methods

(*iii*) for group working and employee participation in group decisions

(*iv*) to enhance employees' long-term capabilities, not just their competence at current duties.

4. Human resource planning (HRP)

This is the process of comparing a company's existing human resources with its forecast need for labour and then specifying the measures necessary for acquiring, training, developing, redeploying or discarding staff. It involves the estimation of labour turnover, the analysis of the consequences of changes in working practices, and the preparation of 'skills inventories' (i.e. detailed listings of all the competences, work experiences and qualifications of current employees – even those characteristics not relevant to present occupations). The purpose of a skills inventory is to inform management of all the jobs that existing employees might be capable of undertaking. Redundancies can sometimes be avoided through careful human resource planning.

5. The four Cs model of HRM

The four Cs model was developed by researchers at the Harvard Business School as a means of investigating HRM issues in a wider environmental context than the mundane and instrumental tasks of recruitment and selection, training, appraisal, maintenance of employee records, and so on (Beer *et al.* 1985). According to the Harvard model, HRM policies need to derive from a critical analysis of:

- the demands of the various stakeholders in a business (*see* **6:29**) and
- a number of 'situational factors'.

Situational factors

These include the state of the labour market, the calibres and motivation of employees. management style (which itself depends in part on the culture of the local community), the technologies used in production and the nature of working methods (e.g. whether specialisation and the division of labour are required). Labour market situations are crucial to the analysis. The labour market comprises all the people seeking work and all the companies, government bodies and other organisations that require employees. Labour markets operate at regional, industry sector, national and (increasingly) international levels. There are sub-markets for various categories of occupation, skill, educational background and other employee characteristics and for different types of task.

Further situational factors that might be relevant are:

- Form of ownership of the organisation (and hence to whom management is accountable)
- Influence of trade unions and employers' associations
- Laws and business practices of the society in which the organisation operates
- The competitive environment
- Senior management's ability to coordinate and control.

Stakeholder expectations and situational factors need to be taken into account when formulating human resources strategies, and will affect HRM policies concerning such matters as remuneration systems, degree of supervision of workers, use of labour-intensive rather than capital-intensive methods, etc. An increase in the intensity of business competition may cause a firm to improve labour productivity, discard employees, restructure administrative systems, and so on. A change in the age structure of the population could lead an organisation to hire more women. Rising educational standards might make it appropriate to redesign jobs in order to give workers more autonomy.

Outcomes to human resources management

According to the Harvard researchers, the effectiveness of the outcomes to human resources management should be evaluated under four headings: commitment, competence, congruence and cost-effectiveness.

1. *Commitment* concerns employees' loyalty to the organisation, personal motivation and liking for their work. The degree of employee commitment might be assessed via attitude surveys, labour turnover and absenteeism statistics, and through interviews with workers who quit their jobs.

2. *Competence* relates to employees skills and abilities, training requirements and potential for higher-level work. These may be estimated through employee appraisal systems and the preparation of skills inventories. HRM policies should be designed to attract, retain and motivate competent workers.

3. *Congruence* means that management and workers share the same vision of the organisation's goals and work together to attain them. In a well-managed organisation, employees at all levels of authority will share common perspectives about the factors that determine its prosperity and future prospects. Such perspectives concern the guiding principles that govern the organisation's work; how things should be done, when, by whom, and how enthusiastically.

To some extent these perceptions may be created by management via its internal communications, style of leadership, organisation system and working methods; but they can only be sustained and brought to bear on day-to-day operations by the organisation's workers. Staff should *feel* they possess a common objective. They need to experience a sense of affinity with the organisation and *want* to pursue a common cause. Congruence is evident in the absence of grievances and conflicts within the organisation, and in harmonious industrial relations.

4. *Cost-effectiveness* concerns operational efficiency. Human resources should be used to the best advantage and in the most productive ways. Outputs must be maximised at the lowest input cost, and the organisation must be quick to respond to market opportunities and environmental change.

Problems with the four Cs approach

The Harvard model suggests that human resources policies should seek to increase the level of each of the four Cs. For example, commitment might be enhanced through improving the flow of management/worker communication, while competence could be increased through extra training. Problems with the four Cs approach are:

- How *exactly* to measure these variables
- Possible conflicts between cost-effectiveness and congruence (especially if the drive for the former generates low wages)
- The huge variety of variables potentially relevant to any given HRM

situation. Often it is impossible to distinguish the key factors defining the true character of a particular state of affairs

- The fact that sometimes a technology or set of working conditions make it virtually impossible to increase the levels of some of the Cs. Certain jobs are inevitably dirty, boring and repetitive; yet they still have to be done.

6. Measuring the employee life cycle

Employees may be categorised according to age, length of service, occupation, educational background, job experience and promotion potential. *Labour turnover* is commonly measured by the ratio of the number of workers who left the firm during a certain period (normally six months or a year) to the average number of workers employed during the same period. If this is relatively constant over time the firm can predict the recruitment needed to keep all existing posts occupied. The problem is that if just one or two posts are filled and vacated many times during a particular period the index becomes artificially high. For instance, if a single job is filled ten times in a year the effect on the index is identical to that of ten people leaving different jobs during that year. To overcome (partially) this problem the 'labour stability index':

Number of employees with more than one year's service
Total number of people employed one year ago

can be used to show the extent to which employees with longer service are leaving the firm. Note that this index does not reveal the average length of service of employees, which should be computed separately for each category of staff.

Another useful exercise is to compute the percentages of a group of employees – all of whom are hired on the same date – who are still with the firm after certain periods. Thus for example, 10 per cent might have left by the end of one year, 25 per cent after two years, 70 per cent after five, and so on. The firm can then predict how long, on average, it takes for (say) half of all workers recruited on a particular date to leave the firm. The exercise can be repeated for various occupational groups.

7. Causes and effects of high labour turnover

High labour turnover may be due to low pay, inadequate holiday entitlement, long working hours or other conditions of employment regarded by workers as unsatisfactory. Other causes include:

(a) excessively monotonous work

(b) absence of promotion prospects

(c) bad recruitment and staff induction procedures

(d) ineffective grievance procedures

(e) poor communications within the organisation.

High labour turnover is undesirable for several reasons. Recruitment and training costs increase, new entrants are relatively unproductive during the early stages of their service, and additional demands are placed on the remaining staff. Morale is typically lower in firms with high labour turnover. Note, however, that certain categories of employee on average exhibit exceptionally high labour turnover rates, notably young workers and those engaged in boring and repetitive duties. Also, workers are more likely to quit their jobs in rapidly expanding industries.

8. Absenteeism

Absenteeism can result from job dissatisfaction, individual inclinations not to attend work, or from bad personal relationships within groups of workers. Job-related factors include poor physical conditions, boredom, inadequate supervision, stressful environments and/or inconvenient working hours. Other determinants of absenteeism include:

(a) the age, sex and length of service of the employee (young people and females have higher absenteeism rates on average than others, *vice versa* for long-serving workers)

(b) the individual's general state of health

(c) the worker's attitude towards employment

(d) availability of sick pay

(e) distance from work and/or travelling difficulties

(f) extent of the employee's family responsibilities.

Note that several of the above factors are interconnected. For example, it is a fact that women on average take more time off work than men, but it is also known that females predominate in many tedious and low-status occupations.

9. Managing absenteeism

The high costs and disruptions to workflows created by absenteeism cause many companies to apply special policies to encourage regular attendance. Costs of absenteeism relate to sick pay, need for overtime working to cover for missing employees, failure to meet project deadlines, management time absorbed in rearranging workloads, etc. Absence control policies may involve:

(a) job design (*see* 15: **26**) and regular job rotation

(b) employee participation in decision making (*see* 15: **27**)

(c) improved recruitment and selection procedures aimed at fitting individuals to jobs

(d) flexitime and job sharing

(e) actions short of dismissal (*see* **42**), e.g. formal warnings, denial of pay increases, etc

(f) bonuses for regular attendance

(g) management exhortations to employees to turn up for work

(h) employee counselling

(i) careful record keeping to identify departments and types of work with the highest absenteeism rates.

ACQUIRING NEW EMPLOYEES

10. Recruitment and selection

The first stage in the recruitment process is the drafting or revision of an accurate job specification for the vacant position, outlining its major and minor responsibilities; the skills, experience and qualifications needed; grade and level of pay; starting date; whether temporary or permanent; and particulars of any special conditions (shift-work, for example) attached to the job. Then the vacancy is advertised in suitable media and/or recruitment agencies are approached.

External recruitment is expensive. It involves advertising, agency fees, distribution of application forms, preparation of shortlists, writing for references, interviewing, payment of travelling expenses, etc. And if the candidate appointed is unsuitable or leaves within a short period the entire procedure has to be repeated.

'Selection' means matching the requirements of a job with the attributes of candidates. This is facilitated by drafting a 'person specification' defining the background, education, training, personality and other characteristics of the ideal candidate. The specification might detail the mental disposition needed for the job, appearance requirements, special abilities (capacity to lead or cope with stress, for example), whether the job is suitable for a highly-motivated person, etc.

11. Interviewing

Shortlisted candidates are then invited for interview. Opinions differ on whether candidates should meet before their interviews.

The advantage is the chance for relaxation and easing of nervousness afforded by conversation. Against this are dangers of candidates being dispirited through meeting other candidates who they might perceive as better qualified than themselves. The purpose of a job interview is to obtain information. Therefore, applicants should be put at ease as quickly as possible and hence into a frame of mind in which they will disclose the maximum amount of information about themselves. Uncomfortable, ill-at-ease candidates will not be as frank as those who are relaxed, confident and in full control of their responses. Accordingly, candidates should be interviewed promptly at the appointed time or, if delay is inevitable, apologies should be offered. Interruptions from telephone calls, secretaries, etc disturb concentration and should be avoided.

12. Rules for conducting interviews

The following rules should be followed when conducting interviews:

(a) Opening remarks should be supportive and uncontroversial.

(b) Questions which simply ask for repetition of information already provided on application forms should be avoided. Rather the interviewer should seek supplementary information to probe in depth the candidate's potential.

(c) Detailed notetaking by interviewers is inadvisable because of its disturbing effects on the interviewee. Candidates should be assessed immediately after their interviews. Otherwise, important points in earlier interviews will be forgotten in the final end-of-session appraisal.

(d) Open-ended questions such as 'what made you decide to do that?' or 'why did you enjoy that type of work?' are usually more productive in obtaining information than direct queries. Generally-worded questions invite the candidate to discuss feelings, opinions and perceptions of events. Simple yes/no questions will not draw out the candidate's opinions. Interviewers should not make critical or insensitive remarks during the interview.

(e) Interviewers should not compare candidates with themselves.

(f) Only job-relevant questions should be asked.

(g) The 'halo effect', i.e. assuming that because a candidate possesses one desirable characteristic (smart appearance or a good speaking voice, for example) then he or she must be equally good in all other areas, must not be allowed to influence the selection.

(h) 'Revealing' questions should not be asked. A revealing question discloses attitudes and beliefs held by the questioner. An example would be 'I like watching football, don't you?'

(i) Inappropriate criteria must not be applied. This could involve, for example, males who interview females associating attractive physical appearance with work ability, or appointing people the interviewer knows socially.

(j) Interviewers should not behave in a pompous manner. This wastes time and contributes nothing to the quality of the interview.

(k) Interview panels should be as small as possible. Overlarge panels create unhelpful dramatic atmospheres, and panel members might ask irrelevant and disconnected questions.

13. Selection testing

Tests are often used where interviews are not possible, e.g. when large numbers of employees are to be engaged within a very short period, and for situations where candidates have no formal qualifications. An effective test will:

(a) be cheap to administer (note that a single test can be given to a roomful of perhaps 40 or 50 people at each sitting, and only a couple of people will be needed to organise and invigilate the test)

(b) measure precisely what it is intended to measure, e.g. an intelligence test should assess intelligence, not learned responses

(c) give consistent results when repeated

(d) discriminate between candidates so that the best candidates obtain high marks and poor candidates do badly

(e) be relevant to the job.

14. Types of selection test

There are four types of selection test: achievement, aptitude, intelligence and personality. *Achievement* tests evaluate an applicant's existing competence – typing tests are a good example. Problems with achievement tests include the following:

(a) They do not evaluate the whole person, only a small sub-section of his or her abilities. A candidate who fails the test is assumed incapable of doing the entire job, which need not be true.

(b) Tests are undertaken in specific test conditions. Success in a driving test proves that the candidate did well over the test circuit, yet he or she may not be a good driver elsewhere.

(c) Candidates who have passed a test might assume they possess knowledge or ability which in fact they do not have. High marks obtained in a test do not guarantee that the successful candidate will do well in the vacant position.

15. Intelligence testing

This is a highly-specialised skill for which extensive training is necessary. The questions asked need to be culturally neutral, independent of general knowledge and past training (otherwise people could learn to become intelligent), while answers given should not depend on environmental factors or be related to the circumstances of the test.

Results should be sensitive to how people feel at the time the test is attempted – whether they are tired, nervous, have the 'flu', etc. Tests should give consistent results when they are repeated, and outcomes should compare with other indicators of ability and records of performance. Methods, problems and the implications of intelligence (and other) testing are discussed in the M&E text *Organisational Behaviour*, to which the interested reader is referred.

16. Personality tests

These seek to identify individual traits such as introversion, extroversion, personal assertiveness, ability to cope with stress and/or expected future patterns

329

of behaviour (management style, potential for leadership, etc). Interpretation of the results of such tests is difficult. Specific problems are that:

(a) Candidates, knowing their personalities are being examined, will attempt to present themselves in ways that create favourable impressions.

(b) Individual attitudes and behaviour can change dramatically over time and according to circumstances.

(c) Assessments relate to observed behaviour and expressed opinion at a particular moment. These might be untypical, so average behaviour is largely ignored.

(d) Because of the subjectivity in interpreting results, candidates might be given very different personality descriptions by differing assessors.

17. Aptitude tests

This category of test is intended to assess candidates' promise; whether, for example, they are suitable for training, or the extent to which they possess qualities that might be subsequently developed. The aptitude being looked for might be physical, intellectual, perceptive or emotional, and the problem arises of how these potentials can be evaluated. One approach is to test existing workers doing similar jobs to discover the qualities needed for success in that type of work. Then candidates might be examined for evidence of these abilities.

18. Biodata

An increasingly common method for selecting employees is to examine the backgrounds of existing 'successful' workers and then recruit people with similar biographical characteristics. Biodata is historic and verifiable information about the individual that is compared against the biodata of a sample of existing successful workers. Use of this method assumes that a person's characteristics are the consequence of certain lifetime experiences, e.g. being the youngest of a large family.

Problems with the biodata technique include choice of appropriate criteria for evaluating candidates (i.e. identifying which *particular* lifetime experiences caused current employees to succeed), and how to ensure that applicants are telling the truth about their personal details.

19. Executive search (headhunting)

This is an increasingly common method for recruiting managerial staff which assumes that the best people will *already* have good jobs. Accordingly recruitment consultants (headhunters) seek to locate (from newspaper and magazine reports, informants, trade association yearbooks, membership lists of professional bodies, etc) suitable candidates and will approach them directly and in strict confidence on behalf of the recruiting firm. The headhunter will:

(a) analyse the vacancy and advise the recruiting company about the type of candidate required and the terms and conditions of employment needed to attract suitable applicants

(b) establish whether targeted individuals are interested in the vacancy at the salary on offer

(c) conduct initial interviews, administer relevant selection tests (*see* **11–14** above), draft candidate profiles for presentation to the recruiting company and offer a recommendation.

Headhunting is commonest in fields where there is an acute shortage of specialist skills, e.g. information technology, financial engineering or advanced manufacturing techniques. The advantages of headhunting are that:

(a) It can be a cheap method of recruitment because only the candidates discovered by the headhunter need be considered (so there are no advertising or administrative costs).

(b) Recruitment consultants have (or should have) expert knowledge of the likely locations of suitable candidates and of the remuneration packages necessary to tempt them away from their current jobs.

(c) Recruiting firms are guaranteed a supply of eminently qualified candidates.

(d) The anonymity of the recruiting firm is preserved until the final stages of the procedure.

20. Problems with executive search

Headhunted individuals might themselves be enticed to leave the recruiting company by other headhunters after a short while. To avoid this some firms impose 'golden handcuffs' on management employees, i.e. large cash bonuses available only if the person remains with the company a certain number of years. Other possible problems are as follows:

(a) The headhunter might acquire confidential information about the infrastructure of the firm. This could be passed on to competitors during a subsequent assignment.

(b) A candidate may offer the headhunter a financial inducement for a recommendation for appointment to the vacant job.

(c) The recruiting firm might expect a headhunter to find a candidate who will solve all its difficulties, when in fact the business is so weak that it is bound to fail.

(d) Headhunters lack detailed knowledge of the vacant position and of the infrastructure and organisational culture (*see* **6:24**) of the recruiting business. Also they are not subject to the same long-run accountability as internal employees of the business.

21. Induction

This is the process of introducing recruits to an organisation. It is important because first impressions can influence employee perceptions of the firm for long periods. Recruits need to know where they should go for help if they experience problems. A new entrant should be told what to do if he or she:

(a) has a problem with money or understanding the wage system

(b) has a medical problem

(c) feels that working conditions are unsafe

(d) does not get on with other people in the department

(e) has difficulty with the work

(f) is bullied or harassed

(g) has a complaint

(h) does not receive adequate training.

Then the recruit should be informed of the firm's organisation structure, expected performance standards, formal disciplinary procedures, and mundane matters relating to lunch breaks, where to make personal telephone calls, etc.

22. Contracts of employment

Under the Trade Union Reform and Employment Rights Act 1993 all employees are entitled to a written contract of employment within 8 weeks of starting work. The following information must be included in the written statement:

(a) names of employer and employee

(b) date when employment began and the date when continuous employment began

(c) pay, or method of calculating pay

(d) intervals at which payment is made, i.e. weekly, monthly, etc

(e) terms and conditions relating to:

   (*i*)   hours of work
   (*ii*) holiday pay, including the pay due on termination of employment
   (*iii*) sick pay
   (*iv*) pension scheme

(f) the length of notice of termination the employee is obliged to give and entitled to receive

(g) a note indicating the employee's right to join, or not to join, a trade union

(h) a description of the manner in which an employee can seek redress of any grievance relating to his or her employment

(i) the title of the job

(j) a note showing whether any period of employment with another employer counts as part of the period of employment for notice purposes

(k) for firms employing more than 20 persons, reference to a document stating the disciplinary rules, and naming a person to whom the employee can apply (and by what method) if he or she is dissatisfied with a disciplinary decision

(l) any collective agreements which directly affect terms and condition

(m) place(s) of work

(n) for temporary jobs, how long the employment is expected to last

(o) for employees working abroad, the period to be spent outside the UK, the currency of payment, any additional benefits payable in consequence of working abroad, and the terms and conditions relating to the employee's return to the UK.

It is not necessary for the written statement to cover all these points in detail; the employee may be directed to documents which are easily accessible for the full particulars. These documents could include, for example, pension scheme handbooks or copies of the works rules.

Employees must be informed in writing of any changes in conditions not more than one month after the change has been made.

Breach of a contract of employment will on the one hand provide the firm with grounds for fair dismissal, and on the other enable the worker to sue for unpaid wages. Once the written statement is issued, the firm cannot alter its terms and conditions without the permission of the individual worker. If it does so it is in breach of contract and the employee can claim to have been unfairly dismissed.

TRAINING

23. Advantages and disadvantages of training

Training should improve workers' competences; equip them for higher-level work; increase the quality of output or performance, and enhance morale. Other reasons for training include the creation of a flexible and adaptable workforce, and less need for detailed supervision. Job satisfaction increases, resulting in higher output, less absenteeism and lower turnover of staff.

The problems with training are as follows:

(a) Training is expensive. Instructors must be employed, and often trainees are not producing while they are being trained.

(b) Staff might leave the firm once they have finished their training.

(c) Possibly, trained and competent employees can be recruited at low cost from outside.

(d) Employees' job expectations increase in consequence of training. If opportunities for rapid advancement do not actually exist then staff may leave the firm in order to practise elsewhere the new competences acquired through training.

24. Assessing training needs

The need for employee training may arise from the introduction of new technologies, or the firm's diversification into different fields. Other causes of the need for training might be poor-quality output, high accident rates, high absenteeism or staff turnover, or unfavourable performance appraisal reports submitted by managers on their subordinates. Note, however, that any one of these might be caused by factors other than inadequate training. A systematic programme of training is of course an integral part of a company's management succession scheme.

Note the difference between 'training', which normally assists people to improve their abilities in a particular job, and 'staff development', which relates to the improvement of a person's overall capacity to pursue a career. Development enhances the general *potential* of the employee.

25. On-the-job versus off-the-job training

On-the-job training occurs at the place of work. It includes verbal instruction, practical demonstrations, specialist short courses and briefing sessions. Trainees perceive the instruction as directly and immediately relevant to their jobs. Often, trainers are supervisors who work in the same department as trainees, so that trainees can learn techniques while actually producing goods. A problem is how best to control the quality of training: supervisors can be extremely bad instructors, and the workplace might not be the best environment in which to learn.

Off-the-job training is undertaken externally in training centres or colleges, or in a section of the firm's premises reserved for this purpose. Trainees may thus concentrate on the instruction given, away from the pressures and distractions of the workplace. Specialist training staff may be employed and the quality of instruction strictly monitored. Trainees learn correct ways of doing things and do not pick up bad working habits. However, trainees may not take seriously the instruction received in an artificially-created work environment, and they might not relate what happens in off-the-job instruction to actual work requirements. Also, full-time instructors can lose touch with current working practices.

26. Principles of training

A number of general principles determine the success or failure of a training course. Trainees must want to learn; they should recognise their own deficiencies and perceive the training offered as relevant for remedying personal shortcomings. The programme should be steady, progressive and not exceed the intellectual capacities of employees. Participants' progress should be regularly monitored and trainees should be able to assess how well they are doing. Training methods should be varied, interesting and require active contributions from course participants. A common mistake is to expect too much progress in too little time.

27. Education and training

Education is concerned with the intrinsic value of information. It seeks to develop an awareness of cause and effect and to foster the ability independently to appraise and criticise material. Thus, education is desirable *in itself* and need not have immediately practicable applications. Training, conversely, is about the *use* of knowledge. It is utilitarian, instrumental and has direct practical objectives. However, training programmes that ignore educational requirements can be counterproductive, since trainees will fail to understand either the wider contexts of the techniques and materials discussed, or the implications of the training and/or the foundations upon which it is based.

28. Skills and knowledge

Knowledge results from the assimilation of facts and experience. Usually it comes from books, listening and conversation. A 'skill', conversely, is a capacity to perform a task competently, and need not be based on knowledge. Thus for example, a skilful machine operator may have no knowledge of the machine's technology, but rather has learned a co-ordinated sequence of actions for efficiently operating the machine. Skills can be *technical* and involve working with physical objects; or *interpersonal* (such as leading others and communicating effectively); or involve decision taking and problem solving or the discovery, processing and dissemination of information.

29. Training methods

The commonest training methods are coaching, lectures, group training, computer-based training and interactive video.

Coaching is one-to-one instruction where, typically, the instructor performs an operation which is then imitated by the trainee. The instructor can vary the pace of the training to suit the capacity of the trainee, and can remedy mistakes instantly. *Lectures* are transmissions of sets of facts and opinions to a large audience, normally without the trainee's participation other than listening and taking notes. They need to emphasise the major points of a topic since only about one third of the material might be remembered. Handouts can reinforce and consolidate the material transmitted.

Group training may involve case studies (simulations of real-life problems), role-playing or group discussion. Participants examine each other's views and learn collectively through pooling ideas and experience. It is essential that participants take group training seriously and that everyone contributes to the exercise. Often, group training involves *action learning* whereby trainees themselves (*i*) collect and evaluate the data needed to solve a (real-life) problem, (*ii*) implement a solution and (*iii*) analyse the consequences.

Computer-based training (CBT) uses software packages that contain instructional material plus exercises to test the trainee's understanding of the topic concerned. Most CBT follows the principles of *programmed learning*, whereby users are not allowed to progress until they have mastered the previous section of the work, e.g. by answering all test questions correctly. CBT enables trainees to work independently and at their own pace, although much self-discipline is needed to complete an entire programme alone. *Interactive video* consists of footage of a simulated interpersonal communication situation (often a conflict situation) that maps out the background to how the situation arose, portrays actors assuming various roles, builds up a climax and then stops abruptly leaving the viewer to provide the next step.

30. T-group training

This is a method of group training that deliberately leaves participants to their own devices. The trainer gives the group a task, and then observes how group members set about establishing a group structure and appointing a leader. However, the trainer does not intervene.

Initially, group members feel helpless. Then they begin to offer suggestions, to pool their knowledge and experience and to create procedures for organising work. Conflicts between members may develop, which somehow or other the group must resolve. Eventually, each member clarifies his or her own role in the system, and rules and leadership structures emerge. At the end of the exercise the trainer explains the dynamics of the processes that have occurred and leads a group discussion.

The advantages claimed for T-group training are that participants:

(a) are made to recognise the need to learn from each other

(b) see how group members react to offers of help

(c) learn through experience the processes of leadership and the efficient allocation of tasks

(d) develop self-confidence in communicating and expressing their views.

Criticisms of T-group training are that it:

(a) takes place in artificially-created environments and thus does not relate to real-life groupwork situations

(b) requires trainees to train themselves (and not everyone is capable of this)

(c) favours extroverted people who easily strike up relationships with others

(d) offers little more than the experiences that people have anyhow through everyday social interactions

(e) is interesting for participants but of no practical value.

MANAGEMENT TRAINING AND DEVELOPMENT

31. Management training

This seeks to improve management performance and to ensure the adequacy of a management succession scheme. Advantages include less need to recruit managers from outside the company (note the high cost of recruiting senior managers), motivation of junior executives, and the creation of more flexible and broad-minded managerial employees. Techniques of management training include short courses, job rotation, planned experience via the systematic delegation of increasingly difficult work to subordinates, coaching and group discussions.

Objections to the value of management training are:

(a) Arguably, many aspects of management can only be learned by doing. Thus there is little point in providing 'academic' management training that has little practical application.

(b) Formal management training cannot inculcate entrepreneurial attitudes. Other methods (*see* **4:3**) are necessary for this.

(c) Training encourages technical specialisation rather than the overall ability to lead.

(d) The environments in which training occurs are artificial and remote from real-life managerial problems.

(e) Management training encourages unrealistic job expectations in junior managerial staff, possibly inducing them to leave the firm.

(f) Normal competition between managerial staff should ensure the survival of the fittest.

32. Content of management training

Implementation of a management training programme requires the assessment of the abilities of current management staff and the creation of schemes to enhance the potential of each individual. Typically, management training is provided in the following areas:

(a) Background knowledge of the company, its trading environment, products, production methods, markets and personnel

(b) Elements of management theory and practice, administrative procedures, sources and uses of finance, the legal environment, and specialist techniques

(c) Analytical skills, specification of objectives, organisation, delegation and control

(d) Interpersonal skills, communication skills, leadership, and co-ordination and motivation of staff

(e) Creative abilities, problem-solving techniques and capacity to initiate new activities.

Much management training is done on short courses conducted in hotels or purpose-built residential training centres. These are particularly useful when staff from different departments or firms are able to compare and discuss their various experiences. Note, however, that participants might greatly enjoy a residential short course, but not really benefit from attendance. They could enjoy the company of classmates, meet new people and be impressed by the physical environment in which a course takes place, yet not learn anything of practical value.

33. Managerial competencies

From 1987 onwards, various UK government bodies funded an attempt to define precisely and systematically the competences that managers need to possess. Statements of these competences were to form the basis for the syllabuses of government-approved management studies courses. The aim was to discover what managers actually do, and hence establish the skills and experiences that trainee managers need to acquire.

Three 'dimensions' of managerial competence were identified:

(a) *Managing resources and systems*, including 'managing people' (staffing, guiding, liaising with others), specific management functions (inventory management, for instance) and financial control. Each element of the dimension is then broken down into detailed activities. Thus, for example, financial control encompasses costing, budgeting, accounting, employee compensation and so on. Staffing incorporates recruitment, interviewing, job analysis, induction, etc.

(b) *Personal effectiveness*, incorporating communication skills, time management, assertiveness, ability to cope with stress, self-awareness, learning capacities and similar personal abilities.

(c) *Environmental sensitivity* in relation to customers, the wider community, economic and commercial institutions, and the welfare of employees. Knowledge of marketing, industrial relations, corporate strategy and the legal aspects of business are included here.

34. Performance criteria

Competence was defined in terms of the trainee's ability to *perform* (rather than simply know about) managerial duties. An 'element of competence' was either (*i*) an action, behaviour or outcome that a person should be able to demonstrate, or (*ii*) a piece of knowledge or understanding needed to complete a task. Associated with each element of competence is a performance criterion that precisely defines expected knowledge or behaviour. Thus, for example, the element 'Able to Select a Job Applicant' has attached to it the following performance criteria:

(a) assemble relevant information on candidates

(b) compare candidates with job specifications

(c) conduct interviews and rank candidates in a fair and logical manner

(d) be able to ask suitable questions while conducting interviews

(e) establish unbiased yardsticks against which candidates are to be assessed.

Eventually, management qualifications will comprise a number of units of competence all related to a particular field.

35. Advantages and problems of the proposed scheme

The authorities hope that national standards will be established that are applicable to all management education and training regardless of where or how it is undertaken. Other advantages are that:

(a) Students will know exactly what is expected of them and what they need to learn and do in order to become competent managers.

(b) Employers will know that all accredited management qualifications cover certain basic elements.

(c) Individuals will be motivated – via the existence of a ladder of management qualifications – to undertake further courses in management.

(d) As students qualify they can become teachers, pass on their competence to others, and eventually create a critical mass of managerial expertise within the UK.

(e) If this (massive) project is successfully completed it will provide a fully-comprehensive taxonomy of all the tasks, duties, knowledge and experience requirements, responsibilities and special abilities needed for all levels of management.

Criticisms of the approach include the following:

(a) Dimensions of competence encompass every imaginable managerial function and task. Colleges and professional bodies already teach and examine in their relevant fields. Simply listing all the things that managers do adds nothing to what is already known, taught and practised.

(b) Entrepreneurial flair, which can be an essential part of successful management, might not be measurable (and hence not easily assessed).

(c) Individuals enter management in so many different ways and from such different backgrounds that no single national curriculum can possibly cater for the (often highly specific) needs of all trainees.

(d) Many of the most successful and innovative of all entrepreneurs and managers have received no management training.

(e) Differentiating between people who are and are not competent in certain aspects of management (especially those concerning interpersonal relations) may not be possible. How for example could a student be examined in the ability to listen, empathise and reassure?

(f) Management, by its very nature, is a fast-changing subject. Inevitably, therefore, rigidly defined statements of competence must quickly become out of date.

(g) The ultimate measure of efficient business management is the rate of profit achieved – regardless of whether the individuals involved are deemed 'competent' in terms of the stated performance criteria.

36. The managerial grid

In 1964 Robert Blake and Jane Mouton devised a method for training managers in the diagnosis of their own and other people's leadership styles. The 'managerial grid' is a taxonomy of management styles classified according to the manager's interest in subordinates as people in comparison with his or her concern for production. Each concern is rated on a scale from one to nine so that a '9,9' manager, for example, is one who possesses both a very high concern for people and a high concern for production. A '1,9' manager, with low concern for production but great emphasis on human relations, pays careful attention to subordinates' human needs, but exerts little effort to ensure that work is actually done properly. Such a manager is likable, enjoys satisfactory relations with subordinates and generates a friendly atmosphere in his or her department. The '9,1' manager on the other hand arranges work as efficiently as possible, with scant regard for subordinates' feelings.

Within the grid defined by the two axes (one showing concern for people, the other concern for production) five managerial types were distinguished:

(a) 1,1: managers who make little effort to get work done or to develop close personal relationships

(b) 9,1: managers who are task-efficient but low on human involvement

(c) 1,9: managers with little regard for task-efficiency but who mix well with subordinates

(d) 5,5: managers who balance task performance with human relations considerations

(e) 9,9: managers who achieve high production from committed, satisfied subordinates.

Grid training tries to help managers identify their inclinations within this framework. Ideally, the '9,9' position should be the desired combination.

37. Outdoor management training (OMT)

The justification for this is the assumption that direct parallels exist between the personal qualities necessary for successful corporate management and those cultivated through participation in outdoor pursuits such as rockclimbing, canoeing, sailing or orienteering, since the essential demands of these activities (planning, organising, team-building, dealing with uncertainty, direction and control) are the same as those needed for business management.

Accordingly, outdoor exercises are sometimes used to train managers in leadership, target setting, communication, co-ordination and the motivation of subordinate staff.

The advantages of OMT are as follows:

(a) Individuals are forced to recognise the importance of clear expression, trust and co-operation among members of a team.

(b) Participants learn about themselves; their strengths and weaknesses, relationships with others and capacity for command.

(c) OMT teaches accountability, since it is impossible to hide mistakes or 'pull rank' when helping other people climb a rockface or cross desolate moorland.

Critics of OMT allege that it has little relevance for modern management methods, which rely heavily on information processing, model formulation and data-interpretation skills. OMT, they argue, encourages 'gifted-amateur' approaches to management. The time devoted to such exercises might be better spent learning about advanced management techniques.

38. Evaluating training effectiveness

Successes achieved in training manual workers can be assessed through output levels, quality of production, time taken to complete tasks and other quantifiable criteria. Evaluating management training is more problematic, however, because improved performance cannot always be directly appraised. Moreover, skills acquired on courses undertaken now might not be applicable in managers' current jobs.

The payoff to investments in training might not be immediately apparent. Improved morale, better personal relationships, greater attachment to the firm and other intangible benefits can result from training but not be measurable in purely financial terms. Note, moreover, that favourable comment from trainees need not indicate an effective programme: enjoyable and popular courses are not necessarily the best. The crucial question is 'what would happen if the firm did not bother training its employees?'

39. Welfare services

Large organisations provide employee welfare services for reasons of social responsibility and to improve employee morale and feelings of attachment to the business. The availability of welfare services, moreover, can be an aid to the recruitment of high-calibre staff. Examples of welfare services include the following:

(a) Counselling (*see* 2:29), including bereavement and retirement counselling

(b) Social and recreational facilities

(c) Assistance with housing or transport

(d) Availability of company loans to employees

(e) Benevolent funds

(f) Legal advice

(g) Long-service grants

(h) Rehabilitation schemes for injured workers

(i) Canteen services

(j) Occupational health screening.

Note the overlap between many 'welfare services' with employee fringe benefits incorporated into remuneration packages.

TERMINATION OF EMPLOYMENT

40. Dismissal

Dismissal is the termination of employment by:

(a) the employer, with or without notice; *or*

(b) the employee's resignation, with or without notice, when the employer behaves in a manner that demonstrates refusal to be bound by the contract of employment (this is termed 'constructive dismissal', i.e. the employer is behaving so unreasonably that the worker has no alternative but to quit); *or*

(c) the failure of the employer to renew a fixed-term contract.

Certain employees have the statutory right not to be unfairly dismissed. This is discussed in 11:**17**.

41. Summary dismissal

Dismissal without notice (termed 'summary' dismissal) is lawful only if the employee's behaviour makes impossible the fulfilment of a contract of employment. Examples are theft, persistent drunkenness, violence, abusiveness to colleagues or customers, wilful disobedience or incompetence that immediately causes damage to the employer's business. Otherwise the notice stated in the employee's contract, or statutory notice (*see* 11:**17**), must be given.

42. The ACAS code

ACAS (*see* 11:**17**) has issued a code of practice on dismissal. This is not legally binding but industrial tribunals will refer to it when deciding whether a dismissal was 'fair'. The code recommends that at least two written warnings be issued prior to dismissal, that the worker be given full details of alleged misbehaviour, have the right to be represented by a union officer and be given the opportunity to appeal.

43. Redundancy

A dismissed employee is redundant when the firm no longer requires work of the type done by the employee. Thus, it is a worker's job that becomes redundant, not a particular worker. By law, criteria for selecting redundant personnel must be fair and objective. Among the criteria commonly applied are length of service, age, capabilities, qualifications, experience, past conduct and suitability for alternative employment within the business. Workers with more than two years' service are entitled to a redundancy payment from their employing firms.

44. Actions short of dismissal

Disciplinary action short of dismissal against employees who behave improperly or who lack effort are lawful provided they do not discriminate unfairly with respect to race, sex, marital status or a person's involvement or non-involvement with a trade union. Examples of such actions are demotion, denial of pay rises, failure to promote certain employees, loss of increments, refusal of requests for time off or the allocation of low-status duties.

EMPLOYEE RELATIONS

45. Management and trade unions

Trade unions are associations of workers formed to protect their interests in employment situations. They differ from 'staff associations' (which are set up by and within the employing firm) in that they are independent of employers and – provided they register as independent unions with the Government Certification Officer – qualify for legal immunity from breach of contract actions in industrial disputes (*see* 11:**21**).

Unions have highly specific objectives, namely to achieve better wages and working conditions for members, job security and improved welfare benefits. Accordingly they seek to negotiate with employers in order to attain these ends. This is normally done through 'collective bargaining' (*see* **45**).

46. Employers' associations

These are associations of firms formed to negotiate with trade unions within a particular industry. Membership of an employers' association implies agreement to abide by its rules, including adherence to pay settlements negotiated by the association with unions. Firms which pay more or less than agreed industry (or national) wage levels are liable to expulsion from the association.

47. Collective bargaining

Through collective bargaining, representatives of groups of workers seek to negotiate with and influence employers on matters relating to pay, working hours and conditions, indeed any issue that affects working life. Collective bargaining recognises the weakness of the individual worker as a negotiating unit and, implicitly, accepts the existence of conflicts of interest between management and other employees. Arguably, collective bargaining assists employing firms as well as workers, for the following reasons:

(a) Management–worker relationships are stabilised.

(b) It can be an efficient way of determining pay and working conditions and for settling disputes. There is no need for individual wage negotiations and official agreements can be expected to stick.

(c) Meetings between management and unions provide a useful forum for discussion of wider issues concerning the progress of the firm.

(d) If unions are not recognised, labour will still make its opinions known in some way, possibly with disruptive consequences – such as absenteeism, lack of effort, non-cooperation and so on.

(e) Compromise is encouraged; opposing viewpoints are openly discussed. Procedural rules covering consultation methods, arbitration and grievance regulations, recognition agreements and so on can help defuse sudden conflicts through forcing parties to meet, discuss and negotiate.

The *disadvantages* to management of collective bargaining include:

(a) reduction of managerial prerogative

(b) delays in taking decisions about human resources

(c) possible increases in labour costs

(d) failure to resolve certain difficulties because of the inability of union representatives to agree among themselves.

Collective bargaining results in *substantive* agreements, covering pay, hours and conditions of work, etc, and *procedural* agreements which regulate the methods applied to settlement of industrial disputes.

48. Control of grievances

Grievances result from external circumstances (e.g. poor working conditions) or from an employee's internal feelings of distress caused, for instance, by bad personal relationships with other workers or the perception of being treated less favourably than everyone else. Externally created grievances may be remedied through altering environmental circumstances: improving conditions, restoring a contractual right, etc. Internally generated grievances may require the counselling of the employee (*see* 2:29) or a move to a different department or job.

Often, grievances are due to misunderstandings rather than to fundamental difficulties. Examples are communication breakdowns, petty jealousies, interpersonal rivalry and departmental disputes. Usually these minor problems can be settled by increasing the flow of information through the organisation, by defining the authority and responsibilities of people and departments more carefully, and by generally promoting co-operation between individuals and sectional groups. Otherwise, a formal grievance procedure is required. The commonest procedure is as follows:

(a) The aggrieved worker must approach his or her immediate supervisor in the first place.

(b) If the grievance remains unsettled the worker nominates a representative (typically a trade union or staff association representative) who takes up the case. This person discusses the matter with the supervisor and, if settlement is still not forthcoming, with the supervisor's boss.

(c) The unresolved issue is now placed before a three-person committee comprising one management and one employee representative plus an independent chairperson mutually agreed by the other two members.

49. Industrial disputes

Disputes arise from a multitude of sources, including demands for higher wages, concerns with the working environment, the speed of assembly lines, grading systems, threats of redundancy and so on. Resolution of disputes may occur through the following means:

(a) Formal grievance procedures (*see* **46**).

(b) Establishment of joint negotiating committees (works committees) that meet at predetermined intervals to deal with problems which have arisen since the last meeting. Both sides promise not to take industrial action prior to a matter being discussed in the works committee.

(c) One side or the other imposing its will, e.g. through management threatening dismissals or employee representatives organising strikes, a work-to-rule, or other industrial action. (Note that firms are legally entitled to sack striking workers, provided *all* strikers are dismissed and not just some of them.)

(d) Arbitration agreements which provide for the appointment of an independent referee to hear and adjudicate cases. Parties agree in advance that the arbitrator's decision shall be final.

50. Pendulum arbitration

This is a form of arbitration in which:

(a) Each party presents its demands to the arbitrator, e.g. the union may ask for an X per cent wage increase whereas the management offers only Y per cent.

(b) The arbitrator then selects one solution or the other – there is no haggling or compromise.

(c) This settlement is binding on both sides.

The advantage claimed for pendulum arbitration is that it forces the parties to be realistic in their demands; there is no splitting the difference as commonly occurs with conventional collective bargaining.

51. New technology agreements

These are accords whereby management and unions jointly consider, negotiate and agree procedures for the introduction of major technological innovations. Such agreements will (hopefully) encourage acceptance of change, reduce uncertainty and involve unions directly at the time a significant change is contemplated. Bargaining then ensues over the amendments to job specifications, working practices and employee reward structures implied by new methods and systems.

The problems with these agreements are that:

(a) They may interfere with managerial prerogative.

(b) Technology is continuously advancing so that having to discuss the implications of each new development can impede the introduction of change.

(c) Refusal to implement vital new technologies may become a bargaining weapon in wider industrial disputes.

52. No-strike agreements

Under the Trade Union and Labour Relations Act 1974 a 'no-strike' clause in an agreement can only be part of individual contracts of employment when the agreement:

(a) is in writing

(b) expressly provides for the inclusion of the clause in individual contracts

(c) is reasonably accessible to the employee at his or her place of work

(d) is made with independent unions only.

The individual worker's contract should include the no-strike clause either expressly or by clear implication.

EUROPEAN DIMENSIONS OF PERSONNEL MANAGEMENT

53. Consequences of the European Single Market

EU workers can seek employment in any member state and freely reside in that country. Individuals may bring their families to the country of their employment and thereafter receive unemployment benefit on the same basis as local workers. They have equal access to public housing and to education for their children, and may retire and continue to reside in their adopted country.

54. EU recognition of professional qualifications

In the past, member states restricted the right of entry to certain professions (e.g. accountancy, law, medicine) to persons who qualified within their own national frontiers. Such restrictions are now being lifted. The training and other requirements for specific professions are being harmonised via the award of Higher Education Diplomas valid and recognised in all Community countries. Anyone possessing the appropriate EU recognised diploma (issued only after at least three years' training) will be free to practise his or her profession in any member state.

55. Further proposals

The European Commission has drafted three proposals (yet to be accepted by the Council of Ministers) that will significantly affect the personnel field. These cover the following issues:

(a) Compulsory alterations in the company law of all member states to give workers a say in running their companies (*see* 3: **28**).

(b) Laws that will force a company domiciled in one country to transmit to its subsidiaries operating in other countries key information about the parent company's current financial position and expected future performance. This information would then be communicated to the employees of the subsidiary firms.

(c) Regulations to grant temporary workers the same legal rights as permanent employees, and to restrict firms' capacities to use large numbers of casual, temporary workers instead of permanent staff.

56. The European Social Charter

The European Commission has produced a draft of a Social Charter which it believes to be necessary to complement the completion of the single internal market for business, goods and services. Acceptance of the provisions of the Charter is voluntary and (at the time of writing) may not be imposed on a member state against its wishes. The Social Charter demands the rights of EU citizens to:

(a) freedom of movement

(b) fair remuneration

(c) freedom of occupation

(d) improvement in living and working conditions

(e) social protection

(f) freedom of association

(g) freedom of collective bargaining

(h) vocational training

(i) equal treatment for men and women

(j) information about their employing firms, consultation between management and employees, participation of workers

(k) protection and safety at work

(l) protection of children and young persons

(m) a decent living standard for the elderly

(n) social integration for disabled persons.

The intention of the Social Charter is to create a social partnership between the two sides of industry. However, if it is adopted, the Charter will be more than a statement of intentions; it will become *legally binding* in all EU countries – which will have to legislate to ensure that these rights are guaranteed within their frontiers. Moreover, the draft Charter requires member states to commit themselves to 'mobilise all the resources necessary' to implement its provisions.

Britain and the social charter

Adoption of the Social Charter by the UK will prove expensive for many British firms. Following Maastricht (*see* 8:20), all the EU countries except Britain determined to implement key elements of the Social Charter via a protocol independent of EU law. Note, however, that many of the employee benefits required by the Charter (e.g. pro-rata pay and equal access to superannuation schemes for part-time workers, protections for the casually employed, a minimum wage, legal rights to vocational training, compulsory employee participation in management decisions, and so on) *already* apply in several industrially advanced EU nations. Hence no additional costs will be incurred by firms within these countries as the provisions become law.

Progress test 16

1. List five common employment interviewing mistakes.

2. What are the characteristics of an effective selection test?

3. Define 'constructive dismissal' and 'summary dismissal'.

4. Explain the difference between education and training.

5. List the advantages of collective bargaining.

6. Define 'human resource planning'.

7. What is the difference between the service role and the advisory role of a personnel officer?

8. Define 'staff development'.

17

THE FUTURE OF MANAGEMENT

1. Emerging issues in management

Management is a fast-changing subject, and new priorities and issues continually emerge. There is particular concern in contemporary management literature for the following matters:

(a) The study of comparative international management and the need for managers to adopt international orientations towards their work

(b) Ethical and environmental issues in management

(c) The 'demographic time-bomb' (*see* **33**)

(d) Changes in the institutional framework of management caused by the completion of the European Single Market

(e) Increasing use of modern management methods by non-profit organisations (*see* **25**) and by government (*see* **26**)

(f) Refocusing of emphasis on to production and operations management, especially quality management (*see* **10:31–37**) rather than on human relations

(g) New forms of organisation structure (*see* Chapter 6)

(h) The increasing importance of women in management (*see* **28–32**)

(i) The special problems confronted by individuals from ethnic minorities who wish to enter management (*see* **34**).

COMPARATIVE INTERNATIONAL MANAGEMENT

2. Definition

Comparative international management (CIM) concerns the analysis of the causes and consequences of differences in management style and practice between nations or groups of nations. Thus, for example, it might examine differences between the USA and Japan, or between Islamic countries and (say) the non-Islamic English-speaking world. The basic *purposes* of management (as outlined in Chapters 1 and 2) are the same in all countries; but the *techniques* used to achieve managerial objectives differ significantly among nations.

3. International differences in management practice

Management style and practice differ between countries for a number of reasons, including:

(a) Disparities in customs, beliefs, attitudes and other aspects of national cultures

(b) Variations in the institutional frameworks within which businesses operate, particularly company structures

(c) Average sizes of enterprises and their forms of ownership

(d) Contrasting management training and education systems (*see* 6)

(e) Differences in contract law, the law relating to employment, health and safety regulations, etc

(f) Differing economic conditions and stages of economic development.

Reasons for studying CIM include the insights it provides into the usefulness of domestic practices, and the fact that differences in style may exert enormous influences on business growth and productivity.

Today, techniques and management know-how are quickly transferred between countries. And the extent to which certain management practices are successfully applied anywhere – irrespective of national frontiers and cultural considerations – gives an indication of whether basic, universally applicable general principles of management (*see* 1:13) actually exist.

4. Cultural and social influences

Cultural factors include religion (*see* 7); attitudes towards industry and towards management as an occupation (*see* 19); and community views on efficiency, the role of profit, savings and investment. Achievement in business is rewarded more in some societies than elsewhere. Willingness to accept risk also differs markedly between countries. Moreover, national management styles depend on *social* factors such as:

(a) Whether there exists a *work ethic* in the country. Higher incomes and increasing productivity create possibilities for greater amounts of leisure; yet in some communities managers (and others) choose to work extremely hard and take little time off regardless of their large remunerations.

(b) *Social class systems.* A high degree of class and/or occupational mobility results in individuals from a wide variety of class and income backgrounds reaching the top in management positions. Class systems affect recruitment policies and procedures, and promotion and salary grading schemes. Rigid class structures cause an oversupply of trained, educated and competent people in lower-level management jobs, since social barriers prevent their moving up the hierarchy.

(c) *Attitudes towards authority*. Paternalistic management styles (*see* 15:1–2) and highly formal interpersonal relationships between superiors and subordinates are likely in countries where deferential attitudes are valued for their own sake. The psychological distance between managers at different levels affects communication, problem-solving and decision-making systems.

(d) Existence or otherwise of strong desires to *accumulate wealth*.

(e) The *role of women* in society.

(f) The *lifestyles* to which members of the society aspire.

5. Technical factors

The materials, equipment and natural resources available within a country can affect the orientation of its businesses. Japan, for example, has no oil, coal or other significant mineral deposits. This forces Japan to import fuel and raw materials and hence to export large quantities of manufactured goods to pay for these imports. Thus, Japanese post-war industrial policy – manifest in the choice of education system, state support for research into information technology, erection of barriers against foreign goods, etc – has *necessarily* focused on the need to succeed in international markets.

6. Education systems

The quality of a country's education system determines the overall calibre of the managers of its businesses. Some important consequences of good or bad basic education systems are as follows:

(a) Poorly educated managers will not be able to understand and apply the latest management techniques, particularly those with a quantitative dimension, and may tend to resist change. They are not likely to read current trade and technical journals and hence may be unfamiliar with the latest technical developments.

(b) Ill-educated individuals frequently possess hostile attitudes towards other groups and cultures. This has implications for recruitment, selection and performance appraisal procedures, and for general equal opportunity matters.

(c) If females receive a different sort of education from males (e.g. girls being taught only non-technical subjects) it becomes difficult for women to enter certain managerial occupations.

(d) It is difficult to introduce technically complex products and processes to organisations where the top management is inadequately educated.

(e) If irrelevant subjects are taught in schools and colleges the country will eventually experience skills shortages in key areas.

(f) Badly educated managers often find it difficult to communicate with (better educated) managers in other countries, leading to fewer export orders.

7. Religious factors

Religion affects culture and may itself be an important determinant of individual behaviour and management style. The following influences are particularly significant:

(a) Religion can form the basis for a class system and hence create a barrier preventing certain groups obtaining management jobs. The Hindu caste system, for instance, once allocated members of each caste to *specific* occupational and social roles. (Discrimination based on caste is now forbidden by the Indian constitution.) Catholic minorities in Protestant countries and Protestant minorities in Catholic countries sometimes complain of discriminatory treatment where appointment to managerial positions is concerned.

(b) The ease with which women can enter management may be affected by religious considerations.

(c) Religious principles can determine attitudes towards the morality of the pursuit of material wealth.

(d) A community's dominant religion might directly affect business practices. Islam (*see* **14**) is a case in point.

(e) Religion can engender patriotic attitudes among business leaders. Japanese Shinto, for example, emphasises respect for the state, for the Japanese people and for national authority. Such influences might encourage co-operation among employee groups and aggressive attitudes towards export marketing.

MANAGEMENT IN PARTICULAR COUNTRIES

8. American management

The USA was the home of scientific management (*see* 1:**3**) and the first country where classical approaches to management (*see* 1:**13**) were extensively applied. Equally, the human relations and contingency schools (*see* Chapter 1) originated there. American writers, moreover, are among the leading innovators in contemporary management thought. While there is no unique US management style, a number of common propositions can be discerned, as follows:

(a) Individualism and the beliefs that free enterprise and the pursuit of self-interest are morally just.

(b) Emphasis on strategy (*see* Chapter 5) and the application of logic and rationality to organisational design.

(c) Commitment to competition and reliance on market mechanisms to allocate resources.

(d) Freedom of employers to hire and fire labour as market conditions change, accompanied by freedom of choice of occupation for workers.

(e) Unitary frames of reference (*see* 2:25) among managers.

9. Transmission of American ideas to Europe

American approaches (especially scientific management) travelled to Europe during the early twentieth century mainly through the adoption by European industry of mass production methods. It was after World War II, however, notably through the US Marshall Aid scheme, that US management techniques became widely used in Europe.

West European governments formed the *European Productivity Movement* (EPM) which organised training in American management methods for European industrialists. The EPM arranged visits to the USA, exchanges, conferences, meetings and training courses featuring American speakers. It also sponsored empirical research into the efficiency of various working methods and published the results. Another major factor in the transmission of American ideas was the success achieved by the large US accountancy companies which in the 1950s set up subsidiaries in Europe and which then diversified into management consulting, using American methods.

10. Transmission of American ideas to Japan

The US occupation of Japan following World War II forced (*i*) the comprehensive democratisation of that country's political institutions, (*ii*) the introduction of wide-ranging business and technical training, and (*iii*) the development of an education system based on equality of opportunity. In the late 1940s, however, Japan faced severe shortages of skills and material resources, had low productivity and an unenviable reputation for low-quality goods. Accordingly, the (then) latest American methods – statistical quality control, work study, target setting, marketing, organisational development, etc – were transported to Japan. Importantly, however, these devices were modified to correspond to existing Japanese lifestyles, customs and cultural traditions. The result was outstandingly successful, and today Japanese firms have a high reputation for quality, reliability and new-product development.

11. Nature of Japanese management

The Japanese management system retains the country's customary respect for status and authority, but in many respects is intensely competitive and egalitarian. There is meritocratic recruitment, extensive staff training and career development, job rotation and much concern for the welfare of employees. It is *not* the case, however, that all Japanese firms offer lifelong employment: only a minority of Japanese employees have full career contracts, and those who do are required to retire at 55. Nevertheless, it is generally true that most workers expect to spend their entire careers with a single employer.

Japanese firms have strong motherhood cultures (*see* 6:21). New recruits are socialised into existing value systems, and the philosophy of the organisation is constantly projected. Workers are made to *feel* an integral part of the organisation. Only people considered likely to fit in with current organisational cultures are recruited. Thereafter, promotion and wage payment systems are based on seniority. Other important features of Japanese management include:

(a) Single union representation of the employees of a particular company

(b) Single status for all grades of employee (managers and operatives dress alike, eat in the same canteen, belong to the same superannuation scheme, etc)

(c) Allocation of tasks and targets to groups rather than individuals

(d) Extensive worker participation in decision making (e.g. through Quality Circles – *see* 10:**36**), with open communication between management and operatives

(e) Trusting employees to complete their duties satisfactorily (for instance, by not constantly inspecting their work)

(f) The expectation that every member of the organisation should feel personally responsible for its success.

12. Advantages and problems with the Japanese approach

Advantages of the Japanese approach to management are as follows:

(a) Slow but steady progression through the management hierarchy (necessitated by the restricted promotion opportunities available in Japanese firms) means that employees acquire, through job rotation and lateral transfers, wide-ranging experience of the company's operations. Generalist management skills are acquired.

(b) Job security and continuous staff development enables managers to follow long-term careers.

(c) Single status stimulates team spirit (*see* 14:**13**) and employee morale.

(d) Consultation with workers ensures that the latter's knowledge of day-to-day operations is applied to management decision making.

(e) Japanese companies' desire to offer long-term employment causes them to seek continuously to expand their overseas market shares in order to provide work for their employees. Accordingly, Japanese companies have an ongoing incentive to invest in sound long-term projects, to modify and adapt products to serve new market segments (*see* 7:**6**), to introduce new products on a regular basis, to market aggressively and to develop efficient international distribution systems.

Difficulties with the Japanese approach (which is sometimes referred to as 'theory Z') include possibilities (*i*) that the emphasis on conformity could itself eventually cause organisational inflexibility and resistance to change, and (*ii*) that seniority-based promotion may block the rapid progress of the most able.

Further problems apply to attempts to transplant Japanese methods into other cultures, e.g. the introduction of Quality Circles (*see* 10:**36**) to firms that do not practise employee participation in any other field.

13. Management in Islamic countries

Under Islam, business management is required (in certain countries legally obliged) to adhere to the following moral principles:

(a) The payment of interest on financial dealings is forbidden, since it is regarded as improper to reward those with excess funds while penalising others (especially the poor) who need to borrow. This applies even to loans between businesses, since it is perceived as unjust to levy interest on organisations that assume risk in order to produce (socially useful) goods and services, yet at the same time provide a return for people who simply lend money.

(b) Business people are expected to place spiritual fulfilment before the attainment of material goods. Muslim theology defines everything a person should believe; Muslim law prescribes everything he or she should do.

(c) The principle of profit sharing is extensively applied. Islamic banks, for example, do not pay interest on deposits but instead distribute to investors 'profit shares' (the values of which are not known in advance) that result from the utilisation of the funds deposited. The banks in turn 'invest' in their borrowers through providing them with financial resources; hence banks do not 'lend' at interest *per se*. 'Dividends' are obtained on these investments, which are then used to pay profit shares to depositors.

(d) Instead of consumer credit being offered to customers via interest-bearing loan agreements or hire-purchase, it is assumed that finance suppliers (the equivalent of finance houses or hire-purchase companies in the non-Islamic world) themselves buy goods on behalf of clients and then *resell* them to clients at a higher price, with clients paying by instalments. The finance supplier's profit mark-up is the Islamic equivalent of interest on consumer credit.

(e) Traders are required to be honest in their dealings. Defects in products must be disclosed prior to sale. Profiteering from artificially created shortages (hoarding) is forbidden.

(f) Written agreements witnessed by two independent outside parties are preferred to informal agreements reached by word of mouth.

Islamic government taxation policies normally seek to redistribute income. Note, however, that Islam has no ideological objections to private enterprise or free markets. Indeed, Islam emphasises the rights of individuals to private property and to inherit wealth. Commerce is seen as a productive activity.

Critics of Islamic approaches to business argue that although religious control over business practices can create community spirit, feelings of belonging and a common purpose among citizens, it may also lead to inefficiency, low economic growth and restricted industrial performance. Also, they point to the under-representation of women in managerial jobs in Islamic states. The proportion of women in management positions is typically much lower than in secular countries.

THE EUROPEAN SCENE

14. European management

The cultural diversity of European nations has prevented the emergence of a set of uniform principles generally applicable to the management of European firms. Nevertheless, certain broad features of European business practice may be discerned, notably:

(a) The widespread use of limited liability (*see* 3:7) and the separation of ownership from the control of large enterprises

(b) General acceptance and adoption of American management practices (*see* 8)

(c) Functional specialisation and the pursuit of subject-based rather than generalist careers. Thus, managers often think of themselves as (say) engineers, accountants, food technologists, etc first and as administrative managers second.

(d) Widespread tendencies towards the decentralisation of large organisations, especially via the establishment of subsidiaries and setting up divisions within firms.

15. Employee participation in management decisions

Employee participation in management decisions and/or the appointment of employee representatives to company board of directors have been common (often legally necessary) in continental countries for many years. However, the form of participation varies from state to state.

Germany has perhaps the most extensive system of worker participation, which operates through 'works councils' and through 'co-determination' (i.e. elected worker directors serving on company boards). Any company with more than five employees may be required by them to set up a works council consisting of worker representatives elected by secret ballot. A works council is empowered to *approve* changes in working hours and conditions, holiday arrangements, training, disciplinary procedures and recruitment methods. It is also legally entitled to be *informed* of (but not to approve) intended alterations in company staffing levels. Councils negotiate with employers over such matters as dismissals, overtime payments, shift-work systems, etc. These activities occur in parallel with trade union initiatives. A works council may place an actual or intended dismissal before a local labour court, which is obliged to hear the council's appeal.

By law, companies employing more than 500 staff must have 33 ⅓ per cent worker representation on their supervisory boards (*see* 1:29). For companies with at least 2000 employees the figure is 50 per cent, although the casting vote lies with the chairperson (who is elected either by a two-thirds vote of the board or by shareholders' representatives alone, depending on the rules of the company).

Additionally, companies employing more than 100 workers have to establish 'economic committees' comprising equal numbers of management and labour representatives. Economic committees discuss marketing, production and financial matters. They cannot take executive decisions as such.

The situation in other EU countries with compulsory worker participation is as follows:

(a) *Belgium.* Corporations with more than 100 employees must establish *worker's councils* comprising equal numbers of management and worker representatives. Councils are required to meet at least once a month to review working conditions and general matters affecting the company.

(b) *Denmark.* The employees of a company with an average of at least 35 workers over the previous three years may elect two directors to its board, or half the number of directors elected by shareholders – whichever is the greater. Any business employing at least 30 persons requires a works council comprising equal numbers of employee and management representatives, provided a majority of the workforce so desires. Works councils communicate information and opinions between management and labour, but cannot veto proposals or take executive decisions.

(c) *France.* Corporations with more than 50 employees must form works committees comprising employee representatives, two of which are entitled to attend meetings of company boards. However, the employee representatives cannot vote at board meetings. Company training plans (which are obligatory for firms with at least 50 workers) must be submitted to and discussed by the works committee.

(d) *Luxemburg.* Public companies with at least 100 workers must have one third of their boards of directors designated by employees. Companies with 150 or more workers are required to set up works councils (with equal representation of management and labour) which participate in decisions concerning health and safety, welfare, recruitment and appraisal procedures, and other personnel policies. They have the legal right to be informed of planned changes in working conditions. A public company employing at least 15 persons is obliged to have 'employee delegates' who are legally entitled to a minimum of three meetings with management each year.

(e) *The Netherlands.* Companies with at least 100 workers must form works councils consisting entirely of employee representatives who have the rights to:

(*i*) information on the company's progress

(*ii*) consultation over management intentions regarding mergers and takeovers and/or organisational restructuring

(*iii*) propose and object to nominations for appointment to the firm's board of directors.

Also the works council can exercise a veto over proposals on recruitment, training, health and safety and related personnel policies.

(f) *Portugal.* Depending on the size of the company a workers' committee of between three and eleven members has to be set up. The committee does not participate in management *per se*, but is entitled to receive relevant information (including financial information) about the company's affairs.

The UK position

Successive UK governments have chosen not to legislate to provide employee representation along continental lines. At the time of writing the British approach leaves labour/management relations entirely to collective bargaining (*see* 16:45). There are no worker directors in major UK firms.

16. Advantages and problems of worker directors

Apart from the general advantages (*see* 15:27) of involving employees in management decisions, the essential argument in favour of worker directors is that since employees spend much of their lives working for and making valuable contributions to employing organisations, they should be entitled – through elected representatives – to some say in how their employers' businesses are run. Also, worker directors can criticise management's intentions and put new interpretations on issues and events. The counterargument is that since firms are owned by entrepreneurs or shareholders who put their personal capital at risk, it is inappropriate for anyone other than directors selected by owners to control a company's assets. Worker directors, moreover, may face substantial difficulties which prevent their being effective in this work.

The problems confronting worker directors include the following:

(a) Possible reluctance of other board members to disclose confidential information to employees' representatives in case it is passed on to union negotiators.

(b) Potential hostility and social ostracism from other directors, who might conduct secret board meetings to decide key issues without the presence of employee representatives.

(c) The possibility that special privileges afforded to worker directors – higher status, preferential treatment, expenses, time off for board meetings – might cause them to lose contact with basic-grade workers.

17. The British approach to management

Britain, as the first country to experience an industrial revolution, has a long and rich history of management thought and innovation. Key contributions to management thinking came from Adam Smith (1723–90), Robert Owen (1771–1858), James Watt (1769–1848), Matthew Boulton (1770–1842), Charles Babbage (1792–1871) and many more.

In *The Wealth of Nations* (1776) Adam Smith analysed the economic effects of (then) new approaches to factory organisation and labour management necessitated by recent technical innovations, the division of labour, the problems attached to the separation of ownership from control, and the managerial implications of the joint-stock company. Robert Owen, an owner of cotton mills, pioneered the provision of welfare services in employment situations. He observed and recorded the relations between working hours, pay and productivity, and experimented with incentive schemes. Owen also developed new systems for the control and training of supervisors, for employee appraisal and the setting of targets for workers. These ideas were adopted by George Palmer (1809–1906), a biscuit manufacturer, who pioneered the implementation of job security and sick-pay schemes, staff development programmes and the use of aesthetically attractive packaging for consumer products.

James Watt and Matthew Boulton were engineers who, in their casting foundry, devised new means for materials planning, controlling quality, costing and management accounting, and for standardising production methods. Also during the early 1800s, mathematician Charles Babbage examined the human skills required for factory operations, new techniques for improving productivity, and methods for reducing the amount of training necessary for operatives. Babbage was an important precursor of F.W. Taylor (*see* 1:3) and the classical school (*see* 1:**13**).

In the late nineteenth and twentieth centuries, however, British managers have adopted mainly American techniques and administrative practices. This followed naturally and logically from the application in the early 1900s of American-style scientific management (*see* 1:3–5) to many UK manufacturing firms. Also, several internationally renowned work study practitioners set up in Britain during the 1920s and 1930s and, importantly, secured the endorsement of several large UK trade associations and government departments. The Gilbreths (*see* 1:**6**) in particular were engaged as consultants to many prestigious British companies.

Labour shortages during World War II stimulated interest in productivity improvement techniques. The government assumed control of all manufacturing industry and this, together with other emergency wartime measures such as food rationing, the compulsory rehousing of people affected by enemy bombing, centralised control over the railways and all natural resources, etc created the need for planning and organising on an unprecedented scale. Operations research (OR) was a British invention of the wartime years. Organisation and methods (*see* 10:**44**) divisions were established in government departments.

18. Management in Britain

The British economy comprises many diverse forms of enterprise. It is thus difficult to identify a unique British management style. Arguably, however, UK business management exhibits the following general characteristics:

(a) Formal hierarchies and bureaucratic structures in large organisations.

(b) Pluralistic frames of reference (*see* 2:**27**) in industrial relations, with a plethora of trade unions representing differing employee categories.

(c) Frequent changes in the ownership of public companies (*see* 3:**9**), resulting in short-term strategic orientations.

(d) Significantly lower levels of management training than the average for major competing nations.

(e) Directive leadership with top-down planning (*see* **5:17**). Control of individuals by immediate superiors rather than self-determination or group control by peers.

(f) A tendency to adopt classical approaches (*see* **1:13**) to organisational design, with unity of command (*see* **1:9**) and conventional line and staff systems.

(g) Functional specialisation of individuals in areas such as finance, personnel, marketing, etc.

(h) Belief that promotion by merit leads to greater efficiency than promotion based on length of service.

Long-run trends in the British economy indicate an overall decline in the country's competitive position, particularly *vis-à-vis* the balance of payments and manufacturing. Critics of British management attribute this to a failure to invest in new methods, poor industrial training, bad industrial relations, and inadequate attention to marketing and quality control. All the UK political parties recognise these problems and have policies for tackling them, though they differ markedly in their recommended solutions.

19. Attitudes towards industry

According to Martin Weiner, UK business has suffered from anti-industrial social attitudes which, he alleges, have spread throughout the British education system. Weiner's thesis is that from the 1850s onwards, families that benefited from industry consciously chose to have their children educated in the arts, the humanities, the traditional professions such as law and medicine, and not in technology. This 'gentrification' of the British middle class created, he argues, a *social climate* hostile to industrial management, and caused the emergence in the late 1800s of an education system fundamentally opposed to the teaching of applied science, business, technical and vocational subjects in schools and universities. He further suggests that once established this attitude spread and, by the turn of the century, affected teachers *throughout* the education system. In consequence, the *type* of knowledge transmitted in education (particularly higher education) could not be directly or immediately applied to industrial management. Few (if any) administrative skills were taught, while attitudes deeply antagonistic to the study of technology, business and administrative management were common.

Criticisms of Weiner's hypothesis relate to its speculative nature (it cannot be proven either way), and to the argument that business *itself* should be responsible for funding training in business and technical subjects. Education, Weiner's opponents assert, should seek to develop the *whole person*. The role of education, they argue, is to nurture the imagination of the young, to develop critical faculties and to transmit and interpret the cultural values of society: education should be above purely vocational skills.

MANAGEMENT EDUCATION

20. National differences in management education and training systems

The USA has recognised the value of business education for many years. There are numerous business schools, and a course in business management is seen as an essential ingredient of the curricula of many other disciplines. Americans learn about management both at college and through company-sponsored training schemes.

European countries either follow the American model or have technically oriented vocational training systems, as in Germany, for example.

21. Germany

The German system does not teach 'academic' management studies *per se* (although 'business economics' is a common and popular subject). Rather, people study science, engineering or humanities first, and then receive extensive management training while in employment. Many Germans follow 'technical apprenticeships' that – as well as imparting technical skills – equip them for administrative management.

Germany is a country that makes things (about a third of its GDP comes from manufacturing) and where technical competence is highly valued. Many senior managers in German industry have risen 'through the ranks' of apprentice, skilled technician, master craftworker and supervisor, then to middle and senior management. A major feature of the German scene, however, is the extremely low representation of women in management. To a limited extent this could result from the technical orientation of German industry (German girls tend to study non-technical subjects at school), but the discrepancy is equally large in service industries where technical/engineering considerations do not apply.

22. Japan

Japanese managers acquire managerial competence on the job through training and experience. It is common for employees to spend their entire careers with a single company, hence accumulating a great amount of experience of various functions. At college, Japanese students tend to study subjects other than business management (the country has only a couple of dedicated business schools and there are no professional bodies similar to those which exist in Britain). Nevertheless, Japanese managers in large companies are typically well educated when they begin their careers.

Individuals with little education can still reach the top, but a much longer period is usually required. The big Japanese corporations invest heavily in employee training. There is extensive coaching, target setting, evaluation and many planned experience programmes. Those who succeed may be placed on a 'horizontal fast track', i.e. they are given more lateral transfers than colleagues of the same cohort, thus equipping them with the greater breadth of experience necessary for top management. Correspondence courses are common and are frequently paid for by employers.

23. France

Engineering has a high status in the French educational system, and many engineers occupy senior management positions. Specialist and high-level business schools also exist. A critically important factor in French management education is that by law *every* French business must belong to its local Chamber of Commerce. This provides Chambers of Commerce with substantial resources, some of which are used for management training for member companies. Additionally there are national training taxes – part of which are passed back to employers to finance the training (including management training) of employees. This money can be used for approved in-house training or to purchase the services of outside management trainers.

24. Britain

British management education comprises a mixture of institution-based courses (leading to degrees, college diplomas or certificates); national qualifications; short courses offered by state colleges and private training companies; and (overwhelmingly) courses leading to the examinations of professional bodies. The continuing popularity of professional qualifications is the consequence of (*i*) the long-standing UK tradition of 'learning while doing', and (*ii*) the fact that membership by examination of a professional body guarantees to employers that the student has attained a nationally recognised standard, so that a professional qualification offers an 'entry ticket' to a job. Also, many arts and humanities graduates find professional bodies a useful way of acquiring business and managerial knowledge. Note, importantly, that British managers receive on average less company-sponsored management training each year than do their counterparts in most of the UK's major industrial rivals.

MANAGEMENT IN GOVERNMENT AND NON-PROFIT ORGANISATIONS

25. The management of non-profit organisations

Non-profit organisations such as museums, schools, art galleries, institutions that cater for the performing arts (ballet companies, for instance), etc increasingly apply modern management methods to their operations. However, non-profit organisations typically possess special characteristics which affect how they have to be managed. The major distinguishing features of non-profit institutions are listed below.

(a) Their objectives cannot always be expressed in terms of desired rates of financial return.

(b) Most non-profit organisations need to maintain an immaculate public image – possibly one not directly associated with aggressively commercial operations.

(c) They frequently rely on government support and hence must be seen to provide a public service.

(d) Typically, non-profit bodies must simultaneously appease several different 'publics'. A school, for example, must satisfy the requirements not only of pupils in terms of the latter's success in passing examinations, but also of parents, local and national education authorities, school inspectors, local employers who recruit school-leavers, neighbours (through minimising noise and damage caused by the misbehaviour of children arriving at and leaving school), teachers, governors and the school's administrative staff.

26. Management and government administration

Possibly the most significant economic phenomenon of recent years has been the widespread introduction of market systems as the primary means for allocating national resources. Countries throughout the world have abandoned long-standing commitments to central economic planning and direct state control. Market forces are today almost universally regarded as the best means for determining what goods are produced, for whom they are produced and the methods of production. This has led to an increase in interest in the application of business management techniques to local and national government. Special considerations relate to these applications, as follows:

(a) The primary aim of government is to serve the public rather than to earn profit, i.e. government *spends* money rather than earns it (revenues occur mainly through taxation). Thus, government needs to ensure that maximum *social* benefit is obtained for each unit of expenditure.

(b) Public services cannot easily define their objectives in quantitive and/or monetary terms. And the measurement of the social effects of government actions may be extremely difficult.

(c) The basic objectives of public policy are liable to alter suddenly (and drastically) in consequence of changes in government or other political factors.

Management techniques commonly applied to government operations include the following:

(a) *Cost/benefit analysis*, i.e. attempting to quantify and assign monetary values to all the social costs and benefits likely to arise from an intended government project.

(b) *Setting internal targets* within each field of government activity, e.g. planned reductions in the time needed to administer a certain function, or increasing the average speed of response to requests for assistance from members of the public.

(c) *Modelling and simulation analysis*. The latter involves the creation of various scenarios containing major relevant variables and constraints and the examination of the likely effect of changes in each scenario. 'What if' questions may then be asked.

(d) *Attempted creation of internal markets,* i.e. having civil and other public servants behave as if they were entrepreneurs. Usually, this requires various government institutions or departments to submit 'bids' for 'contracts' issued by the central administration. Bids are based on cost per unit of activity needed to achieve stated objectives, e.g. the teaching cost per student of running a certain course in an educational establishment. The main problems with internal markets are:

(i) deciding what to do with institutions/departments whose bids are unsuccessful

(ii) assessing the reliability of the cost levels quoted in bid estimates and whether they are feasible

(iii) establishing meaningful cost centres (*see* 9:6) around which bid estimates can be constructed

(iv) assessing the relationships between costs and the quality of the service provided.

Another difficulty is relating 'as if' market systems to the job security traditional in public service. In commercial situations, those who are unsuccessful are quickly out of work. Applying the same principle to public sector institutions might result in some public services – fire stations, schools, colleges, hospitals, etc – closing down in certain areas.

27. Management of public sector institutions

Running public sector institutions (hospital trusts, for example) *as if* they were private sector firms is said to have the following advantages:

(a) Institutions become more flexible. They encounter fewer bureaucratic constraints imposed by outside bodies, can vary the size of their workforces more easily, and are free to pursue activities that bring in the maximum amount of revenue.

(b) The need to restrict expenditure to an institutional budget causes a public sector organisation to apply (possibly for the first time) strict financial discipline and stringent management controls.

(c) Institutions can create incentives for individual employees via performance-related pay.

(d) Institutions are less vulnerable to employee industrial action co-ordinated at the national level, because industrial relations negotiations occur *within* the unit concerned.

Critics allege, however, that the following problems apply to institutional self-management:

(a) As publicly funded organisations, institutions have no incentives to make profits for distribution to owners and employees, yet they are held accountable for their activities *as if* the profit motive were present. Institutions face many penalties for poor performance, but are eligible for very few rewards.

(b) The divorce of units from national or local government control denies institutions access to ancillary services and management expertise previously available from a central body.

(c) Senior employees of institutions are compelled to adopt a managerial role and devote their attention to budgeting, staff appraisal, administration of bureaucratic procedures, etc at the expense of their professional duties *vis-à-vis* health care, education or whatever.

(d) Often, the individuals who find themselves in charge of self-managing units have received no management training and have no experience whatsoever of business administration. They are not familiar with managerial concepts or terminology, which possibly makes them extremely vulnerable to 'quick-fix' gimmicks that would not be adopted by private companies.

(e) Lack of clear objectives might create much confusion concerning the fundamental purpose of the institution.

WOMEN MANAGERS

28. Women in management

The number of women in UK management has increased over the last quarter century, although women are still underrepresented in management work. Women face special problems when pursuing managerial careers, including the following:

(a) The need to balance continuity of employment (and hence the acquisition of managerial skills and experience during the early stages of a career) against requirements to take time out from the workforce for childbearing and initial child rearing. A woman who leaves the workforce for (say) four or five years to have a family is then that many years 'behind' her male contemporaries when she resumes her career. Note how management recruitment and development programmes are typically designed for young college leavers rather than for slightly older women with families.

(b) Possible discriminatory sexual stereotyping by existing male senior managers, who might assume that a woman's role is to look after home and family and not to manage organisations.

(c) Preassumptions that family commitments will cause a woman to take more time off work than male colleagues.

(d) Lack of child-care facilities for working mothers. Note that in Britain (unlike certain states in the USA) no tax relief is available to individuals who need to employ others to help look after their children.

(e) The existence within organisations of male networks, informal communication systems, and power groups that men can use to help each other and to provide support and understanding when things go wrong.

(f) Lack of female role models for women managers to emulate. Note how the higher the level to which a woman rises within an organisation, the fewer female colleagues of equivalent rank she is likely to have.

29. Recruitment, appraisal and promotion problems

There is evidence to suggest that women managers are more common in certain types of management job (personnel, for instance) than others. Also, females are better represented in the managements of service industries than in manufacturing. This could be due in part to unfair discrimination in recruitment and promotion procedures, and possibly to biases in performance appraisal (*see* 12:**30**).

Factors militating against women being recruited to undertake management jobs and/or their achieving promotion might include:

(a) Low aspirations among women themselves, leading them not to apply for higher-level positions

(b) Perceptions by existing senior managers that women have low aspirations

(c) Assumptions (by men) that women are not very good at taking decisions

(d) Male prejudices that 'feminine' characteristics of supportiveness, sensitivity, being good at human relations, etc are inappropriate for people in positions of authority

(e) Male selection panels evaluating candidates against masculine values and norms

(f) Media portrayal of women as sex objects rather than as thinking and responsible people

(g) Possible failure of male superiors to delegate demanding work to female subordinates, hence denying them the experience needed to undertake higher-level duties

(h) Male superiors' possible preconceptions that women lack commitment to long-term careers, that money spent on training will be wasted, and that women possess outside interests that will interfere with work

(i) Possible perceptions that if a woman is promoted to a senior position her (predominantly) male subordinates will resent being accountable to a woman.

30. Appraisal difficulties

To the extent that most senior managers are male, performance appraisal means that men appraise women. A possible problem here is that male appraisers who dislike the idea of women managers might (unconsciously) apply inappropriate preassumptions to their assessments of female subordinates' qualities. For example, traits considered desirable in a man might be regarded as undesirable in a woman, e.g. a forceful male subordinate may be classed as 'assertive' (a positive characteristic) whereas a forceful woman might be described as 'bossy'. A man who frequently loses his temper might be seen as a 'demanding taskmaster'; a woman as 'likely to become hysterical'. If moreover a male appraiser considers women to be (say) 'emotional', then he could tend to notice examples of emotional behaviour in female subordinates, while unconsciously ignoring emotional characteristics in males! Other biased preassumptions might be that:

(a) Whereas excellent work completed by male subordinates is due to ability, successes achieved by females are due to chance and/or help given by male colleagues.

(b) The restrained and unobtrusive management styles adopted by some women managers (which are highly effective in many circumstances) indicate lack of initiative and low leadership ability.

Such difficulties could result in women being directed towards careers in areas regarded as more suitable for females. Unfortunately, however, these jobs usually offer fewer opportunities for advancement through line management than do the positions typically occupied by males.

31. Possible solutions

The UK *Equal Opportunities Commission* (EOC) suggests four measures that large companies might adopt in order to encourage increased female participation in management:

(a) Adherence to EOC codes of practice on the avoidance of unfair sex discrimination.

(b) Active encouragement of women to apply for higher-grade managerial posts.

(c) Implementation of flexitime and job-sharing arrangements.

(d) Special training for women managers.

EOC codes of practice are endorsed by the government, but are not legally binding. They will be looked at by a court called upon to adjudicate a case, and a firm that failed to follow recommendations embodied in an EOC code of practice will normally be regarded as having behaved improperly. Nevertheless, a code of practice cannot be legally enforced; it is simply a set of guidelines and examples of good procedure.

Special all-female *training courses* recognise the unique problems facing many women managers and hence may incorporate material (assertion training, for example) specially designed to help overcome them.

32. Positive discrimination

More direct attempts to improve female representation in the higher levels of management have been implemented in the USA, notably through 'fast-tracking' schemes introduced by companies, and 'affirmative action' programmes initiated by the federal government.

(a) *Fast tracking* is a method for achieving roughly equal proportions of males and females in senior positions within an organisation that initially has very few women managers. Females are recruited and put on to separate training and promotion systems where advancement occurs automatically – as of right provided certain training and other targets are attained. A number of 'milestones of progress' towards the occupancy of a senior management position are identified, and the precise requirements for reaching each milestone carefully defined. Management must then justify not promoting females to progressively higher levels.

(b) *Affirmative action programmes* exist in the USA but not in Britain. They apply to firms that do business with national or local government. Under these schemes, individual organisations can be compelled to achieve specific equal opportunity targets (e.g. recruit so many women or ethnic minority workers within the next 12 months) as a condition of continuing to receive public contracts.

THE DEMOGRAPHIC TIME-BOMB, AGEISM AND THE PROBLEMS CONFRONTING ETHNIC MINORITIES

33. The demographic time-bomb

The average age of the population in Britain and most other industrialised countries is steadily increasing. This will have the following consequences:

(a) Additional demand for products consumed by middle-aged and elderly people and reduced consumption of goods normally purchased by the young.

(b) Recruitment difficulties in relation to young workers, plus possible skills shortages in certain fields.

(c) Fewer young families and hence less demand for housing (i.e. fewer 'first-time buyers') resulting in spillover effects on house prices, the demand for mortgages and hence the financial services market overall.

(d) The need to retrain older workers and extend training to high-unemployment ethnic minority groups.

(e) Greater female participation in the workforce.

(f) Possibly an oversupply of people in middle management.

(g) Probably a reduction in age discrimination by employers.

Age discrimination is illegal in the USA but not (at the time of writing) in Britain. Ageism has been criticised as unfair on the grounds that older people make good workers, with lower-than-average absenteeism, lateness and labour turnover rates. Older employees, moreover, tend to be more satisfied with their jobs, possibly because their expectations are lower and they are better adjusted to work routines than are younger workers. There are, however, disadvantages to firms that engage a high proportion of older employees, notably that:

(a) Such companies may be unattractive to young people because of lack of immediate short-term promotion prospects.

(b) Older workers may be unfamiliar with and resistant to new technologies.

(c) Since older workers are less likely to quit their jobs, attempts to reduce the size of a labour force through natural wastage can become extremely difficult. A freeze on recruitment means that *younger* people (who leave more frequently) are not replaced, thus further increasing the average age of remaining workers. This creates staffing crises when older cohorts retire.

34. Ethnic minorities

The legal definition of an 'ethnic minority' currently applied by UK courts is that it is a group distinguished from others by a 'sufficient combination' of shared customs, beliefs, traditions and characteristics derived from a common or presumed common past, even if the distinctions are not biologically determined. Thus, Jews and Sikhs have both been accepted as distinct 'ethnic' groups by the English judiciary.

Ethnic minorities are greatly underrepresented in management. Unfair discrimination might be a factor causing this. Arguably, the following difficulties contribute to under-representation:

(a) Ignorance of existing managers about the latent abilities and potential of ethnic minority candidates.

(b) Inappropriate stereotyping.

(c) Undervaluation of the contributions of ethnic minority employees.

(d) Discourtesies to ethnic minority individuals (jokes, name calling and so on) that occur behind their backs but which, nevertheless, may prejudice the opinions of the current management.

Responses to these difficulties could involve:

(a) Adherence to codes of practice issued by the *Commission for Racial Equality*.

(b) Incorporation of anti-discrimination clauses into firms' disciplinary rules, with explicit provision for the suspension and ultimate dismissal of employees who engage in discriminatory behaviour.

(c) Positive action programmes whereby people from minority groups are either encouraged to apply for jobs in areas where they are underrepresented or are given special help and training to enable them to develop their abilities and skills.

ACADEMIC DEVELOPMENTS IN MANAGEMENT STUDIES

35. Modern approaches to management studies

The trend in the academic teaching of management is towards rigorous analysis, close argument and empirical research. This requires some degree of abstraction, using symbols and theories to establish sets of conclusions from carefully defined assumptions. Such an approach offers conciseness and precision, and imposes the need for disciplined thinking. Equally, however, it can lead to the separation of the 'pure' management theorist from the realities of mundane everyday problems of operational management, planning, co-ordination and control. Abstract management theories that contribute little (sometimes nothing) to the efficient and (where appropriate) profitable governance of modern organisations have little value.

One immediate consequence of the scholastic academicisation of management studies has been a shift in the nature of the vocabulary used to describe advanced theoretical developments in the field.

36. All the 'isms'

Advanced literature in management studies increasingly carries words and phrases normally associated with scientific methodology and reasoning, reflecting heightened scholastic interest in the subject. For reference, some of the basic 'isms' and related expressions are briefly outlined below.

(a) *Behaviourism.* This is the assertion that an individual's actions are determined by environmental stimulus-response factors.

(b) *Determinism.* Deterministic views of behaviour insist that all observed occurrences are the inevitable outcomes of preceding events. For example, 'economic determinism' alleges that all economic and commercial conduct is the consequence of economic forces. Determinism implies that genuine 'choices' are not really available, because everything depends on external forces.

(c) *Empiricism.* Empiricists argue that the best means for gaining fresh knowledge or developing theories are observation, measurement and practical experimentation.

(d) *Ethnocentrism.* This is the tendency to regard one's own nation, group or culture as superior, and to compare the standards of other nations, groups or cultures against this belief. Ethnocentrism contrasts with *polycentrism*, which regards other nations, groups and cultures as different but of equal value; and with *geocentrism*, that sees some but not all nations, groups and cultures as being of equal status.

(e) *Holism.* Holistic approaches assert that the whole of a system is more than the simple sum of its constituent parts, and that the system's totality has its own unique characteristics. Synergy (*see* 2:8) is a manifestation of holism.

(f) *Logical positivism.* Adherents of logical positivism allege that the only statements which are truly valid are those arrived at through systematic analysis and/or which can be verified through empirical observation and testing.

(g) *Metaphysics.* This is the branch of knowledge that deals with the first principles of a subject, especially those principles which can only be explained or discovered through abstract reasoning. It requires speculation rather than empirical research.

(h) *Methodology.* The methodology of a subject is all the procedures of enquiry, techniques of analysis, and rules and methods used to study its content.

(i) *Phenomenology.* Phenomenological views of human behaviour suggest that conduct cannot be straightforwardly explained through scientific analysis and observation. This implies that individuals are essentially unpredictable and subjective, and that each person is motivated by a unique set of (complicated) factors. Hence the approach contradicts both *behaviourism* and *rationalism*.

(j) *Positivism.* Positivistic approaches insist that the only genuine knowledge is that which is discovered through scientific observation (rather than through imagination and/or speculation). *Logical positivism* (*see* above) is a close derivative of this view.

(k) *Rationalism.* This sees behaviour as the outcome of logical thought and objective reasoning (and not necessarily of past experience).

(l) *Reductionism.* Reductionism means the resolution of complex issues into simple constituent parts. Sometimes it is used as a term of abuse against people who oversimplify complicated issues.

(m) *Reification.* This concerns the conversion of abstract views into concrete (and hopefully testable) propositions.

(n) *Relativism.* Relativism is the proposition that knowledge, beliefs and concepts (e.g. of right and wrong) have meaning only in relation to an individual's particular situation, so that it is impossible to define truly objective general standards. Accordingly relativism implies that people cannot *rationally* decide what is good or bad. Rather, opinions (and hence decisions) depend on individual circumstances, personal experience and the culture in which the person lives. The term 'naive relativism' has been applied to the idea that since opinions are personal, their value can only be assessed against personal standards (i.e. the belief that it is only one's own opinion that is important).

(o) *Teleology.* Adoption of a teleological approach to a subject involves the search for grand designs, common unifying principles and general laws to explain observed phenomena.

Progress test 17

1. How can cultural factors affect management style?

2. Outline the main characteristics of British management education.

3. What are the implications for management of the 'demographic time-bomb'?

4. List the essential features of the Japanese approach to management.

5. How does the management of non-profit organisations differ from the management of profit-seeking enterprises?

6. List the major features of the Islamic approach to management.

7. What measures can companies adopt to encourage greater female participation in management?

8. Distinguish between positive discrimination and affirmative action.

APPENDIX 1

REFERENCES AND BIBLIOGRAPHY

Adair, J. (1983), *Effective Leadership*, Gower.

Alderfer, C.P. (1972), *Existence, Relatedness and Growth: Human Needs in Organisational Settings*, The Free Press, New York.

Allport, F.H. (1924), *Social Psychology*, Houghton Mifflin, Boston.

Ansoff, H.I. (1979), *Strategic Management*, Macmillan.

Ansoff, H.I. (1990), *Implanting Strategic Management*, Prentice-Hall.

Argyris, C. (1957), *Personality and Organisation*, Harper and Row.

Argyris, C. and Schon, D. (1978), *Organisational Learning: A Theory of Action Perspective*, Addison-Wesley.

Barnard, C. (1938), *Functions of the Executive*, Harvard University Press.

Beer, M, Spector, B.A., Lawrence, P.R. and Walton, R.E. (1985), *Human Resource Management*, The Free Press.

Belbin, R.M. (1981), *Management Teams: Why They Succeed or Fail*, Butterworth-Heinemann.

Blake, R.R. and Mouton, J.S. (1964), *The Managerial Grid*, Gulf Publishing.

Bowen, D.E. and Lawler, E.E. (1992), 'The empowerment of service workers: what, how and when', *Sloan Management Review*, Spring 1992, 31–39.

Brown, A. (1995), *Organisational Culture*, Pitman.

Burns, T. and Stalker, G.M. (1961), *The Management of Innovation*, Tavistock Publications.

Christopher, M., Payne, A. and Ballantyne, D. (1991), *Relationship Marketing*, Butterworth-Heinemann.

Clark, N. (1994), *Team Building: A Practical Guide for Trainers*, McGraw-Hill.

Collins, B. and Payne, A. (1991), 'Internal services marketing', *European Management Journal*, 9 (3), 261–270.

Deming, W.E. (1988), *Out of the Crisis*, Cambridge University Press.

Denison, D. (1990), *Corporate Culture and Organisational Effectiveness*, Wiley.

Drory, A. and Romm, T. (1990), 'The definition of organisational politics: a review', *Human Relations*, Nov. 1990, 1133–54.

Drucker, P.F. (1954), *The Practice of Management*, Harper and Row.

Drucker, P.F. (1989), *Managing for Results*, Heinemann.

Drucker, P.F.(1987), *The Effective Executive*, Harper and Row.

Eagly, A.H. and Johnson, B.T. (1990), 'Gender and leadership style: a meta-analysis', *Psychological Bulletin*, September 1990, 233–256.

Eagly, A.H. and Karau, S.J. (1991), 'Gender and the emergence of leaders: a meta-analysis', *Journal of Personality and Social Psychology*, May 1991, 685–710.

Farrell, D. and Petersen, J.C. (1988), 'Patterns of political behaviour in organisations', *Organisation Studies*, 9 (2), 406–407.

Fayol, H. (1916), *General and Industrial Management*, English translation Pitman 1949.

Fielder, F.E. (1967), *A Theory of Leadership Effectiveness*, McGraw-Hill, New York.

Follett, M.P. (1942), *Dynamic Administration: Collected Papers of Mary Parker Follett*, Harper.

Fox, A. (1966), 'Industrial Sociology and Industrial Relations', *Royal Commission on Trade Unions and Employers' Associations Research Paper No. 3*, HMSO.

French, J.R.P., and Raven, B.H. (1959), 'The bases of social power', in D. Cartwright, (ed), *Studies in Social Power*, University of Michigan Press.

Furnham, A. (1990), *Personality at Work: the Role of Individual Differences*, Routledge, Chapman and Hall.

George, W.R. (1990), 'Internal marketing and organisational behaviour', *Journal of Business Research*, Vol. 20, 63–70.

Gier, R.N. (1979), *Understanding Scientific Reasoning*, Holt, Rinehart and Winston.

Gilbreth, F.B. and Gilbreth, L. (1914), *The Psychology of Management*, Sturgis and Walton.

Gilbreth, F.B. and Gilbreth, L. (1916), *Fatigue Study*, Sturgis and Walton.

Glaser, B.G. and Strauss, A.L. (1967), *The Discovery of Grounded Theory: Strategies for Qualitative Research*, Chicago, Aldine.

Grant, J. (1988), 'Women as managers: what they can offer to organisations', *Organisational Dynamics*, Winter 1988, 56–63.

Gronroos, G. (1994), 'Quo vadis, marketing? toward a relationship marketing paradigm', *Journal of Marketing Management*, Vol. 10, 347–360.

Guest, D. (1987), 'Human resource management and industrial relations', *Journal of Management Studies*, 24 (5), 503–21.

Hall, D.T. (1976) *Careers in Management*, Goodyear, Calif.

Hammer, M. and Champy, J. (1993), *Re-engineering the Corporation: A Manifesto for Business Revolution*, Nicholas Brealey.

Hamner, W.C. (1974), 'Reinforcement theory and contingency management in organisational settings', in Tosi, H.I. and Hamner, W.C. (eds), *Organisational Behaviour and Management: A Contingency Approach*, Chicago, St Clair Press.

Handy, C. (1976), *Understanding Organisations*, Penguin.

Handy, C. (1989), *The Age of Unreason*, Pan.

Harvey, J. (1974), 'The Abiline paradox: the management of agreement', *Organisational Dynamics*, 3(1).

Hersey, P. and Blanchard, K.H. (1989), *The Management of Organisational Behaviour*, 3rd edn., Prentice Hall.

Herzberg, F. (1966), *Work and the Nature of Man*, New York, World Publishing Co.

Hull, C.L. (1943), *Principles of Behaviour*, New York, Appleton Century Croft.

IRRR (Industrial Relations Review and Report) (1994), 'Team building and development', *Employee Development Bulletin*, 55, July 1994, 2–11.

Ishikawa, K. (1985), *What is Total Quality Control?*, Prentice-Hall.

Janis, I.L. (1972), *Victims of Groupthink*, Houghton Mifflin.

Juran, J.M. (1988), *Juran on Planning for Quality*, The Free Press.

Kanter, R.M. (1983), *The Change Masters*, Simon and Schuster.

Katz, R.L. (1974), 'Skills of an effective administrator', *Harvard Business Review*, Sept/Oct. 1974, 90–101.

Ker, S. and Jermier, J.M. (1978), 'Substitutes for leadership. Their meaning and measurement', *Organisational Behaviour and Human Performance*, Dec. 1978, 375–403.

Kotler, P. (1991). *Marketing Management: Analysis, Planning, Implementation and Control*, 7th ed., Prentice-Hall.

Kotter, J.P. and Schlesinger, L.A. (1979), 'Choosing strategies for change', *Harvard Business Review*, March–April 1979.

Lawrence, P.R. and Lorsch, J.W. (1967), *Organisation and Environment*, Harvard University Press.

Legge, K. (1989), 'Human resource management: a critical perspective', in J. Storey (ed.), *New Perspectives on Human Resource Management*, Routledge.

Levinson, D.J. et al. (1978), *The Seasons of a Man's Life*, New York, Knopf.

Lewin, K. (1948), *Resolving Social Conflict*, Harper.

Lewin, K., Lippitt, R. and White, R.K. (1939), 'Patterns of aggressive, behaviour in experimentally created social environments', *International Journal of Social Psychology*, vol. 10.

Likert, R. (1961), *New Patterns of Management*, McGraw-Hill.

McClelland, D.C. (1961), *The Achieving Society*, Van Nostrand Reinhold.

McGregor, D.V. (1960), *The Human Side of Enterprise*, McGraw-Hill.

Manz, C. and Sims, H. (1987), 'Leading workers to lead themselves: the external leadership of self-managing work teams', *Administrative Science Quarterly*, Vol. 32, 106–107.

Maslow, A.H. (1954), *Motivation and Personality*, Harper and Row.

Mayo, G.E. (1945), *The Human Problems of an Industrial Society*, Harvard University Press.

Mintzberg, H. (1973), *The Nature of Managerial Work*, Harper and Row.

Mintzberg, H. (1979), *The Structuring of Organisations*, Prentice Hall.

Moult, G. (1990), 'Under new management', *Management Education and Development*, 21 (3), 171–182.

Ohmae, K. (1982), *The Mind of the Strategist*, McGraw-Hill.

Ohmae, K. (1985), *Triad Power: The Coming Shape of Global Competition*, The Free Press.

Ouchi, W. (1981), *Theory Z: How American Business Can Meet the Japanese Challenge*, Addison-Wesley.

Parasuranman, Al, Zeithmal, V.A. and Berry, L.L. (1988), 'SERVQUAL: a multiple item scale for measuring consumer perceptions of service quality', *Journal of Retailing*, 64 (1), 12–40.

Parker, S.R. (1971), *The Future of Work and Leisure*, MacGibbon and Kee.

Peters, T.J. (1987), *Thriving on Chaos*, Alfred A. Knopf.

Peters, T.J., and Waterman, R.H. (1982), *In Search of Excellence*, Harper and Row.

Perrow, C. (1970), *Organisational Analysis: A Sociological View*, Tavistock Publications.

Piercy, N. and Morgan, N. (1991), 'Internal marketing: the missing half of the marketing programme', *Long Range Planning*, Vol. 24, 82–93.

Polya, G. (1945), *How to Solve It*, Princeton University Press.

Porter, L.W. and Lawler, E.E. (1968), *Managerial Attitudes and Performance*, Irwin-Dorsey.

Porter, M.E. (1980), *Competitive Strategy*, The Free Press.

Porter, M.E. (1985), *Competitive Advantage*, The Free Press.

Porter, M.E. (1990), *The Competitive Advantage of Nations*, Macmillan.

Salaman, G. and Butler, J. (1990), 'Why managers won't learn', *Management Education and Development*, 21 (3), 183–191.

Schein, E H. (1965), *Organisational Psychology*, Prentice-Hall.

Schein, E.H. (1985), *Organisational Culture and Leadership*, Jossey-Bass.

Schneider, B., Parkington, J.J. and Buxton, V.M. (1980), 'Employee and customer perceptions of service in banks', *Administrative Science Quarterly*, Vol. 25, 252–267.

Schramm, W. (1954), *The Process and Effects of Mass Communication*, University of Illinois Press.

Shannon, C. and Weaver, W. (1949), *The Mathematical Theory of Communication*, Illinois University Press.

Sherif, M., Harvey, O.J., White, B.J., Hood, W.R., and Sherif, C. (1961) *Intergroup Conflict and Co-operation*, University of Oklahoma Press.

Simon, H.A. (1960), *Administrative Behaviour*, Macmillan.

Sorge, A. and Streeck, W. (1988), 'Industrial relations and technical change', in Hyman, R. and Streeck, W. (eds), *New Technology and Industrial Relations*, Blackwell, 19–47.

Soujanen, W.W. (1966), *The Dynamics of Management*, Holt, Rinehart and Winston.

Stubbs, D.R. (1985), *How to Use Assertiveness at Work*, Gower.

Taguchi, G. (1986), *Introduction to Quality Engineering*, Asian Productivity Council.

Tannenbaum, R. and Schmidt, W.H.(1958), 'How to choose a leadership pattern', *Harvard Business Review*, March–April, 1958.

Taylor, F.W. (1911), *The Principles of Scientific Management*, Harper.

Tolman, E.C. (1932), *Purposive Behaviour in Animals and Men*, New York, Appleton Press.

Training Commission: Occupational Standards Branch, (1989), *Classifying the Components of Management Competencies*, Training Agency, Sheffield.

Trist, E.L. and Bamforth, K.W. (1951) 'Some social and psychological consequences of the Longwall method of coal getting', *Human Relations*, Vol.4.

Tuckman, B.W. (1965), 'Developmental sequences in small groups', *Psychological Bulletin*, June 1965, 384–399.

Vroom, V.H. (1964), *Work, and Motivation*, Wiley.

Warde, A. (1990), 'The future of work', in Anderson, J. and Ricci, M. (eds), *Society and Social Science*, Open University Press.

Waterman, R.H. (1987), *The Renewal Factor*, Bantam.

Weber, M. (1947), *The Theory of Social and Economic Organisation*, The Free Press.

Weiner, M. (1981), *English Culture and the Decline of the Industrial Spirit*, Cambridge University Press.

Weiner, N. (1948), *Cybernetics*, MIT Press.

Woodward, J. (1965), *Industrial Organisation*, Oxford University Press.

Wyatt, S., Frost, L., and Stock, F.G.L. (1934), *Incentives in Repetition Work*, Medical Research Council, HMSO.

APPENDIX 2

GLOSSARY OF MANAGEMENT TERMS

ABC analysis (Pareto analysis). The classification of items (stock, for example) into three categories (high, medium, low) according to their value or frequency of use. Frequently, about 20 per cent of items account for around 80 per cent of value or use.

Abilene paradox. The situation that arises when a group decision is taken without any one of the individuals taking it being committed to the outcome. Each person mistakenly believes that the other people really want the decision, and hence do not wish to block the outcome they believe other participants want.

Above-the-line advertising. Advertising in media that pay commissions to advertising agencies providing them with business. Examples are newspapers and magazines, television and poster site companies. Other advertising media (e.g. direct mail) are said to be 'below the line'.

ACAS (Advisory, Conciliation and Arbitration Service). A government agency that (*i*) attempts to conciliate in industrial disputes and to achieve out-of-court settlements in cases of alleged unfair dismissal, and (*ii*) publishes Codes of Practice on employment matters.

Accounting. The systematic recording, analysis and interpretation of financial data.

Acid test ratio (quick ratio, liquidity ratio). The ratio of liquid assets to current liabilities.

Administration order. A means for avoiding *bankruptcy* or company liquidation through a County court appointing an independent person to administer the finances of an individual or a business. Creditors cannot enforce judgments against the debtor while the order is in operation.

Affirmative action programmes. United States public purchasing policies whereby supplying firms' continuing access to public sector contracts can be made conditional on their achieving certain prespecified equal opportunity targets, e.g. to increase female representation in the workforce by 30 per cent within the next 12 months.

Agent. Someone who undertakes assignments on a client's behalf but then 'drops out' of resulting contracts with third parties. Agents bind their *principals*, but are not liable for principals' debts if the latter default.

Algorithm. A set of standard rules and procedures for solving a certain class of problem.

Alienation. The estrangement of the employee from his or her work, causing the worker to feel that work is not a relevant or important part of life.

APACS (Adaptive Planning and Control Sequence). A technique developed by the Marketing Science Institute for formulating marketing plans.

Articles of association. A document specifying the rules and conditions governing internal relations between directors and members of a company, e.g. shareholders' voting rights, share transfer regulations, election of directors, etc.

Attachment of earnings order. A court order against a debtor compelling the debtor's employer to pay that person's wages to the court (for distribution to creditors) and not to the employee.

Authorised (nominal) share capital. The total value of shares a company is allowed to issue.

Autonomation. A production system in which machinery is self-monitoring and itself signals the need for attention when problems arise.

Balance sheet. A statement of a business's fixed and current assets and long and short term liabilities on a given day.

Bankrupt. A private person or sole trader declared insolvent by a County court and whose financial affairs are placed in the hands of a *trustee* who sells off the bankrupt's assets to raise money to pay the latter's debts.

Behaviour expectation scales (behaviourally anchored rating scales). A method of *performance appraisal* in which the assessor pinpoints various aspects of the appraisee's conduct considered typical of that person when completing particular types of work.

Bills of exchange. A document prepared by a supplier which, once signed ('accepted') by the customer, provides evidence of the existence of a debt.

Biodata. Information about a job applicant's personal background collected in the belief that particular life experiences create attitudes and personalities that make people suitable for certain types of job.

Body copy. The main text of an advertisement, as opposed to the headline, *tag line* or illustration.

Bonus shares. Free additional shares distributed to existing shareholders to compensate them for past profits retained within a business rather than being paid out as dividends.

Brainstorming. A technique for generating new ideas, without considering their feasibility. The practicability of all the ideas generated is evaluated later.

Brand. A name, logo, trade mark or other device used to identify a company's product and to distinguish it from the products of competitors.

Brand leverage. Use of favourable brand images currently attached to an existing product to launch and market an entirely different type of product.

Budgets. Intentions concerning and limits upon the amounts of money that may be spent by various people or departments on certain functions or activities. The term is also applied to expectations of outcomes, e.g. the phrase 'sales budget' might be used to describe anticipated sales revenues.

CADCAM. Computer-aided design and computer-assisted manufacture.

Capacity planning. A technique for relating the intensity of a firm's production operations to the forecast level of demand for its products.

Capital employed. The extent of the capital invested in a business, measured either as the value of its *net assets* or as shareholders' *equity* plus long-term debts.

Cash flow forecasts. Predictions of the timing and values of all cash receipts and payments expected to occur over future months.

Chain of command. The line of authority that runs from the apex of an organisation to its base and which carries information and instructions to lower levels.

Change agent. A person or institution (often an external management consultant) responsible for initiating and implementing organisational change.

Chaos theory. The proposition that since disorder and confusion are endemic to business situations, managements should accept that 'anything can happen' and hence not attempt to plan and control long-term future activities. Rather, organisations need to be able to learn from past and current events and develop rapid and flexible responses to fast-changing environments.

CIM (computer-integrated manufacture). Advanced CADCAM systems extended to include all aspects of production planning, operations, packaging and despatch.

Classical approach. A *school of thought* that insists that certain general and universally valid management principles should be applied to all administrative and organisational situations.

Close company. A limited company controlled by five or fewer shareholders. Such companies are legally required to distribute most of their investment incomes to shareholders.

Closed and open systems. Closed systems can survive without interacting with their environments; open systems cannot.

Closed-loop systems. A control mechanism in which data on current performance automatically adjust operations in order to rectify divergences between planned and actual output or activity.

Closed shop. An organisation or section of an organisation in which all employees are members of a trade union and where there exists some means for preventing individuals who are not union members from being employed.

Code of practice. A document published by a government agency, professional body, trade association or other authority, which outlines model procedures for good practice in a certain field and which offers examples of good and bad behaviour.

Co-determination. The system of worker participation in company management used in Germany. It provides for employee representation on *supervisory boards*, plus works councils and the provision of management information to workers.

Collective bargaining. Negotiations between managements and employee representatives, normally involving trade unions.

Commercial paper. Unsecured IOUs issued by large corporations.

Common law. Law that derives from custom and tradition rather than from Acts of Parliament.

Confirming houses. Foreign trade intermediaries who, as *principals*, guarantee the payments of overseas buyers who are not sufficiently known in the UK for British firms to supply them on credit.

Constructive dismissal. The resignation of an employee in direct consequence of the employing firm's misbehaviour and/or failure to abide by a contract of employment (e.g. if the employee is sexually harassed).

Content theories. Motivation theories which focus on the precise definition and explanation of the needs that motivate people to behave in certain ways.

Contingency theory. The proposition that management styles and organisational structures should be tailor-made to suit the requirements of each individual management situation. Thus it is the antithesis of the *classical approach*.

Control. The process of (*i*) establishing standards and targets, (*ii*) monitoring activities and comparing actual with target performance, and (*iii*) implementing measures to remedy deficiencies.

Convertibles. Company *debentures* that carry the option of conversion into company shares at some time in the future, prior to the maturity of the debenture.

Co-operative. A business that adheres to the principle of one vote per member rather than one vote per share. Members may be employees or, in the case of a 'retail co-operative', customers of the firm.

Core worker. A full-time, permanent and (normally) superannuated employee.

Corporate plan. A long-term plan describing how the organisation intends deploying its total resources in order to achieve its *mission*.

Cost accounting. The computation of the costs of a business and the analysis of deviations of actual from expected costs.

Cost-benefit analysis. The study of all the costs and benefits expected from a project, including the allocation of monetary values to intangibles such as increased job satisfaction or the lower quality of life resulting from pollution.

Cost of sales. The value of a firm's stock of goods at the start of a trading period plus purchases during that period less stock on hand at the period's end.

Council of Ministers. The major decision-making body of the EU, consisting of a Minister from each member country (although the Ministers change according to the matter being discussed).

Crash cost. The additional expenses (overtime, higher input prices, etc) required to complete a project in less time than initially intended.

Critical incidents. Examples of exceptionally good or bad performance considered by senior managers when appraising subordinates.

Critical path. The sequence of activities which, if not completed on time, will hold up the completion of an entire project.

Current assets. Stocks, debtors and cash in hand and at the bank.

Current ratio. The ratio of current assets to current liabilities.

Cybernetics. The study of control systems and, in particular, the interrelations of machines and humans in the process of control.

Dawn raid. The purchase on open markets of a large part of a company's voting share capital in a very short period (e.g. a single morning) usually as a precursor to an attempted hostile takeover.

Debenture. A loan to a company, normally (but not necessarily) fixed term and fixed interest, secured against its assets.

Decision support system. All the software, models, *algorithms* and computerised information processing methods and systems used to solve problems and take decisions within an organisation.

Delayering. The rationalisation and *downsizing* of a management structure through the complete removal of one or more layers of middle management.

Delegation. The assignment to a subordinate of duties accompanied by the authority needed to complete them.

Demographic time-bomb. The eventual effects of current trends in the age structure of the population, e.g. fewer young and recently qualified workers, decline in demand for youth products, fewer contributors to pension schemes, etc.

Department. A set of activities and subordinates under a manager's jurisdiction.

Depreciation. Loss in the value of an asset through wear and tear. Tax relief for depreciation is called a 'writing-down allowance'.

Differentiated marketing. The practice of serving many *market segments* and modifying products, advertisements and other promotional messages to meet the particular needs of each segment. This differs from 'concentrated marketing' which focuses on a single market segment, and 'undifferentiated marketing' that ignores differences in market segments and instead attacks all of them with the same product and advertisements. The marketing of Coca-Cola is an example of the undifferentiated approach.

Direct marketing. Selling through direct mail, telephone calls, catalogues, and cut-outs in newspaper and magazine advertisements.

Director. Technically a person elected by the shareholders of a company to protect their interests. In practice the word is commonly used to describe any top administrator of a large organisation.

Double loop learning. Learning that involves challenging the basic assumptions about how tasks should be undertaken and whether particular standards and objectives are relevant to a job.

Downsizing. Reduction of the size of a firm's workforce, typically involving voluntary or involuntary redundancies. It is sometimes referred to as 'rightsizing'.

Economies of scale. Reductions in unit production costs that result from large-scale operations, e.g. discounts obtained on bulk purchases, benefits from applying the division of labour, integration of processes, ability to high-quality staff, establishment of research facilities, etc.

Empowerment. The process of giving employees the power to complete tasks and attain objectives independently, without having to refer to management for permission to take certain actions.

End-user computing. The creative manipulation of computer packages and systems by employees who have no special qualifications or expertise in computing or information technology.

Entrepreneur. The initiator and organiser of business activity, who decides how resources are to be deployed and who carries the risks of the business.

Environmental scanning. The analysis of an organisation's economic, market, legal, technological and other environments in order to predict and respond to external change.

Equity. Technically the *ordinary shares* of a business. In practice the word is used to describe any kind of share capital.

Equity theory. The proposition that employees' beliefs about whether they are fairly treated in relation to (*i*) their efforts, and (*ii*) how other workers are treated, are primary determinants of motivation.

Ergonomics. The study of the relationships between employees and their working environments and how the latter can be adapted to meet human capabilities and needs.

Ethical investment funds. *Unit trusts* that either (*i*) decline to invest in countries considered morally undesirable, or (*ii*) will only invest in companies that adhere to certain principles.

Ethics. Fundamental moral principles, judgements and values governing individual and/or group behaviour.

European Commission. Effectively the civil service of the EU. The Commission initiates proposals to the *EU Council of Ministers* where, if accepted, they become Directives that are binding on all member states. The Commission also issues non-binding Recommendations on various matters.

European Economic Interest Group (EEIG). A non-profit-making subsidiary of at least two EU businesses in different countries formed to conduct market or other research, to establish common distribution facilities, or for some other collective purpose or project.

European Social Charter. A list of basic social and employment rights intended for incorporation into the constitutional laws of EU members.

Executive search (headhunting). The use of external recruitment consultants to locate and approach suitable candidates (already employed by other – possibly competing – companies) for management positions.

Expectancy theory. The assertion that the effort an employee expends in trying to satisfy a need will depend on that person's expectation of his or her effort being followed by an outcome which brings desirable rewards.

Expert system. A computer package that mimics the problem solving methods of a human expert.

Export merchants. Intermediaries in foreign trade who buy goods in the UK and resell them in foreign markets.

Factoring. The sale to an outsider of debts owed to a business.

Fast tracking. A promotion system whereby certain preselected employees are put on to accelerated training, planned-experience and management development programmes which guarantee advancement provided certain targets are met.

Feedback and feedforward control systems. In a feedback system, information from the output of the system is automatically transmitted to the input stage so that remedial action can be implemented if required. With a feedforward system, likely problems are predicted and current activities altered now in order to overcome them.

Felt-fair methods. Techniques of *job evaluation* that apply overall general assessments to the grading of employees' work.

Final accounts. The trading and profit and loss accounts, manufacturing account (where appropriate) and balance sheet of a business.

Financial engineering. The techniques and procedures through which enterprises seek to finance their long-term operations at the lowest aggregate interest cost.

Financial futures. Options taken out now to borrow money in future periods at fixed rates of interest specified today in the futures contract.

Fishbone diagram. A diagram used to illustrate relationships between the causes of a problem, typically under five headings: materials, working methods, machinery, measurements, and human resources.

Fixed assets. Assets such as land, buildings and motor-vehicles that are purchased for use within a business rather than for resale at a profit.

Fixed and floating charges. A fixed charge is security for a loan when the security relates to specific named assets (buildings or vehicles for example). Floating charges represent security against all the company's assets, so that lenders have no claim over particular assets if the borrower's business fails.

Flexible manufacturing. Computer-controlled machining and other techniques that enable the manufacture of small batches of output, each modified to suit the requirements of particular market segments while continuing to obtain manufacturing *economies of scale*.

Flexitime. The practice of allowing employees to decide their own starting and finishing times subject to their completing a predetermined minimum number of hours each week.

Fordism. Another name for *scientific* management.

Forfaiting. A means for obtaining immediate cash payment, via an intermediary (normally a bank), for goods to be provided to a customer in future periods under a long-term contract, typically against the security of the goods to be supplied. The word 'forfait' means 'surrender of rights'.

Four Cs model. See *Harvard model*.

Frame of reference. The attitudes and psychological influences that determine how a person perceives issues and events.

Franchise. An exclusive right to use the name, products, business methods, logos, etc of another organisation within a specified geographical area.

Fraud. Misrepresentation made (*i*) deliberately, or (*ii*) without believing the statement to be true, or (*iii*) recklessly or carelessly.

Frustration. The consequence of interference with an individual's attempt to achieve his or her desired objectives. It is commonly associated with lack of control over working methods.

Functional authority. The authority of a *staff manager* to control the activities of people in other departments to the extent that these activities relate to his or her particular function.

Garnishee order. A court order against a debtor which compels named people and institutions that owe money to the debtor to pay this to the court (for distribution to creditors) and not to the debtor.

Gearing. The ratio of debt to *equity* capital in a company. A firm that borrows heavily in relation to its share capital is said to be highly geared.

Golden handcuffs. Remuneration arrangements whereby certain significant rewards do not become available until an employee has remained with a firm for an agreed minimum period.

Golden parachute. An incentive offered to existing directors of a takeover target to induce them not to oppose the takeover.

Goodwill. The difference between the sale value of a business and the value of its *net assets*, i.e. that part of its worth attributable to it being a going concern.

Grapevines. Informal and unofficial communication channels that often arise in large organisations.

Greenmail. The purchase of a significant minority shareholding in a company followed by its resale at a higher price to major shareholders in the company in exchange for the predator abandoning the attempted takeover.

Gross profit. The value of sales less *cost of sales* and direct costs of production.

Group cohesion. Group members' willingness to co-operate and work together as a *team* and the extent to which they share common goals and perspectives.

Group norms. Group members' shared perceptions of correct behaviour; of how work should be completed; attitudes towards management and other groups, etc.

Group technology. The geographical arrangement of factory processes, plant and equipment into relatively self-contained units that minimise the distances between each related process or item of equipment.

Halo effect. The assumption, when conducting an employment interview, that because a certain candidate possesses one desirable characteristic then he or she must be equally worthy in other respects.

Harvard model of human resources management. An approach to HRM that emphasises the importance of *stakeholders* in an organisation and the 'situational factors' of (*i*) the labour market, (*ii*) employee motivation, (*iii*) management style and (*iv*) the technologies used in production. The effectiveness of HRM policies are evaluated under four headings: employee commitment, employee competence, congruence (i.e. whether management and workers share the same perceptions of the organisation goals), and cost-effectiveness.

Headhunting. See *executive search*.

Heuristics. A technique for applying *ad hoc* rules of thumb to the solution of complex problems. Results are regarded as provisional and subject to alteration as circumstances change. The game of chess is an example.

Hierarchy of needs. A sequence of needs which A.H. Maslow claimed individuals attempt to satisfy in sequential order. There are five levels: physiological, security, affection, esteem, and *self-actualisation*.

Higher education diploma. An educational qualification, obtained after at least three years' study, that is recognised in all EU countries.

Hire-purchase. A means for purchasing goods through instalments. Ownership of the goods does not pass to the buyer until the final payment has been made.

Holding company. A company with majority shareholdings in several other companies.

Honeycomb organisation. An approach to organisation design that involves self-contained cells which can be set up or disbanded at will.

Horizontal fast track. A planned-experience job rotation scheme which gives the employee a larger number of postings (all at the same level of responsibility) within a given period than normal for employees on a particular grade.

Human relations approach. A *school of thought* which suggests that human, psychological and group influences are critical determinants of employee attitudes and behaviour.

Human resources management. Those aspects of management which deal with the human side of enterprise and with employees' relations with their employing firms. It covers, *inter-alia*, elements of industrial psychology, *personnel management*, training and industrial relations.

Hygiene (maintenance) factor. An aspect of the working environment which, if satisfactory, an employee does not notice but which, if it is less than satisfactory, causes employee displeasure and low morale. Hygiene factors do not motivate employees.

Hypothecation. The practice of pledging goods or property as security for a debt without transferring possession or title to them. Lenders have a lien on the pledged assets, i.e. they can keep the goods until the debt has been settled.

Industrial engineering. Techniques for improving the quantity and quality of output and the speed of production.

Industrial tribunal. A three-person court, with a qualified solicitor or barrister in the chair plus two lay members, that hears cases relating to alleged unfair dismissal, health and safety at work, equal opportunities and related employment matters.

Information technology. The acquisition, processing, storage, analysis and dissemination of information using computers.

Insolvency practitioner. An individual, licensed under the 1986 Insolvency Act, who advises insolvent persons or businesses about the courses of action necessary to honour their debts. All receivers, administrators, trustees or others holding formal bankruptcy/company liquidation appointments must be licensed insolvency practitioners.

Intense distribution. A distribution system with a large number of retail outlets.

Interactive video. A training method requiring trainee participation in role-play situations depicted in a video.

Internal marketing. Application of the techniques of marketing to the internal operations of the firm, especially in relation to human resources management (e.g. motivation of employees to produce better quality output).

Internal markets. A means for allocating resources within large organisations (including the public services) whereby managers are expected to behave *as if* they were entrepreneurs and subject to market forces. Divisions of the organisation submit competing bids for work. Successful bids are rewarded with internal 'contracts' for the supply of in-house services.

Intrapreneurship. Adoption of entrepreneurial attitudes and approaches to management by employees of large organisations.

Inverted management pyramid. An approach to organisation and management that turns upside down the conventional organisational hierarchy, placing customers at the top of the system and hence recognising the crucial importance of customer contact staff for the welfare of the enterprise.

Investment trust. A public limited company that purchases shares in other companies and makes further investments in any area it believes will yield a high return (property for example). The trust pays dividends to its own shareholders from the revenues it receives from its investments.

Invoice discounting. A means for raising short-term finance whereby (*i*) the discounting company purchases the client firm's invoices as they are issued to customers, (*ii*) the client then collects the outstanding balances under its own name (though acting as an *agent* of the discounting company), and (*iii*) repayment of the money owed to the discounting company occurs from the money collected from customers as and when they settle their accounts.

Job enlargement. Allocation to a worker of a wider variety of tasks of approximately the same level of difficulty.

Job enrichment (vertical job enlargement). The allocation to a worker of (*i*) additional responsibility, (*ii*) more complex and difficult tasks, and (*iii*) greater scope to make decisions.

Job evaluation. The process of placing jobs in order of their relative worth so that employees may be paid fairly.

Job extension. A term which embraces both *job enrichment* and *job enlargement*.

Joint and several liability. The (unlimited) liability of members of a partnership for all debts accrued by any one partner on behalf of the firm. If some partners have no assets on termination of the partnership, its creditors can claim all they are owed from the remaining partners.

Junk bond. A debenture or other bond secured against worthless assets, possibly other junk bonds.

Just-in-time systems. Purchasing and/or inventory management procedures which schedule the arrival of supplies at the precise moment they are needed for processing, and not before.

Kaizen system. An approach to employee participation, based on *Quality Circles*, that encourages groups of workers continually to improve the work of their sections via a cycle of 'planning, doing, checking and actioning'.

Kanban system. A method of *just-in-time* control over work in progress whereby each stage in the production process calls for supplies at the precise moment they are needed, rather than holding inventories. Hence, materials are 'pulled' through the system and not 'pushed' into stocks.

Labour stability index. A measure of labour turnover showing the percentage of the firm's employees with at least one year's service.

Labour utilisation budget. That part of a company's *production budget* which deals with the costs of employing, deploying and servicing labour (e.g. training and recruitment costs).

Leadership. The ability to influence the thoughts and behaviour of others.

Learning organisation. A business operating in a turbulent environment that requires regular transformations in working methods, so that the firm needs continuously to train and develop its employees in order to facilitate the introduction of new systems.

Letter of credit. A document issued by an importer's bank accepting liability for settling the importer's debts up to a stated amount in specified circumstances and on certain conditions.

Leverage buy-out. A company takeover financed by borrowed funds.

Limited liability company. A business in which the liability of the owners (shareholders) for the firm's debts is restricted to the value of their investment in the company.

Line manager. A manager possessing executive authority to take and implement decisions.

Liquidation of a company. Either the winding-up of a solvent company, or the equivalent of *bankruptcy* for an insolvent limited company.

Logical systems analysis. A method of *systems analysis* which begins from a specification of the target output of a system and then identifies the inputs and procedures needed to generate that output.

Logistics. Analysis of the costs, efficiencies and feasibilities of the various modes of transport and temporary storage needed to move goods to their destinations, safely and with minimal pilferage and materials loss.

Management buy-out. The purchase of an existing firm or division of a business using funds raised by its current management. This differs from a 'management buy-in' whereby the finance for the purchase is arranged by an outside team which thereafter contributes to the operational management of the business.

Management by exception. A control technique that requires management intervention only when operations vary from predetermined norms by more than a prespecified value.

Management by objectives. A top-down control technique whereby corporate objectives are segmented into departmental targets and then into goals for sections and, ultimately, for individual employees.

Management earn-out. A company takeover or *management buy-out* in which the provision of external funds is conditional on the acquired business achieving preset profit targets over an agreed period following the takeover.

Management information system. The methods and procedures whereby an organisation procures, integrates and interprets the internal and external information needed for effective decision taking, planning and control.

Management science. The application of statistical and *operations research* methods to managerial problem solving and decision making.

Management style. The ambience towards employees displayed by an individual manager or by an entire management team.

Managerial grid. A management training method designed to help managers identify their own and other people's leadership styles.

Managerial prerogative. The right of management (which represents the owners of a business) to manage without interference from employees.

Managerial responsibility. The conscious restraint of an organisation's power in order to help others.

Manufacturing account. The account in which a manufacturing business calculates the costs of acquiring input materials, manufacturing wages and factory overheads.

Manufacturing automation protocol. Integration via computers of assembly lines and offices at different locations into a single *closed-loop* manufacturing system.

Manufacturing resource planning. An extension of *materials requirements planning* that incorporates computerised purchasing, *capacity planning*, automated stores procedures and other aspects of operational control.

Marginal cost. The additional cost of producing one extra unit of output. For example, if it costs a total of £5500 to produce 947 units and £5525 to produce 948 then the marginal cost of the extra unit is £25.

Market segmentation. The practice of dividing a market into sub-units defined by demographic, geographic or lifestyle characteristics.

Marketing concept. The proposition that the supply of goods and services should be a function of the demand for them.

Marketing mix. The combination of marketing elements used in a given set of circumstances, normally listed under four headings: promotion, price, product and place.

Marketing services industry. The industry that provides ancillary services to marketing departments in companies. It encompasses advertising and PR agencies, list brokers, fulfilment houses, etc.

Materials requirements planning. A computerised production scheduling technique which analyses end products and required delivery dates to determine the raw materials, components and sub-assemblies needed to satisfy customers' orders on time.

Matrix organisation. A system for organising managers from different departments into teams constructed to complete specific projects or oversee particular functions.

Mechanistic organisations. Bureaucratic organisations with fixed and highly formal hierarchies, administrative procedures and communication systems.

Memorandum of association. One of the documents used to form a limited company. It specifies the objects (contractual powers) of the business plus details of its share capital.

Merchandiser. A supplier's representative who assists retailers select and apply the best methods for presenting a product to customers at the point of sale, e.g. by advising on the optimum shelf position for the good.

Mezzanine finance. Forms of business finance that lie between ordinary shares and secured *debentures*. Examples are preference shares and unsecured or partially secured loans.

Mission statement. A brief explanation of the fundamental purpose and objectives of the firm, including how it wishes to relate to its environments, *stakeholders*, and to other groups and organisations.

Modernism. A term used to describe the manner in which modern society is organised and the belief that the rational application of scientific research is capable of solving the world's problems.

Morphological analysis. A *brainstorming* technique intended to generate ideas geometrically via cross-referencing concepts.

Mortgage. A loan secured against tangible assets (usually property) whereby the borrower possesses and uses the assets but does not own them until after the final mortgage repayment.

Mortgage debenture. A *debenture* secured against a *mortgage* on property owned by a borrowing firm.

Motherhood culture. An approach to management development that emphasises in-house training, the retention of employees for long periods, internal promotion and the use of existing staff rather than outsiders for the administration of new projects.

Motivation. All the drives, forces and conscious or unconscious influences that cause an employee to want to behave in a certain manner.

Multi-option facility. A financing arrangement whereby a consortium of lenders make available to a borrower a certain amount of funds over a long period. Each member contributes varying sums for short periods during the term of the agreement.

Net assets. Fixed plus current assets less current liabilities.

Net profit. *Gross profit* less administrative and other expenses, with or without adjustment for tax and interest payments.

Network analysis. A planning technique that breaks a project down into logically ordered components and estimates the minimum time needed for its completion.

New technology agreement. An accord whereby management and unions jointly consider, negotiate and agree procedures for the introduction of major technical innovations.

Novation. The substitution of a new legal obligation for an old one with the consent of all the parties concerned, e.g. an incoming member of a partnership agreeing to take over all the business debts of a retiring partner, subject to the approval of current creditors of the firm.

Open-account trading. Settlement of international credit transactions by means of cheque or electronic money transfer and without recourse to *bills of exchange* or *letters of credit*.

Open-loop system. A *feedback* mechanism requiring human intervention to remedy difficulties.

Operational research. According to the UK Operational Research Society, 'the application of the the methods of science to complex problems arising in the direction and management of large systems of people, machines, materials and money in industry, business, government and defence.'

Operations management. Management of all the processes necessary to transfer tangible resource inputs into outputs of goods and services. It is particularly concerned with *industrial engineering* and the organisation of manufacturing.

Optimised production technology. An approach to manufacturing that focuses on the identification and removal of bottlenecks in material flows.

Ordinary shares. Shares that have no special rights or privileges in relation to dividends or the division of assets on dissolution of a company. Ordinary shares with votes are called 'B shares'; those without, 'A shares'.

Organisation and methods (O & M). The application of work study to clerical and administrative procedures.

Organisation charts. Diagrams showing patterns of authority, responsibility and communication within organisations.

Organisational politics. Negotiations and settlements that occur among the members of an organisation in consequence of the existence of conflicting interests between sections and employees of the firm.

Organisational culture (climate). The totality of all the attitudes, norms, beliefs, and perspectives shared by the majority of the members of an organisation.

Organisational development (OD). The process of periodically reviewing the adequacy of a firm's organisation structures, communication systems, authority and responsibility systems, etc in relation to its present needs.

Organistic organisations. Flexible and relatively informal organisations with fast and effective internal communications, overlapping responsibilities and willingness to accept change.

Original motion. A proposition put to a committee for debate and resolution.

Over the counter (OTC) share dealings. Transactions in the shares of companies not recognised by the *Stock Exchange*.

Parkinson's law. The proposition that employees will expand their work unnecessarily to make it last as long as the maximum time available for its completion.

Partnership. A collection of between two and twenty people (ten for banking firms) who form, manage, and are jointly responsible for the debts of a business without limited liability.

PAYE (pay as you earn). The taxation system introduced in 1944 to enable employees to pay their income tax as they receive their wages and to place the administrative responsibility for tax collection on employing firms.

Pendulum arbitration. A technique for fixing the level of pay increase to be awarded to workers whereby management and (usually) a trade union each submit to an independent arbitrator figures that each side believes to be reasonable. The arbitrator selects one figure or the other: no haggling is involved.

Perceptual map. A diagram used to identify the market *position of a product* as perceived by consumers of that type of good.

Performance appraisal. The systematic examination of an employee's recent successes and failures at work and/or the assessment of that person's suitability for promotion or training.

Peripheral workers. Part-time or casual employees hired and fired according to the organisation's current labour requirements.

Person culture. An organisational culture sometimes found in organisations which exist to serve the people within them, e.g. consultancy firms or professional organisations.

Personnel management. That part of *human resources management* concerned with staffing, with meeting the needs of people at work and with the practical rules and procedures governing relationships between employees and the organisation.

PERT (programme evaluation review technique). A method of *network analysis* used where the durations of the major activities of a project are uncertain.

Peter principle. The proposition that since individuals are often promoted in consequence of successes achieved in their current jobs they will rise through the ranks of an organisation until eventually they occupy positions in which they are incompetent. Then they cease being promoted and remain as incompetent employees indefinitely.

Piece rate wages. Employee remuneration based on the number of units of output the worker produces rather than time spent on the job.

Pluralism. An approach to industrial relations which asserts that the best way to achieve consensus is to recognise that parties to negotiations necessarily possess conflicting interests and differing attitudes and views.

PODSCORB. The acronym for the basic management functions of planning, organising, directing, staffing, co-ordinating, reporting and budgeting.

Polysensuality. Consumers' desire for a total consumption experience, e.g. to smell fresh bread or coffee at the point of sale as well as merely purchase the good.

Portfolio analysis. A technique for deciding which of its products a company should retain, develop or abandon.

Position of a product. Consumers' perceptions of a product, compared to competing products, in relation to such variables as price, quality, reliability, attractiveness, and so on.

Post-Fordism. Changes in working methods necessitated by the shift from standardised mass production towards customised production for niche markets using the techniques of *flexible manufacturing, total quality management*, and the employment of *peripheral workers*.

Post-modernism. The proposition that today's world is so different to how it used to be that there are few connections between what occurred in the past and what is likely to happen in the future.

Power culture. An *organisational culture* based on a single authority figure, as in a small business that begins to expand. There are few rules or procedures and all important decisions are taken by a handful of people.

Preference shares. Non-voting shares which (*i*) carry a fixed rate of dividend payable from a company's profits before *ordinary shareholders* receive any dividend and (*ii*) take precedence over ordinary shareholders for the repayment of capital when the company is wound up.

Preproduction programming. Work planning, *process engineering*, and choosing the rate and quantity of production.

Price-earnings ratio. The current market price of a share divided by its earnings during the last reported accounting period.

Principal. In the context of trade, the person ultimately responsible for fulfilling an obligation. In the context of investment, the initial sum of money invested.

Process engineering. Choice of production methods, tools and equipment.

Process theories. Approaches to motivation which examine the thought processes that underlie individual motivation to behave in a certain manner.

Product life-cycle hypothesis. The proposition that products, like people, are conceived, grow, mature, decline and die.

Production budget. A *budget* that details the expected costs of creating the outputs specified in a firm's sales forecast.

Profession. A field of activity entry to which is restricted to persons possessing predefined qualifications and experience based on several years of serious study.

Profit and loss account. The account in which a business's *net profit* is computed.

Programmed decisions. Decisions taken automatically according to predetermined criteria, e.g. the decision to place an order to replenish the firm's stock of a certain item whenever some specified minimum inventory level is reached.

Psychographics. A *market segmentation* method which divides markets using psychological and (particularly) lifestyle criteria.

Psychological contract. An informal unwritten understanding between a worker and his or her employing firm concerning how the person should be treated and how he or she should interrelate with company management.

Psychometric tests. Selection tests that seek to quantify psychological dimensions of job applicants. Examples are tests of intelligence, personality and motivation.

389

Purchase agreement. A credit agreement that provides a loan for a specific purpose. The lender may then be held equally liable with the supplier for any defect in the item purchased.

Quality assurance standards. Published standards for application within companies to ensure that certain prespecified minimum quality requirements are met, e.g. that only materials of a particular type and quality will be used in manufacture.

Quality Circle. A discussion group, usually comprising production operatives under the guidance of a specially trained group leader, that meets periodically to consider, analyse and resolve quality and production control difficulties.

Quoted (listed) companies. Public limited companies recognised by the *Stock Exchange* and whose shares are traded on the main market of the exchange.

Rational decision model. An *algorithm* of the steps needed to make logical decisions. Rational decision making also involves the analysis of barriers to effective decision making and the environments in which decisions are made.

Red circling. The practice in *job evaluation* of continuing to pay current salary levels to individuals whose jobs have been graded into lower wage categories, but paying a reduced rate to the people who eventually take over the high-salaried employees' jobs.

Redundancy. A dismissal situation in which the firm's requirements for the employee to carry out work of a particular kind has ceased or diminished or is expected to do so.

Re-engineering. The radical redesign of business systems and processes in order to improve their performance. It aims to remedy fundamental deficiencies rather than simply speeding up existing processes.

Relationship marketing. An approach to marketing that emphasises the importance of establishing long-term relationships with customers based on trust and mutual co-operation, hence creating repeat orders and encouraging customer loyalty to the supplying firm.

Resale (retail) price maintenance. Refusing to sell products to retailers who will not undertake to charge prespecified minimum prices.

Reservation of title (Romalpa) clause. A term in a contract of sale whereby the supplier retains ownership of goods delivered to customers until they have been fully paid for. If the customer defaults having resold the goods to third parties, the supplier may reclaim the goods from these third parties.

Retail audit. A market research technique of continuously monitoring the items sold by a selected sample of retail outlets.

Revealing question. An interview question which indicates the preferences of the person asking the question, e.g. 'I enjoy watching tennis, don't you?'

Reverse buy-out. A procedure whereby a private or unquoted public limited company takes over a *quoted* company and then itself becomes a subsidiary of the latter.

Rights issue. An offer by a company to sell additional shares to existing shareholders at an attractive price.

Role culture. An *organisational culture* based on highly bureaucratic rules and procedures.

Safety representative. An employee selected by his or her trade union to undertake safety inspections at an employing firm's premises and to complete other duties as specified in the Health and Safety at Work Act 1974.

Sale and leaseback. An agreement whereby a business sells its premises to an outsider for a modest price in return for the right to occupy these premises at a low rent for a predetermined period.

Satisficing behaviour. Decision taking based on easily applied rules of thumb that result on average in acceptable (albeit possibly sub-optimal) outcomes.

Schematic models. Decision models based on graphs, charts, rules and algorithms. These differ from 'mathematical models' that present analogues of the numerical relations between variables.

School of thought. A collection of writers, thinkers, and practitioners of a subject who all adhere to the same fundamental principles and doctrines in relation to that subject.

Scientific management. An approach to management based on the work of F.W. Taylor that emphasises the the division of labour, work measurement, close supervision of operatives, *piece rate wage systems* and fitting workers to jobs.

Secondary picketing. Picketing by workers of a firm not directly involved in an industrial dispute.

Self-actualisation. The highest need of a human being, namely the need to fulfil and extend his or her potential to the maximum extent.

Sensitivity analysis. The study of the key assumptions upon which intended actions are based. These assumptions are systematically altered and 'what if' questions then asked.

Seven-S system. A technique for analysing an organisation's effectiveness under seven headings: strategy, structure, systems, style, staff, skills, and shared values.

Shamrock form of organisation. An organisation system based on three distinct groups of employee: *core workers, peripheral workers*, and outside contractors.

Share dilution. The consequence of a company issuing additional share capital, but not increasing its total profits. Profits must now be distributed to a greater number of shareholders, resulting in lower dividends per share.

Simulation analysis. A quantitative decision-making technique that systematically alters the parameters (limiting factors) and assumptions of a model and examines the consequences.

Single loop learning. The learning necessary to enable an employee to apply existing methods to the completion of a job.

Skimming. A high-price policy that seeks to 'skim the cream' off the top end of a market through offering a de-luxe version of the product to high-income consumers.

Sleeping partner. A member of a partnership who contributes capital but has no say in its management. Sleeping partners can register with the Registrar of Companies and obtain limited liability in relation to the partnership's debts.

Sole trader. A one-person business operating without limited liability.

Span of control. The number of direct subordinates reporting to a manager.

Staff manager. A manager who advises line executives but does not take or implement final decisions.

Stakeholder. A person or group with a vested interest in the behaviour of a company.

Standard costing. The computation of expected values for materials usage, input prices, labour needed for production, machine time and expenses, etc and subsequent comparison of these predictions with actual costs.

Standing committee. A committee that meets at predetermined intervals to consider matters relating to a certain subject (health and safety, for instance) that have arisen since the previous meeting.

Standing orders. Rules and procedures governing the conduct of a meeting or committee.

Stock Exchange. A market place for shares and debentures. The exchange is a private business owned by its members.

Strategic business unit (SBU). A grouping of a business's activities taken (usually) from different divisions or subsidiaries. The SBU is then treated as a self-contained entity for the purposes of planning and control.

Strategic management. The determination of where the organisation should be headed, the specification of general corporate objectives, and the overall selection of policies for guiding the firm.

Stress. A syndrome comprising physiological and psychological reactions to mental tension. Stress is not a measurable entity; its existence is only apparent through its consequences.

Substantive motion. A motion that has been amended by resolution of a committee. It replaces the *original motion* to which it relates.

Summary dismissal. Dismissal 'on-the-spot' without notice or payment in lieu of notice.

Supervisor (first line manager). A manager who controls non-managerial employees but is controlled by other managers.

Supervisory board. The upper level of a two-tier board of directors, taking general strategic decisions.

Sustainable development. That rate of economic development which enables the present generation to satisfy its requirements without compromising the ability of future generations to meet their needs.

Swap agreement. An arrangement whereby the borrower of funds has the right to exchange one type of interest rate obligation for another at certain prespecified points during the period of a loan.

SWOT analysis. Detailed examination of a business's strengths and weaknesses, and the opportunities and threats it confronts.

Synectics. A problem-solving technique that narrows down the range of options available to the decision taker until the optimum solution is discovered.

Synergy. The situation where people working together are collectively more productive than the sum of their individual contributions.

Systems analysis. Detailed examination of the methods, procedures, functions and activities of organisations in order to achieve stated objectives.

Systems approach. *A school of thought* which views organisations as conglomerations of interrelating subsystems that collectively relate to the outside world.

T-group training. A group training method in which the instructor takes a back seat and encourages group members to assist and learn from each other while completing group tasks.

Tactics. The practical methods for implementing strategic decisions.

Tag lines (strap lines). Brief catchphrases that run across the bottoms of many press advertisements.

Taguchi methods. Quality management systems which emphasise the need to minimise variability in production rather than constantly checking and measuring output.

Task culture. An *organisational culture* that is project orientated, flexible and responsive to change. Job satisfaction is high and there is much group cohesion.

Team. A working group the members of which voluntarily co-operate, co-ordinate their activities and enthusiastically strive to achieve group activities.

Technology. The utilisation of the materials and processes necessary to transform inputs into outputs.

Theory X and Theory Y. Assumptions about human nature supposedly held by managers, e.g. whether workers are naturally idle and require close supervision and control (theory X), or inherently hard working and capable of self-direction (theory Y).

Tort. A civil wrong (e.g. libel, trespass, negligence) which causes damage to other people.

Total quality management (TQM). Integration of practical techniques of quality control (inspection, sampling, etc.) with a firm's overall strategies and tactics in order to create an *organisational culture* that is conducive to the continuous improvement of quality.

Trade credit. The practice of delaying payments to creditors in order to release short-term business funds.

Trading account. The account in which a business computes its *gross profit*.

Trait theory. A *leadership* theory which asserts that certain people are born with or otherwise acquire personal qualities (e.g. assertiveness) that make them effective leaders.

Transactional leadership. A style of *leadership* that focuses on providing subordinates with the resources and management assistance necessary to complete their tasks, rather than attempting to motivate subordinates per se.

Transformational leadership. Charismatic *leadership* that inspires subordinates to levels of *motivation* considerably higher than currently required.

Triad of regional economic groups. The three regions of North America, Western Europe and Japan that dominate the World economy.

Triple I organisation. A learning organisation based on 'ideas, information and intelligence'.

Trustees. Individuals or organisations who assume responsibility for administering the resources of others. Examples are *unit trusts, investment trusts,* and trustees of bankrupt persons.

Unit trust. An organisation managed by a trust that uses investors' money to purchase a wide range of securities. Thus each unit in the trust bought by a member of the public represents a broad spread of investments.

Unitarism. The belief that management and labour have identical interests and hence may be expected to pull together towards common objectives. Willingness to co-operate is taken for granted; dissent cannot be understood.

Unity of command. The situation in which each person has just one boss.

Unlisted securities market. Sub-sections of the *Stock Exchanges* of certain European countries through which companies that fail to meet the requirements for a full quotation may raise money by selling shares.

Value added tax (VAT). A tax levied at each stage in the production and distribution process. A business charges VAT to its customers but may reclaim the VAT it pays when purchasing its own supplies, i.e. it pays tax only on 'value added' to inputs.

Value analysis. The critical examination of a product's functions to establish whether these functions could be fulfilled by an item with a lower manufacturing cost.

Venture capital. A minority shareholding in a young business taken by an outside body, e.g. a merchant bank. Usually the VC agreement provides for (*i*) the resale of the shares to the company on a prespecified future date at a (high) predetermined price, and (*ii*) some involvement of the VC provider in the management of the company.

Warrant of execution. A court order against a debtor enabling a court bailiff to seize the debtor's goods to the value necessary to clear his or her outstanding balances.

White knight. A third party approached by the target of a hostile takeover and invited to purchase a majority shareholding in the target firm to prevent it being taken over by anyone else.

Working capital. Current assets less current liabilities.

Works council. A means for involving employees in management decision making via regular meetings between management and employee representatives.

Workspace premises. Units of floorspace in large open plan buildings that serve as premises for small businesses. Common services (telephone switchboard, conference rooms, etc) are shared by the building's occupants.

Zero-base budgeting. A budget allocation method which assumes that no money whatsoever will be allocated to any given department or function at the start of each year. Thus, department managers must justify each and every demand for resources.

INDEX